INSTITUTE OF LANGUAGES, CULTURES AND SOCIETIES
UNIVERSITY OF LONDON

BITHELL SERIES OF DISSERTATIONS
VOLUME 50

RECLAIMING THE NATION
THE LEFT-WING PATRIOTISM OF *DIE WELTBÜHNE*
IN THE WEIMAR REPUBLIC

INSTITUTE OF LANGUAGES, CULTURES AND SOCIETIES

BITHELL SERIES OF DISSERTATIONS

Launched in 1978 by the then Institute of Germanic Studies, the Bithell Series of Dissertations is designed to help young scholars publish recent work of high quality which has been accepted for the award of a research degree by a University in the United Kingdom or the Republic of Ireland. Volumes 14 to 41 were published in conjunction with the Modern Humanities Research Association. From 2015 onwards, publication has been resumed by the Institute of Languages, Cultures and Societies (ILCS). For a list of previous volumes in the series, see https://ilcs.sas.ac.uk/publications/bithell-series-dissertations.

Theses for possible inclusion in the series are considered by the Bithell Editorial Board on a rolling basis. Recommendations for theses to be considered should be made by the supervisor and/or examiners, should be accompanied by a copy of the Examiners' Report and Abstract, and sent to Professor Godela Weiss-Sussex at the Institute of Languages, Cultures and Societies, School of Advanced Study, University of London, Senate House, Malet Street, London WC1E 7HU, or by email to godela.weiss-sussex@sas.ac.uk.

Editorial Board

Professor Judith Beniston (University College London)
Professor Laura Bradley (University of Edinburgh)
Professor Charles Burdett (ILCS Director, *ex officio*)
Professor Sarah Colvin (University of Cambridge)
Dr Steffan Davies (University of Bristol)
Professor Angus Nicholls (Queen Mary University of London)
Dr Anne Simon (ILCS – *Series Editor*)
Professor Godela Weiss-Sussex (ILCS – *Chair*)

Reclaiming the Nation

The Left-Wing Patriotism of *Die Weltbühne* in the Weimar Republic

by
Jack Arscott

Institute of Languages, Cultures and Societies

2025

Published by the
Institute of Languages, Cultures and Societies
School of Advanced Study, University of London
Senate House, Malet Street, London WC1E 7HU
https://ilcs.sas.ac.uk/

© Jack Arscott, 2025

The author has asserted his right under the Copyright, Designs and Patents Act 1988 to be identified as the author of this work.

All rights reserved. No part of this publication may be reproduced, stored in a retrieval system, or transmitted, in any form or by any means, electronic, mechanical, photocopying, recording or otherwise, without the prior written permission of the author and the publisher.

Cover image: Inscription on the west elevation of the Reichstag, Berlin.
Photo © Savh, 2 November 2011 (via Wikimedia Commons CC BY-SA 3.0)

First published 2025

ISBN 978-0-85457-287-8
ISSN 0266-7932

CONTENTS

	Acknowledgements	vii
	Note on Referencing	ix
	Introduction	1
1.	Regionalist Patriotism	25
2.	Internationalist Patriotism	89
3.	Socialist Patriotism	161
	Conclusion	233
	Bibliography	241
	Index	257

ACKNOWLEDGEMENTS

This book is based on my doctoral thesis, written during three fruitful years at the Institute of Languages, Cultures and Societies, University of London, courtesy of a scholarship from the *Friends of Germanic Studies*. The monograph itself was made possible by the generous support of the Modern Humanities Research Association in the form of a Research Scholarship in the Modern European Languages. My greatest debt of all, however, is to Professor Godela Weiss-Sussex, whose supervision of my MPhil dissertation at Cambridge proved to be the start of several collaborations. As my primary PhD supervisor, Godela's uncanny ability to second-guess my own reservations about my work, coupled with her peculiar knack for keenly interrogating my reasoning or choice of words without breaking my spirit, found the perfect foil in Dr Catherine Smale, my secondary supervisor. Catherine is a veritable repository of relevant, up-to-date secondary literature and was always quick to give credit where she felt it was due.

These things are never just a handful of years in the making, however. This book is therefore also dedicated to my first-ever German teacher, Astrid Masson, whose devotion to our classes and conspiratorial sense of humour turned German from a bolt-on A-Level subject to my choice of degree in a matter of months. It would also be remiss of me to overlook the seminal role of Dr Caroline Summers and the rest of the German Department at the University of Leeds, my much-loved *alma mater*, without whom I might never have taken an interest in inter-war German literature. Leeds is also to thank for my meeting Alex Clifford, now an increasingly prolific author in his own right, who has the dubious distinction of being one of the only people willing to talk to me at length about the finer points of Weimar politics; the fact that he is happy to do so while tramping Hadrian's Wall or the South Downs seals my debt of gratitude. My gratitude also goes to Monja Stahlberger for being both an endlessly patient listener and an expert in snagging a table in a crowded café at lunchtime; to Dr Peter Böthig for throwing open the archives of the Kurt Tucholsky Literaturmuseum in Rheinsberg for two restorative summer months; to my family for never questioning that this project was the right thing to do; and to the European Union for enabling me and many others to broaden our cultural and emotional horizons over many years. Without E.U. funding I could neither have taken up a Deutscher Akademischer Austauschdienst (DAAD) scholarship to attend a summer school on German language and culture under the auspices of the Ruprecht-Karls-Universität Heidelberg in 2013 nor embarked upon a year's study abroad at the Ludwig-Maximilians-Universität München through the ERASMUS programme from 2014 to 2015.

Special mention is owed to my dear friend Flavia di Battista, who has lit the way along the winding path of academia for over a decade. No matter what I do, you will always be one step ahead.

NOTE ON REFERENCING

Throughout and without exception, this monograph relies on the comprehensive series of reprints of *Weltbühne* originals produced by Athenäum in 1978. This collection encompasses the period from 1918 to 1933 and devotes a volume to each year; each volume is labelled according to its year in the sequence of publication dating back to the foundation of the *Schaubühne* in 1905. This rationale is complicated by the fact that the Athenäum series considers the nine-month period after the renaming of the journal as *Die Weltbühne* in April 1918 effectively to mark a fourteenth year, as opposed to being a continuation of the thirteenth year. A further quirk of the Athenäum series is that, departing from this assumption, each of these volumes is divided into half-years, with the page numbering starting again at the beginning of each six-month period. This pagination system necessitates an idiosyncratic referencing system, whereby anything published between April and June 1918 is cited as 14.1, plus the page number/s, and anything thereafter as 14.2 etc. On this basis, the volume for 1919 is divided into 15.1 and 15.2 and so on. For example, the reference 15.1 (1919), 467–70 refers to the first half of the relevant Athenäum volume (in this instance, that covering 1919).

INTRODUCTION

This book reveals the long-overlooked flowering of left-wing German patriotism in the fifteen years separating the end of the First World War and Hitler's rise to power. The eventual triumph of Fascist nationalism has tended to overshadow the prevalence in much left-wing writing during the Weimar Republic of alternative patriotic blueprints that clashed with the Nazi interpretation of nationhood.[1] In fact, the weekly theatre review turned left-wing political journal *Die Weltbühne* was a leading forum for the development, intermingling and occasional collision of three definitions of patriotism that were fundamentally progressive in spirit: regionalist, internationalist and Socialist.[2] As such, its output in the inter-war period

---

1   The founder of the Fascist ideology was the Italian dictator Benito Mussolini, whose Partito Nazionale Fascista took effective control of the Kingdom of Italy in 1922 and established a one-party state within four years. The name of the party derived from the word 'fasci', which had been in use in Italy since the 1870s to connote a variety of insurgent political groups and in turn originated from the tightly bound cluster of wooden rods, or 'fasces', wielded by a magistrate's lictors (officers) in Ancient Rome in token of the judge's unshakeable power to sentence Roman subjects. Like most Fascist movements, Adolf Hitler's Nationalsozialistische Deutsche Arbeiterpartei (NSDAP), widely known as the Nazi Party, although Socialist, established totalitarian state control of society, glorified military violence and sought to purge the country of all groups which did not conform to its racial, political and moral ideal of nationhood. In Nazi Germany this translated to Hitler's arrogation of absolute power to himself as *Führer* (a deliberate echo of Mussolini's title, *Il Duce*), the use of paramilitary groups – the *Sturmabteilung* (SA) and *Schutzstaffel* (SS) – to repress opposition and sow terror in the wider population, eventually complemented by the introduction of mandatory membership of the *Hitlerjugend*, and the implementation from 1941 of the *Endlösung*, or Final Solution, which authorized the extermination of European Jewry in Nazi concentration camps.

2   In this book the terms 'progressive' and 'regressive' reflect a fundamental attitude both to the system change in German domestic politics after the First World War in particular and to the shifting landscape of international relations in general at that time. Thus the attribution to a writer or a group of the label 'progressive' indicates that they are, broadly speaking, in favour of parliamentary democracy, peace and multilateral dialogue, whereas 'regressive' refers to those forces in inter-war German society which yearned for the return of an autocratic leader, longed for Germany to take up arms to avenge the perceived injustice of the Treaty of Versailles and refused to accept the new borders. Put simply, then, 'progressivism' here means the embrace of republicanism, the rejection of war as

presents a tailor-made case study for this project, which explores the commonalities and contradictions generated by these three schools of idealistic patriotic thought.

Upon its definitive pivot to politics in the febrile climate of early 1918, the journal shed its former name, *Die Schaubühne*, and rapidly established itself among the foremost platforms for left-wing dissent during Germany's transition to democracy. Edited by Siegfried Jacobsohn from the inception of its forerunner in 1905 until his death in 1926, whereupon the editorship transferred first to Kurt Tucholsky and then to Carl von Ossietzky, *Die Weltbühne* published a range of journalistic and literary work, from polemics to sober political analysis to satirical commentary, sketches and poems. It owed allegiance to no one party but consistently and trenchantly repudiated conservative attitudes, from xenophobia through militarism to outright revanchism. Contemporary observers and later historians alike appended various labels to its writers in reference both to the well-educated, bourgeois milieu from which they were frequently recruited and the markedly left-of-centre political constituency to which they hoped to appeal. Of these monikers, the most persistent has proved to be 'linke Intellektuellen', though this epithet does not fully capture the radical reputation many of them enjoyed.[3]

The left-wing orientation of *Die Weltbühne* could not be circumscribed by any party doctrine, be it that of the Unabhängige Sozialdemokratische Partei Deutschlands (USPD) or the Sozialdemokratische Partei Deutschlands (SPD). On the face of it, the most natural political ally of the broadly pacifist journal might appear to have been the USPD, which had broken away from the majority SPD in 1917 in protest at the support of the movement for the German war effort. Already saddled with this historical albatross, its larger cousin was regarded as almost irredeemably cursed by association with the strong-arm tactics of Germany's imperial era from the moment *Reichswehrminister* Gustav Noske called in irregular paramilitary troops to crush violently an episode of mass civilian unrest in the capital in January 1919. The strong vein of ideological puritanism in USPD ranks, which hindered the eventual reabsorption of the party into the SPD until 1922, centred on the former's suspicion of the latter's pragmatism once installed in government, an attitude it was inclined to equate with the forsaking of the seminal notion of *Klassenkampf*. Since it was itself invested in upending the distribution of power in Weimar society, *Die Weltbühne* could not remain

---

the conventional means of solving international conflict and the acceptance of new geopolitical realities, while 'regression' encompasses restoration, revanchism and revisionism.
3   Istvan Deak, *Weimar Germany's Left-Wing Intellectuals: A Political History of the 'Weltbühne' and Its Circle* (Berkeley, CA: University of California Press, 1968), p. 2.

untouched by this internecine strife, which played out at high volume in the pages of the competing party presses.[4] At the same time, however, it was unencumbered by any sense of collective responsibility and consequently found itself at liberty to air ideas that few editors of *Vorwärts* or *Die Freiheit*, the official organs of the SPD and USPD respectively, would have dared to float for fear of provoking the anathema of party leaders. Ultimately, the only party to which *Die Weltbühne* ever felt able to swear allegiance did not exist: a Socialist unity party capable of condensing the entire German Left into a potent electoral force.

The significance of *Die Weltbühne* to public discourse in Weimar Germany cannot be expressed in numbers. Diverse sources, while differing in their precise calculations, agree that circulation figures never exceeded sixteen thousand.[5] At the same time, however, there is a striking degree of unanimity on the influence exerted by the journal on the political climate of the inter-war period, even if this cannot be easily quantified. Thus few would dispute either Friedhelm Greis and Stefanie Oswalt's judgement that it is now regarded as '*das* publizistische Forum der intellektuellen, bürgerlichen Linken der Weimarer Republik',[6] or Ronald Taylor's identically emphasized anointing of the journal as '*the* organ of progressive intellectual opinion throughout the Weimar Republic',[7] any more than they would underestimate the fact that 'die Schriften von Tucholsky und Ossietzky', evidently regarded as inseparable, together comprised the ninth *œuvre* to be cast into the flames at the Nazi book burnings in 1933.[8] Nor was Hitler's party the first to take umbrage at the merciless campaigning and trickle of damaging revelations issuing from the *Weltbühne* offices, latterly to be found on the Kantstraße in the Berlin neighbourhood of Charlottenburg. As recently as 1931 Ossietzky had been sent to prison for facilitating treason and the betrayal of military secrets with the publication of Walter Kreiser's article 'Windiges aus der

---

4   Kurt Koszyk, *Zwischen Kaiserreich und Diktatur. Die sozialdemokratische Presse von 1914 bis 1933* (Heidelberg: Quelle & Meyer, 1958), pp. 67–152.
5   Kurt Koszyk, *Deutsche Presse 1914–1945. Geschichte der deutschen Presse. Teil III*, Abhandlungen und Materialien zur Publizistik, 7 (Berlin: Colloquium, 1972), p. 285; Fritz J. Raddatz, '*Das Tage-Buch*'. *Portrait einer Zeitschrift* (Königstein/Taunus: Athenäum, 1981), p. 5; Friedhelm Greis and Stefanie Oswalt, 'Die Geschichte der Zeitschrift', in *Aus Teutschland Deutschland machen. Ein politisches Lesebuch zur 'Weltbühne'*, ed. by Friedhelm Greis and Stefanie Oswalt (Berlin: Lukas, 2008), pp. 13–23 (p. 18); Ian King, '"Das Bürgertum erliegt der Wucht...". Tucholsky zwischen Bürgertum und Arbeiterbewegung', in *Kurt Tucholsky und der 'Weltbühne'-Kreis zwischen Bürgertum und Arbeiterbewegung*, ed. by Ian King (Leipzig: Ille & Riemer, 2016), pp. 25–47 (p. 30).
6   Greis and Oswalt, 'Die Geschichte der Zeitschrift', p. 13.
7   Ronald Taylor, *Literature and Society in Germany, 1918–1945*, Studies in Contemporary Literature and Culture, 3 (Brighton: Harvester, 1980), p. 26.
8   Greis and Oswalt, 'Die Geschichte der Zeitschrift', p. 21.

deutschen Luftfahrt' (1929), which had exposed the Republic's re-stocking of its air force in contravention of the Treaty of Versailles (1919).[9] The so-called '*Weltbühne*-Prozeß' was soon followed by a trial for defamation and a second court appearance in quick succession for Ossietzky; this time the presiding judge found in favour of the defendant, deciding that star columnist Tucholsky's statement 'Soldaten sind Mörder' in an article from 1931 had not been directed at the German *Reichswehr* in particular.[10]

To grasp the importance of its contribution to Weimar political debate, then, one need not necessarily subscribe to Kurt Koszyk's view that such 'Außenseiter-Zeitschriften' as *Die Weltbühne* 'das Bild der Weimarer Republik derart geprägt, daß sie zeitweilig mit ihren Namen identifiziert wurde'.[11] Instead, it is perhaps sufficient to understand that long-form weekly journals, chief among them *Die Weltbühne* and Stefan Großmann's *Das Tage-Buch*, did not depend on circulation and advertising revenue for their impact as much as did the competing daily titles of the large publishing houses then clustered together in the capital's newspaper quarter in Friedrichstadt, none of which could match the seven-figure print runs then common in England, America and France.[12] Indeed, Koszyk's description of the 'Außenseiter-Zeitschriften' as purveying 'eine ausgesprochene Minderheitenpublizistik, deren Gewicht vorwiegend darin bestand, daß sie die Auffassungen einer politischen Elite zum Ausdruck brachte' should not be construed as an attempt to trivialize their effect.[13] On the contrary, the refusal of Jacobsohn, Großmann, his successor Leopold Schwarzschild or the editor of *Die Aktion* Franz Pfemfert to bow to popular tastes or solicit fickle business interests enabled them directly and at length to address politically contentious issues with a conscientiousness that could not fail to be uncomfortable for Weimar leaders.

Even Ullstein's high-circulation weekly *Berliner Illustrirte Zeitung* (*BIZ*), which could sell approaching two million copies per issue, could hardly claim to be as politically disruptive as the independently operating *Weltbühne*. An otherwise broadly celebratory retrospective collection of *BIZ* articles, published by Ullstein itself in 1982, concedes that the paper had been:

---

9 Heinz Jäger [pseudonym], 'Windiges aus der deutschen Luftfahrt', *Die Weltbühne*, 25.1 (1929), 402–07.
10 Ignaz Wrobel, 'Der bewachte Kriegsschauplatz', *Die Weltbühne*, 27.2 (1931), 191–92 (p. 192).
11 Koszyk, *Deutsche Presse 1914–1945*, pp. 283–84.
12 Modris Eksteins, *The Limits of Reason: The German Democratic Press and the Collapse of Weimar Democracy*, Oxford Historical Monographs (Oxford: Oxford University Press, 1975), p. 74.
13 Koszyk, *Deutsche Presse 1914–1945*, p. 285.

im Krieg ausdrücklich national, im Frieden nüchtern und niemals aggressiv. Wenn die 'Illustrirte' den Präsidentschaftskandidaten Paul von Hindenburg nur als Feldmarschall vorstellte, seinen Rivalen Karl [sic] Marx aber als Staatsmann, so war das für die Haltung des Blatts bereits eine auffallend starke politische Äußerung.[14]

The political reticence of the mass-market *BIZ* stands in stark contrast to the stated aims of its considerably smaller counterparts, whose political partisanship was no less forceful for their professed independence from party doctrine. Pfemfert, for example, had closed the first issue of his fortnightly *Die Aktion* in 1911 with the following manifesto:

> 'Die Aktion' tritt, ohne sich auf den Boden einer bestimmten politischen Partei zu stellen, für die Idee der Großen deutschen Linken ein. 'Die Aktion' will den imposanten Gedanken einer 'Organisierung der Intelligenz' fördern [...]. [...] Bei vollkommener Unabhängigkeit von Rechts und von Links ist 'Die Aktion' eine Tribüne, von der aus jede Persönlichkeit, die Sagenswertes zu sagen hat, ungehindert sprechen kann. 'Die Aktion' hat den Ehrgeiz, ein Organ des ehrlichen Radikalismus zu sein.[15]

Even by the humble standards of contemporary periodicals, Pfemfert's journalistic venture was ultimately a resounding commercial failure, saddled as it was from at least 1923 onwards with debt and the debilitating health problems that would prevent its editor and principal contributor from even maintaining a monthly production cycle after 1925. Nonetheless, Pfemfert's early ambition is strongly reminiscent of Fritz J. Raddatz's summary of the tenets underpinning *Das Tage-Buch*, whose launch in 1920 was accompanied by Stefan Großmann's appeal for 'eine Verschwörung der schöpferischen Köpfe'.[16] *Das Tage-Buch* was predicated, Raddatz observes, on:

> die drei wesentlichen Grundsätze einer Wochenschrift: Verlegerische Unabhängigkeit, politische Radikalität – die durch die Person Leopold Schwarzschilds militant republikanisch, vehement anti-marxistisch und später brisant antifaschistisch zugleich war – und den Versuch, eine Bühne zu bilden für die intellektuellen Debatten der Zeit.[17]

---

14 Christian Ferber, 'Für jedermann: Anmerkungen zu einer öffentlichen Einrichtung' (Vorwort), in *'Berliner Illustrirte Zeitung'. Zeitbild, Chronik, Moritat für jedermann, 1892–1945*, ed. by Christian Ferber (Berlin: Ullstein, 1982), pp. 5–10 (p. 8). The reference is to the candidate of the Catholic Zentrumspartei, Wilhelm Marx.
15 Ursula Walburga-Baumeister, *'DIE AKTION' 1911–1932. Publizistische Opposition und literarischer Aktivismus der Zeitschrift im restriktiven Kontext*, Erlanger Studien, 107 (Erlangen: Palm & Enke, 1996), p. 94.
16 Stefan Großmann, 'Zum Anfang', *Das Tage-Buch*, 10 January 1920, p. 1.
17 Raddatz, *'Das Tage-Buch'*, pp. 7–8.

It should be noted that Pfemfert was a staunch Marxist, but the ostentatiously proclaimed editorial independence, the radical aspirations and the desire to serve as a forum for elevated political debate perceived by Raddatz in the rival *Tage-Buch* could otherwise be lifted straight from the personal mission statement of the editor of *Die Aktion*.

The special status of *Die Weltbühne* resided in the incorruptibility that characterized its interventions in current affairs. While Pfemfert's ideological inflexibility compromised his quest undiscriminatingly to represent a transcendental 'Große deutsche Linke', not even the subversive self-sufficiency of *Tage-Buch* could satisfy Ossietzky's compulsion to hold power to account. A major factor in the eventual succumbing by the future editor of *Die Weltbühne* to Jacobsohn's overtures to give up his role as contributing editor to *Tage-Buch* and write leader articles for him instead was Ossietzky's frustration that Großmann's outfit, unlike Jacobsohn's, had pulled its punches on the revelations about the illicit arming and training of a 'Schwarze[n] Reichswehr'.[18] Of the broadly financially independent weekly journals, *Die Weltbühne* was most able to free itself from the shackles of self-censorship and narrow party doctrine.

Indeed, it is the devout passion with which *Die Weltbühne* pursued its untethered political course that marks it out from its competitors. In describing Leopold Schwarzschild's methods after succeeding Großmann as editor of *Tage-Buch*, Fritz Raddatz attributes to him the same aloof, unemotional circumspection with which Ossietzky is sometimes credited in his capacity as editor of *Weltbühne*. Noting that everything at Schwarzschild's *Tage-Buch* 'auf kühler, genauester, gleichsam mikroskopischer Untersuchung [basiert]',[19] Raddatz paints a picture of clinical abstraction in which there is no room for political bias:

> Schwarzschilds Methode ist die eines Arztes, angewandt auf die Gesellschaftswissenschaft. Er ist vollkommen frei von jeglicher Ideologie […]. Er ist lediglich ein höchst akkurater Beobachter – und kann mit stringenter Logik solchermaßen beobachtete Details zu einem Krankenbild grausamer Schärfe zusammenfügen.[20]

For his part, Ossietzky was sometimes regarded not only as a distant, unfeeling character with whom Tucholsky, for one, could not strike up a

---

18 Raddatz, '*Das Tage-Buch*', p. 12; Kurt R. Grossmann, *Ossietzky. Ein deutscher Patriot* (Munich: Suhrkamp, 1963), p. 97.
19 Raddatz, '*Das Tage-Buch*', p. 72.
20 Raddatz, '*Das Tage-Buch*', pp. 72–73.

rapport, but as a ruthlessly logical writer untroubled in the prosecution of his arguments by personal sympathies.

However, it is Ossietzky's idealism which emerges as the overwhelming constant in many first-hand memories of him. Among the quotations most frequently adduced in support of Ossietzky's personal integrity is his explanation of his decision not to abscond after being sentenced to an eighteen-month jail term at the end of the 'Weltbühne-Prozeß': 'Der Oppositionelle, der über die Grenzen gegangen ist, spricht bald hohl ins Land herein'.[21] The corollary to Ossietzky's willingness to martyr himself for the cause of democratic republicanism is his acute awareness of his own symbolic importance as figurehead of the Weltbühne crusade against the Weimar Republic's right-wing regression.[22] In his own estimation, Ossietzky could only be an insurgent who 'seine ganze Person einsetzt' and never 'lediglich ein höchst akkurater Beobachter' in the Schwarzschild mould.[23]

By the same token, many hagiographies of Ossietzky exonerate him from any suspicion of being 'frei von jeglicher Ideologie'. Thus, upon the former's death, Thomas Mann relished the possibility that Ossietzky 'mit der Zeit ins legendäre Maß eines Menschheitskämpfers und Märtyrers wachsen könnte',[24] thereby underlining both his unimpeachable moral rectitude and his missionary vigour. For his part, fellow journalist Berthold Jacob claims to have been struck by the resemblance between Ossietzky and an engraving of the sixteenth-century knight Ulrich von Hutten that he had first glimpsed in 1905; if Jacob admired in the latter 'das Auge durchdringend und feurig',[25] he was impressed on meeting Ossietzky in 1922 by his 'feurigen stahlblauen Augen, die sich, bei besonderem Anlaß, hell illuminieren konnten'.[26] Ossietzky's predecessor, whose sudden death at forty-five briefly propelled a grieving Tucholsky into the editor's chair, seems to have exuded a similarly pugnacious spirit. In an article marking the twenty-fifth anniversary of the journal, Siegfried Jacobsohn's protégé remembered: 'Er hatte Lust zu kämpfen, er hatte das flinke Florett und eine tödlich treffende Hand. Er war ein ritterlicher Gegner – doch wohin er schlug, da wuchs kein Gras mehr'.[27] Strikingly, his posthumous biographer, Kurt R. Grossmann, similarly described Ossietzky

---

21 Carl von Ossietzky, 'Rechenschaft', Die Weltbühne, 28.1 (1932), 689–709 (p. 691).
22 As his case shows, the latter increasingly manifested itself in political justice and the suppression of dissent.
23 Ossietzky, 'Rechenschaft', p. 692.
24 Thomas Mann, 'Ossietzky zu Tode gemartert', Deutsches Volksecho, 14 May 1938, pp. 4–5.
25 Berthold Jacob, Weltbürger Ossietzky. Ein Abriß seines Werkes (Paris: Carrefour, 1937), p. 7.
26 Jacob, Weltbürger Ossietzky, p. 8.
27 Kurt Tucholsky, 'Fünfundzwanzig Jahre', Die Weltbühne, 26.2 (1930), 373–82 (p. 374).

as 'ein[en] ritterliche[n] Fechter'.[28] The common denominator in profiles of the two longest-serving editors of Weltbühne is thus their easily aroused combative instinct, allied in both cases to a chivalric code of honour.

Not for nothing, however, is Die Weltbühne most readily identified with the chameleon figure of Kurt Tucholsky, who provided the initial impetus for the political turn of Die Schaubühne as early as 1913. A deft practitioner of many literary forms from the novella to the cabaret chanson, the mordantly witty Tucholsky contributed 1,552 articles to the journal in the inter-war period alone, availing himself of a quartet of pseudonyms in order to give free rein to the range of different emotional responses elicited in him by the cultural and political vicissitudes of his time.[29] Of these, the predominant persona was the peevish Ignaz Wrobel, whose fierce denunciations of reactionary prejudice and hypocrisy distilled a generalized sense of frustration within Weltbühne ranks that the democratic German state which had emerged after the abdication of the Kaiser was, as Tucholsky himself put it in an article of the same name, a 'zufällige Republik',[30] or, in Ossietzky's still more provocative words, 'eine unmögliche Republik'.[31]

Prominent though it was, the risk of fixating on the adversarial attitude displayed by the journal towards most Weimar governments lies in over-interpreting it. The overwhelming majority of its contributors were fundamentally in favour of republican democracy. Contrary to Golo Mann's malign characterization of the 'ungebundene[n] Linksliteraten' of the German press,[32] the Weltbühne stable had no quarrel with the Weimar Republic in principle, but rather with the way in which it was felt to be betraying democracy in practice. Indeed, Die Weltbühne was unrelenting in its opposition both to the remnants of monarchism and to the waxing Fascism that, in its estimation, bedevilled German public life and jeopardized the republican order. In spite of its own grave reservations about the widely unpopular Treaty of Versailles, the journal also protested against the systematic undermining of the agreement by a succession of coalition governments, while it was partly revelations about the clandestine rearmament of the skeleton Reichswehr under the tutelage of the Red Army in Siberia that in 1935 earned the editor responsible, Carl von Ossietzky, the Nobel Peace Prize, which he accepted from the Nazi concentration camp at Esterwegen (Prussia).

---

28 Grossmann, Ossietzky. Ein deutscher Patriot, p. 109.
29 Elmar E. Holly, 'Die Weltbühne' 1918–1933. Ein Register sämtlicher Autoren und Beiträge, Abhandlungen und Materialien zur Publistik (Berlin: Colloquium, 1989), pp. 39–41.
30 Kurt Tucholsky, 'Die zufällige Republik', Die Weltbühne, 18.2 (1922), 25–30.
31 Carl von Ossietzky, 'Seeckt und Severing', Die Weltbühne, 22.2 (1926), 559–62 (p. 562).
32 Golo Mann, Deutsche Geschichte des 19. und 20. Jahrhunderts (Frankfurt a.M.: Fischer, 1958), p. 707.

Five years after Mann's broadside Harry Pross countered that any republic which allowed itself to be brought to its knees by such criticism had no right to call itself a republic.[33] Pross's verdict, borrowed from Ossietzky, may be provocative, but his defence of the honest intentions of *Die Weltbühne* displays a shrewder understanding than Mann's of the motivation of the journal. What Pross had grasped was that the staunch republicanism of the stalwart commentators in the journal can be measured precisely by their sporadic hostility towards those politicians entrusted with Germany's democratic experiment. However, this insight did not catch on. For all that Mann's arguments were soon regarded in some quarters as a transient phenomenon of 1960s American scholarship,[34] Modris Eksteins renewed the offensive in 1975 when pointedly observing that left-liberal newspaper editors shared with none other than Joseph Goebbels an understanding of the role of the journalist as that of a biased opinion-former rather than an impartial *in*former.[35] In search of evidence for the implication that left-wing publications had ultimately poisoned the mind of the Weimar population against republicanism just as effectively as the much more numerous right-wing press, Eksteins eventually cites the cases of Theodor Wolff, popular editor of the *Berliner Tageblatt*, and Hellmut von Gerlach, his equally esteemed counterpart on *Die Welt am Montag*, who not only frequently contributed to *Die Weltbühne* but assumed the acting editorship following Ossietzky's arrest in 1932. Both men had resigned, four years apart and in quite different circumstances, from the Deutsche Demokratische Partei (DDP), which Wolff had helped found in 1918; Eksteins chastises both decisions as guided by purely negative impulses, 'rather than a positive desire to achieve greater independence on political matters for the newspapers which the two men edited'.[36] Not content with this, he proceeds to overstate his case:

> The withdrawal of these leading journalists from the DDP symbolized the retreat of many idealistic republicans and democrats from the politics of the Weimar Republic. The DDP, in many respects, embodied the goals and ideals of the Republic; not without justification did it proclaim itself 'the true party of the constitution'. Disengagement from it also signified disengagement from the realities of the Republic.[37]

---

33 Harry Pross, *Literatur und Politik. Geschichte und Programme der politisch-literarischen Zeitschriften im deutschen Sprachgebiet seit 1870* (Olten: Walter, 1963), p. 107.
34 Harold L. Poor, 'Kurt Tucholsky and the Question of the Destructiveness of the Intellectual Left in the Weimar Republic', in *Perspectives & Personalities: Studies in Modern German Literature (Honoring Claude Hill)*, ed. by Ralph Ley and others (Heidelberg: Winter, 1978), pp. 313–19.
35 Eksteins, *The Limits of Reason*, p. 74.
36 Eksteins, *The Limits of Reason*, p. 100.
37 Eksteins, *The Limits of Reason*, p. 100.

Eksteins is not alone: too many scholars have succumbed to the temptation to pin the blame for the collapse of Germany's first democracy on its democratic critics, apparently banking on the intriguingly counter-intuitive nature of this verdict to incite the curiosity of their readers.

The turn of this century witnessed a backlash against this stubborn thesis, with Peter Queckbörner labelling Alf Enseling's condemnation of the ideological intransigence of the journal in 1962 a 'Vorwurf aus der Steinzeit der Publizistik'.[38] Momentum swung back the other way, however, with the publication of Riccardo Bavaj's work *Von links gegen Weimar* (2005), in which Bavaj curiously accuses *Die Weltbühne* of growing more, not less, radical over the Weimar period, even to the point of abandoning its faith in parliamentary democracy altogether and fostering anti-republican sentiments. Bavaj's claim that the journal strayed 'zusehends in die Nähe des deutschen Kommunismus' and thereby turned its back on the Weimar system stands reality on its head.[39] Indeed, such untenable claims are testament to the dangers of over-identifying journals with their most vociferous writers: Bavaj's principal body of evidence is the work of Alphons Steiniger, a unique figure whom it would be misleading to cast as in any way representative.

The disingenuousness of Bavaj's case against the *Weltbühne* is underscored by the selective nature of his citation from the secondary literature. The first line of the foreword to *Von links gegen Weimar* refers admiringly to Kurt Sontheimer's study from 1962 of anti-democratic thought in the Weimar period; and Bavaj eventually quotes Sontheimer to the effect that the left-wing intellectual press '*nicht* dazu beigetragen hat, diesen Parteien den Rücken zu stärken'.[40] What Bavaj conveniently leaves out is Sontheimer's subsequent clear distinction between the Republic's nationalist assailants and its left-wing critics, whom Sontheimer celebrates as 'humanitäre Sozialisten, aufrechte Streiter für eine freie, menschenwürdige und gerechte Gesellschaftsordnung'.[41] Bavaj's reluctance to acknowledge the gap between consciously seeking to bring down a state and finding fault with its representatives is exemplified by

---

38 Alf Enseling, '*Die Weltbühne*'. *Organ der intellektuellen Linken*, Studien zur Publizistik, 2 (Münster: Fahle, 1962), p. 134; Peter Queckbörner, '*Zwischen Irrsinn und Verzweiflung*'. *Zum erweiterten Kulturbegriff der Zeitschrift 'Die Schaubühne'/'Die Weltbühne' im Ersten Weltkrieg*, Analysen und Dokumente, 41 (Frankfurt a.M.: Lang, 2000), p. 25.
39 Riccardo Bavaj, *Von links gegen Weimar. Linkes antiparlamentarisches Denken in der Weimarer Republik*, Politik- und Gesellschaftsgeschichte, 67 (Kempten: Dietz, 2005), p. 415.
40 Kurt Sontheimer, *Antidemokratisches Denken in der Weimarer Republik. Die politischen Ideen des deutschen Nationalismus zwischen 1918 und 1933* (Munich: Nymphenburger, 1962), p. 389. This is then cited in Bavaj, *Von links gegen Weimar*, p. 417.
41 Sontheimer, *Antidemokratisches Denken*, p. 390.

his telling omission of the word 'jedoch' in between his citation of Sontheimer's observation that right-wing commentators 'ihr literarisches Zerstörungswerk an der Republik trieben' and the latter's description of left-wing despair at the perceived 'Degeneration und Abfall' of the republican system.[42] In the original, this all-important adverbial conjunction serves to establish an opposition between the intentions of these two groups,[43] but in Bavaj's account Right and Left are yoked together as if both were bent on the destruction of the democratic order. It would be stretching generosity to declare this an oversight.

Although Bavaj dedicates twenty-three pages of his book to an excessively earnest study of Kurt Tucholsky as a 'Paradebeispiel eines solch radikalen Denkens der Kompromisslosigkeit',[44] it need hardly be said that the *Weltbühne* strategy for exposing the nationalist world view and preparing the ground among its readership for its own patriotism cannot be reduced to Ignaz Wrobel's colourful character assassinations, any more than to the mischievous lyrics of another of his alter egos, Kaspar Hauser. It was broad-based, encompassing closely drawn profiles of business leaders, atmospheric industrial reportage and thorough indictments of legal injustice from the pen of such USPD luminaries as Heinrich Ströbel and Felix Stössinger, with regular columnists including the future architect of the constitution of the German Democratic Republic, Alphons Steiniger, the later co-founder of the *Frankfurter Allgemeine Zeitung* Erich Dombrowski and high-profile intellectuals from Kurt Hiller to Otto Flake. However, the thread running through a critical mass of the journal's output is the conviction that the future of the German nation depended on a programme of drastic reform that would enshrine democracy in the German body politic and release the nation's captive progressive spirit from authoritarian oppression.

Much as *Die Weltbühne* could afford to be considerably more forthright than most daily newspapers and was unusual even among left-wing journals in its willingness to adopt uncompromising political positions, its patriotism fell on already-fertile ground at a time when Left and Right frequently and vociferously crossed swords in the name of the national interest. Benjamin Ziemann's study of the republican patriotism of ex-servicemen from 2013 demonstrates the strong currency of the national idea in left-wing circles in the post-war period. At the outset of a volume that sifts a wide variety of soldierly sources, Ziemann argues:

> 'Patriotic pacifism' is indeed an appropriate term for the political core values of the Reichsbanner members in particular, as they abhorred

---

42 Bavaj, *Von links gegen Weimar*, p. 417.
43 Sontheimer, *Antidemokratisches Denken*, p. 389.
44 Bavaj, *Von links gegen Weimar*, p. 415.

war, criticised armaments and were convinced that the Republic represented a better Germany which had left the legacy of Prussian militarism behind.[45]

The concept of patriotic pacifism and its competing iterations are discussed at some length in Chapter 2; it is cited here merely as an example of the extent to which conventional expressions of patriotism, such as militarism, were subject to challenge in the Weimar period as political progressives reacted faster and more creatively than their imperialist opponents to the system-change symbolized by the Weimar constitution. Their ability and desire to equate the new order with a patriotic ideal reflect the urgency with which the republican Left took the rhetorical fight to the nationalist Right in the struggle for moral custody of the national cause.

Appearing a year before *Contested Commemorations*, *The Weimar Moment*, the volume edited by Leonard V. Kaplan and Rudy Koshar, identifies several more areas in which republican actors confronted right-wing propaganda about what could be considered consistent with patriotic values. Thus Peter E. Gordon interprets philosopher Ernst Cassirer's address on the ninth anniversary of the Weimar Constitution in 1928 as 'a legitimation of republican constitutionalism against the nationalist prejudice that condemned the republic as essentially *un-German*',[46] based on the premise that 'the very idea of a republican constitution derives from principles native to German philosophy in general and German idealism in particular'.[47] This claim, lent an explicitly religious inflection, would be repeated in the following decade by the legal scholar Carl Joachim Friedrich in an attempt to prove the Calvinist origins of representative democracy.[48] Turning away from disputes over the inherently national qualities of republican government, another chapter even cites the aforementioned '*Weltbühne*-Prozeß' at length to highlight the stubborn prevalence in Weimar courtrooms of an anachronistically nationalistic understanding of treason, albeit without linking the application and enforcement of international law to a polemical reformulation of

---

45 Benjamin Ziemann, *Contested Commemorations: Republican War Veterans and Weimar Political Culture*, Studies in the Social and Cultural History of Modern Warfare, 36 (Cambridge: Cambridge University Press, 2013), p. 13.
46 Peter E. Gordon, 'German Idealism and German Liberalism in the 1920s: Remarks on Ernst Cassirer and the Historicity of Interpretation', in *The Weimar Moment: Liberalism, Political Theology and Law*, ed. by Leonard V. Kaplan and Rudy Koshar, Graven Images (New York: Lexington, 2012), pp. 337–44 (p. 341).
47 Gordon, 'German Idealism', p. 339.
48 Udi Greenberg, 'The Limits of Dictatorship and the Origins of Democracy: The Political Theory of Carl J. Friedrich from Weimar to the Cold War', in *The Weimar Moment*, ed. by Kaplan and Koshar, pp. 443–64 (p. 454).

the national interest such as was often to be found in the pages of the *Weltbühne*.[49] Democratic Germans were therefore entitled to argue that, to the same extent as promoting the republican principle meant honouring one's German inheritance, to commit treason for the sake of preventing war was to discharge one's responsibilities to one's living compatriots.

It is increasingly clear that the Weimar period was a time of intense ontological debate concerning such visceral notions as national loyalty and duty. Almost half a century ago Ronald Taylor offered a tantalizing glimpse of the particular role of *Die Weltbühne* in this patriotic discourse, remarking that:

> the intellectualism of the *Weltbühne* circle did not include a denigration of true patriotism, and they were as concerned as any right-wing nationalist to see the restoration of German well-being and self-respect. It depended on where one sought these qualities.[50]

Taylor's failure to elaborate on this profound point is understandable within the confines of an overview, but the observation seems to have prompted little in the way of prolonged engagement in the decades since. It is, accordingly, a key concern of this study to demonstrate precisely how *Die Weltbühne* succeeded in making a vital contribution to the cultivation of a new patriotic idiom by putting at its disposal a clear vocabulary, by turns affirmative and antagonistic, for articulating a progressive answer to the right-wing nationalist challenge.

Patriotism versus Nationalism

This is the first study of *Die Weltbühne* to move beyond the question of the journal's republican credentials and closely examine its complex relationship with patriotism. Previous research into the journal, to which twenty-first century scholarship has contributed only a modest number of dedicated studies,[51] has tended to focus either on the personalities of its editors or on its short-term stance on specific domestic or international issues.[52] Although

---

49 Peter Caldwell, 'Sovereignty, Constitutionalism, and the Myth of the State: Article Four of the Weimar Constitution', in *The Weimar Moment*, ed. by Kaplan and Koshar, pp. 345–70 (pp. 357–62).
50 Taylor, *Literature and Society in Germany, 1918–1945*, p. 27.
51 Queckbörner, *'Zwischen Irrsinn und Verzweiflung'* (2000); Greis and Oswalt (eds), *Aus Teutschland Deutschland machen* (2008).
52 W. B. van der Grijn Santen, *'Die Weltbühne' und das Judentum. Eine Studie über das Verhältnis der Wochenschrift 'Die Weltbühne' zum Judentum, hauptsächlich die Jahre 1918– 1926 betreffend* (Würzburg: Königshausen & Neumann, 1994).

such limitations can be seen as a reflection of the status of the journal as a weekly publication dealing mainly in current affairs, the near-total absence from this list of any attempt to chart the development of a single idea over the final fifteen years of the presence of the paper on German soil creates a gap in our understanding of its legacy that demands to be filled.[53] This is another way in which it is hoped this study will reinvigorate scholarly engagement with *Die Weltbühne*, as the sheer volume of its output over its lifespan offers substantial scope for further detailed investigations on a variety of other recurring themes. Few, if any, though, can be said to have defined the activity of the journal to the same degree as did its conflicted attitude to Germany itself.

In order to appreciate the radical nature of the break by *Die Weltbühne* with traditional patriotism, it is necessary first to understand how the term had conventionally been understood. Only once the generally accepted meaning of the term and its nexus of mental associations have been established can the reader appreciate the extent to which patriotic sentiments in *Die Weltbühne* confound the expectations that, in many quarters, cling to the notion of patriotism to this day. Deriving from the Greek *patris*, meaning land of one's fathers, via the Latin *patria* and the French *patriotisme*, the term patriotism denotes, at its most basic level, love of one's country. However, it has often aroused suspicion on account of its frequent deployment as a synonym for nationalism, whereby it has accrued associations of aggression, xenophobia and self-aggrandizement rooted in such historical precedents as the vanquishing of the Weimar state by Fascist nationalism. Accordingly, one late-twentieth-century English definition hints at the collocation of the term with extremism by rendering it as 'love of or *zealous* devotion to one's country';[54] while another, dating from the beginning of the millennium, adds 'concern for its defence' before directing the reader to the entry for nationalism, which duly offers patriotism as a synonym.[55] Yet another dictionary, printed a year before the first, likewise errs on the side of negativity, declaring the patriot to be 'one who truly, *though sometimes injudiciously*, loves and serves his fatherland', albeit granting the adjective 'patriotic' an interest in 'the public welfare'.[56] In the world after Hitler it is hardly surprising that many

---

53 An exception is Dieter Lang's meticulously researched *Staat, Recht und Justiz im Kommentar der Zeitschrift 'Die Weltbühne'* (Frankfurt a.M.: Lang, 1996), which spans the entire Weimar period, dealing primarily with specific cases and legal controversies under thematic rubrics.
54 *The Shorter Oxford English Dictionary*, ed. by C. T. Onions (London: Guild, 1987), p. 1529.
55 *Collins English Dictionary*, ed. by Diana Treffry, 4th edn (2000), p. 1138.
56 *Chambers Concise 20th Century* Dictionary, ed. by G. W. Davidson, M. A. Seaton and J. Simpson (Edinburgh: Chambers, 1986), p. 714.

academics should have followed lexicographers in imputing sinister motives to any avowal of patriotic commitment.

Of these denunciations, few can have been as emphatic as that of American philosopher George Kateb. At the outset of a work bearing the uncompromising title *Patriotism and Other Mistakes* (2006), Kateb asks:

> What is patriotism? It is love of one's country. How is patriotism most importantly shown? Let us not mince words. The answer is that it is most importantly shown in a readiness, whether reluctant or matter-of-fact, social or zealous, to die and to kill for one's country. These two answers constitute the most common understanding of patriotism.[57]

In his determination to prove the moral bankruptcy of patriotic loyalty, Kateb does not trouble to distinguish between patriotism and nationalism. From his unequivocal description of the former as 'a commitment to the system of premature, violent death',[58] it is a short distance to the verdict with which he denies his subject even the potential for being a constructive force: 'Patriotism is on a permanent moral holiday, and once it is made dynamic, it invariably becomes criminal'.[59]

In recent years, however, resistance to such a simplistic characterization of patriotism has steadily grown. In 2007 Jan-Werner Müller explored the capacity of constitutional patriotism to foster an affirmative national consciousness predicated on pride in one's country's hard-won membership of a rules-based international order. As Müller explains, the notion of constitutional patriotism was first defined by Dolf Sternberger in the *Frankfurter Allgemeine Zeitung* on the occasion of the thirtieth anniversary of the West German constitution on 23 May 1979,[60] before being developed by Jürgen Habermas.[61] Sternberger's seminal article, the bulk of which is concerned with demonstrating and endorsing the benevolent reach of the *Grundgesetz* into various facets of quotidian life, ends on a warning against complacency: 'Eine gewisse maßvolle Unzufriedenheit ist dem Staat förderlich. Sie mindert nicht die Treue, die der Verfassung geschuldet wird. Gegen erklärte Feinde jedoch muß die Verfassung verteidigt werden, das ist patriotische Pflicht'.[62] In its emphasis on dissent as a viable expression

---

57 George Kateb, *Patriotism and Other Mistakes* (New Haven, CT: Yale University Press, 2006), p. 7.
58 Kateb, *Patriotism and Other Mistakes*, p. 8.
59 Kateb, *Patriotism and Other Mistakes*, p. 13.
60 Jan-Werner Müller, *Constitutional Patriotism* (Princeton, NJ: Princeton University Press, 2007), p. 25.
61 Müller, *Constitutional Patriotism*, pp. 28–29; p. 34.
62 Dolf Sternberger, 'Verfassungspatriotismus', in *Schriften*, ed. by Dolf Sternberger, 12 vols in 13 (Frankfurt a.M.: Insel, 1977–96), x, *Verfassungspatriotismus* (1990), pp. 13–16 (pp. 15–16).

of patriotic sentiment, this concept echoes the constructive criticism of their country by writers in *Die Weltbühne*, borne along as this was by an 'adversarial relationship with democracy's enemies, real or presumed' such as that later encouraged by Sternberger.[63] For his part, Müller counters Kateb's charge that 'the patriot always gives his side the benefit of every moral doubt'[64] by stressing the importance to constitutional patriots of their country's adoption of 'universal moral values', from civil liberties to anti-discrimination laws.[65]

Meanwhile, in his lecture 'In Defense of a Reasonable Patriotism' (2018) William Galston takes issue directly with Kateb's insistence that patriotic love automatically implies disdain for other countries, arguing that 'it is perfectly possible to love one's own without becoming morally narrow, or unreasonable, let alone irrational'.[66] Patriotism resides for Galston in complete candour vis-à-vis the moral standing of one's country, that is to say, in 'caring enough about one's country to try to correct it when it goes astray'.[67] Re-imagined as rationale rather than religious faith, patriotic pride loses its congenital quality and acquires a strict conditionality. Indeed, in answer to Kateb's charge against patriotism of criminality, one might argue that, whereas the nation need not justify its actions to the nationalist, in the eyes of the patriot it is permanently on probation.

The difference between the patriotism on display in the pages of *Die Weltbühne* and the nationalism with which patriotism is often confused was stark. The nationalist understanding of the German national interest, which contributors to the journal strenuously challenged, dated back to the *Kaiserreich*. This nationalism can be broken down into two distinct forms: state-based and citizen-based, or, more properly, subject-based. The former, the imprint of which *Weltbühne* writers regarded as permeating Weimar society long after its imperial object had ceased to exist, glorified Prussian conquest in the name of a collective German destiny. A raft of studies dealing specifically with the German nationalist tradition[68] support

---

63 Müller, *Constitutional Patriotism*, p. 25.
64 Kateb, *Patriotism and Other Mistakes*, p. 13.
65 Müller, *Constitutional Patriotism*, p. 36.
66 William Galston, 'In Defense of a Reasonable Patriotism' <https://www.brookings.edu/research/in-defense-of-a-reasonable-patriotism/> [accessed 25 June 2020].
67 Galston, 'In Defense of a Reasonable Patriotism'.
68 Bernhard Viel, *Utopie der Nation. Ursprünge des Nationalismus im Roman der Gründerzeit*, Blaue Reihe Wissenschaft, 6 (Berlin: Matthes & Seitz, 2009), p. 46; Michael Hughes, *Nationalism and Society: Germany 1800–1945* (London: Arnold, 1988), p. 17; Roger Chickering, *We Men Who Feel Most German: Cultural Study of the Pan-German League 1886–1914* (Boston, MA: Allen & Unwin, 1984), p. 26.

the generally held view,⁶⁹ argued most cogently by Ernest Gellner in his landmark work *Nations and Nationalism* (1983),⁷⁰ that nationalist rulers confronted with the problem of their own popular legitimacy have tended to present themselves in the role of secular 'Great Redeemer' anointed to re-establish the links between their wayward compatriots and a glorious past.⁷¹ Gellner's description of the populist function of nationalism is particularly striking in that it simultaneously depicts state-based nationalism as drily bureaucratic in content and mythic in form:

> Nationalism is not the awakening of an old, latent, dormant force, though that is how it does indeed present itself. It is in reality the consequence of a new form of social organization, based on deeply internalized, education-dependent high cultures, each protected by its own state.⁷²

In the *Kaiserreich*, born out of Prussia's victory over France in 1871, the need for a founding myth translated into an authoritarian propaganda offensive that invoked the self-sacrifice of a supposedly homogenous German people on the battlefield in order to consolidate the grip of an overwhelmingly Prussian social elite on political power.

Official nationalism in the German Empire duly contrived its own iconography in the form of monuments celebrating either Bismarck or the first Kaiser Wilhelm, as well as those recording the act of unification itself.⁷³ As Abigail Green points out, most such monuments were commissioned and funded not by public subscription but by private individuals.⁷⁴ Nonetheless, this fact merely underlines the extent to which some imperial subjects had internalized the state's appetite for ceremonial self-fashioning. Roger

---

69 Ernest Renan, *Qu'est-ce qu'une nation? Conférence faite en Sorbonne, le 11 Mars 1882* (Paris: Calmann Lévy, 1882; repr. Barcelona: Flammarion, 2011); Karl Deutsch, *Nationalism and Social Communication* (Cambridge, MA: MIT Press, 1972).
70 Ernest Gellner, *Nations and Nationalism*, New Perspectives on the Past, 2nd edn (Ithaca, NY: Cornell University Press, 2008 [1983]).
71 The original Great Redeemer was Jesus Christ, who is said to have died upon the Cross to absolve mankind of its sins. In the secular variation on the theme, nationalist leaders promised the people whom they wished to govern that under their rule they would transcend their compromised recent past and return to an original state of purity or perfection.
72 Gellner, *Nations and Nationalism*, p. 46.
73 Abigail Green, *Fatherlands: State-Building and Nationhood in Nineteenth-Century Germany*, New Studies in European History (Cambridge: Cambridge University Press, 2001), p. 315.
74 Green, *Fatherlands*, p. 313.

Chickering takes a particularly cynical view of the attempts by the imperial regime to win the support of its subjects:

> The nationalism officially propagated in the new Empire was a civic religion; the national community that was to be the object of civic loyalty was coterminous with the new political entity that had emerged in the heart of Europe. Although it could build on political traditions that extended at least as far back as 1848, this 'official nationalism' had shallow roots. The symbolism of the new nation-state was meagre and included, as Theodor Schieder has pointed out, little more than a flag, an army (which was not really national), and the monarchy.[75]

Events such as the *Kaiserparaden*, the Kaiser's annual inspection of the troops in four separate regions of his empire, or the citizen-led institution of Sedan Day, a regular anniversary in honour of the decisive victory over the French forces in 1870, reflect the dependence of state-based nationalism on historical symbolism, however specious it may have been. The glamour of the army was exploited at regular intervals to conjure what Alon Confino has called 'a timeless national memory invented in the second half of the nineteenth century for a timeless nation, unified in 1871'.[76] This carefully staged nationalist fervour apparently left little room for introspection or visions of the future.

For the most part, these blind spots were shared by the grass-roots chauvinists of the nationalist associations. Proponents of subject-based nationalism typically formed rigidly hierarchical associations and clubs whose prominent members were overwhelmingly prosperous, usually Protestant, individuals hailing from the university-educated middle and upper classes and acting in a private capacity.[77] They met regularly to debate, produce newsletters or thrash out a consensus on the basis of which the organization could then lobby government on matters such as colonial expansion in West Africa or the strengthening of the imperial fleet. Like their counterparts in government, these activists were intent on preserving many aspects of the status quo. This reactionary nationalism revolved around a *deutschnational* world view which Chickering summarizes thus:

> The navy, the colonies, the language, and Germans struggling to preserve their ethnic integrity all ultimately meshed with one another to symbolize the defense of culture, authority, and order at home and abroad. The patriotic societies shared a common fear of threats

---

75 Chickering, *We Men Who Feel Most German*, p. 26.
76 Alon Confino, 'The Nation as a Local Metaphor: National Memory and the German Empire, 1871–1918', *History and Memory*, 1 (1993), 42–86 (p. 78).
77 Chickering, *We Men Who Feel Most German*, p. 188.

to these symbols. The ideologies of all these organizations were informed by a common vision of conflict between the forces of order and disorder, whether this conflict be played out in terms of rivalry for naval power and empire, or in the progressive subversion of one language and culture by another.[78]

Notwithstanding the obvious interest of these associations in the protection of Germany against cultural or territorial disintegration, this passage also hints at a bone of contention between state- and subject-based nationalism in the *Kaiserreich*. At its most extreme, the latter forcefully advocated the territorial expansion of the German Empire, to which end it called for an ethnic crusade against Slavs, Jews and any other racial group whose presence on the European mainland was deemed to hamper the construction of a contiguous German superstate.[79] As Chickering shows, members of the *Alldeutscher Verband* shared with their Marxist adversaries the belief that conflict between groups was the driving force of human civilization.[80] There the similarities ended, however, as Pan-Germanists held ethnicity, and not class, to be the standard under which humanity was fated to go into battle.

German nationalism in the decades before the First World War, then, had two faces: the complacent self-mythologizing of the imperial state and the restless ethnic paranoia of the nationalist associations.[81] Frustration with 'the limits of official nationalism' in *deutschnational* circles did not put a brake on the ambitions of these associations,[82] which foresaw the absorption of the German diaspora into a vast German realm spanning the European mainland between Belgium and Romania.[83] Dictated as it was by the notion of mortal enmity between races, the inexorable logic of this programme demanded a total victory culminating in the colonization of all European lands in which an etymologically Germanic tongue was spoken.[84] Under this plan the *Kaiserreich* was to seize all available sea ports *en route* to achieving world domination at the expense of the British, American and Russian powers. The historical distortions necessary to justify so sweeping a campaign of reclamation resulted in

---

78 Chickering, *We Men Who Feel Most German*, p. 187.
79 Chickering, *We Men Who Feel Most German*, p. 1.
80 Chickering, *We Men Who Feel Most German*, p. 77.
81 'Complacent' because the state regarded ceremonies alone as sufficient to inculcate national pride in its citizens.
82 Green, *Fatherlands*, p. 330.
83 Chickering, *We Men Who Feel Most German*, p. 188.
84 Felicity Rash, *German Images of the Self and the Other: Nationalist, Colonialist and Anti-Semitic Discourse, 1871–1918* (London: Palgrave Macmillan, 2012), p. 63.

an 'Überspannung der germanischen Idee',[85] which Georg Steinhausen identified in 1913 as characteristic of the worst excesses of the nascent German imagined community.[86]

Arguments centred on shared linguistic or ethnic heritage, not in themselves indicative of a nationalist viewpoint, were thus abused by nationalists in support of destructive foreign-policy aims. This cause took human form in the person of the German *Pionier*. All the major nationalist associations, chief among them the Pan-German League, routinely published pamphlets evoking the splendid isolation of a German nation assailed on all sides by foreign conspirators. The 'pioneer' was a popular conceit to illustrate this imagined encirclement. Mobilized with especial frequency against the dread figure of the Slavic migrant labourer, the 'pioneer' represented the last bastion of valiant German resistance against barbarian invasion.[87] Such flights of xenophobia, which conveniently defined the 'pioneer' in opposition to his enemies, cast the German in heroic caricature while relieving the reader of the burden of filling in the outlines.[88]

Despite the broad scholarly consensus to which this rough anatomy of the two predominant forms of nationalism in pre-war Germany attests, few Germanists have evinced much interest in building upon it by distinguishing between the neurotic nationalism of the *Kaiserreich*, be it state- or association-driven, and the radically different patriotism with which the German left wing experimented in the post-war period. The effect of this has been to create the impression that little had changed in the interim, instead of allowing for the possibility that new forms of attachment to the German nation might have grown out of the collapse of the pre-war regime.

In *Nationalism and Society: Germany 1800–1945* (1988), Michael Hughes takes a tentative step towards shifting the dial. Patriotism, he argues, 'can exist as purely passive national sentiments not necessarily determining men's political behaviour'. Nationalism, on the other hand, has 'two essential ingredients: sentiment and action'.[89] Reaffirming this putative difference, Hughes insists that nationalism 'must contain an element of aspiration.

---

85 Georg Steinhausen, *Geschichte der deutschen Kultur*, 2 vols (Leipzig: Bibliographisches Institut, 1904–13), II (1913), p. 493.
86 For this concept see Benedict Anderson, *Imagined Communities: Reflection on the Origin and Spread of Nationalism* (New York: Verso, 2016 [1983]).
87 Chickering, *We Men Who Feel Most German*, p. 83.
88 Because the pioneer existed as a counterfoil to the figure of the Slavic migrant labourer, he was not modelled on a real person with natural human limitations or weaknesses and was not equipped with any distinguishing characteristics beyond his exaggeratedly heroic 'Germanness'.
89 Hughes, *Nationalism and Society*, p. 16.

Like Peter Pan it never grows up: if it does, it disappears. Nationalism involves dissatisfaction with the existing situation and the desire to change it by the achievement of national goals'.[90] Ultimately, this distinction between an energetic nationalism and a self-indulgent patriotism grievously underestimates the potential of patriotism as a motor for political change. Hughes even pays lip service to the untested assumption that patriotism is merely xenophobia without the will to action.[91] By contrast, this study shows that German patriotism in the inter-war period could be both highly political and emphatically progressive. The example of the left-wing *Die Weltbühne* does not merely call for a re-assessment of knee-jerk assumptions of equivalence between patriotism and nationalism, but also demonstrates that patriotism can function as a viable progressive alternative to nationalist political projects.

This book deconstructs left-wing patriotism as it manifests itself in *Die Weltbühne* by isolating its three distinct variants: regionalist, internationalist and Socialist. Since these descriptors do not refer to closely circumscribed cultural or political programmes with designated spokespeople, studying them inevitably throws up tensions and contradictions. As prevailing trends, however, they together form the backdrop to a large portion of the interwar output of *Die Weltbühne* and, as such, constitute an indispensable key to understanding the relationship of the journal with the German national idea. Taken together, the three categories of left-wing patriotism identified in this study of *Die Weltbühne* constitute a novel means of conceiving of this phenomenon.

The regionalist streak in the *Weltbühne* corpus reveals a pronounced tendency to challenge simplistic views of German nationhood and instead project a more diverse national identity less susceptible to nationalist generalizations. More explicit still is the unwavering commitment of the journal to internationalism, which frames its columnists' repeated endorsement of a new leadership role for Germany in world affairs that would actively exploit its status as a militarily defeated nation. The Socialism of *Die Weltbühne* is an axiomatic part of its legacy; however, as elucidated here for the first time, the journal mounted Socialist arguments not only for their own sake but out of the conviction that Socialism was the only political ideology that could save Germany from self-destruction. This monograph dedicates a chapter to each of these three forms of patriotism, highlighting both points of intersection and areas of divergence to present a comprehensive picture of the complex and crowded eco-system of left-wing patriotism cultivated in *Die Weltbühne*.

90 Hughes, *Nationalism and Society*, p. 17.
91 Hughes, *Nationalism and Society*, p. 16.

Structure of the Monograph

The first chapter starts by exploring an eclectic assortment of texts, including a polemic, several sentimental essays and two poems, which invoke the regional idea of *Heimat* to charge Germany's military and business elite with jeopardizing their country's territorial integrity. In the wake of the Treaty of Versailles, which imposed heavy losses on Germany's western and eastern borders, dismay made itself felt across the political spectrum. In *Die Weltbühne* this consternation did not express itself in demands for the return of rightfully German territory, but in the registering of an inalienable emotional ownership of the lost lands and the denunciation of those Germans whom journal authors held responsible for the depletion of their country or, indeed, for their own dispossession. On the basis of a thorough review of the discourse on *Heimat*, the first half of this chapter thus argues that the private *Heimat* often serves as the principal touchstone for acts of collective identity-building and not as a tool of division. The second half of the chapter turns away from the aftershocks of Versailles and considers the slight but significant *œuvre* of Wilhelm Michel, as well as two more poems and a prose ode, as documents of a patriotic particularism centred on communities and regions that remained within Germany's borders after the war. These pieces are bound together by what they reveal about the capacity of the regional *Heimat* to foster a sense of national belonging.

The second chapter is the most ambitious in scope. Divided into three parts, it seeks to present a cross-section of what is, superficially, the most paradoxical facet of the journal's patriotism: its internationalism. To this end, it begins with a close reading of three lengthy series published in *Die Weltbühne* in 1922 that reflect the conflicted attitude of the journal towards France by treating the vexed Franco-German relationship from three radically different standpoints. The next two sections dissect the fixation in the journal on Germany's international moral rehabilitation and its unstinting support of pacifism, resolving in the process the ostensible tension between internationalism and patriotism by identifying fear for Germany's future as the main driver behind the vociferous globalist rhetoric of *Die Weltbühne*. Since consensus existed neither on the precise co-ordinates of the moral compass that would save German sovereignty, nor on how the patriotic dividends of pacifism should be pitched to a sceptical imagined readership, the analysis unpicks the tangled web in which the internationalist patriotism of the journal is ensnared and scrutinizes each strand in turn. At the level of the text itself, particular interest is taken in how the language of reconciliation and atonement intertwines with the idiom of self-preservation and outright exceptionalism, particular attention being drawn to the dramatic phraseology of the reformed mercenary Carl Mertens and the campaigning pacifist intellectual Kurt Hiller as markers of the perceived urgency of Germany's predicament.

The third chapter follows the evolution of the Socialist stance displayed by *Die Weltbühne*, tracing its moderation in tone from the rhetoric of revolution to the nostrums of reform. The iconoclastic enthusiasm with which the journal greeted the fall of the *Kaiserreich* and the dawn of the democratic age peaked in excited appeals for Germans to fulfil their historical destiny and finally redeem the hopes of their revolutionary ancestors by ushering into being a truly just society in which privilege and penury would be a distant memory. The centrepiece of the section on revolutionary patriotism is a controversial series, authored by an anonymous former officer in the Imperial Army, which combines the revisionist patriotism of prominent left-wing radicals from the *Weltbühne* stable with the fraternalist imperatives of international Communism. The next section explores the social-democratic turn in the post-1919 *Weltbühne* against the backdrop of three instances of civil unrest: the Kapp Putsch of 1920; the March Action of 1921; and the simmering tensions in the Ruhr between 1920 and 1925. This section pays especially close attention to the immoderate language in which moderate republicanism was frequently couched, locating a patriotic fervour in the virulent anti-extremism of the journal's leader writers; the currency in these articles of the *Volkskörper* discourse illuminates the state of flux in which the notion of the progressive is perpetually caught.[92] Thus, whereas the first chapter attests to the designs of the journal for holding Germany together in a spiritual sense and the second documents its efforts to keep the Weimar Republic alive as an independent state, the third ultimately reveals the desire of *Die Weltbühne* to tend to the physical health of the German nation.

---

92 A distant off-shoot of the Classical notion of the 'body politic', the *Volkskörper* was a nineteenth-century metaphor for the German nation that gained in currency after the First World War as Germans digested the lasting physical and territorial impact of the conflict. Though it lent itself through its biological overtones to the racial pseudo-science of the Nazi regime, the term was by no means confined to right-wing commentators during the Weimar period. Echoing the German concept's origins in nineteenth-century demography, the Left eagerly exploited its evocative power to articulate eugenically charged arguments for the cleansing of the political consciousness of the German working classes and bourgeoisie in particular.

CHAPTER 1

Regionalist Patriotism

In her study of transborder German nationalism in the post-war era, Erin R. Hochman poses a series of recurring questions that had, she insists, already been preoccupying Germans across the political spectrum for over a century when the dust settled on the First World War in 1919:

> Beginning in the early nineteenth century, in response to the French Revolutionary and Napoleonic Wars, contemporaries spoke of the existence of a 'German Question' that needed to be resolved. The German Question historically encompassed a multitude of issues related to geography, politics and population: Where should the boundaries of a German nation-state be drawn? What form of government would be best suited to a German nation-state? Who could be considered members of a German nation?[1]

On one hand, these questions expose the fault lines running beneath the geographical constellation that the First World War had left behind. Far from definitively settling the conundrum of how far German territory extended, the Treaty of Versailles had merely succeeded in re-opening debates surrounding a number of liminal spaces on or beyond Germany's western and eastern frontiers. At the same time, the instability of German identity was palpable within the borders of the Weimar Republic as well, as Germans strove to come to terms with the transition to democracy and the accompanying disappearance of traditional levers of authority.

However, these dramatic challenges to the already precarious German sense of self did not find the German population psychologically unequipped. As the nation state they thought they knew was transformed inside and out and questions continued to outnumber answers, many Germans fell back on a national idea that held within it the germ of an ideal: *Heimat*. Even the writers from the *Weltbühne* stable, for whom pre-war Germany was far from an object of nostalgia, were sufficiently perturbed by post-war trends and developments to project an alternative to the heavily mythologized,

---

1 Erin R. Hochman, *Imagining a Greater Germany: Republican Nationalism and the Idea of Anschluss* (Ithaca, NY: Cornell University Press, 2016), pp. 4–5.

imagined national community beloved of their political adversaries, with its shallow, Prussian-infused yearning for world domination. Thus *Heimat* rapidly became the rhetorical antidote of choice to the crude, backward-looking nationalism of the reactionary Right and its bourgeois sympathizers.

It is worth noting that the word *Heimat* had not always conjured up a mental image of the nation, let alone of a politicized national entity. In its earliest dictionary definition, recorded in the eighteenth century, the term denotes nothing more than '[den] Ort, das Land, wo jemand daheim ist'.² As Jost Hermand and James Steakley explain in the preface to their collection of essays from 1996, this soon changed utterly, though not in a way conducive to clarifying its meaning:

> By 1900, *Heimat* had come to mean virtually anything: a romantic nostalgia for preindustrial conditions; a conservative emphasis on various characteristic ethnic attributes; a feeling of ecological responsibility for a particular region; a leftist-utopian desire for shared ownership of the territory where one resided; an aversion for the ugliness brought about by industry; a glorification of the German peasantry as the wellspring of national health; and much more.³

Two years after the appearance of this volume Elizabeth Boa and Rachel Palfreyman iterated that there had never been a consensus on what the term designates, other than a vague, purportedly untranslatable, quality of *home* 'in the sense of a place rather than a dwelling',⁴ a fact reflected in its having been envisaged both as a recognizable regional space and as an idealized national realm.⁵ By 2005 the blandly geographical meaning originally ascribed to *Heimat* had become so overlain with inference that Johannes von Moltke could justly describe it as 'burdened with emotional connotations almost to the breaking point'.⁶ Joachim Klose would subsequently describe *Heimat* as a subjective entity that signified something different to everyone.

---

2   Joachim Klose, '"Heimat" als gelingende Ordnungskonstruktion', in *Die Machbarkeit politischer Ordnung. Transzendenz und Konstruktion*, ed. by Werner J. Patzelt, Edition Politik, 8 (Bielefeld: Transcript, 2013), pp. 391–416 (p. 392).
3   Jost Hermand and James Steakley, 'Preface', in *Heimat, Nation, Fatherland: The German Sense of Belonging*, ed. by Jost Hermand and James Steakley, German Life and Civilization, 22 (New York: Lang, 1996), pp. i–ix (p. vii).
4   Elizabeth Boa and Rachel Palfreyman, *Heimat – A German Dream: Regional Loyalties and National Identity in German Culture 1890–1990*, Oxford Studies in Modern European Culture (New York: Oxford University Press, 2000), p. 1.
5   Confino, 'The Nation as a Local Metaphor'.
6   Johannes von Moltke, *No Place Like Home: Locations of Heimat in German Cinema*, Weimar and Now: German Cultural Criticism (Berkeley, CA: University of California Press, 2005), p. 8.

Heimat, he declares, is 'immer Heimat *für jemanden*, also *daseinsrelativ* – etwa so, wie das Farben im Verhältnis zur Farbwahrnehmung sind'.⁷ Klose's simile echoes Alon Confino's older analogy, in which the countless iterations of *Heimat* resolve into 'a mirror that reflect[s] the beholder'.⁸

Nonetheless, it is precisely the ambiguity of the term that would prove so attractive to its political exponents and the link between *Heimat* and the nation was well established by the inter-war period with which this book is concerned. As Boa and Palfreyman explain in the introduction to their study of the 'protean Heimat mode', this link was not straightforward.⁹ Its complexity, they rightly point out, derives from the historical appeal of the idea of *Heimat* both to biological nationalists and to patriotic social reformers. The first of these groups pressed the concept into service for violent and sometimes criminal ends. The ideology of *Blut und Boden* propagated in its name by the Nazis and their forerunners reduced the *Heimat* from a fluid space ripe for political experimentation to a closely circumscribed place delimited by ethnicity.¹⁰

In *Heimat, Space, Narrative*, which applies Marc Augé's theory of space and place to the concept of *Heimat*, Friederike Eigler gestures to this exclusionary history. Taking as her point of departure Augé's definition of *place* as a site on which repeated use bestows an anthropological significance lacking in the *non-place*, Eigler emphasizes the reactionary potential of any place accruing an excess of social meaning: 'Across disciplines and languages, the German concept of Heimat is often used as short hand for regressive, narrow, or nostalgic notions of place; that is, it is employed in binary opposition to dynamic notions of space'.¹¹ Such sentimental manipulation of the idea of *Heimat*, underpinned by a deeply conservative understanding of the ideal community, reached a climax in the war propaganda of the German imperial government. Posters entreating loyal German subjects to make loans (*Kriegsanleihen*) to the war effort inflamed the *Heimatgefühl* of their viewers in order to win them over to the national cause. One typical example cited by Confino depicts a largely unspoilt rural landscape decorated with the slogan 'Schützt eure Heimat!' and the image of a sword-wielding knight in the foreground.¹² This evocation of a mediaeval protector is an example of

---

7   Klose, '"Heimat"', p. 392.
8   Confino, 'The Nation as a Local Metaphor', p. 77.
9   Boa and Palfreyman, *Heimat*, p. 17.
10 Boa and Palfreyman, *Heimat*, p. 7.
11 Friederike Eigler, *Heimat, Space, Narrative: Towards a Transnational Approach to Flight and Expulsion*, Studies in German Literature, Linguistics and Culture, 147 (Rochester, NY: Camden House, 2014), p. 22.
12 Confino, 'The Nation as a Local Metaphor', p. 70.

the 'timeless national memory' which, according to Confino, the *Kaiserreich* strove to create.

On a spatial as well as a temporal level, right-wing treatment of the idea of *Heimat* at this historical juncture relied on an elastic interpretation of the semantic limits of the concept. On one hand, it invoked 'a limited terrain that affords its inhabitants respite and protection from incursions originating in the more intangible and abstract spaces beyond its boundaries'.[13] On the other, it hoped in so doing to increase public identification with a larger German nation by presenting this national community as one that could be conceived of within 'the spatial horizon of *Gemeinschaft* as structured exclusively through local relations among family members, neighbors, friends, or members of a congregation'.[14] If this war-time strategy succeeded where, according to Abigail Green, the political unification of 1871 had largely failed,[15] any resulting sense of national citizenship remained a negative one in which membership was open only to those who already belonged to the national *Gemeinschaft*.

These wartime campaigns built on an existing folk memory that had been furnished with stereotype images of a uniformly pleasant regional *Heimat* for decades. According to one contemporary observer, the liberal theorist Paul Krische, the chief perpetrator of this pre-war charm offensive was the tourist industry. Feigning ignorance of the twin realities of rapid industrial development and sweeping urbanization, local tourist boards propositioned day-trippers with cloyingly nostalgic postcards carrying a dated image of the provincial *Heimat*:

> Ein Bild mit der Unterschrift Heimat zeigt durchweg einen Blick vom Berge auf ein Tal mit Dörfern zwischen fruchtbaren Fluren und einem altertümlichen Städtchen im Vordergrunde, mit Resten von Stadttürmen und der Stadtmauer, mit vielerlei Erkern, hochragenden Giebeln und ineinandergeschachtelten Dächern.[16]

One's overriding impression on reading this passage, which tellingly describes the view *from* and not *of* a mountain, is of hallowed ground consecrated by centuries of unchanging human activity. Such landscapes, as Confino argues in his essay on pre-war *Heimat* imagery cited above, had 'human dimensions, and suggested companionship between man and nature'.[17] At their centre the

---

13 Von Moltke, *No Place Like Home*, p. 11.
14 Von Moltke, *No Place Like Home*, p. 13.
15 Green, *Fatherlands*, p. 337.
16 Paul Krische, *Heimat! Grundsätzliches zur Gemeinschaft von Scholle und Mensch* (Berlin: Paetel, 1918), p. 30.
17 Confino, 'The Nation as a Local Metaphor', p. 64.

immutable and harmonious *Heimatstädtchen* stood in opposition to 'nature that inspired awe and challenged – or seemed to defy – men and women, such as big mountains and rivers', in the process radiating an atmosphere of contentment and self-sufficiency impervious to the suggestive power of dramatic natural scenery.[18] The pre-industrial contours of the little old town in Krische's image enshrine, therefore, a fantasy world in which human endeavour is suspended in a state of perennial repose existing outside time and yet instantly accessible to those who need it.

Krische's ironically poetic description of the stereotypical *Heimat* answers a need similar to that catered for by what Shelley Baranowski calls the 'rural myth'. In her study of the East Prussian *Junkertum* during the Weimar period, Baranowski explores the efforts made by such landowners to equate their quasi-feudal estates with 'a sense of place, an identification with nature, indeed a *Heimat* that no other residence, no matter how attractive, could offer'.[19] This rearguard action was stirred by a widespread fear of rampant industrialization and unchecked urbanization. While both Left and Right repudiated the dehumanizing consequences of metropolitan life and assembly-line employment, the latter, in the form of the traditional landed gentry, endeavoured to keep modernity at bay instead of seeking to reform it. Baranowski locates a significant point of convergence between Pomeranian landowners and the scarcely less conservative Prussian Evangelical Church in their shared abomination of the modern metropolis:

> [The Prussian Evangelical Church] saw urban civilization and all of its consequences as its greatest menace. In brief, the cities meant republicanism, pluralism, mechanization, Americanization, sectarianism, experimentation in education, and moral decay, particularly in its confusion of the proper boundaries between the sexes. Such ills [...] spread their tentacles eastward, threatening to penetrate the remotest hamlet with their poison. Because church leaders were accustomed to associating Germany's strength as a nation with the preservation of a healthy rural life, the threat of the cities, in their minds, was serious indeed.[20]

This demonization of the city as a pernicious force of liberalization hostile to the national interest lies at the heart of the rural myth.[21] As the fear of pluralism and sectarianism suggests, reinforcement of the rural community

---

18 Confino, 'The Nation as a Local Metaphor', p. 64.
19 Shelley Baranowski, *The Sanctity of Rural Life: Nobility, Protestantism, and Nazism in Weimar Prussia* (New York: Oxford University Press, 1995), p. 60.
20 Baranowski, *The Sanctity of Rural Life*, p. 102.
21 Baranowski, *The Sanctity of Rural Life*, p. 6.

against urban influence also implied a distinctly anti-Socialist retention of a pre-capitalist *Ständestaat* predicated on the exploitation of agricultural labour. According to this reading, Germany's survival was conditional upon the denial both of individual freedoms and of the prospect of social mobility. The rural myth thus effectively encouraged an insular form of regionalist patriotism, which demanded the fortification of the *Heimat* rather than its enlargement.

However, this depiction of *Heimat* as an amulet brandished to ward off nebulous outside forces and forestall the march of time does not tell the whole story of a fiercely contested idea. Nor do Hermand and Steakley omit to translate the anatomization of the term cited above into concrete political imperatives, arguing that:

> three fundamental orientations can be distinguished: 1) a definite repudiation of the forced automation and rationalization of German industry in the mid-twenties, which once again elevated Germany to the second-strongest industrial power of the world; 2) an ever-stronger longing for a truly German national state and, ultimately, for a Third Reich; and 3) as a backlash to this, a leftist demand that the term Heimat finally be transformed into a socioeconomic reality.[22]

Signalling his proximity to the third orientation, in *Heimat!* Krische takes issue with the tendency of the *Heimatbewegung* to harbour:

> ein Vorurteil gegen alle neuen Kräfte der menschlichen Kultur und eine Außerachtlassung der obersten Erkenntnis, daß die Gemeinschaft von Scholle und Mensch etwas dauernd Arbeitendes ist, bei dem es auch ständig Geburt und Tod gibt, Neuerstehen und Vergehen, wie überall in der Natur.[23]

As this corrective to the reactionary instincts of right-wing sentimentalists suggests, Krische's contribution to *Heimat* discourse is to re-cast the regional *Heimat* as a seat of ceaseless collaborative activity sustained by a fluid succession of custodians. In Krische's hands the individual *Heimat* itself ceases to be an emblem of cultural stasis jealously handed down the same ethnic line from one generation to the next and becomes, to use Boa and Palfreyman's term, protean. By allowing for demographic change, he disputes the notion of *Heimat* as a tribal family heirloom, foreshadowing by five years Eduard Spranger's attempt to redefine the *Heimatgefühl* as a state of communion that occurs 'erst dann, wenn man sich in [diese gegebene

---

22 Hermand and Steakley, 'Preface', pp. vii–viii.
23 Krische, *Heimat!*, p. 33.

Geburtsstätte] hineingelebt hat',[24] or, as Krische himself had put it, 'wenn man längere Zeit an einem neuen Orte weilt und sich in ihm einlebt'.[25] *Heimat* is thus re-configured as a porous *space* open to new arrivals, as opposed to a watertight *place* the interior of which cannot be breached.

Krische's desire to expose *Heimat* to the agents of change resounds almost a century later in Joachim Klose's proposal for revising the popular understanding of *Heimat*. Instead of seeing it as a static location enclosed within a non-negotiable perimeter, Klose suggests re-imagining the *Heimat* as a liminal space in which different cultural currents can overlap. Drawing on the Old High German meaning of *Ort*, which formerly denoted 'den örtlichen oder zeitlichen Anfangs- oder Endpunkt, im engeren Sinne das vordere oder hintere Ende, die Grenze, den Rand oder die Seite',[26] Klose distinguishes between brittle borders and supple 'edges': 'Grenzen schneiden Heimat von ihrer Umwelt ab und verriegeln den Weg zu weiteren Schichten von Beheimatung. Ränder hingegen sichern eine prinzipielle Offenheit von Orten und von Heimat'.[27] Crucially for our purposes, however, Klose's work is not a mere rehashing of Krische's arguments. Instead, Klose builds on his liberalization of the idea of *Heimat* by declaring love of the regional *Heimat* to be a prerequisite for a broader patriotism:

> Es leuchtet ein, dass Heimatbewusstsein, seinerseits eine Voraussetzung für bereitwillige Verantwortungsübernahme, gerade für eine Demokratie nötig ist. Doch zu den tragenden Sinnschichten solcher 'Beheimatung in der Demokratie' müssen dann noch Republikanismus und Patriotismus kommen. 'Heimat' ist politischem Handeln nämlich vorgelagert, umschließt es aber noch nicht, und Gemeinsinn ist nur eine Ressource freiheitlicher Politik, doch noch nicht diese selbst. Heimat und auf sie bezogener Gemeinsinn müssen deshalb ihrerseits transzendiert werden, wenn es um die Konstruktion einer freiheitlichen Ordnung geht. Was da als nächste Schicht herangezogen wird, etwa der 'Verfassungspatriotismus', wird seinen 'Sitz im Leben' freilich erst dann finden, wenn eine feste Verbindung zur Wirklichkeitsschicht der 'Heimat' gelingt.[28]

The generosity of spirit and sense of civic duty which Klose deems the *Heimatgefühl* to be uniquely capable of instilling presents a stark contrast to its characterization by Peter Blickle just over a decade earlier as 'the

---

24 Eduard Spranger, *Der Bildungswert der Heimatkunde. Rede zur Eröffnungssitzung der Studiengemeinschaft für wissenschaftliche Heimatkunde* (Berlin: Hartmann, 1923), p. 11.
25 Krische, *Heimat!*, p. 53.
26 Klose, '"Heimat"', p. 403.
27 Klose, '"Heimat"', p. 404.
28 Klose, '"Heimat"', p. 412.

permission to remain asleep in a disindividualizing world'.[29] Indeed, Klose presents the small-scale *Heimat* not only as the keystone in the national edifice but as the foundation of a patriotic consciousness.

Klose was not the first to suggest that the possession of a *Heimatgefühl* might enable the cultivation of an authentic social solidarity for which the exclusion of certain groups would be counter-productive. In her study of Palatinate *Heimat* activism, which describes the inter-war *Heimatbewegung* as nothing less than 'the political unit's attempt to root itself firmly in local life while at the same time claiming membership in the nation',[30] Celia Applegate demonstrates that regional identity did not necessarily exist in a vacuum, instead serving as a potential precondition for patriotism. The following passage depicts such regional patriotism as an intriguing combination of contrary impulses: reform and self-preservation:

> Heimat rhetoric and Heimat activities encouraged a public-mindedness, a desire for moral elevation, and, not least of all, *a search for security in a society ridden by crisis*. Heimat defined a certain kind of identity, neither private nor partisan but 'political' in its dependence on a common public space: to be conscious of one's Heimat and solicitous of its welfare was continually to seek the implications of action that followed from the sharing of a land and a historical tradition.[31]

Any attempt on the part of left-wing writers in the Weimar period to reclaim *Heimat* activism as an emancipatory force along these lines therefore held the potential for a radical re-appraisal of its political versatility. Johannes von Moltke is among those critics to point out that the longstanding association of the concept of *Heimat* with a monolithic notion of *Gemeinschaft* has led to its being exploited as a touchstone to ward off external interference with conventional power relations.[32] In Applegate's conception, however, *Heimat* is indifferent to distinctions of class, confession or even place of birth, requiring from its inhabitants the humility to prioritize the protection of their shared environment over their own interests.

The capacity, observed by Applegate and Klose in turn, of the *Heimatgefühl* to instil a sense of moral responsibility in its holders corresponds neatly to Moritz Föllmer's essay on evocations of a national *Volksgemeinschaft* in the

---

29 Peter Blickle, *Heimat: A Critical Theory of the German Idea of Homeland*, Studies in German Literature, Linguistics, and Culture (Rochester, NY: Camden House, 2002), p. 68.
30 Celia Applegate, *A Nation of Provincials: The German Idea of Heimat* (Berkeley, CA: University of California Press, 1990), p. 106.
31 Applegate, *A Nation of Provincials*, p. 151.
32 Von Moltke, *No Place Like Home*, p. 13.

inter-war period. Föllmer writes that patriotic appeals in the Weimar era called on listeners 'to meet the demanding challenge of setting aside their own interests and needs in favour of higher principles of behaviour', adding that 'this search for a new moral order was a defining feature of German society between the two world wars'.[33] Whereas Föllmer ultimately judges such unifying slogans as the *Volksgemeinschaft* to have failed to construct an idea of nationhood sufficiently resilient to withstand Nazi populism, Applegate is more interested in what might have been. *Heimatliebe*, she argues, is not inherently incompatible with patriotism. On the contrary, it is its genesis.

Far from shrinking the nation to familiar proportions in the manner of Germany's wartime leadership, some activists from the Palatinate *Heimatbewegung* related to their region on an ever-grander scale until it became one with the nation: 'Identification with the nation did not [...] require that all peasants, hometownsmen, and other unregenerate localists shed themselves of their premodern burden of provincial culture. Nationalism could embrace their smaller worlds; Germanness could encompass their diversity.'[34] This passage eloquently describes the growth out of particularism of a larger emotional commitment, here unhelpfully called 'nationalism'. Indeed, Applegate's vision is of a national *Heimat* comprising a multitude of idiosyncratic regional *Heimaten*, as opposed to a single bucolic hinterland awash with interchangeable little towns untouched by the outside world. The abiding image of her case study is that of a chrysalis of political consciousness out of which a mature German patriot emerges when the time is right. According to this formula, the first sphere of activity is the family unit, followed by the local community, which is then surrounded in its turn by the nation.[35]

As we have seen, the work of Klose and Applegate goes against the grain of nationalist portrayals of the *Heimat*, which tend to represent this microcosmic Germany either as a quiescent childhood village synonymous with 'a memory of the simple things one took for granted, of kinship, commitment and continuity',[36] or as a beleaguered earthly paradise in defence of which any self-respecting German must take up arms. Such proponents of cultural pessimism advanced a world view in which the only solution appeared to be to contract in upon oneself in defence of one's time-honoured and inviolate moral and

---

33 Moritz Föllmer, 'The Problem of National Solidarity in Interwar Germany', *German History*, 23 (2005), 202–31 (p. 204).
34 Applegate, *A Nation of Provincials*, p. 13.
35 Applegate, *A Nation of Provincials*, p. 159.
36 Confino, 'The Nation as a Local Metaphor', p. 71.

biological assets.[37] Attendant associations of parochialism,[38] xenophobia or even, in the case of agricultural estates in East Prussia, feudalism remain powerful to this day, ensuring that the mention of *Heimat* continues to summon the image of 'a never-never land, where Germans found a second Germany, impervious to politics, one of harmonious relationships, to compensate for the deficiencies and conflicts of the first, and real, Germany'.[39] By contrast, this chapter shows that the idea of *Heimat* serves certain *Weltbühne* writers as an irresistible framing device for the articulation of a progressive patriotism. Although not principally a study of the idea of *Heimat*, this book therefore attests to the benefits of a more nuanced approach which allows for the possibility of an understanding of *Heimat* rooted in a tangible reality firmly removed from the fantasies of right-wing nationalism.

From the beginning to the end of the Weimar period *Die Weltbühne* teems with evocations of *Heimaten* of both national and local proportions. The allure of the idea of *Heimat* to *Weltbühne* columnists can be provisionally explained by the fact that, even in the broadly republican pages of this journal, the German state which had emerged out of the confusion of military defeat was not embraced wholeheartedly. In their search for a Germany that would be a more faithful reflection of their own political convictions, the writers discussed here therefore looked closer to home for inspiration. Wary of a Weimar regime that they regarded as both intolerably compromised by its perceived proximity to an unscrupulous capitalist elite and undermined from birth by a monarchist state apparatus, these columnists sought to free the notion of *Heimat* from the vice-like grip of right-wing ideology. In his essay 'Heimat' (1929), which first appeared in the satirical volume *Deutschland, Deutschland über alles*, Kurt Tucholsky rued the fact that the idea of *Heimat* had been so distorted in nationalist books, films and lyrics, 'daß man sich beinah schämt, zu sagen: man liebe seine Heimat'.[40] This chapter therefore demonstrates how *Heimat*, understood here as an intimate, small-scale microcosm of an imagined German society, was pressed into service in *Die Weltbühne* to articulate a communitarian vision of patriotism predicated on individual responsibility to one's local neighbourhood.[41]

---

37 Baranowski, *The Sanctity of Rural Life*, p. 60.
38 Green, *Fatherlands*, p. 334.
39 Confino, 'The Nation as a Local Metaphor', p. 75.
40 Kurt Tucholsky, 'Heimat', in *Deutschland, Deutschland über alles* (Berlin: Neuer Deutscher Verlag, 1929), pp. 226–31 (pp. 226–27).
41 This idea is not without traction today. In *Reclaiming Patriotism* (Charlottesville, VA: University of Virginia Press, 2019), the Israeli-American sociologist Amitai Etzioni defines a progressive patriotic model predicated on what he calls 'liberal communitarianism', a world view which strives to realize the common good while upholding individual rights.

The *Heimat* Without

Against the backdrop of Erin Hochman's tripartite 'German Question', this first section examines how three essay-length contributions to *Die Weltbühne* exported a progressive image of *Heimat* into German-speaking parts of Europe then, or soon to be, under the control of foreign countries, thereby creating a spiritual Germany beyond the borders of the actual nation state. As one of the articles explored below attests, this hypothetical Germany frequently encompassed the inhabitants of the First Austrian Republic, which many insisted on calling *Deutschösterreich* in defiance of the legal injunction against this name established by the Treaty of Saint-Germain-en-Laye of September 1919. Indeed, according to Hochman the prohibition of an Austro-German union, or *Anschluß*, by the Treaty prompted democratically minded Germans who might otherwise have been reluctant to contravene a legally binding diktat to emphasize an alternative form of national belonging to state citizenship:

> Just as republicans used the [pro-*Anschluß* Österreichischen-Deutschen] Volksbund to advance their claims about democracy, they also viewed the Volksbund as a way to construct a more inclusive Greater German national community. In championing Austrians' rights in Germany, republicans made it clear that they did not simply believe in a civic form of nationhood. 'National belonging' (*Volkszugehörigkeit*) mattered more to them than 'state belonging' (*Staatszugehörigkeit*).[42]

Given the currency of such supra-political forms of identity, it is small wonder that the imaginative longing of the *Weltbühne* writers did not stop at the borders of those territories legally enshrined as German in the post-war treaties. The role of sentiment in these articles cannot be discounted, but their most striking feature is the layer of progressive patriotism in which they are cloaked. The *Heimat* in question, not necessarily the writer's own, often serves as a canvas for the projection of a more humane Germany than either the imperial regime that had forfeited the land or its uninspiring and compromised successor.

The first of the three articles under discussion is Arnold Zweig's essay 'Oberschlesische Motive' (1921), which anticipates the concession of his native Upper Silesia to Poland the following year.[43] Next are four contributions written under three pseudonyms over a four-year period to illuminate Kurt Tucholsky's personal and multi-faceted relationship with the historically

---

42 Hochman, *Imagining a Greater Germany*, pp. 225–26.
43 Arnold Zweig, 'Oberschlesische Motive', *Die Weltbühne*, 17.1 (1921), 247–49.

German province of the Courland (Kurland), which German soldiers refused to vacate until it was finally awarded to Latvia in 1920. The final case study is Otto Flake's essay on the Austrian region of the Steiermark in which the German Flake mourns the reassignment of the territory south of the River Mura to Yugoslavia after the fall of the Austro-Hungarian Empire.[44] Whether it is the author's own or that of an intimate acquaintance, Upper Silesia, the Courland and Styria are all described as 'Heimat' in these articles. Resentment towards the nation that stands to inherit the region is conspicuous by its absence in the case of Tucholsky and only flares up in Zweig's article on one occasion, despite Flake's essay being more openly hostile to the erosion of the German cultural sphere represented by Styria's concession to Slovenia.

It would be disingenuous to claim that *Die Weltbühne* was entirely impervious to undiluted anti-Slav sentiment in its response to changes to Germany's eastern frontier. In fact, the journal exhibited sporadic intolerance towards movements for self-determination in Central Europe, especially in the first half of the Weimar Republic. The areas ceded to the Slavic states of Poland, Czechoslovakia and Yugoslavia quickly became a lightning-rod for a form of anti-Slav nationalism that asserted, often explicitly, the superiority of 'greater German', or *großdeutscher*, culture over the majority cultures in the new states.[45] Indeed, the scorn with which contributors sometimes met irredentism in Central and Eastern Europe in this period had more in common with the xenophobia of the pre-war 'Ostpionier' discourse mentioned in the introduction than with any progressive re-interpretation of the concept of *Heimat*.[46] Their assumptions infiltrate even the more moderate expressions of regionalist patriotism discussed in this section, albeit clothed in those instances in less incendiary language. Flake's essay on Styria, the third case study to be discussed, is more closely aligned to this world view than its delicate style would initially suggest.

In 1920 Walter Kollenka cast doubt on the right to exist of the new Czechoslovakian state, which had inherited three-and-a-half million German speakers in the Sudetenland following the dissolution of the Austro-Hungarian Empire formalized in the Treaty of Saint-Germain-en-Laye. In a foreshadowing of Zweig's choice of words in 'Oberschlesische Motive',[47] the so-called 'Sudetendeutschen' are portrayed as having to atone for 'die

---

44 Otto Flake, 'Südsteiermark', *Die Weltbühne*, 21.2 (1925), 160–68.
45 *Großdeutsch* was a common term used to refer both to demands for a political *Anschluß* between Germany and Austria and to the shared cultural orbit of the two peoples dating back to the pre-war empires.
46 Chickering, *We Men Who Feel Most German*, p. 83.
47 Zweig, 'Oberschlesische Motive', p. 249.

Sünden ihrer nationalistischen Väter', whose provocations had inflamed the latent patriotic passions of the majority Czech population in Bohemia and Moravia.⁴⁸ The tenor of Kollenka's piece nonetheless leaves little doubt over whose claim he supports: he greets the language policy of the new state with a condescension that scarcely conceals his annoyance. In response to the obligation for German civil servants to learn Czech, he observes: 'Kein Wunder, daß ein Staat, der an solchen Zuständen krankt, im Ausland an Prestige verliert, nirgends Vertrauen findet und bis zur Lächerlichkeit herabsinkt'.⁴⁹ The desire of the Czechoslovakian regime to enforce a uniform language is thereby cast as a presumption which is destined not to be taken seriously by outside observers. Kollenka's tone is, however, clearly a defence mechanism against a perceived infringement of the eastern frontier of *Großdeutschland*.

An article from 1921 by Arno Voigt, a member first of the Unabhängige Sozialdemokratische Partei Deutschlands (USPD) and then of the Kommunistische Partei Deutschlands (KPD), provides a further example of this nationalist hauteur. Upbraiding the secessionist member of the Preußischer Landtag Wojciech Korfanty for pressing the Polish claim on Upper Silesia, Voigt twice deploys infantilizing language to belittle the Polish cause. First, he describes the reconstituted Polish nation as one that has 'politisch bisher stets versagt [...] und in kindisch ungeduldiger Weise den Erfolg erheulen will'.⁵⁰ Voigt then concludes by branding Korfanty 'eines jener eiteln Gewächse, wie sie auf dem Boden des Chauvinismus entstehen, der letzten Endes nichts andres ist als kindische Großmannssucht'.⁵¹ Voigt's oblique approval of Korfanty's patriotism, which prompts him to concede with grudging respect that the latter is 'gewiß ein Patriot',⁵² does not prevent him from judging the Poles and finding them wanting in comparison with 'das nüchterne, arbeitsame deutsche Volk'.⁵³ The Poles' efforts to assert themselves are thus doomed to be ridiculed, whereas German rule is presented as a natural reflection of the Germans' superior virtue.

The charge of chauvinism, common to both articles, is as revealing of these columnists' preconceptions as it is of their lack of self-awareness. Tellingly, Kollenka pre-empts Voigt's imputation of chauvinism vis-à-vis the Poles by raising the spectre of a Czech government operating under the influence of

---

48 Walter Kollenka, 'Die Deutschen in der Tschechoslowakei', *Die Weltbühne*, 16.1 (1920), 635–38 (p. 635).
49 Kollenka, 'Die Deutschen in der Tschechoslowakei', p. 637.
50 Arno Voigt, 'Korfanty', *Die Weltbühne*, 17.1 (1921), 303–06 (p. 303).
51 Voigt, 'Korfanty', p. 306.
52 Voigt, 'Korfanty', p. 303.
53 Voigt, 'Korfanty', p. 303.

an unbridled nationalism that manifests itself in 'Haß und Chauvinismus'.[54] Although he does not entirely exonerate the minority German population in the Sudetenland of contributing through their own inflammatory rhetoric to the 'von Nationalhaß geschwängerte[n] Atmosphäre Tschechiens',[55] Kollenka appears to base his dislike of the new republic on the premise that Czech patriotism is intrinsically unreasonable and therefore a sign of intemperance. While the *Sudetendeutschen* do not have to justify their claim to predominance, any Czech challenge is automatically liable to incur accusations of unwarranted self-aggrandizement.

This combination of cultural snobbery and displacement anxiety scarcely dissipated as the years went on; nor was it confined to the Slavic populations of Central Europe. In 1926 long-serving contributor Hans Glenk wrote a disparaging piece about Hungarian culture, 'Zurück zum Balkan', in which he attributes that nation's artistic achievements and cosmopolitanism to its large Jewish minority, whom he polemically declares to be 'die ewigen Ostpioniere der deutschen Sprache'.[56] In an echo of the language used by Kollenka and Voigt at the beginning of the decade, Glenk blames the reluctance of older Hungarians to speak German on 'Chauvinismus',[57] an indirect consequence of a law from 1904 that had removed German from the school syllabus and introduced Hungarian as the universal language of instruction. Lamenting the oppression of the country's German minorities which this legislation supposedly represented, Glenk finds solace only in conscripting the Hungarian Jews in an imagined national mission of linguistic expansion that explicitly takes up, if only in his choice of words, the fantasy fostered by pre-war nationalist associations of the eastward-bound German pioneer. Having established the decisive influence of Budapest's Jewish population as patrons of the performing arts and practitioners of literature, Glenk duly calls into question the very existence of an independent Hungarian culture:

> Sie [die Juden] sind es, denen Budapest Ansehen und Anschein einer Weltstadt verdankt, auf ihnen ruht die 'ungarische' Kultur. Auf ihnen und den Siebenbürger Sachsen, den Deutschstämmigen, die das sachlichere, im Allgemeinen mehr der Wissenschaft zugewandte und sie fördernde Gegengewicht bilden. Auf dem Untergrund des Magyarentums aber schwimmt diese ganze Kultur wie Öl auf dem Wasser – unverbunden.[58]

---

54 Kollenka, 'Die Deutschen in der Tschechoslowakei', p. 635.
55 Kollenka, 'Die Deutschen in der Tschechoslowakei', p. 638.
56 Hans Glenk, 'Zurück zum Balkan', *Die Weltbühne*, 22.1 (1926), 88–95 (p. 92).
57 Glenk, 'Zurück zum Balkan', p. 92.
58 Glenk, 'Zurück zum Balkan', p. 93.

According to Glenk, Hungarian culture exists only in inverted commas; it is a Judeo-German creation masquerading as organically Hungarian. By crediting the Transylvanian German minority with introducing intellectual rigour into Hungarian culture, Glenk subtly suggests that the future of Hungary is in doubt. After all, at the time of writing, this German-speaking exclave had long since been transferred to Romania under the Treaty of Trianon. Glenk also foresees the deliberate eradication of the Jewish population from Hungary, an event which he claims would consign the country to the culturally inferior Balkan, or Southern European, sphere of influence. This prophecy, which gives the article its name, confirms a trend of rising insecurity among *Weltbühne* columnists concerning the diminished cultural weight of *Großdeutschland* in Central Europe.

Upper Silesia

The patronizing air adopted by such contributors as Kollenka, Voigt and Glenk towards the new neighbours of the Weimar Republic derives from a scarcely concealed contempt for the right or capacity of Czechoslovakia, Poland and Hungary to exist. However, such absolutism would prove the exception in *Die Weltbühne*. By declining to seek political redress in the form of the restitution of lost land, the highest-profile writers of the journal generally kept a safe distance from any 'revisionistische[n] Konsens' such as that said to have united right-wing commentators and a critical mass of politicians within the left-wing parties regarding Weimar Germany's eastern border.[59] This did not, however, mean that the German Question posed by Hochman at the beginning of this chapter held no interest for them. What it actually meant was that they sought the answer outside the political sphere of international treaties and diplomatic wrangling.

Arnold Zweig's piece on the erstwhile East Prussian province of Upper Silesia lays claim to a cultural ownership unaffected by geo-political niceties. A sizeable coal-rich expanse described in a leader article in late 1921 as 'die wirtschaftliche Zentrale Europas', Upper Silesia was the subject of protracted discussions after the war.[60] In March 1921, after delegates at the Paris Peace Conference had twice proposed that the bulk of the region become part of the renascent Poland, an inconclusive plebiscite was held in the vain hope of definitively settling the question of its governance. Writing weeks ahead of this

---

59 Heinrich August Winkler, 'Im Schatten von Versailles. Das deutsch-polnische Verhältnis während der Weimarer Republik', in *Deutsche und Polen. 100 Schlüsselbegriffe*, ed. by Ewa Kobylińska, Andreas Lawaty and Rüdiger Stephan (Munich: Piper, 1992), pp. 95–103 (p. 100).

60 [Anon.], 'Wie Oberschlesien verloren ging!', *Die Weltbühne*, 17.2 (1921), 441–45 (p. 445).

fruitless referendum, Zweig, who had spent his school years in the industrial city of Kattowitz, contests Poland's entitlement to the region. Nonetheless, 'Oberschlesische Motive' can no more be confused with a nationalist tract than it can with a plea for the Upper Silesian right to self-determination. The latter cause was championed by a group calling itself alternately the Bund der Oberschlesier or Związek Górnoślązaków. Founded in 1919, the movement promoted German-Polish harmony within an autonomous state.[61]

When the League of Nations finally granted the industrial heartlands in the east of the province to the Polish Republic in the summer of 1922, it dealt a heavy blow both to Germany's material wealth and to the country's self-esteem. The mixed feelings on display in 'Oberschlesische Motive', however, indicate that even Germans with a personal stake in the matter had long been aware that the destiny of Upper Silesia was not a straightforward question of moral right or wrong, let alone of uncontested territorial primacy. Torn between chastizing the lawless behaviour of his own country and admonishing the Polish state for its audacity, Zweig fears for his regional 'Heimat', 'die in der Erbschaft der Sünden eines vergewaltigenden Staates verloren gehen kann an einen andern Staat, der sie nicht geschaffen hat, nie hätte schaffen können, und dessen Anrecht auf sie weder natürlich noch sittlich ableitbar ist'.[62] His vehement disqualification of Poland as the heir to his homeland indicates Zweig's susceptibility to what Shelley Baranowski considers a modern German tendency to 'superimpose nationalist claims on the fluidity of medieval Europe'.[63] The Kingdom of Prussia had not acquired its part of Upper Silesia until 1742, thus becoming the sixth ruler to administer the territory since the Early Middle Ages.[64] Zweig's unequivocal dismissal of the Polish claim conveniently passes over this multi-layered history as though its pre-German past had left no trace.

At the same time, however, Zweig is acutely aware that Upper Silesia was not necessarily taken seriously by his compatriots. He could even be referring to Arno Voigt when, in reference to the peripheral status of his homeland in the German consciousness, he drily observes: 'Heute lächelt im Reiche Niemand mehr geringschätzend und gönnerisch, wenn das Wort "Oberschlesien" ausgesprochen wird'.[65] In Voigt's article the sudden

---

61 Maria Gierlak, 'Deutsche Presse in Polen 1919–1939. Forschungsstand, -postulate und -desiderate', in *Grenzdiskurse. Zeitungen deutschsprachiger Minderheiten und ihr Feuilleton in Mitteleuropa bis 1939*, ed. by Sibylle Schönborn (Essen: Klartext, 2009), pp. 67–80.
62 Zweig, 'Oberschlesische Motive', p. 249.
63 Baranowski, *The Sanctity of Rural Life*, p. 18.
64 The previous five were, in turn, the Polish House of Piast, the Kingdom of Bohemia, the Holy Roman Empire, the Kingdom of Hungary and the Habsburg Crown.
65 Zweig, 'Oberschlesische Motive', p. 248.

metamorphosis of the area into a nationalist touchstone appears to be born of cynicism rather than conviction. The author, to whom Upper Silesia signifies merely the technical superiority of the German nation over its less advanced rivals, describes the appeal of the region to Korfanty in terms that might have been gleaned from a geography textbook:

> Bis nach Oberschlesien, wo noch 1903 kein einziger Pole in den deutschen Reichstag gewählt wurde, will er sein Vaterland ausdehnen: aus dem strichweise in dichtest besiedeltes Land, aus Agrargegend in ein Industriezentrum, vom Osten zum Westen. Den Bergwerksdirektoren und Hüttenbesitzern soll in Gestalt von Analphabeten und Lehmkuhlbewohnern das Saatkorn einer neuen Welt aufgepflanzt werden.[66]

On close inspection, Voigt's witheringly sarcastic denunciation of Korfanty's aspirations reveals little about Upper Silesia besides its primary characteristics, thereby reducing the region to an economic asset seen from a bird's-eye view. So important is the area as a token of German geo-political dominance, in fact, that Voigt is content to reserve judgement on the social implications of its subordination to heavy industry. By aligning himself with the pit owners over the supposedly primitive Poles, Voigt suspends his political allegiances for the sake of national solidarity against a common enemy.

By contrast, Zweig's patriotic attachment to his region, which any state but the German one 'nie hätte schaffen können', does not involve compromising on his political convictions.[67] In fact, his principled opposition to the exploitation of the industrial proletariat is an integral part of the constructive criticism in which his patriotism manifests itself. Whereas Voigt derisively portrays the Poles as living in caves, Zweig describes the arid, interchangeable living quarters of the densely populated industrial zone as 'Anstalten zum Arbeiten und Behaustsein', thereby rendering the physical fabric of the workers' settlements a moral indictment of functionalist German values.[68] For Zweig, these buildings are monuments to a utilitarian mindset that sacrifices human happiness to the ceaseless production of goods. He steadily reinforces this message as the article progresses, condemning the assembly-line model for enriching absentee owners 'ohne Glanz, Freude, Ruhe, Daseinsgefühl dort zu verbreiten, wo [die Arbeit] geleistet ward'.[69] Zweig's rhetorical crusade against materialism culminates in the final paragraph, as

---

66 Voigt, 'Korfanty', p. 303.
67 Zweig, 'Oberschlesische Motive', p. 249.
68 Zweig, 'Oberschlesische Motive', p. 248.
69 Zweig, 'Oberschlesische Motive', p. 248.

he claims to read in the topography of the Upper Silesian townscape the antisocial, lonely existence of its inhabitants.

The closing line makes no explicit mention of the struggle for Upper Silesia, instead redoubling its moral condemnation of capitalism. The region's moral dissipation, it is implied, is to blame for any future political problems: 'Hinter der ästhetisch neutralen Oberfläche des Motivs steht noch der ganze drohende, nach Erkenntnis rufende, zur Einkehr ermahnende Tatbestand einer Sittlichkeit, die uns bis hierher gebracht hat: und unratsam dürfte es sein, ihn zu überhören'.[70] According to Zweig, the domination of the local economy by large corporations has alienated the Silesians from one another, replacing the communitarian principles of mutual support with the impersonal doctrine of productivity. For all that it may attest to a lack of foresight, Zweig's portrayal of this doctrine as *drohend* and *nach Erkenntnis rufend* suggests that the danger of Upper Silesia ending up in Polish hands is of secondary importance to its colonization by capitalism. The urgent calamity facing Upper Silesia is its people's complicity in the commercial exploitation of their *Heimat*; the existential threat looming over them is not ethnic infiltration but ethical collapse.

Conversely, Zweig's initial show of outrage over Poland's alleged moral transgressiveness is comparatively short-lived and, indeed, relatively tame in the context of the journal's frequently scathing view of Slavic self-determination in the post-war years. In a brief foreword Zweig explains that 'Oberschlesische Motive' had originally been commissioned by a friend in 1920 to serve as a preface to an illustrated map of Upper Silesia but was returned to its author without explanation. Given that the offending article is in part a denunciation of pre-war Germany's vainglorious pursuit of power and prosperity, it seems likely that the reason for the rejection lay in its lack of conventional patriotism. The Polish presence in Upper Silesia is not dwelt upon in the first part of 'Oberschlesische Motive', with Zweig reflecting instead on the contamination of his homeland by factory compounds and their pollutants:

> Ich kenne diese Landschaft. Das zweite Jahrzehnt meines Lebens wurde von ihr geprägt, von dieser aufreizend magern und herben Gegend, degradiert zur Umgegend für Industrie, zur Umgegend von Städten wie herausgeschnitten aus beliebigen Großstädten der Jahrhundertwende, die sich arbeitsam ins Getreideland und den schönen Wald wie eine Erkrankung der lebendigen Erde einfraßen häßlich wie Krätze.[71]

---

70 Zweig, 'Oberschlesische Motive', p. 249.
71 Zweig, 'Oberschlesische Motive', p. 247.

At the linguistic level, the most arresting feature of this potted history of industrialization is Zweig's eventual relinquishment of control over syntax as he strives to communicate the shock of the disfigurement of Upper Silesia by man-made forces. Sandwiched between two similes of disease, the baleful verb *einfraßen* is almost entirely obscured by the author's emotional response to the incursion it represents. The soil of his *Heimat* is being poisoned by homemade urban sprawl and the building blocks of the munitions industry, a self-inflicted contagion the most devastating symptom of which is the postwar break-up of German territory. Zweig's perspective thus mirrors that of contemporary *Heimat* activists for whom 'Germany was threatened not by an invading army, but by "native vandals" – a home-grown class of capitalists who had become more thoroughly indifferent to it than any distant culture could'.[72] The infection of the Upper Silesian countryside is portrayed as the cause of its possible amputation from the rest of Germany, not an effect of its mooted foreign occupation.

Although this lament apportions a large part of the blame for the deterioration of the region to its abusive German protector, there is one clear sign that Zweig is not a neutral observer in the dispute over Upper Silesian sovereignty. By beginning his reminiscences with the words 'Ich kenne diese Landschaft', he stakes a claim that is impervious to any change in the status quo. In the context of the forthcoming referendum, this is by definition a challenge to Polish designs on Upper Silesia. This bias does not, however, diminish the pity Zweig feels for the predominantly Polish industrial workforce. He stops short of idealizing the Polish coal and steel workers, whom he describes as 'nicht weniger, nicht mehr' than the muscle in the body of Upper Silesia,[73] but still identifies them as bearing the physical brunt of the alteration to the landscape.

The commercially motivated desecration of the hills and fields of Zweig's youth does not discriminate between national groups, acting upon both the native population and those 'deren Sprache uns Niemand lehrte oder nahelegte, deren Lebensform uns Niemand deutete, und deren Recht auf bessere Daseinsbedingungen uns verdeckt wurde vom Germanisierungstaumel eines sich vermessenden und über alle Grenzen schwellenden Staates'.[74] It is evident from this passage that Zweig's strength of feeling about the Germanness of Upper Silesia does not extend to demonizing his country's rival for control over the region. The perceived audacity of

---

72 William Rollins, '*Heimat*, Modernity, and Nation in the Early Heimatschutz Movement', in *Heimat, Nation, Fatherland*, ed. by Hermand and Steakley, pp. 87–112 (p. 102).
73 Zweig, 'Oberschlesische Motive', p. 248.
74 Zweig, 'Oberschlesische Motive', p. 248.

the Polish state in pressing its claim to his *Heimat* is now ascribed to the generalized acquisitiveness of the *Kaiserreich*, to the expansionist ambitions of which he assigns a natural limit. Nor is the faint obscenity inherent in the image of the German Empire sprawling into territory to which it had no right a distant memory: the mantle has simply been transferred to the industrial elite, which has survived intact into the democratic era. The coal and steel magnates' restless exploitation of any available land is what Zweig now seems to have in mind when he raises the spectre of the German state bursting its banks in nationalistic frenzy.

In Zweig's telling, Upper Silesia is simultaneously coveted by a nation with no entitlement to it and under attack from within in the form of industrialization. The encroachment of mines on the Silesian countryside blurs into the movement of troops across no-man's-land, as the delicate eco-system regulating provincial life is sacrificed to the unsentimental demands of mineral extraction: the pits pockmarking the earth's surface and the corrosive, discolouring fumes emanating from the power stations and hanging in the air above call to mind first-hand accounts of trench warfare such as Ernst Jünger's *In Stahlgewittern* (1920) or Erich Maria Remarque's best-selling novel *Im Westen nichts Neues* (1929);[75] the symbols of death and human suffering are close at hand, represented most viscerally by 'die drohend und klagend aufgestreckten Gerippe der Fördertürme' and the jaundiced trees stained yellow by the gases.[76] Jünger bears witness to an even starker scene of desolation, describing the transformation of a small parcel of northern French countryside into one in which:

> buchstäblich kein Strauch, kein winziges Hälmchen mehr zu sehen [war]. Jede Handbreit Bodens war umgewühlt und immer wieder umgewühlt, die Bäume entwurzelt, zerfetzt und zu Mulm zermahlen, die Häuser weggeblasen und zu Pulver zerstäubt, Berge abgetragen und das Ackerland zur Wüste verwandelt.[77]

In the year following the publication of Jünger's war memoir, Zweig reaches for a similarly apocalyptic register to convey the destruction of his native landscape. Try as he might to find a terrible beauty in the nocturnal light-show provided by the factories, 'die aufflammenden Horizonte, wenn nachts die Hochöfen rund um die Stadt ihre glühenden Eisenflüsse speien' conjure an atmosphere of exploding mortar shells and mustard gas instantly

---

75 Ernst Jünger, *In Stahlgewittern. Aus dem Tagebuch eines Stoßtruppführers* (Leisnig: Meier, 1920); Erich Maria Remarque, *Im Westen nichts Neues* (Berlin: Propyläen, 1929), pp. 60–61.
76 Zweig, 'Oberschlesische Motive', p. 248.
77 Jünger, *In Stahlgewittern*, p. 60.

suggestive of the Western Front.[78] Indeed, Remarque's hero himself describes the literal bombardment of his trench in the aestheticizing tones of somebody narrating a firework display:

> Eine ungewisse, rötliche Helle steht am Horizont von einem Ende zum andern. Sie ist in ständiger Bewegung, durchzuckt vom Mündungsfeuer der Batterien. Leuchtkugeln steigen darüber hoch, silberne und rote Bälle, die zerplatzen und in weißen, grünen und roten Sternen niederregnen. Französische Raketen schießen auf, die in der Luft einen Seidenschirm entfalten und ganz langsam niederschweben. Sie erleuchten alles taghell, bis zu uns dringt ihr Schein, wir sehen unsere Schatten scharf am Boden. Minutenlang schweben sie, ehe sie ausgebrannt sind. Sofort steigen neue hoch, überall, und dazwischen wieder die grünen, roten und blauen.[79]

For his part, Zweig grudgingly admits that he is not insensible to '[dem] magischen Glanz feuriger Buntheit' created by the mingling of the sunset with the factory fumes and concedes that he will never forget 'diese roten und veilchenfarbenen Wolken, deren nach Sonnenuntergang tiefes Leuchten die Antwort der Atmosphäre ist auf die Schwängerung mit Kohlenstaub und Gasen'.[80] Both explicitly and implicitly, then, his metaphor-laden denunciation of heavy industry links it to military aggression and thereby back to the 'Germanisierungstaumel' that allegedly obscured the fundamental rights of the resident Polish population and culminated in the slaughter of the First World War. Even without the symbiotic relationship between the military and the manufacturing tycoons being made explicit, the reader is forced to conclude that Germany is a nation at war with itself.

Zweig's answer to this self-immolation is to mount an intellectual counter-offensive that seeks to reinstate a sense of symbiosis between the workers and the land. As the eastern heartland of German industry, Upper Silesia is to lead by example, serving as a template for a more sustainable collaboration with the regional *Heimat* that could be replicated on a national scale:

> Aber man ändere die Gesinnung durch die Umkehr zu wahrem, beseeltem und von Grund auf änderndem Sozialismus, man erziehe die Keime des Gemeingefühls, welche selbst in dieser heutigen deutschen Gesellschaft warten, und die durch die Not der Bedrohung mit Verlust vielleicht – dreimal vielleicht – zum Schwellen kommen können: und die künftigen Bauten einer künftigen Industrie werden plötzlich selber eine neue Gestalt zeigen, die sich zur heutigen Gestalt

---

78 Zweig, 'Oberschlesische Motive', p. 248.
79 Remarque, *Im Westen nichts Neues*, p. 62.
80 Zweig, 'Oberschlesische Motive', p. 248.

verhält wie die schaffende Arbeit zur ausgebeuteten Arbeit, wie die schenkende Erde zu jener, die zu zerfallenden Tälern und narbigen Flächen eines Bruchfelds geschändet wird.[81]

The reference to 'die künftigen Bauten einer künftigen Industrie' demonstrates that Zweig does not believe in the pastoral idyll evoked by aristocratic proponents of the aforementioned 'rural myth' in order to entice potential farm labourers back from the city. The Socialist rebirth of German society he envisages evidently entails making existing working opportunities more humane rather than reversing the Industrial Revolution. This appeal for Germany to learn from its mistakes makes liberal use of naturalistic metaphor to illustrate the boundless potential of grass-roots Socialism. All the same, the cautious optimism of Zweig's vision depends not on a literal return to an agrarian economy but on the flowering of what Applegate calls 'a publicness defined by the effort to achieve commonality, mutual dependence, and responsibility'.[82] Both in Applegate's image of ever-multiplying spheres of belonging and in Zweig's work-based programme for moral renewal, the impulse is local and the scope nationwide.

Indeed, Zweig is careful to point out that Upper Silesia does not exist in a vacuum but instead forms an integral part of the wider German nation. In the following passage his description of the 'Reich' as wounded and feverish reflects his drastic view of the treaty negotiations, which he evidently considers already to have stretched Germany to breaking point:

> Möglicher Verlust der Heimat und das Vernichtende dieses Verlustes für das im Wundfieber zitternde Reich geben dem oberschlesischen Motiv, dieser kargen Landschaft, diesem industriellen Werkbau plötzlich ein Relief, das ihnen früher abging, und das sie mit allem Recht in den Kern einer Konzeption setzt.[83]

If the disputed status of Upper Silesia has finally forced Germans from other parts of the country to acknowledge their responsibility to it, the raised profile of his homeland has also prompted an epiphany in Zweig himself. He thus advocates a regional patriotism based on a radical departure from the prevailing economic orthodoxy. Upper Silesia is to be the forerunner of a nationwide adoption of Socialism that will shield Germany from any further incursions into its sovereign territory by rendering war an impossibility. Two different entities are at stake in 'Oberschlesische Motive'. One is Upper Silesia itself, exposed to the risk of being cut adrift in a foreign land, and the other is a wider

---

81 Zweig, 'Oberschlesische Motive', p. 249.
82 Applegate, *A Nation of Provincials*, p. 150.
83 Zweig, 'Oberschlesische Motive', p. 249.

German nation in mortal danger. Crucially, the fates of the regional *Heimat* and the national community are presented as umbilically connected. Without the advent of Socialism, both will perish.

The Courland

Whereas Arnold Zweig seeks to recast Germany in the fantasy image of a region that would soon be awarded to another nation, four pieces written by Kurt Tucholsky between mid-1919 and 1923 challenge modern Germany to remodel itself on an erstwhile German protectorate that had belonged to a succession of other imperial powers for approximately half a millennium at the time of writing. Tucholsky's idealization of the Courland, which encompasses the western half of modern-day Latvia, leads him via what he calls 'die baltische Frage' towards an answer to the third quandary contained within Hochman's 'German Question'.[84] In the first and last articles in the sequence, 'Ein untergehendes Land' and 'Frühlingsvormittag', Tucholsky effectively enfolds the German diaspora into his patriotic vision, thereby loosening the criteria for membership of the German nation.[85]

The Duchy of Courland, which bordered East Prussia until the dissolution of the latter at the end of the Second World War, had been a possession of the Russian Empire since the late eighteenth century. After the downfall of the ruling Teutonic Order in the late fifteenth and early sixteenth centuries, sovereignty over the Courland had passed first to the Polish-Lithuanian Commonwealth and then to the Russian Tsar.[86] Its appeal to Tucholsky lay not least in the distinctively German flavour of its cultural traditions, a legacy that dated back to the settlement of the area in the late twelfth century by the *Schwertbrüderorden*.[87] A large, mostly flat plain on the Baltic Sea coast, the Courland had little of the industrial significance of the smaller Upper Silesia. Nonetheless, a steady influx of estate-owning aristocratic and religious elites from across North-West Germany had created the conditions

---

84 Peter Panter, 'Ein untergehendes Land', *Die Weltbühne*, 15.2 (1919), 11–14 (p. 12).
85 Peter Panter, 'Frühlingsvormittag', *Die Weltbühne*, 19.1 (1923), 341–42.
86 The Teutonic Order (*der Deutsche Orden*) was a Catholic military order (now purely religious) that developed out of a fraternity founded by German merchants in Acre *c*. 1191 and had as its main task the provision of help and medical care to sick pilgrims in the Holy Land. It subsequently undertook to spread Christianity in north-eastern Europe and in the first half of the thirteenth century established the *Deutschordensstaat*, which encompassed the length of the Baltic coast as far east as Estonia. The headquarters of the Order were in Marienburg (modern Malbork), south-east of Gdańsk.
87 Established in 1202 for the purposes of exporting Christianity to Livonia, a region that would be subsumed in the sixteenth century into Estonia and Latvia, the *Schwertbrüderorden* was absorbed by the Teutonic Order in 1237.

for an ancestrally German ruling class to establish itself in the region in the seven hundred years since the arrival of the German knights in the early decades of the thirteenth century. In spite of the decline of their chivalric forebears, these *Deutschbalten* remained substantially in the majority in urban areas until a steady decline set in from the middle of the nineteenth century onwards.

In the two middle reflections, 'Kurländisches Landknechtslied' and 'Die baltischen Helden', Tucholsky assumes the personas of the sardonic poet Kaspar Hauser and the acerbic commentator Ignaz Wrobel to launch a more direct assault on his compatriots' behaviour,[88] but the prevailing perspective is that of the sentimental Peter Panter, under whose name both 'Ein untergehendes Land' and the later 'Frühlingsvormittag' appear. At the time of publication of the first three articles, the territory was still the subject of a tug-of-war between Russian, German and ethnically Latvian forces stemming from the signing of the Treaty of Brest-Litovsk on 3 March 1918. This pact saw Russia's Bolshevik government formally hand the Courland over to Germany, thereby strengthening the latter's grip on the area. In 1915 the Courland had been occupied by German Eighth Army soldiers under the command of Otto von Below, in whose regiment Tucholsky had served until his transfer to Romania in 1918. Supplemented by mercenaries, many of these soldiers remained in the Courland beyond the Armistice before finally making way for an indigenous Latvian government in August 1920.

Having been billeted in the region for two years, during which time he met Mary Gerold, the woman who would become his second wife, Tucholsky clearly harboured an interest in the Courland that goes deeper than any abstract sense of cultural affinity with its German minority. To an extent, the

---

88 Tucholsky had originally contrived his four pseudonyms – Peter Panter, Theobald Tiger, Ignaz Wrobel and Kaspar Hauser – to conceal the fact that as many as four articles in any given issue of the journal might be by him. He named his prickliest and most temperamental persona Wrobel after the author of an arithmetic textbook with which he had struggled as a boy, adding the Christian name Ignaz because of its abrasive sound. Harking back to the foundling boy who appeared on the streets of Nuremberg in 1828 claiming to have spent his first sixteen years locked in solitary confinement in a dark cell, Kaspar Hauser's contributions direct an uncomprehending gaze on the world before him in order to cast society in an unfamiliar and unflattering light. Tiger and Panter were inventions of a law lecturer of Tucholsky's designed to serve as imaginary opposite numbers in hypothetical civil lawsuits; in Tucholsky's hands Tiger became a versifier and Panter an author of feuilletons and cultural critic. For Tucholsky's own account, see Kurt Tucholsky, 'Starter, die Fahne –! Ab mit 5 PS', in *Kurt Tucholsky: Panter, Tiger & Co*, ed. by Mary Gerold-Tucholsky, 2nd edn (Hamburg: Rowohlt, 1955 [1954]), pp. 8–10. The article first appeared in *Die Weltbühne*, 23.2 (1927), 964–66 under the title 'Start'. It was the foreword to Tucholsky's *Mit 5 PS* (Berlin: Rowohlt, 1928) and appeared in the journal partly for promotional purposes.

Berlin-born outsider inevitably deals in stereotypes in his writings on the region: the wider *deutschbaltische* population is treated as a sympathetically homogeneous mass. However, his personal links with the area put him in a position to elaborate a regionalist patriotism predicated on the exemplary German qualities of the Courland. Through the beloved figure of Mary Gerold, whose positive attributes are always taken as a reflection of her Baltic-German origins, Tucholsky is even able to imagine the Courland as an alternative *Heimat* to his native Berlin. Indeed, the earliest of the four pieces under discussion here, 'Ein untergehendes Land', concludes with the citation in its entirety of 'Holderbaum' by the Baden-Württemberg poet Christian Wagner (1835–1918), with its line 'Das reinste Glück hängt an der Heimatscholle'.[89] Tucholsky's affection for Wagner's work is clear from his obituary of the recently deceased poet earlier in the same year, in which he credits Wagner's genius to the fact that he was 'ein Deutscher [...] und die ewige Musik in sich hatte'.[90] Bryan P. Grenville notes Tucholsky's 'lifelong affection for "Bauerndichtung"' and singles out Christian Wagner for special mention.[91] For all that Grenville insists Tucholsky had no time for 'Heimatdichter', who allegedly merely feigned intimacy with nature, Wagner's eulogy of the 'Heimatscholle' suggests that the division was not, in fact, clear-cut.

The central premise of 'Ein untergehendes Land', which derives some of its key insights from a recently published history of the Courland by a little known Baltic German called Hans Vorst, is that the *Deutschbalten* are the heirs to a morally superior German culture alien to the modern Germany that now covets it. Tucholsky contends that the peoples of the German diaspora, including the Transylvanian Germans admired by Hans Glenk in 'Zurück zum Balkan', have gradually refined the customs and attitudes of earlier generations to a literal art form, raising the possibility of a portable national *Heimat* unconstrained by geography. It seems to be no coincidence that expatriate German communities have perfected their native qualities outside the political borders of the German nation state:

> Es ist nun ganz merkwürdig zu beobachten, wie die Deutschen, die die Geschichte und der Zug der Welt vom Vaterlande abgesplittert hatten, sich im Ausland alles oder nichts bewahrten, *sich zu immer bessern Deutschen fortentwickelten* oder ganz und gar in den fremden Volksteilen aufgingen. Verloren wir sie, so war das kein Wunder bei

---

89 Christian Wagner, 'Holderbaum', in *Gedichte*, 2nd edn (Munich: Müller, 1913 [1913]), p. 75.
90 Peter Panter, 'Christian Wagner', *Die Weltbühne*, 15.1 (1919), 182–83 (p. 182).
91 Bryan P. Grenville, *Kurt Tucholsky: The Ironic Sentimentalist*, German Literature and Society, 1 (London: Wolff, 1981), p. 68.

einer Politik, die in den Landsleuten nur Untertanen und Objekte zum Regieren sah – behielt sie auch das Land nicht, so zogen sich doch hie und da spinnewebdünne Fäden vom Mutterboden zur fremden Kolonie, die auch die Jahrhunderte nicht zu zerstören vermocht hatten.[92]

Tucholsky's evocation of a qualitative process of *Fortentwicklung* suggests that physical remoteness from their ancestral homeland has enabled German exiles to come close to an ill-defined apotheosis of Germanness. This claim treats German identity as both prescriptive and provisional in that it is subject to infinite improvement while remaining recognizably and exclusively *sui generis*. By effectively granting the Baltic German population of the Courland honorary citizenship of a timeless, intangible German *Kulturnation*, Tucholsky questions the primacy of the political border as a means of organizing human society.

The notion of *Fortentwicklung* resurfaces later in the article in reference to the aforementioned *Siebenbürger Sachsen*. For their part, the *Deutschbalten* are said to match their Transylvanian counterparts in their loyalty to a more sympathetic German culture than that fostered by 'das deutsche Kaiserreich Wilhelminischer Prägung' then holding the Courland hostage.[93] Supposedly a relic of early nineteenth-century rural German life, the traditional Curonian character which Tucholsky distils from Vorst's book is defined by a voracious appetite for self-improvement free from the intellectual arrogance of metropolitan Germans. Tucholsky's use of the past tense in the following passage suggests, however, that the latter is in the ascendancy:

Wie die Siebenbürger Sachsen die besten Seiten des guten alten Deutschtums, das hierzulande längst untergegangen ist, fortentwickelt haben, so gab es in Kurland noch das deutsche Landleben aus dem Anfang des neunzehnten Jahrhunderts. Nur ist der Landbewohner niemals ein 'Onkel aus der Provinz', weil er mit den großen Städten, wie Riga und Dorpat, in reger Verbindung stand, und weil er sehr viel las und sehr viel wußte. [...] Man war ein bißchen spießig, aber sehr solide und in allen äußern Dingen von einer erstaunlichen Kultur, wie sie auf dem Lande fast nur noch in England zu finden ist; man war beharrend (ich möchte absichtlich das Wort 'konservativ' vermeiden), aber doch rege und voll Interesse für alles, was Kunst und die Wissenschaften hergaben – man war fromm, dabei frisch und stark und gleich weit entfernt von diesem entsetzlich altjüngferlichen Protestantismus mit den zusammengekniffenen Lippen wie von dem frechen Monismus der großen Städte, in denen der Koofmich

---

92 Panter, 'Ein untergehendes Land', p. 11. My italics.
93 Panter, 'Ein untergehendes Land', p. 11.

'uffjeklärt' war und alles besser, viel besser wußte ... Mit einem Wort: es waren Menschen. Richtige lebendige Menschen.[94]

Tucholsky's ideal German is an intriguing compound of restless energy and *Bodenständigkeit*. Simultaneously receptive to the intellectual life of the city and inured to the cynicism of its dubious merchants, or *Koofmich*s, the Curonians are inspired by a wholesome piety that never descends into asceticism. This portrait of exemplary nuance, with its carefully cultivated balance of restraint and licence, is depicted as a testament to the possibilities of *Fortentwicklung* when a community is allowed to evolve independently of its origins. Far from pandering to a reactionary myth of rural quietude, Tucholsky describes the *Deutschbalten* as a culturally cosmopolitan caste whose rural way of life is enlivened by communication with the urban centres.

If the Upper Silesian countryside reflects the moral bankruptcy of its German occupants to Arnold Zweig, the unspoilt Curonian landscape appears to Tucholsky as the foremost emblem of the success of the expatriate German community in developing a vernacular independence of temperament within a palpably German cultural tradition. This accomplishment is imperilled, however, by the presence of an actual army whose strong-arm tactics are the literal complement to Zweig's metaphorical capitalist invasion force. In 'Ein untergehendes Land' the untouched acres of the Courland thus become the front line in a dual sense for a clash between two Germanies: the delicately poised and self-contained diaspora of the *Deutschbalten* and the boorish band of mercenaries who refused to vacate the region after the end of the First World War. Tucholsky's gloomy prophecy 'daß der feine Reiz des Landes endgültig dahin ist, wenn die fade Reichssauce sich über Felder und Auen ergießen wird' casts a pre-emptive shadow over his rhapsodic tribute to the bucolic charms of the Courland:[95]

> Und haben sie auch die Kultur fast entzwei geschlagen: eins können sie nicht morden, und das ist die landschaftliche Schönheit des Landes. Es ist, wie wenn der liebe Gott einmal hätte zeigen wollen, wie man es machen muß: alles ist so klar und sauber und eindeutig und so unsagbar deutsch. Es ist fast als sei Deutschland eine Skizze, und Kurland, das sei erst das fertiggestellte Werk.[96]

In Tucholsky's reading, the custodians of the Curonian countryside have preserved the unique aesthetic sensibilities of their German ancestors and

---

94 Panter, 'Ein untergehendes Land', p. 13.
95 Panter, 'Ein untergehendes Land', p. 13.
96 Panter, 'Ein untergehendes Land', p. 14.

improved upon their work. Once again the Courland appears as a time capsule of elevated German culture in the face of which the soldiers claiming the area on behalf of the modern German state appear as the emissaries of a philistine regime.

There is, in fact, a clear continuity in Tucholsky's post-war writings on the Courland with the pre-war ambivalence of the journal vis-à-vis Germany. In reference to its pre-1918 iteration, *Die Schaubühne*, Alf Enseling points out 'daß sich die Kritik auch früher nicht gegen den Kern des deutschen Volkscharakters gerichtet hatte, sondern nur gegen gewisse Entartungen an der Oberfläche'.[97] For Tucholsky, militarism is one such perversion, now as before. He therefore scathingly quotes the speculators who had traversed the region in wartime to the effect that there was 'noch so viel zu machen' in a region they clearly regarded as a greenfield site ripe for the intervention of town planners and platoon commanders.[98] What this blueprint did not allow for, however, was that the Courland was already, in his estimation, the culmination of a particular expression of the German genius.

Although the Weimar Republic had succeeded the *Kaiserreich* in the previous year, Tucholsky does not acknowledge the regime change in his writing. At the end of 'Das untergehende Land', his future wife makes a sudden appearance as the antithesis of the German society she mistakenly idealizes. Mary's absence from Tucholsky's life mirrors the disappearance of the independent Baltic-German culture of which she is a cherished exemplar:

> Und du? Wo magst du jetzt sein? Damals, als ich dich kennen lernte, wolltest du mit aller Gewalt aus Riga fort und aus diesem Lande, das dir so klein erschien und so eng. Und ich lächelte und sagte, du wüßtest gar nicht, was du da an Kurland hättest. Steck einmal die runde Nase in unser Deutschland, und du wirst erschrocken zurückprallen. Weißt du, was du an deinem Heimatlande gehabt hast, kleine Dame?[99]

The image of the Courland in the person of Mary Gerold recoiling on contact with Tucholsky's Prussified Germany attests to an insoluble antagonism between the lovers' rival cultures. Instead of facilitating 'den Weg zu weiteren Schichten von Beheimatung', the encounter of the German diaspora with the vestigial *Kaiserreich* is a collision of two incompatible German *Heimaten*.[100] As explained in the introduction to this volume, Joachim Klose's reappraisal of *Heimat* as a potential space for cultural exchange depends on re-imagining

---

97 Enseling, *Die Weltbühne*, p. 64.
98 Panter, 'Ein untergehendes Land', p. 13.
99 Panter, 'Ein untergehendes Land', p. 14.
100 Klose, '"Heimat"', p. 404.

political borders as permeable 'edges' to be transcended. To Tucholsky, however, the border had proved itself to be a symbol of confinement, both constraining a restless Mary and immuring two Germanic cultures until they had become mutually incomprehensible.

In October of the same year Tucholsky divides his sympathies between both *Heimaten* to rail against the depredations of the German soldiers who have remained in the Courland beyond the Armistice. He claims that their ranks have since been swelled by 'thousands' of opportunists driven purely by the desire to defer the responsibilities of civilian life. In the second line of the article 'Die baltischen Helden' Tucholsky accuses his erstwhile comrades of having, at a single stroke, exploited the native population of the Courland and abandoned their compatriots to their fate:

> Offizier und Mann sogen mit vereinten Kräften an dem Mark des [kurländischen] Landes, und durchaus nicht immer im Interesse des Landes, sondern sehr oft im eignen. [...] Während die Not in der Heimat stieg und stieg, lebten die Besatzungstruppen, und ganz besonders das Offiziercorps, in Kurland weit besser und reicher, als sie jemals in der ausgehungerten Heimat vermocht hätten. Nichts zog sie hierher – alles hielt sie dort.[101]

The soldiers of the Imperial Eighth Army, whose war-time antics supposedly did not serve any higher ideal than their own sensual fulfilment, are described as vampirically sucking dry the dwindling bone marrow of the Courland even as their German homeland withers away for lack of attention. Tucholsky treats both misdeeds with pathos, but the false perspective adopted in the final line, which retroactively removes him from the scene of the alleged crime, suggests that his loyalties lie ultimately with Germany. In conjunction with the distant pronoun 'sie', his use of the word 'hierher' to refer to Germany and 'dort' to denote the Courland creates the fleeting impression that he had never left Germany, thereby absolving him of complicity in the excesses of the imperial soldiery.[102] The Courland, Tucholsky's temporary home, briefly loses its familiarity in the process, defined merely by what it is not: the *Heimat*.

Twice in the course of 'Die baltischen Helden' Tucholsky cites distasteful poetry as what he evidently deems incontrovertible proof of the parasitic attitudes of the mercenary soldiers. The preface to the article, drawn from a version of the mercenary song 'Sollt ich einem Bauern dienen', announces its anonymous author's preference for earning his keep not in

---

101 Ignaz Wrobel, 'Die baltischen Helden', *Die Weltbühne*, 15.2 (1919), 500–04 (p. 500).
102 In other words, Tucholsky was himself present in the Courland while this perceived exploitation was going on but writes as if he had not been. His deliberate deployment of the words 'hierher' and 'dort' create the same illusion.

the fields, but 'wo man von den Waffen spricht'.[103] This extract is innocent, however, by comparison with another poem from a soldier's magazine published in German-occupied Mitau,[104] which Tucholsky reproduces in its entirety.[105] The unnamed author of the call-to-arms boasts openly of sexual conquests with Curonian farm girls and fantasizes darkly about peppering Russian soldiers with bullets.

The influence on Tucholsky of such texts is clear from a pastiche published under the name of Kaspar Hauser in the same issue of *Die Weltbühne*. Entitled 'Kurländisches Landknechtslied', this poem scorns the suffering of the *Heimat* and baldly states the mercenaries' intentions:

> Nach Hause? Pah – das gehn wir nicht!
> Wir wolln uns Weiber kaufen.
> Wir fressen unser Leibgericht
> und saufen, saufen, saufen!
>   Ha, Kadja, welch ein schönes Land!
>   Und reich mir deine Hand![106]

As well as ridiculing the idea that German soldiers have beaten a path to the Courland for the national cause, Tucholsky's parody mocks the idea that any of them sincerely appreciate the natural beauty of the region. Turning to his girlfriend, whom he has presumably 'bought', the mercenary briefly eulogizes their surroundings, only instantly to drop the subject and demand that Kadja take his hand. Having fallen in love with a local woman and written admiringly about the Curonian landscape, Tucholsky is repelled by the blind gluttony and lust that prompt his fellow Germans to treat the women they find there as mere sex objects and effusions about the countryside as transparent pretexts for empty physical intimacy.

Be it Mary Gerold's or Tucholsky's own, the Germanic *Heimat* is at the mercy of German militarism in both 'Das untergehende Land' and 'Die baltischen Helden'. Instead of existing to serve the national interest, the army

---

103 [Anon.], 'Sollt ich einem Bauern dienen?', in *Sammlung Deutscher Volkslieder welche noch gegenwärtig im Munde des Volkes leben und in keiner der bisher erschienenen Sammlungen zu finden sind*, ed. by Wilibald Walter (Leipzig: Rein, 1841), pp. 13–16.
104 The city of Mitau, now Jelgava, lies 25 miles south-west of the modern Latvian capital of Riga. It had served for over two centuries as the capital of the Courland under the Polish-Lithuanian Commonwealth. The magazine to which Tucholsky refers is *Die Trommel* and he dates the unattributed poem to October 1919, the same month in which 'Die baltischen Helden' appeared. The publication does not appear to have survived.
105 Wrobel, 'Die baltischen Helden', p. 503.
106 Kaspar Hauser, 'Kurländisches Landknechtslied', *Die Weltbühne*, 15.2 (1919), 486.

and its mercenary rump seem to see their activity as an end in itself, with no discernible purpose beyond perpetuating the privileges of the soldiers:

> Sie wollen ihr altes Leben weiterführen. Sie wollen fortsetzen, was sie 1914 begonnen, und durch vier Jahre getrieben haben: geschäftig zu sein, ohne stark zu arbeiten, zu disponieren, ohne eine Verantwortung zu tragen [...] – sie wollen das Mißverhältnis zwischen Leistung und Löhnung nicht aufgehoben haben und auch fürder in einer Gemeinschaft, ja, in einem kleinen Staat leben, wie er sonst nirgends zu finden sein kann, weil er unrettbar zusammenbrechen müßte.[107]

By describing garrison life in the Courland effectively as an alternative jurisdiction in which fugitive Germans are at liberty to indulge themselves with impunity, Tucholsky punctures the myth of soldierly self-sacrifice. The micro-state the occupiers have fashioned for themselves appears as Wilhelmine Germany in miniature, an anti-*Heimat* in which members simply help themselves to the resources on offer without giving anything in return. Explicitly absent from Tucholsky's description is any sense of the 'commonality, mutual dependence, and responsibility' which Applegate equates with affirmative *Heimatliebe* and the progressive patriotism it can engender.[108] The national interest is also conspicuous by its absence from this portrait of the army's motives, leaving a patriotic void that responsible republicanism must fill.

In Tucholsky's view, the Weimar state does not rise to this challenge in the ensuing four years. In 'Frühlingsvormittag', published in 1923, Tucholsky ultimately revives from 'Ein untergehendes Land' the image of the Courland as the finished article to Germany's rough copy in order to illustrate the inexpungible Germanness of the Latvian province. However, the reader's attention is first drawn to the fact that this cultural holdover is an anomaly stranded for the past two-and-a-half years in independent Latvia. An innocent stroll on north German soil with the recently arrived Mary Gerold, to whom the piece is dedicated, demonstrates the unbridgeable divide between the lovers' *Heimaten*. Indeed, their political separation merely confirms the temperamental gulf between their inhabitants. In contrast to Germans, Tucholsky insists, people from the Courland are not permanently fixated on their public image: 'Ihr überlegt gar nicht so viel. Ihr seid hübsch, und damit gut. Und ihr geht, schreitet, lacht, fahrt und trinkt so, wie es euch eure kleine Seele eingegeben hat – ohne darüber nachzudenken, wie das wohl "aussieht".[109] The stilted and self-conscious Germans with whom Tucholsky draws this flattering,

---

107 Wrobel, 'Die baltischen Helden', p. 501.
108 Applegate, *A Nation of Provincials*, p. 150.
109 Panter, 'Frühlingsvormittag', p. 342.

if slightly paternalistic, comparison seem to belong to the same bourgeois class whose obsession with property has left its mark on the landscape through which he and Mary are walking. Whereas 'Das untergehende Land' describes the wanderer's view across the undulating fields of the Courland as uninterrupted by man-made structures almost as far as the eye can see, the route pursued by the Germany-bound lovers in 'Frühlingsvormittag' is studded with evidence of human ownership and its accompanying legal stipulations. Turning in wry surprise from the only pond they pass not to be guarded by a sign proclaiming 'Verboten', Mary promptly steps into a puddle in a new pair of shoes and takes her annoyance out on her companion. 'Aber dann', Tucholsky pointedly relates, 'ist das vorbei ...'.[110] Unlike the signs forbidding entry, Mary's spontaneous reaction does not threaten consequences. Her insouciance stands out in a German culture that is apparently excessively burdened with prohibitions.

In light of his aversion to relatively inoffensive proclamations of private property, it is hardly surprising that Tucholsky is appalled by the German seizure of land in the Courland. Indeed, cultural rapprochement with the *Deutschbalten*, and not the forcible re-absorption of the Courland into the German state, is the prize squandered by military overreach and bungled diplomacy. When Mary regales him with tales of the long walks that can be taken in the Courland, he immerses himself in bitter-sweet recollections: '– und mir wird das Herz weit, wenn ich an das schönste Land denke, das wir beide kennen: Gottes propprer Protzprospekt für ein unglücklicherweise nicht geliefertes Deutschland'.[111] The metaphor may be similar but it is now encumbered with the sobering realization that Germany has not lived up to the potential embodied in its Baltic-German diaspora. In Tucholsky's original image imperial Germany had been the sketch and the Courland the final draft.[112] Four years later, it seems the democratic Republic has long since missed the deadline for corrections.

The pro-active patriotism of Arnold Zweig, who in 1921 had still held out hope for his home region to show Germany the way to absolution, gives way here to the reactive patriotism of Kurt Tucholsky. By 1923 it is clear that Tucholsky's dream of a Baltic-infused Germany is not going to transpire. However, his loathing for the dominant German culture, which he regards as inseparable from Prussian militarism, does not amount to an outright rejection of his home country. Instead, what the Courland offers is a glimpse of an alternative German society guided by a drastically different relationship with the natural world, the citizens of which are characterized

---

110 Panter, 'Frühlingsvormittag', p. 342.
111 Panter, 'Frühlingsvormittag', p. 342.
112 Panter, 'Ein untergehendes Land', p. 14.

by moderation and a desire for self-improvement. This is the polar opposite of the sybaritic abandon of the occupying German soldiers. To judge by Tucholsky's fraternal sentiments towards the *deutschbaltisch* diaspora, the preponderance of militant Germans both within and outwith the borders of the post-war state constitutes the triumph only of a particular subset of the German nation. His patriotic enthusiasm thus lies dormant, waiting for the humane spirit of their expatriate cousins to evince itself in a German people whose baser instincts have, for the time being, prevailed.

Styria

In 1925 the Lorraine-born Otto Flake presented his take on the German Question following a visit to one of the eastern frontiers of German-speaking Europe. Flake, a long-standing and regular contributor to *Die Weltbühne* considered at length in the next chapter, had just returned from the Steiermark. The vast wine-growing region had belonged exclusively to the Austro-Hungarian Empire until the Treaty of Saint-Germain-en-Laye (1919) had turned the River Mura into a border between two new states: the First Austrian Republic to the north and the Kingdom of the Serbs, Croats and Slovenes to the south.[113] During his stay with a gentleman farmer on the Austrian side of the river, Flake had observed first-hand the transfer to Slovenian administration of towns and villages until recently under the jurisdiction of the Austrian half of the Habsburg Empire. It is hard to ascribe a political orientation to the flurry of sometimes contradictory impressions contained within the resulting article, 'Südsteiermark', but its general pro-*großdeutsch* tendency can be deduced from the author's readiness to echo Arno Voigt and Walter Kollenka in attributing the Slavic will to self-determination to 'Chauvinismus'.[114] Like Tucholsky before him, Flake takes up Hochman's question concerning who is entitled to claim membership of the German nation and polemically throws it open to interpretation. The *Heimat* he wishes to enfold into his *Großdeutschland* is an audacious compound of prosaic reality and egalitarian fantasy centred on an agricultural river basin now split down the middle by the very waterway to which it owes its historical prosperity.

---

113 Petra Kramberger, 'Das Jahr 1929 in der deutschsprachigen Presse der Untersteiermark aus Maribor, Celje und Ptuj', in *Grenzdiskurse*, ed. by Schönborn, pp. 113–26 (p. 118). Kramberger briefly explains here that the absolute monarchy out of which the state of Yugoslavia would arise in 1929 had first taken the form of a constitutional monarchy in which each of the three main ethnic groups was explicitly represented.

114 Flake, 'Südsteiermark', p. 163.

Although Flake was not himself an Austrian, his article can only be understood in the context of the ethnic tensions incubated by the lopsided composition of the Austro-Hungarian Empire and unleashed by its collapse upon the end of the First World War. In a chapter exploring the cultural ramifications of the political power shift in the Untersteiermark, which lay due south of the area in which Flake stayed, Petra Kramberger writes that the Slovenians instantly capitalized on the fall of the Empire to assert the political primacy of the numerically superior Slovenian population. The clutch of towns in which German citizens predominated had been known as 'das deutsche Festungsdreieck der Untersteiermark', not least because political power over the rest of the region had been concentrated here.[115] By sacking all German-speaking civil servants and teachers, closing German-language schools and banning German street signs, the resurgent Slovenian majority hoped 'alle Spuren der deutschen Vergangenheit zu tilgen'.[116] This was the heightened atmosphere that greeted Flake on his arrival at the border in 1925.

As it was for Kollenka with regard to the new Czech state, for Flake the most immediate affront associated with the concession of southern Styria to Slovenian tutelage resided in the privileging of the Slovenian language over the German one on the southern bank of the Mura. Indeed, Flake's reflections on Styria provide compelling evidence for the influence of the German philosopher Johann Gottlieb Fichte's (1762–1814) notion of the German *Kulturnation* on non-political conceptions of nationhood into the Weimar period. Flake's overall debt to Fichte's *Reden an die deutsche Nation* (1808) is plain from the title of his series *Deutsche Reden* (1922) alluded to above, but a cursory glance at a passage from Fichte's own *Reden* will suffice to show their particular relevance to the soft linguistic imperialism on show in Südsteiermark.

Decades ahead of unification, Fichte explicitly distinguishes between the 'Staat', represented by German-speaking principalities and 'Reiche', and the wider 'Nation', which included German minorities abroad. In his telling, members of this diasporic 'Nation' pursued customs and nurtured institutions revealing of their German origins. These far-flung compatriots lived on, he claims, in the imagination of legally German subjects:

> Soweit die deutsche Zunge reichte, konnte jeder, dem im Bezirke derselben das Licht anbrach, sich doppelt betrachten als Bürger, teils seines Geburtsstaates, dessen Fürsorge er zunächst empfohlen war, teils des ganzen gemeinsamen Vaterlandes deutscher Nation. [...]

---

115 Kramberger, 'Das Jahr 1929 in der deutschsprachigen Presse', p. 113.
116 Kramberger, 'Das Jahr 1929 in der deutschsprachigen Presse', p. 119.

Kein deutschgeborner Fürst hat es je über sich vermocht, seinen Untertanen das Vaterland innerhalb der Berge oder Flüsse, wo er regierte, abzustecken und dieselben zu betrachten als gebunden an die Erdscholle.[117]

For Fichte, the German language possessed an almost magical power that made it capable of conjuring in its speakers a sense of profound kinship with fellow ethnic Germans whom they had never seen. Such a mystical belief in the unifying power of the German tongue may, in fact, account for Flake's intercession in this article on behalf of a people whose historical sense of its own Germanness was, by his own admission, by no means universal or straightforward.

The possibility of an Austro-German *Anschluß* lies directly beneath the surface in this article. Flake's insistence on calling the young Austrian state 'Deutschösterreich' in defiance of the legal injunction against such nomenclature in the Treaty of Saint-German-en-Laye hints at his desire for the cultural community of *Großdeutschland* to become a political reality.[118] Declarations of Austro-German fraternity pre-dated the collapse of the Hohenzollern and Habsburg empires: in his speech 'Österreich im Spiegel seiner Dichtung' (1916) the Austrian writer Hugo von Hofmannsthal had addressed his compatriots' hereditary 'Dualismus des Gefühles, unsere Zugehörigkeit zu Österreich, unsere kulturelle Zugehörigkeit zum deutschen Gesamtwesen'.[119] Whether or not such evocations of a *Kulturnation* necessarily translated into political ambition depended on the individual, though unification of the two German-speaking states was prominent among the early objectives of German negotiators at the peace talks[120] and Hochman observes a groundswell of support among Austrians for the idea after the First World War.[121] Hofmannsthal's own ambivalence about the political implications of his words may detract somewhat from the certainty of his pronouncement: 'Unsere geistige Haltung gegenüber dem deutschen Nationalstaate, von dem wir Unbegrenztes zu empfangen und dem wir Unschätzbares zu geben haben, ist

---

117 Johann Gottlieb Fichte, *Reden an die deutsche Nation* (Berlin: Realschulbuchhandlung, 1808), pp. 273–74.
118 Flake, 'Südsteiermark', p. 160.
119 Hugo von Hofmannsthal, 'Österreich im Spiegel seiner Dichtung', in *Gesammelte Werke in Einzelausgaben*, ed. by Herbert Steiner, 4 vols (Frankfurt a.M.: Fischer, 1950–55), *Prosa*, III (1952), 333–49 (p. 345).
120 Klaus Schwabe, 'Germany's Peace Aims and the Domestic and International Constraints', in *The Treaty of Versailles: A Reassessment after 75 Years*, ed. by Manfred F. Boemeke, Gerald D. Feldman and Elisabeth Glaser, Publications of the German Historical Institute (Cambridge: Cambridge University Press, 1998), pp. 37–68 (pp. 45–46; p. 59).
121 Hochman, *Imagining a Greater Germany*, p. 71; p. 84.

deutlich vorgeschrieben'.[122] His entitlement to speak on behalf of a politically significant number of his compatriots, however, seems secure. Indeed, the concept of citizens of the Weimar Republic, curiously known as *Reichsdeutsche*, uniting with their Austrian counterparts around a single constitution remained in wide circulation throughout the 1920s; Hochman shows that the popularity of this idea was, in fact, only enhanced by its prohibition. Noting Hitler's subsequent ideological appropriation of the *Anschluß*, she argues for the widening of our historical understanding of the concept to encompass a progressive 'desire to unite peacefully members of a German nation into a single state based on the Weimar constitution'.[123]

Flake's affinity with Hofmannsthal's German 'Gesamtwesen' is clear from the first line, which reads: 'Ich sah ein Städtchen in dem Zustand, den es zur Zeit Goethes gehabt haben muß'.[124] Radkersburg, which lies on the Austrian shore of the River Mura, is thereby instantly invested with a generically German atmosphere that is only enhanced by the reference in the following line to marauding Ottoman armies attacking up the River Drava in the Middle Ages *en route* to Vienna. Flake then goes further, declaring the town to be 'der südöstlichste deutsche Ort'.[125] In spite of this tribalism a curious feature of 'Südsteiermark' is Flake's alternating between subjective and objective perspectives, the latter manifest in his sober ability to distinguish 'Das, was immer ist und die Perioden über sich ergehen läßt, den Boden, den Ort, die Bauten, und Das, was den Boden, den Ort, die Bauten für ein paar Jahre übernimmt, die Menschen'.[126] His occasional adoption of this external viewpoint, which accords no special importance to the Austrian claim to the Südsteiermark, co-exists uneasily with his professed empathy with his locally born friend.

It is small wonder that a world view which regards Austrian territory as simply and unproblematically German should mobilize the common German language against the Slovenian pretender. Thus Flake's first reaction upon crossing the border is to register his unease at the sight of Cyrillic lettering on municipal signage in the town of Gornja Radgona, which he stubbornly calls Oberradkersburg.[127] This, he opines in unwontedly technocratic language, is 'eine Erschwerung des Verkehrs'.[128] The next line betrays what is actually at

---

122 Hofmannsthal, 'Österreich im Spiegel seiner Dichtung', p. 347.
123 Hochman, *Imagining a Greater Germany*, p. 37.
124 Flake, 'Südsteiermark', p. 160.
125 Flake, 'Südsteiermark', p. 160.
126 Flake, 'Südsteiermark', p. 162.
127 Until the Treaty of Saint-Germain-en-Laye, Gornja Radgona had formed part of the Radkersburg settlement.
128 Flake, 'Südsteiermark', p. 163.

stake for Flake: 'Auch die Tschechen sind sich ihres slawischen Charakters bewußt, ohne doch jenes Alphabet einzuführen'.[129] For all his professed concern over the adverse fiscal consequences of erecting a border between the vintners of Radkersburg and their vineyards, Flake is clearly most troubled by the fear of cultural displacement. Imposing the Cyrillic alphabet on the unpractised Austrians is made to resemble the first act in a pan-Slavic plot to graft a uniformly Slavic character onto Germanic Styria.

Flake's linguistic insecurity belongs to a long tradition of imagined correlation between the political and linguistic ascendancy of the nation that had especially firm roots in the Germanophone sphere. According to Joseph Jurt, the status of the German language was vigorously debated whenever the *Kulturnation* felt its standing in the world to be under threat. The Prussian court of Friedrich II, and the Prussian Academy in particular, recognized the potential of language as an instrument of political 'soft power':

> Offensichtlich wurden Sprache und Literatur, aber auch die Wissenschaften als zentrale Elemente der nationalen Identität, der Bedeutung einer Nation eingestuft. Die politische und kulturelle Dimension erscheinen in einem Reziprozitätsverhältnis. Die politische Bedeutung einer Nation trägt zur Ausbreitung ihrer Sprache und ihrer Kultur bei, strahlt aber auch wieder auf diese zurück.[130]

Having established the depth of the perceived symbiosis between the cultural renown of a nation and its political primacy, Jurt applies it to Fichte's deification of the German language in his *Reden*. Dismissing Romance languages as insubstantial and derivative, Fichte prophesies: '[D]agegen wird der deutsche Geist neue Schachten eröffnen und Licht und Tag einführen in ihre Abgründe und Felsmassen von Gedanken schleudern, aus denen künftige Zeitalter sich Wohnungen erbauen'.[131] The tool for this work of excavation is to be the uncompromised German language.

Jurt interprets Fichte's assertion that the supposed purity of the German language would ultimately enable its speakers to prevail over their Western European adversaries as a defence mechanism in the face of Napoleonic invasion: 'In einem Augenblick politischer Schwäche, der gleichzeitig ein kultureller Höhepunkt war – darin war Deutschland singulär –, betrachtete man die Kultur als kompensatorische Größe und die Sprache als Fundament

---

129 Flake, 'Südsteiermark', p. 163.
130 Joseph Jurt, *Sprache, Literatur und Nationale Identität. Die Debatten über das Universelle und das Partikuläre in Frankreich und Deutschland*, Mimesis, 58 (Berlin: De Gruyter, 2014), p. 101.
131 Fichte, *Reden an die deutsche Nation*, p. 168.

der Nation'.¹³² In view of the losses incurred by Germany and Austria at Versailles and Saint-Germain respectively, Jurt's explanation of Fichte's claims of cultural supremacy as a reaction against French occupation maps with uncanny precision onto Flake's neurotic monitoring of the German language in the Südsteiermark. After leaving Gornja Radgona behind and passing through a handful of villages, Flake observes in a tone of barely suppressed satisfaction that court proceedings and church services are still conducted in German; indeed, his approval of the fact that Yugoslavian is no more than an 'Unterrichtsgegenstand', whereas German remains the language of instruction, offers a hint of the national power relationship he deems proper in the region.¹³³ Fichte's Napoleonic nemesis is replaced here by a less tangible threat to a more debatable claim: German predominance in the ill-defined geo-political zone known as Mitteleuropa.

The assumption of *großdeutsch* entitlement to seniority in Mitteleuropa underpins Flake's essay. As Martin Ruehl explains, the notion of 'Mitteleuropa' was open to almost as many interpretations as the term *Anschluß*, or indeed the related notion of *Großdeutschland* itself, membership of which could be bestowed through 'language, culture, history, the shared and burdensome experience of the Great War, ethnicity, and an individual decision to join the German Volk'.¹³⁴ Ruehl notes that Mitteleuropa served as:

> a synonym for German supremacy on the continent [sic], whether in Friedrich Naumann's more federalist, economic plans, the aggressively annexationist claims of the Pan-Germans during the First World War, or the irredentist rhetoric of the Weimar historian Wilhelm Schüßler, who called for a drastic revision of the boundaries imposed on Germany by the Treaty of Versailles and the recuperation of 'German national space' ('deutscher Volksraum') in Eastern and South Eastern Europe.¹³⁵

Entirely innocent of the expansionism of the nationalist associations discussed in the introduction, Flake also stops just short of Schüßler's irredentism. Nonetheless, his keenly observed summary of a festival in Radkersburg takes in one speaker's wish that the post-war treaties not prove the final word on the border question, as well as dwelling on the fact that one

---

132 Jurt, *Sprache, Literatur und Nationale Identität*, p. 188.
133 Flake, 'Südsteiermark', p. 164.
134 Hochman, *Imagining a Greater Germany*, p. 46.
135 Martin A. Ruehl, 'Aesthetic Fundamentalism in Weimar Poetry: Stefan George and his Circle, 1918–1933', in *Weimar Thought: A Contested Legacy*, ed. by Peter E. Gordon and John P. McCormick (Princeton, NJ: Princeton University Press, 2013), pp. 240–72 (p. 256).

dancing troupe had flown the black-red-gold tricolour of the Weimar state while 'not a single one' had displayed an Austrian flag.[136] Flake's emphasis on these contributions suggests that he is not a neutral observer, but instead takes the part of the hypothetical *großdeutsch* state.

In one disarmingly candid passage Flake confesses to what he considers an inescapable human weakness: national bias. In what follows, he casts aspersions on the post-war treaties, even suggesting that they are the latest in a long line of settlements to discriminate against the Germans:

> Solange die Völker den Boden zum Gegenstand ihrer Gier machen, wird der Reisende nicht umhin können, sich über jeden Streifen zu freuen, der für die eigne Nation gerettet wurde, und bei jedem, der verloren ging, Bedauern zu empfinden.
>
> Diese Gefühle haben etwas Infantiles, aber wenn man sich um Das, was ist, kümmert, sind sie gegeben, und bei jedem Gang durch die Fluren tritt ein absoluteres Gefühl auf, das für Gerechtigkeit. Es wäre lächerlich, immer nur von den Deutschen zu erwarten, daß sie sich verschachern lassen.[137]

This passage is striking for its juxtaposition of self-knowledge and abject susceptibility to the irrational appeal of herd loyalty. After venturing a succinct explanation of state-based nationalism, Flake immediately casts off any such cool objectivity. His own biography makes this particularly noteworthy: Flake was born in Metz only nine years after the city had been granted to the German Empire along with the rest of Lorraine at the end of the Franco-Prussian War (1870–71). His insinuation that the Germans are perennial victims therefore rests upon a highly selective approach to recent history.

On one hand, his admiring acknowledgement of the role of Italian stonemasons in the construction of Radkersburg, together with his evocation of the ghosts of Croatian, Turkish and Hungarian regiments that had passed through over the preceding centuries, proves that Flake is sensitive to the vicissitudes of history.[138] On the other, his solicitude for 'Das, was ist' outweighs these niceties. Instead of regarding human settlements as palimpsests of their past owners, Flake offers a reformulation of Fichte's claim that places are repeatedly formed anew by the people occupying them and not the other way around. In an attempt to allay fears that the dispersal

---

136 Flake, 'Südsteiermark', p. 166.
137 Flake, 'Südsteiermark', p. 163.
138 Flake, 'Südsteiermark', p. 162.

of Germans around the world would dilute the essence of the German *Volk*, Fichte had declared:

> Der Mensch wird leicht unter jedem Himmelsstriche einheimisch, und die Volkseigentümlichkeit, weit entfernt, durch den Wohnort sehr verändert zu werden, beherrscht vielmehr diesen und verändert ihn nach sich. [...] Sieger und Herrscher und Bildner des aus der Vermischung entstehenden neuen Volks waren doch nur die Germanen.[139]

Whereas Fichte had sought to pre-empt paranoia about Germany's cultural dissolution by asserting that Germans had always succeeded in subjecting other peoples and places to their will, Flake applies the same logic retrospectively to de-legitimize the actual diminishment of *Großdeutschland*. By way of justifying his partisan feelings about Styrian sovereignty, Flake again feigns distance from his subject, this time by deploying the impersonal pronoun *man*: 'Man kann eine Landschaft an sich auf Sinne und Geist wirken lassen; aber die genaueste Phantasie wird neben dem allgemein Seienden auch das spezifisch Gewordene suchen, anders gesagt: sich für Besitz und Besitzer interessieren.'[140] What emerges from this passage is a perceived hierarchy of ownership; Flake's unapologetic defence of 'Das, was ist' could just as well be rephrased as concern for 'Das, was eben war'. Styria's historical custodians, enumerated by Flake himself in an earlier part of the essay, have forfeited their candidacy. On the Slovenian side of the border he duly lets fall several ambiguous remarks that lend themselves to a political interpretation. Hearing the clatter of a wooden scarecrow in the wind, Flake looks around for storks. Realizing his mistake and seeing only herons on the riverbank, he reflects morosely: '[D]er Storch gehört zu den aussterbenden Vögeln.'[141] If the threatened status of the stork is intended to mirror the dwindling *großdeutsch* influence in the region, however, its migratory habits and proverbial part in the birth of the next generation may offer the German observer a glimmer of hope for the future.

However, the political substance of 'Südsteiermark' is not exhausted by the crossfire of national claim and counter-claim. Flake's essay is, in fact, just as much a Socialist fable as it is an assertion of cultural sovereignty. Just as his relationship with Mary Gerold enables Kurt Tucholsky to see the Courland from an inside perspective, so Flake's insight into his host's life as a livestock farmer offers him a glimpse of the Styrian *Heimat*. Returned from elective

---

139 Fichte, *Reden an die deutsche Nation*, pp. 117–18.
140 Flake, 'Südsteiermark', p. 163.
141 Flake, 'Südsteiermark', p. 164.

exile in Argentina, where he had spent the war years, Flake's friend has apparently experienced a dual epiphany. Turning his back on the exploitative ranch economy of the pampa and the overtures of the European metropolis, he has resolved to regain his place in his native community through honest labour: 'Er kehrte zurück, nun fähig, in der Heimat bodenständig zu werden, im engen Kreis zu wirken; Natürliches muß man unter den Füßen haben, ganz wie die Leute da in der Kleinstadt, nur wissender, freier, weniger gierig'.[142] The provincial *Heimat* is here portrayed as the only setting in which the integrity of Flake's friend could flourish, whereas the town is a claustrophobic hive of egotism and mutual surveillance. This idealization of rural life corresponds both in outline and particulars to what Shelley Baranowski has called the 'rural myth', with Flake even rhapsodizing about the smell of the cowshed.[143] Promoted by the landed gentry on East Prussian estates and elsewhere, the rural myth 'asserted without contradiction the common bonds of rural society and the common goals of all agricultural producers at the same time it upheld social stratification as a necessity'.[144] This was a self-serving creed calculated to shore up a teetering social order against the destabilizing tremors of social mobility and political liberalization unleashed by the twin phenomena of industrialization and urbanization.

Notwithstanding these similarities, the outward resemblance of 'Südsteiermark' to this conservative propaganda offensive is misleading. Baranowski argues that, in projecting an agrarian utopia 'as a distinctive, genuine, and wholesome way of life that was vital to Germany's future as a great power', apologists for the estate model chose to ignore the forcible co-opting of the lower classes on which this economy depended.[145] In 'Südsteiermark', by contrast, the key symbolic encounter is with an elderly noblewoman who is busy working the fields of her own estate on the other side of the border. Admittedly, Flake prefaces this brief meeting by comparing the sunflowers to miniature solar eclipses, thereby co-opting the crops themselves into a laconic commentary on the decline of the traditional social hierarchy. However, any rueful value judgement one might be inclined to infer from this metaphor is instantly undermined by the appearance of the labouring aristocrat, as well as by the fact that Flake struggles even to remember what her title had been: 'eine Baronin oder Gräfin, ich vergaß es'.[146]

In conjunction with his elaborate endorsement of the anti-materialist epiphany that brought his host back to his homestead, Flake's casual

---

142 Flake, 'Südsteiermark', p. 161.
143 Flake, 'Südsteiermark', p. 161.
144 Baranowski, *The Sanctity of Rural Life*, p. 6.
145 Baranowski, *The Sanctity of Rural Life*, p. 6.
146 Flake, 'Südsteiermark', p. 164.

acceptance of the presence of an aristocrat among the 'alten Recherinnen' in the hay fields suggests an almost utopian belief in the power of a rural subsistence economy to dissolve distinctions of rank and negate the need for competition.[147] Finding in Radkersburg and its surrounds the antithesis to 'diese[m] Kleine[n] und Gehässige[n] in den Städten, diese[m] Einanderüberwachen', he even surrenders his critical faculties in a sun-drenched setting that could pass for a caricature of a bucolic idyll.[148] Sitting at ease among new friends 'in der Szenerie Pans und der bacchantischen Götter' and partaking of a local champagne,[149] he momentarily gives himself up to 'den Geistern des Weines' and begins to muse upon the modern process of civilization that has allegedly delivered soulless mechanization and mutual alienation instead of true happiness.[150] Flake's alcohol-induced certainty that he has found the antidote to this malaise in the matter-of-fact friendliness and plentiful self-sufficiency of his hosts soon passes, but his sobering realization that this is probably wishful thinking scarcely weakens the political parable the episode is intended to illustrate.

It would, therefore, be grossly simplistic to see in 'Südsteiermark' an apologia for the rural myth, though its reactionary gaze can be felt. Noting the history of the farm as an appendage to an aristocrat's townhouse in Radkersburg, Flake adds approvingly: 'Ich sah alte Stiche des Hofes; fast Alles ist, wie es war'.[151] In spite of the poignant undertow of this remark, it would be a distortion of Flake's well-established republican sympathies to read imperial nostalgia into the all-pervading elegiac mood in 'Südsteiermark'. Recounting a visit to a castle in Muraszombat (present-day Murska Sobota), now the northern-most city in the Kingdom of the Serbs, Croats and Slovenes, Flake describes the new regime's policy of land re-distribution as 'ein berechtigtes Prinzip', thereby condoning the expropriation from the fallen aristocracy.[152]

At the same time he is conflicted by the wider repercussions of this expulsion. In the master bedchambers and living quarters of the castle, which is partly occupied by Russian White Army generals assigned to the new border checkpoints, he is visited by 'ein Gefühl der Indiskretion, weil das Alles noch eben benutzte Räume sind'.[153] Such a reaction, more usually associated with the vacation of a room following its occupant's death than with its abandonment by a landlord who has voluntarily taken up residence

---

147 Flake, 'Südsteiermark', p. 164.
148 Flake, 'Südsteiermark', p. 161.
149 Flake, 'Südsteiermark', p. 165.
150 Flake, 'Südsteiermark', p. 164.
151 Flake, 'Südsteiermark', p. 160.
152 Flake, 'Südsteiermark', p. 167.
153 Flake, 'Südsteiermark', p. 168.

in a foreign capital, may seem out of place. However, the individual earl's fate is hardly the point: the visitor's discomfort is generated by what the former's absence represents. Indeed, the symbolism is heavy: the deserted rooms stand for nothing less than the cannibalized 'Volksraum' of *Großdeutschland*. On another level, meanwhile, the decline of German influence in Styria threatens to bring down the curtain once and for all on the pre-modern romantic pastoral glimpsed by Flake on his peregrinations.

Conclusion

The defining trait shared by all three authors discussed in this section is their tendency to perceive Germanophone culture as a fluid entity that grows and expands independently of Germany's political form. By interrogating the foundations of the modern German state, these writers revive the dichotomy between 'Volkszugehörigkeit' and 'Staatszugehörigkeit' underpinning Johann Gottlieb Fichte's early-nineteenth-century tract *Reden an die deutsche Nation*. Indeed, Fichte's claim that national boundaries were powerless to contain the shared cultural bond uniting ethnic Germans acquires new relevance in the context of post-war border changes:

> Dies nun ist in höherer, vom Standpunkte der Ansicht einer geistigen Welt überhaupt genommener Bedeutung des Worts ein Volk: das Ganze der in Gesellschaft miteinander fortlebenden und sich aus sich selbst immerfort natürlich und geistig erzeugenden Menschen, das insgesamt unter einem gewissen besondern Gesetze der Entwicklung des Göttlichen aus ihm steht.[154]

Fichte elaborates on this definition of divinely sanctioned nationhood in the same lecture, describing the 'Vaterland' as a spiritual entity unconstrained by official borders:

> Volk und Vaterland in dieser Bedeutung als Träger und Unterpfand der irdischen Ewigkeit und als dasjenige, was hienieden ewig sein kann, liegt weit hinaus über den Staat im gewöhnlichen Sinne des Wortes – über die gesellschaftliche Ordnung, wie dieselbe im bloßen klaren Begriffe erfasst und nach Anleitung dieses Begriffs errichtet und erhalten wird.[155]

It may surprise modern readers that Fichte's religious mystification of national identity should resonate in a left-wing journal. Crucially, however,

---

154 Fichte, *Reden an die deutsche Nation*, p. 251.
155 Fichte, *Reden an die deutsche Nation*, p. 257.

these echoes did not represent a 'Fichte-Renaissance', as Felicity Rash and others have called the rediscovery of the philosopher by supporters of the First World War in 1914.[156] Unlike their rivals on the right wing, the writers under discussion here refrained from demanding the return of historically German lands. Instead, the lost *Heimat* stood as both a sober indictment of the country's past moral failings and an impassioned plea for its future redemption.

The *Heimat* Within

The first section of this chapter shows the ways in which the idea of a regional *Heimat* could be exported into contested areas on or beyond Germany's borders as a totem of cultural Germanness. This section now demonstrates the stabilizing potential of the *Heimat* as a locus of German identity within a country whose cohesiveness was frequently doubted in the pages of *Die Weltbühne* throughout the Weimar period. Even after Germany's territorial losses under the post-war treaties, the sheer size and geographical spread of its population was regarded as a barrier to any widespread sense of unity emerging in what was often referred to as the 'Sechzig-Millionen-Volk'.[157] Indeed, it was still topical in 1921 for Walter Mehring to point out the difficulty for Germany's wartime leaders 'sechzig Millionen Menschen zu beherrschen, die weniger von einander wußten als zwei Fachwissenschaftler verschiedener Nationen, und deren Nationalgefühl so wenig Gemeinsames hatte wie das eines friesischen Fischers der dänischen Grenzen und eines Bergarbeiters im Ruhr-Revier'.[158] By the end of the decade, so little had changed in the journal's perception of the shallowness of the German national consciousness that Kurt Tucholsky could still declare:

> [E]s ist ja nicht wahr, daß die sechzig Millionen immer ein einziges Ding sind; gespalten sind sie, durch den Klassenkampf zerrissen, in ihren Anschauungen, ihrem Herkommen, ihrer Abstammung so weit voneinander unterschieden, daß man schon auf das Heimatgefühl, das ganz und gar unpolitisch ist, zurückgreifen muß, um wirklich sagen zu dürfen: Deutschland.[159]

---

156 Rash, *German Images of the Self*, p. 37.
157 Karl Rothammer, 'London', *Die Weltbühne*, 17.1 (1921), 267–69 (p. 268); Ein Stabsoffizier, 'Der neue Krieg', *Die Weltbühne*, 16.2 (1920), 446–50 (p. 449).
158 Walter Mehring, 'Die welsche Grenze', *Die Weltbühne*, 17.2 (1921), 306–09 (p. 306).
159 Ignaz Wrobel, 'Ein besserer Herr', *Die Weltbühne*, 25.1 (1929), 953–60 (pp. 956–57).

Given the bewildering variety of groups into which Germans were apparently subdivided, it is hardly surprising that the supposedly unifying 'Heimatgefühl' in which Tucholsky vested so much hope should sometimes also have manifested itself negatively. This section begins by exploring two articles which highlight the aggressively insular tone that *Heimatliebe* could take. The purpose of this digression is to draw attention to the capacity of *Heimatliebe* to obscure the author's sense of kinship with the German nation at large, before exploring a larger corpus of pieces that cultivate an affirmative identification with a regional *Heimat* as a basis for progressive patriotism. The difference between the two articles discussed below and the xenophobic texts examined at the beginning of the chapter (i.e., those by Kollenka, Voigt and Glenk) is that they openly disapprove of, rather than flagrantly promote, the attitudes in question. Published months either side of Tucholsky's 'Der bessere Herr', these two interventions express amused wonderment at the parochialism they perceive.

The first, 'Ruhrprovinz', is by Erik Reger, who had worked as the press-relations manager for the Essen-based steel manufacturing giant Friedrich Krupp AG from 1919 to 1927. On a visit to the workers' colonies of Germany's western industrial heartland, Reger reflects ironically on the petty nature of the exceptionalism nurtured by the townsfolk of the Ruhr. The residents of Essen, Mülheim and Hamborn are portrayed as inordinately proud of their association with public figures such as the steel magnate Hugo Stinnes, or nationally recognized firms such as the writer's former employer. For its part, Buer, which had recently acquired city status courtesy of a merger with Gelsenkirchen, is mockingly described as 'bekannt durch seinen Protest gegen Meyers Lexikon (weil darin über Buer nur zwölf Zeilen stehn)'.[160]

The inevitable consequence of this municipal amour-propre is a feverish competition for prominence, which Reger calls 'particularism': 'Partikularismus ist, wenn eine Stadt nicht einsehen will, daß die Hegemonie der Nachbarstadt ein Naturgesetz sei; wenn sie im Gegenteil sagt: baust du ein Hochhaus, mache ich eine Ausstellung'.[161] The self-aggrandizing impulse driving such expressions of *Heimatliebe* has no need of a national context to furnish it with a sense of purpose. Indeed, the particularism that Reger describes is jealously parochial in scope, placing pride in one's city over solidarity with the wider population of the *Ruhrgebiet*, let alone with the 'Sechzig-Millionen-Volk' as a whole. Thus resentment over the greater tourist cachet of the North-Rhine-Westphalian cities of Cologne and Düsseldorf is surpassed in its ferocity by internecine rivalry: 'Zwischen Dortmund und Essen herrscht

---

160 Erik Reger, 'Ruhrprovinz', *Die Weltbühne*, 24.2 (1928), 918–24 (p. 919).
161 Reger, 'Ruhrprovinz', p. 919.

erbitterte Fehde: über das Bier. Die Devise von Essen, Abend für Abend in Flammenschrift gegenüber dem Hauptbahnhof geschrieben: "Treibt Lokalpatriotismus! Trinkt Essener Biere!"'.[162] The city authorities' conflation of 'Lokalpatriotismus' with the act of buying homegrown refreshments instead of those made in the neighbouring town lends a measure of justice to Reger's equation of particularism with 'Einkreisungspolitik'.[163] Instead of exploiting their acutely felt sense of local belonging to burnish their wider patriotic credentials, the mayors of the *Ruhrgebiet* are depicted as interested only in enhancing the prestige of the town under their purview: 'Sie stecken auf der Generalstabskarte Interessensphären ab und stehlen sich gegenseitig mit Hilfe ministerieller Beziehungen die fetten Bissen aus den Landkreisen weg'.[164] This is 'Lokalpatriotismus' without the patriotic component. The towns of the Ruhr are imagined not as tiles in a national mosaic, but as fortified islands inspired by no deeper mission than their own expansion. Such hostilities therefore leave intact what Heinrich Ströbel had, in the final leader article of 1919, disparagingly called the 'partikularistischen Flickenstaat'.[165]

Less than a year after 'Ruhrprovinz' was published, an article by Arthur Seehof ridiculed the perceived small-mindedness of such 'Lokalpatriotismus'. In 'Freiheitskampf in Mörs' Seehof marvels at the ability 'ein[es] mörser [sic] Patriotenherz[ens]' to treat the mooted absorption of part of Mörs by the larger Duisburg as though it were an infringement of German sovereignty by France or Belgium.[166] Seehof quotes an article from a recent issue of the *Kölnische Volkszeitung* reporting on an emergency public meeting on the plans. After paraphrasing a series of dramatic representations in which speakers had characterized the break-up of Mörs as a crime, the unnamed author describes the moment in which an exchange between a local lawyer and the Mayor of Duisburg was disclosed:

> Wie eine Bombe schlug die Mitteilung des Rechtsanwalts Giese aus Mörs ein, der eine Unterredung mit Herrn Doktor Jarres hatte, worin dieser ihm sagte, daß Duisburg sich wehren müsse gegen die Überflügelung und Erdrückung von Düsseldorf und Essen. Duisburg könne nicht als Stadt zweiter Ordnung dastehen und müsse sich Gebietserweiterung holen, wo es solche nur finde. Mit Entrüstung nahm man von dieser Mitteilung, die die nackte Großmannssucht Duisburgs offenbarte, Kenntnis.[167]

---

162 Reger, 'Ruhrprovinz', p. 922.
163 Reger, 'Ruhrprovinz', p. 919.
164 Reger, 'Ruhrprovinz', p. 919.
165 Heinrich Ströbel, 'Alt-Preußen und Neu-Deutschland', *Die Weltbühne*, 15. 2 (1919), 777–81.
166 Arthur Seehof, 'Freiheitskampf in Mörs', *Die Weltbühne*, 25.2 (1929), 237–38 (p. 238).
167 Seehof, 'Freiheitskampf in Mörs', p. 238.

Seehof evidently regards the congregation's indignation as laughably out of proportion to a proposal to allocate part of one German town to another. Nonetheless, the absence of any neighbourly fellow feeling in this passage is merely the negative corollary to the expressions of patriotic exceptionalism discovered by Celia Applegate in her investigation of the Weimar-era Palatinate, which found its culmination in a heightened commitment to the wider German nation. Whereas the Palatinate supposedly distinguished itself through its unreserved commitment to a larger entity than itself, the 'Lokalpatriotismus' diagnosed by Reger and Seehof in turn radiates no further than its immediate orbit.

In what follows, such navel-gazing pride is contrasted with an assortment of texts, including two poems, that take the local *Heimat* as a point of departure for forming a deeper relationship with Germany. Indeed, alongside scepticism of the virtues of *Lokalpatriotismus*, *Die Weltbühne* was also home to a strain of *Heimat* discourse that held out the possibility of building national consciousness on a bedrock of regional sentiment. Some of the pieces under discussion here take a critical stance, addressing the conservative ideal rather than the progressive idea expounded by Tucholsky and Zweig earlier in this chapter. Taken together, however, they productively complicate the concept of community, thereby supplementing the geographically wide-ranging articles from the opening section by a re-interpretation of *Heimat* from a domestic perspective. These texts demonstrate that regionalist patriotism has no need of a foreign Other against which to define itself, but can flourish equally well in ostensibly stable surroundings.

The Palatinate Writ Large

Among the most intriguing editorial decisions made at the *Weltbühne* was to provide a platform for the elaborate patriotic manifesto of Wilhelm Michel. With only twenty pieces to his name, Michel wrote fewer than half the number of articles composed by Arnold Zweig and Otto Flake, but the body of work he left behind is a more coherent whole than that of many of his contemporaries. Michel, three of whose pieces are discussed here and two in the final chapter, was among the most unabashedly patriotic columnists of *Die Weltbühne* in the early years of the Weimar Republic. He was also the author of a pamphlet called *Verrat am Deutschtum*,[168] to which Otto Flake dedicated an approving review in an issue from mid-May

---

168 Wilhelm Michel, *Verrat am Deutschtum. Eine Streitschrift zur Judenfrage* (Hanover: Steegemann, 1922).

1922.[169] The eponymous betrayal is anti-Semitism, which Michel bemoans as contrary to a German national character that is, in Flake's paraphrase, 'durch Prädestination und Naturell Leistung im Dienst der Gerechtigkeit'.[170] Branding German anti-Semites 'Kellerassel' and 'Leichenfledderer',[171] Michel insists that Germanness is, in fact, synonymous with an instinct for all-encompassing magnanimity:

> Deutsch fühlen heißt alle Dinge, Fragen, Menschen, Sonnen und Planeten aus ungeheurer Liebeskraft umfassen. Deutsch denken heißt welthaft und lebenschöpferisch denken. [...] Siegen darf der deutsche Geist nur nach Art der Sonne in jener Parabel, nicht nach Art des Sturmwinds.[172]

Coming only four years after the Armistice, this bold claim hints at an aggressively progressive rehabilitation of German identity, which Michel reinforced in November with a candidly patriotic leader article entitled 'Glaube an Deutschland'.[173] Disowning Wilhelmine imperialism, the legacy of which he repeatedly attacks in his contributions to the journal, Michel instead articulates 'einen deutschen geistigen Imperialismus' founded on his belief in the German people's inexhaustible capacity for re-invention.[174] In so doing, he evokes a mystical German nationhood capable of adapting to the recent shock of democratization: 'Die Weltstunde ist dem, was deutsch ist, günstig, weil alle Zeiten des Werdens dem deutschen Wesen geheim verwandt sind'.[175] Michel's German genius is at once impervious to the passage of time and intuitively responsive to revolutionary tremors.

This flirtation with essentialist nationalism must be set alongside Michel's call for 'einen andern Nationalismus'[176] from the militarist one embodied by Ludendorff and his opening statement, repeated at the beginning of the third paragraph: 'Glaube an Deutschland heißt: Glaube an eine Kraft, nicht an ein Gehäuse oder gar ein Ornament'.[177] This dynamic interpretation of Germany as a nation in flux, as opposed to the backward-looking iconography favoured by conventional nationalists, is a key element in the left-wing patriotism of *Die Weltbühne* more broadly. Equally characteristic of such rhetoric, though,

---

169 Otto Flake, 'Michel über Michel', *Die Weltbühne*, 18.1 (1922), 514.
170 Flake, 'Michel über Michel', p. 514.
171 Michel, *Verrat am Deutschtum*, p. 10.
172 Michel, *Verrat am Deutschtum*, pp. 25–26.
173 Wilhelm Michel, 'Glaube an Deutschland', *Die Weltbühne*, 18.2 (1922), 537–38.
174 Michel, 'Glaube an Deutschland', p. 538.
175 Michel, 'Glaube an Deutschland', p. 538.
176 Michel, 'Glaube an Deutschland', p. 538.
177 Michel, 'Glaube an Deutschland', p. 537.

is his desire to present Germany's democratic transition as the fulfilment of the nation's natural destiny. Michel defends this process in the teeth of royalist opposition:

> Was spielen die Abstrakta 'Demokratie' und 'Republik' bei ihnen für eine Rolle! Aber nicht um eine beliebige oder abstrakte Demokratie handelt es sich für uns, sondern um eine deutsche Demokratie und um unsre Republik; um eine Form aus unserm Geist und Blut, angemessen der Weltstunde und durchflammt von unsrer Geschichte.[178]

Instead of subordinating the national interest to fashionable universal principles, Michel's political allies wish to infuse the ascendant idea of republican democracy with impeccably German qualities. The sceptics who see no future in such a system of governance are called upon to recognize it for the compound of German 'Geist und Blut' it represents. If the republican 'Geist' flows in the German people's bloodstream, it is an offence against nature to seek to halt its circulation. Anti-Semitism and anti-republicanism are thus acts of national treachery. Establishing a political system that guarantees personal and political freedoms, on the other hand, is portrayed as a profoundly German deed.

This is the backdrop to two further articles by Michel the following autumn in which he outlines his vision for a united German republic. In a leader published in late October 1923 he laments the fact that the Weimar regime had neglected to arrogate all the political power in the state to itself following the November Revolution (1918–19), instead leaving certain federal privileges intact.[179] Indeed, the *Zweideutigkeit* of the title 'Reichsdämmerung' simultaneously points backwards and forwards in time, evoking both the theoretically moribund Wilhelmine state and its successor 'Reich', the fledgling Weimar Republic. The failure of the latter to make a clean break with the former had allegedly preserved, to its own detriment, the fractious truce on which the imperial regime had rested:

> Dieses Reich ist kein einheitlicher Körper mit einer einheitlichen, alle Glieder gleichmäßig durchdringenden Idee oder Seele. Dieses 'Reich' ist ein Konglomerat, errichtet auf der militärischen Kraft und Hegemonie Preußens, und außerdem errichtet auf der stillschweigenden Voraussetzung ungestörter Prosperität.[180]

---

178 Michel, 'Glaube an Deutschland', p. 537.
179 Wilhelm Michel, 'Reichsdämmerung', *Die Weltbühne*, 19.2 (1923), 397–400.
180 Michel, 'Reichsdämmerung', p. 397.

This anachronistic *Staatsform* is a close match for the immutable 'Gehäuse' in which Michel refuses to believe. What he seeks instead is a unifying national idea recognizable to all Germans, regardless of precise provenance. His unwavering conviction that such an idea is awaiting discovery is conditional upon the subsuming of the individual states into an overarching 'Reich' the inherent legitimacy of which enforces loyalty from its citizens. In Michel's uncompromising view, Germans have a binary choice: 'In Deutschland sind entweder die Einzelstaaten real, oder das Reich ist real'.[181] This decision will determine whether the 'Dämmerung' of the title ultimately signals the dawning of the Weimar Republic or its imminent extinction.

The apparent simplicity of this choice identifies the proud *Pfälzer* Michel as an unorthodox spokesperson for those *Weltbühne* columnists who might be termed 'one nation' Germans. In his study of the journal Alf Enseling numbers Michel among a majority of writers who advocated 'die Konzeption des Einheitsstaates' at the expense of regional affiliations, contrasting them with a minority of so-called 'Unitarier', led by Hans Schwann, who promoted 'den [nationalen] Aufbau von der kleinsten Zelle her, von den Kulturzentren'.[182] These contrasting approaches to nation-building deploy strikingly similar language, with both claiming that their model is 'organic'. Thus Schwann endorses a more even distribution of power among Germany's state governments because it would represent 'neben *einer organischen Umbildung der einzelnen Teile*, das Auflösen des starren Staatsgedankens zugunsten des halbstarren Systems'.[183] He even emphasizes its 'größere Beweglichkeit und Anpassungsfähigkeit'.[184] Michel also believes in an incessantly shape-shifting patriotism, but his is predicated on the recognition of his compatriots' shared characteristics rather than seeking impetus from their particularities. For him, the Weimar Constitution is, therefore, an overdue statement of common purpose:

> Es handelt sich in der Weimarer Verfassung durchaus um die Realisierung Deutschlands, um die Herstellung einer echten, organischen Schicksalsgemeinschaft 'Deutsches Volk', und damit im weitesten Sinne um eine viel echtere 'Wiederherstellung des Reiches', als die Gründung von 1871 hatte bewirken können oder wollen.[185]

---

181 Michel, 'Reichsdämmerung', p. 398.
182 Enseling, *Die Weltbühne*, p. 79.
183 Hans Schwann, 'Friedrich Wilhelm Foerster', *Die Weltbühne*, 25.1 (1929), 813–17 (p. 817). My italics.
184 Schwann, 'Friedrich Wilhelm Foerster', p. 817.
185 Michel, 'Reichsdämmerung', p. 398.

In spite of its optimism this passage reveals a tension in Michel's thinking between radicalism and regeneration. The post-war legislature is entrusted with the task of eliciting a repressed sense of communion from the estranged members of a dormant nation. Its right to exist is ordained by fate; its composition is 'organic'. At the same time, the German people must be written into existence in order to fulfil its destiny; it must break new ground in order to go back to its roots.

Indeed, the creative thinking required for the German nation to 'realize itself' along republican lines is ostensibly at odds with Michel's longing for the 'Wiederherstellung' of the Holy Roman Empire.[186] However, his predilection for the word 'Reich' does not only reflect his yearning for what he regards as a golden era of German unity. Enseling explains that there was a general consensus among *Weltbühne* writers that the Weimar Republic, and not the *Kaiserreich*, had assumed 'die eigentliche Nachfolge des alten deutschen Reiches [...], dessen Wahlkaisertum demokratisch interpretiert wurde'.[187] Transplanted into the modern German nation state, the supposedly democratic features of the Holy Roman Empire would not necessarily have been consonant with Michel's preference for an 'Einheitsstaat'. Austin Harrington stresses the absence in the Continental empire of any one centre of gravity, concluding that Weimar-era Germans were torn:

> between loose-knit Holy Roman Empire and close-knit (Protestant) German nationhood. Modern German history in this sense seemed to alternate insolubly between tendencies to centralism and decentralism, centripetalism and centrifugalism, empire and provincialism, totality and fragmentation.
>
> [...]
>
> The result by 1900 was that [...] Germans found themselves in a hiatus position in world history between a no-longer-valid idea of

---

186 The Holy Roman Empire was a loosely bound alliance of nominally vassal states in Central and Western Europe dating back to the coronation by Pope Leo III of Charlemagne as Holy Roman Emperor in Rome on Christmas Day 800. The power to elect the Emperor was vested in the hands of the Seven Electoral Princes, or *Kurfürsten*: the Archbishops of Mainz, Trier and Cologne; the King of Bohemia; the Count Palatine of the Rhine; the Duke of Saxony; and the Margrave of Brandenburg. The prime duty of the Emperor was to protect the Catholic faith. Apart from one interruption (the Wittelsbach Charles VII, r. 1740–45), from 1438 onwards the title remained in the House of Habsburg. The dissolution of the Empire was sealed by the abdication of Francis II in 1806 after a major defeat by Napoleon at the Battle of Austerlitz and in the wake of the latter's occupation of the German lands.

187 Enseling, *Die Weltbühne*, p. 79.

religious civilizational imperium and a not-yet-existent condition of national statehood.[188]

The devolution of political power in the Holy Roman Empire, or what Harrington calls 'centrifugalism', is precisely what Michel wishes to see abolished through the model of the 'Einheitsstaat'. All the same, in an article published a month after 'Reichsdämmerung' Michel makes a solemn vow of fealty to the spirit of the Holy Roman Empire, even arguing that the modern *Pfälzer*, of whom he is one, live in natural accordance with the name of their province, 'der uns als "Pfalz" (palatium = Kaiserpalast) unmittelbar ans Reich bindet, nicht an einen Landesvater oder an eine Landesregierung'.[189]

The immediate context for such ostentatious declarations of belonging in 'Pfalz, Bayern, Deutschland' is the simmering Rhenish independence movement. A historical dependency of the Bavarian Crown straddling the Rhine and encompassing the coalfields of the Saar, the Pfalz was directly implicated in this secession struggle on account both of its geography and its historical relationship with neighbouring France. It had been occupied by Napoleonic forces until its restitution to the House of Wittelsbach in April 1816 in the wake of the Congress of Vienna (1814–15). As Conan Fischer has shown in his study of the Ruhr Crisis, the post-war separatist movement in the Bavarian Palatinate received an unexpected boost in October 1923 with the public backing of the French prime minister Raymond Poincaré,[190] only for an arson attack by separatists on Pirmasens town hall the following February to bring an end to its protracted 'death agonies'.[191]

Against this backdrop, Michel's insistence that the Palatinate is inexorably drawn to the middle of a force field of Germanness is scarcely less politically charged than those articles discussed in the first section:

> Die Pfalz ist Grenzland, aber sie hat keine zentrifugale, sondern eine rein zentripetale Tendenz. Alles in ihr drängt geistig zum warmen, nährenden Mittelpunkt des Deutschtums. Wer in der Pfalz ist, der ist tiefer und herzlicher in Deutschland, als wer in Pommern oder Westpreußen weilt.[192]

As well as echoing Harrington's mechanical language, this passage resembles with uncanny precision Celia Applegate's blueprint for patriotic *Heimatliebe*

---

188 Austin Harrington, *German Cosmopolitan Social Thought and the Idea of the West: Voices from Weimar* (Cambridge: Cambridge University Press, 2016), pp. 85–86.
189 Wilhelm Michel, 'Pfalz, Bayern, Deutschland', *Die Weltbühne*, 19.2 (1923), 470–74 (p. 471).
190 Conan Fischer, *The Ruhr Crisis, 1923-1924* (Oxford: Oxford University Press, 2003), pp. 243–49.
191 Fischer, *The Ruhr Crisis*, p. 248.
192 Michel, 'Pfalz, Bayern, Deutschland', p. 474.

in the Weimar-era Palatinate. Contending that 'the [*Heimat*] trend favoured the state, not the hometown, and the fate of Heimat, the seat of "civic virtue and order", was bound up with the state', Applegate makes provincial consciousness a prerequisite for any sense of national belonging.[193] For his part, Michel even goes so far as to insist that his fellow *Pfälzer* are more receptive than their countrymen from other parts of the Republic to the magnetic powers of Germanness by dint of first identifying with their embattled provincial origins. Their resultant sense of oneness with a mystical and all-encompassing *Deutschtum* is the antithesis of the mean spirit of competition to which Erik Reger would attribute 'Lokalpatriotismus' in 1928. Similarly, Michel's unwavering conviction that his specific *Heimat* is endowed with peculiar quantities of patriotic dedication presents a stark contrast to the self-regarding pride nurtured within the 'mörser [*sic*] Patriotenherze[n]' described by Arthur Seehof.

In the very first sentence of 'Pfalz, Bayern, Deutschland' Michel pleads for the possibility of national and regional loyalties co-existing in harmony in his adoptive homeland:

> Wir Pfälzer haben seit Jahrtausenden so viele Herren und Herrlein gehabt, teils gleichzeitig, teils nacheinander, daß diese sich für unser Gefühl gegenseitig neutralisiert und uns nur zwei echte Orientierungspunkte gelassen haben: die tiefe und, wie man ruhig zugeben kann, überschwängliche Liebe zur Heimat und die unausrottbare Treue zum Deutschtum, die Treue zum Reich.[194]

This statement of dual allegiance is far from banal in a climate in which two different forms of separatism were also under discussion, one proposing to turn the Rhineland into a sovereign state under German protection and the other to amputate the territory from Germany altogether. Written at a moment of high tension, 'Pfalz, Bayern, Deutschland' therefore represents Michel's attempt to exonerate the Palatinate from blanket charges of disloyalty to Germany.

With his claim of Palatinate exceptionalism, Michel nears Schwann's bottom-up formula for constructing national consciousness. This partly accounts for his jealous guardianship of the Palatinate *Heimat* against its obtrusive Bavarian counterpart. The Bavarian authorities, whom Michel suspects of themselves wanting to break up the German nation by seceding, stand accused of indoctrinating Palatinate schoolchildren with the charms of Bavarian heritage. This is achieved by the simple expedient of issuing

---

193 Applegate, *A Nation of Provincials*, p. 9.
194 Michel, 'Pfalz, Bayern, Deutschland', p. 470.

schoolbooks that, under the titles 'Geschichte' and 'Heimat' respectively, glorify the achievements of the Wittelsbach dynasty and celebrate Bavarian landscapes:

> aber kein Sterbenswörtchen von pfälzischer Landschaft oder Geschichte zu melden weiß. Eine Abteilung 'Heimat' richtet man in einem Schulbuch doch nur deshalb ein, damit das Heimatgefühl gefördert und bewußt gemacht wird. Hier aber tritt einzig das Streben zutage, einen fremden Volksschlag ausschließlich für die Reize der altbayrischen Stammlande zu interessieren.[195]

Admittedly, the description of the *Pfälzer* and the Bavarians as 'fremde Volksschläge' is hard to reconcile with Michel's evocation in 'Reichsdämmerung' of an organic 'Schicksalsgemeinschaft' inspired by the 'Gedanke des deutschen Gesamtvolkes'.[196] However, his repeated protestations that the *Pfälzer* are 'echte Reichsländer',[197] 'reichsunmittelbare Rheinfranken'[198] and 'nur Deutsche',[199] and that each of them is 'in erster Linie Pfälzer und Deutscher',[200] reveal such divisive language to be an indirect means of stressing the congenital commitment of the *Pfälzer* to the German *Einheitsstaat*. The Palatinate is a stronghold for 'one nation' Germans; it is its Bavarian overlord which exercises a corrosive influence.

Germany in Miniature

Whereas Wilhelm Michel's work for *Die Weltbühne* was both polemical and firmly rooted in current affairs, a high volume of contributors to the journal did indeed evoke something close to the apolitical 'Heimatgefühl' which Kurt Tucholsky declared in 1929 to be the only binding agent available to the otherwise divided German people.[201] In doing so, they laid claim to a private vision of Germany that was inseparable from their immediate surroundings. There now follows a sample of three engagements with the idea of *Heimat* in which Germany appears in familiar microcosm refracted through the prism of each author's intimate personal experience.

---

195 Michel, 'Pfalz, Bayern, Deutschland', p. 472.
196 Michel, 'Reichsdämmerung', p. 398.
197 Michel, 'Pfalz, Bayern, Deutschland', p. 470.
198 Michel, 'Pfalz, Bayern, Deutschland', p. 470.
199 Michel, 'Pfalz, Bayern, Deutschland', p. 471.
200 Michel, 'Pfalz, Bayern, Deutschland', p. 473.
201 Wrobel, 'Ein besserer Herr', pp. 956–57.

In the penultimate issue of 1920 a short article by the film critic Hans Siemsen appeared under the title 'Ich liebe Deutschland'. The choice of title intrigues because any expectations of a tribute to Germany in general are, in fact, disappointed almost straightaway. Beginning with the blandly sentimental affirmation 'Ja, ich liebe es mehr als irgendein andres Land der Erde', the article abruptly strikes a contrarian note, rebuffing the overtures of the Alps, the Rhine and Berlin on the grounds that none of these German landmarks is without parallel elsewhere in the world.[202] In the space of a single introductory paragraph, an article whose title and opening gambit had promised naïvety thus reveals itself as a gentle critique of the superiority complex which supports traditional patriotism.

Siemsen's professed love of Germany is not competitive, deriving as it does not from Germany's imagined supremacy over other countries, but from his involuntary attachment to one part of it. His affections are reserved for the purportedly barren terrain of northern Germany, with its monotonous topography and sluggish seasonal rhythms. Weighing up the more obviously arresting landmarks of the south, he finds 'die lieblichen sanften Täler mit kleinen Flüssen und kleinen Städtchen' wanting in comparison with his less celebrated *Heimat*.[203] Indeed, Siemsen's description of these hollow bucolic charms echoes Paul Krische's impatience with those politically reactionary portrayals of the semi-rural *Heimat* that invariably show 'ein Tal mit Dörfern zwischen fruchtbaren Fluren und einem altertümlichen Städtchen im Vordergrunde'.[204] There is little room in Siemsen's Germany for universally appreciated idylls.

Conversely, he makes no attempt to exaggerate the appeal of his *Heimat* to the uninitiated. Apart from its ancestral allure, the attraction of the north to Siemsen lies precisely in its banality:

> Die deutsche Landschaft, die ich am meisten liebe, liebe ich nicht, weil sie schön und seltsam und lieblich, sondern weil sie von alledem nichts ist. Ich weiß auch nicht, ob Jemand, der weit herkäme, von Rußland, von Spanien, von Frankreich oder aus Japan, ich weiß nicht, ob ein Fremder die Landschaft, die ich meine, lieben würde. Er würde sie vielleicht verachten. Ich liebe sie. Es ist meine Heimat.[205]

This straightforward statement of devotion is impervious to nationalist appropriation because it depends on pure chance. Accident of birth has

---

202 Hans Siemsen, 'Ich liebe Deutschland', *Die Weltbühne*, 16.2 (1920), 740 (p. 740).
203 Siemsen, 'Ich liebe Deutschland', p. 740.
204 Krische, *Heimat!*, p. 30.
205 Siemsen, 'Ich liebe Deutschland', p. 740.

conferred upon the author an affinity with a landscape apparently lacking in any objective advantages. Indeed, by emphasizing the subjectivity of his feelings, Siemsen relieves himself of any obligation to explain his emotional response to northern Germany.

In the last paragraph he summarizes his contradictory relationship with the landscape of his *Heimat* in terms that could be applied to the conflicted patriotism exhibited by a great number of columnists whose work is explored in the course of this book. Having given a fastidious account of the arrival of spring in his home region, contrasting the tentative blooming of the first flowers here with the abundant 'Paradiesgarten' of the south,[206] he answers his own question in a curiously defiant negative:

> Schön? Nein – aber rührend. Das ist die Landschaft, die ich am meisten liebe, unter deren Armut ich leide, die ich verspotte, und nach der ich mich sehne, wenn ich wo anders, wenn ich in schönern Ländern bin. Das ist die Landschaft, zu der ich immer aus allen Ländern, aus Frankreich, aus Algier, aus Japan und Java und aus all meinen Träumen zurückkehren will – wie man nach Hause zurückkehrt.[207]

It is clear by now that Siemsen is under no illusions about the natural beauty of his *Heimat*. The urge to mock co-exists, however, alongside a recurring nostalgia that overlooks northern Germany's aesthetic imperfections and sees only what the region represents: the reassuring solidity of home. Realism, and not the mythologizing view of nationalism, remains the prevailing mode until the end of the article. Siemsen's *Heimat* is the unmoving counterpoint to his foreign travels, the firm ground that waits at the end of each far-flung flight of fancy.

By this point Siemsen has acquainted the reader with this humble terminus. After three paragraphs of negation, his *Heimat* commands barely three lines: 'Es ist die arme, norddeutsche Ebene, die dürftige Wiese, das einfache Feld, ein wenig Heide, ein wenig Wald und die Kartoffelfelder vor den Toren der Stadt'.[208] The fleeting reference to an unnamed town, the potato patches of which evoke a pre-industrial subsistence economy, highlights a telling feature of 'Ich liebe Deutschland': the windswept, overcast acres dear to Siemsen are otherwise untouched by the identifying markers of a specific place. No city or large town obtrudes on the uninterrupted rural expanse of this 'Deutschland'. Indeed, his decision to confine himself to describing the natural landscape arguably enables Siemsen to project an

---

206 Siemsen, 'Ich liebe Deutschland', p. 740.
207 Siemsen, 'Ich liebe Deutschland', p. 740.
208 Siemsen, 'Ich liebe Deutschland', p. 740.

antithetical German dreamscape onto the tourist-brochure image of fertile soil and sublime summits that Krische finds so tiresome. Whether or not he consciously creates an alternative utopia to the southern one, Siemsen's omission of specific place names makes it possible to see his article as a love letter to an idea of Germany that is no less valid for being overlain with the unsung characteristics of his northern *Heimat*.

Siemsen's clear-sighted tribute to northern Germany pre-empts Kurt Tucholsky's oft-cited essay 'Heimat', which first appeared in his aforementioned collaboration with the pioneering creator of subversive photo montages John Heartfield, namely *Deutschland, Deutschland über alles* (1929). The abiding message of 'Heimat' is compressed into the line: '[E]s gibt ein Gefühl jenseits aller Politik, und aus diesem Gefühl heraus lieben wir dieses Land'.[209] This is itself a poetic reformulation of the same author's line from the same year about the apolitical nature of the 'Heimatgefühl'.[210] As in 'Ich liebe Deutschland' nine years earlier, the Germany described in 'Heimat' is not an undifferentiated earthly Eden. Tucholsky even cautions: 'Es besteht kein Grund, vor jedem Fleck Deutschlands in die Knie zu sinken und zu lügen: wie schön!'.[211] The difference between the two pieces is that Tucholsky is unable to resist the temptation to romanticize northern Germany. Granting to every German 'sein Privat-Deutschland',[212] he continues in a style that borders on stream of consciousness:

> Meines liegt im Norden. Es fängt in Mitteldeutschland an, wo die Luft so klar über den Dächern steht, und je weiter nordwärts man kommt, desto lauter schlägt das Herz, bis man die See wittert. Die See – Wie schon Kilometer vorher jeder Pfahl, jedes Strohdach plötzlich eine tiefere Bedeutung haben ... wir stehen nur hier, sagen sie, weil gleich hinter uns das Meer liegt – für das Meer sind wir da.[213]

This passage, which is followed by lingering reminiscences about the north German beech wood, vindicates on a deeper level Tucholsky's statement that each German has his own 'Privat-Deutschland'. Indeed, the very same sea wind that, in Siemsen's telling, drives the ragged clouds remorselessly over the fields seems to Tucholsky to speak an intelligible language which reveals itself to the walker when its gusts meet the foliage of the beech trees. The same part of Germany is capable both of serving as a salutary antidote to the exotic dream worlds of Siemsen's imagination and of inspiring in Tucholsky

209 Tucholsky, 'Heimat', p. 227.
210 Wrobel, 'Ein besserer Herr', pp. 956–57.
211 Tucholsky, 'Heimat', p. 226.
212 Tucholsky, 'Heimat', p. 228.
213 Tucholsky, 'Heimat', p. 229–30.

a pantheistic reverence that transports him into an immaterial realm of communion with what, to his predecessor writing in 1920, had been nothing more than 'ein wenig Wald'.

This contrast in sensibility is reconciled, however, by the slippage in each case between the writers' specific north German *Heimat* and the encircling national *Heimat* to which it belongs. Just as Hans Siemsen apparently sees no contradiction between his titular 'Deutschland' and his own 'Privat-Deutschland', Tucholsky explicitly dedicates 'Heimat' to 'dem Land, in dem wir geboren sind und dessen Sprache wir sprechen'.[214] He then ends his essay on the bullish proclamation that the atomization of the German people into a multiplicity of irreconcilable political ideologies can be mediated through 'die stille Liebe zu unserer Heimat'.[215] For Tucholsky, the innate Germanness of the 'Heimat' is non-negotiable, meaning that *Heimatliebe* automatically embraces two objects: the part and the whole.

The same slippage is evident in a poem written over two years after Siemsen's piece by the cultural critic Frank Warschauer, 'Die Heimat ist schön'.[216] Both here and in 'Ich liebe Deutschland' the itinerary of foreign travel transcends the narrow frame of reference suggested by the setting. Siemsen has visited France, Algeria, Japan and Java; Warschauer's narrator is called back to the eponymous 'Heimat' from his peregrinations in Greece, Turkey and Chile. In neither case does the peripatetic speaker trouble to name a German way station, inviting the conclusion that Germany and the point of departure are synonymous in their minds; the national *Heimat* does not need to be stated. However, despite the authors' shared assumptions their precise centres of gravity are almost incomparably different. Whereas 'Ich liebe Deutschland' plays out in a northern German landscape of unknown proportions, 'Die Heimat ist schön' relates the history of four generations of a family through its association with a single street.

The opening line establishes a tone of irony that instantly undermines the title and pervades the rest of the poem: 'In der verfluchten Schlucht, in der ich geboren bin | da sitze ich immer noch, weiß der Teufel wieso'.[217] The narrator's comparison of his home neighbourhood to a forsaken ravine conjures the image of an oubliette from which he is unable to escape, no matter how hard he tries. The following lines, which evoke his sheltered childhood, introduce a corresponding note of youthful frustration:

---

214 Tucholsky, 'Heimat', p. 226.
215 Tucholsky, 'Heimat', p. 231.
216 Frank Warschauer, 'Die Heimat ist schön', *Die Weltbühne*, 19.1 (1923), 164.
217 Warschauer, 'Die Heimat ist schön', p. 164.

> Hier hatte schon mein Vater seinen Schneiderladen
> mit Gasbeleuchtung. Die Gesellen sahen immer aus
> wie Käsebrote, die schon eine Weile gelegen haben.
> Sonntags ging der Vater meistens mit uns spazieren
> in den Nebenstraßen, zuweilen sogar bis zum Kullenberger Platz
> eine Stunde lang, zuweilen auch anderthalb.
> Das tat ihm gut, seine Leberschmerzen
> wurden dadurch bedeutend geringer.[218]

The atmosphere of stagnation in this passage seems to confirm that this is to be a satire on contentment. The jaundiced complexion of the clerks is presented as a natural consequence of too much time spent in the dingy confines of the gas-lit tailor shop, while their employer's liver complaint also appears as an oblique indictment of the cramped conditions in which he works. The mention of the family's weekly constitutionals only serves to emphasize the stifling nature of the teenage narrator's upbringing, during which the streets parallel to the family business constituted the perimeters of the known world and a one-and-a-half hour walk was a rare adventure.

Into adult life this urban *Heimat* appears to be inimical to the narrator's quest for space and the freedom to roam. Even the thought of future generations of children playing at trains in the street outside the house, as he had done before them, juxtaposes the static and repetitive reality of town life with infant dreams of unconstrained movement. Relating his return home from South America, the narrator duly reworks the image of subterranean imprisonment for which the 'Schlucht' had stood in the first line:

> Was mich betrifft,
> so bin ich schon in Griechenland und der Türkei gewesen,
> wo ich auch den Sultan gesehen habe, und zwar Achmed Ali den
> Dritten,
> der vor vier Jahren starb. Was glauben Sie, wie ich mich
> angestrengt habe,
> etwas andre Luft in die Nase zu bekommen! Indessen
> so ein Keller hat Arme, die sind stärker
> als Herz und Kopf und sieben Männer und Freunde,
> die einem helfen, nach Valparaiso zu kommen.[219]

The implication here is that the insatiably curious traveller has been carried home against his will by the gravitational pull of provenance, issuing this time

---

218 Warschauer, 'Die Heimat ist schön', p. 164.
219 Warschauer, 'Die Heimat ist schön', p. 164.

from a cellar rather than a ravine. Back in his accustomed spot, he has resigned himself to his fate.

However, an abrupt change in tone at this juncture reveals that the irony of the poem is intended to come at the narrator's own expense and not that of the *Heimat*. Indeed, it is not the title but the opening line that shows itself to be disingenuous. The characterization of his neighbourhood as 'eine verfluchte Schlucht' is suddenly cast in a new light, exposing it as an old saw that the narrator has taken to recycling in conversation until it has ceased to be true. For all that his sedentary lifestyle lacks either the variety or stimulation of his itinerant days, his satisfaction with his domestic arrangements is sincere:

> Ich bin glücklich zurückgekehrt von allen Abenteuern
> und sitze jetzt Sonntag vormittag wie gewöhnlich im Eßzimmer.
> Meine Frau wird gleich kommen. Drei Kinder sind nicht zu viel
> für die Wohnung, es reicht grade. Wirklich komfortabel![220]

The well-travelled patriarch does not attempt to conceal the almost parodic ease of his home life, even choosing the word 'komfortabel!', with its Franco-English roots, to emphasize the ineffable perfection of a household for which the German word 'bequem' would presumably have been insufficient. The neighbouring roof, framing the patch of sky that spares him the inconvenience of obtaining a daily weather report, fulfils the same function now as that performed by the 'Nebenstraßen' of his childhood: the demarcation of the point beyond which he need not stray to sustain his quality of life. Far from a pastiche of *spießbürgerlich* complacency, though, it transpires that 'Die Heimat ist schön' is a wry corrective to the tendency to disparage one's place of origin.

Warschauer's narrator is a knowing witness to the limitations of such a life as his, but his ambivalence does not prevent him from contemplating with an almost playful pleasure the prospect of his family sinking still deeper roots in the *Heimat*. The perpetuation of the ancestral line is introduced as a *fait accompli*:

> Morgen wird Claire konfirmiert. In ein paar Jahren
> bekommt sie ein Kind voraussichtlich oder vier,
> und so geht ein ganzes Geschlecht aus, ein Stamm, eine Wucherung
> von der verfluchten Schlucht, in der ich geboren bin.[221]

As a dutiful Christian daughter, Claire is expected to perform her prescribed child-rearing role so diligently as to launch not just a brood but an irrepressible

---

220 Warschauer, 'Die Heimat ist schön', p. 164.
221 Warschauer, 'Die Heimat ist schön', p. 164.

'Wucherung' into the world, thereby guaranteeing the cycle of departure and return of which the narrator's life is the latest iteration. Warschauer's choice of preposition evokes the possibility of temporary escape for each offspring. Whereas 'Die Heimat ist schön' begins *in* the ravine, the future grandchildren are expected to chart a path *out*, albeit to return at a later date. The repetition in the final line of the phrase with which the poem begins clarifies how it is to be understood: not as a condemnation of the narrator's *Heimat* but as a self-aware comment on the general reluctance to admit to *Heimatliebe*.

This poem warrants inclusion less for its explicit patriotism than for its mild rehabilitation of the community-based idea of *Heimat*, which is not the hermetically sealed outpost that it initially appears. The call of the clan may have conditioned the cosmopolitan narrator's decision to return to the homestead to raise a family, but he does not see his *Heimat* as a world unto itself which his descendants will have no wish to leave. Its frontier with the outside world is as permeable as that envisaged by Joachim Klose in his reappraisal of the 'edge' of the *Heimat* as a point of cultural exchange.[222] For its part, the national *Heimat* does not feature by name here, but its inviting presence is undeniable. 'Die Heimat ist schön' thus represents Warschauer's attempt to free the idea of *Heimat* from its nationalist associations by recasting it as an open-ended personal narrative rather than a perfectly preserved tableau of predetermined communal custom.

In much the same way as the lack of geographical information in 'Die Heimat ist schön' makes it virtually impossible to identify the narrator's neighbourhood, Hans Reimann's poem 'Heimat' (1926) provides a deliberately generic snapshot of a small community that is almost entirely devoid of distinguishing features.[223] While Frank Warschauer's Kullenberger Platz does not exist, the sights and sounds observed by Reimann could be characteristic of innumerable provincial German villages of the period. The intention is surely to conjure an unmistakeably German atmosphere whose carefully established equilibrium would only be disturbed by the addition of specific details.

This atmosphere is not what it might at first seem, however. Indeed, in Reimann's case the irony is more straightforward than in Warschauer's. Doubt as to the conventional nature of the former's *Heimat* creeps in from the first line, with its jarringly incongruous reference to a poster advertising the Thüringia-based chocolate brand Mauxion: 'Friedhof, Kirche, Mauxion-Plakat'.[224] This strategy of mischievous juxtaposition prevails throughout

---

222 Klose, '"Heimat"', p. 404.
223 Hans Reimann, 'Heimat', *Die Weltbühne*, 22.1 (1926), 616.
224 Reimann, 'Heimat', p. 616.

the poem, which deploys rhyming couplets to comic effect. In this way such symbols of continuity as churchyards, with their attendant connotations of family plots and weekly congregations, vie for attention with the trappings of modernity, from electricity cables to telegraph wires. The cadence usually falls on a phenomenon of relatively recent vintage, thereby humorously undermining the popular association of the local *Heimat* with unchanging custom. The transition from an era of arduous field work to the age of labour-saving devices, for example, is encapsulated in the couplet: 'Weide, Gräser, Burgruine, | Kühe, Ochsen, Mähmaschine'.[225] This *Heimat* is no timeless idyll untouched by the tempo of twentieth-century technology.

The question of Reimann's relationship with the concept is made harder to answer by the structure of the poem, which contains only two verbs and no complete sentences. 'Heimat' consists, in fact, of little more than a list of superficial impressions arranged in a provocative order, the effect of which is to underline the twin debt owed by the village to the forces of tradition and innovation, without positioning its author either as an unreconstructed cultural reactionary or as an unbending social progressive. What is not in doubt is the remoteness of Reimann's poem from any uncritical nationalist ode to the provincial German *Heimat*. In the final four lines he twice checks any misinterpretation of his words through the deflationary use of brackets:

> Rote Dächer, Schornsteine, Rauch,
> Handwerksbursche (schnarchend auf Bauch),
> Pappel-Allee (gepflanzt von Napoleons Hand) ...
> Schönes Land, grünes Land, deutsches Land![226]

The passing reference to Napoleon's lasting legacy, followed so swiftly by the exclamation 'deutsches Land!', definitively punctures any pretence of unbroken Germanic influence on the classical *Heimat*: the hybrid status of this one is not only temporal but also cultural. Despite the presence of a Bismarck monument, an emblem of the stereotypical Germanness of the village, its outward appearance bears the distinct traces of French intervention. The advertisement for chocolate bearing the name of the mid-nineteenth-century French entrepreneur André Mauxion is the benign complement to the bitter-sweet memory of earlier French occupation presented by the avenue of poplar trees.

Nearly all the pieces discussed in this section, with the notable exception of Wilhelm Michel's 'Pfalz, Bayern, Deutschland', express a pronounced

---

225 Reimann, 'Heimat', p. 616.
226 Reimann, 'Heimat', p. 616.

ambivalence about making the regional, or indeed hyper-local, *Heimat* the object of one's affections. Hans Reimann's polemical incorporation of French influences in 'Heimat' points to the perceived nationalist monopoly on the concept, an awareness exhibited by Frank Warschauer in 'Die Heimat ist schön' with his open-minded narrator's defensive adoption of the pejorative phrase 'verfluchte Schlucht' to refer to his neighbourhood. The pair's oblique acknowledgement of the fraught nature of the term ought not to distract, however, from their obvious reluctance to relinquish it. Hans Siemsen's refusal to idealize his *Heimat* prevents him neither from professing his love for it, nor from conflating it with Germany as a whole, but it falls to Wilhelm Michel to articulate an unequivocally left-wing claim on the idea, explicitly and dogmatically tying his own *Heimatliebe* to a patriotic longing for a German democratic republic that would definitively consign the *Kaiserreich* to history.

Conclusion

This chapter demonstrates that regionalist patriotism manifests itself in two distinct contexts in *Die Weltbühne*. Most space is dedicated to the international sphere, in which various territories which the columnists of the journal considered culturally German found themselves amputated from the Weimar state by the post-war treaties. The annexation of German land occasions Arnold Zweig, Kurt Tucholsky and Otto Flake to bemoan the discrepancy between the diminished *Staatsnation* and the scattered *Kulturnation*. However, their articles should be read not as revanchist calls-to-arms, but as rueful parables on the consequences of military overreach and runaway industrial capitalism. The alleged betrayal of German culture by the nation's leaders is felt in these articles at a regional level, making tangible the debasing of a hallowed national inheritance by less than half a century of imperial aggression. The first half of the chapter is, therefore, a story of national self-harm in which the self-appointed defenders of the German national interest are cast as the villains.

In the next section the horizons of the investigation narrow to focus mainly on shorter texts about smaller communities inside Germany's borders. This section, with its restricted purview, brings into focus the idea which holds all the articles in this chapter together: *Heimat*. The possibility of exploiting the notion of *Heimat* as a vehicle for left-wing regionalist patriotism is not entirely unheard-of in Weimar scholarship. Indeed, the material explored in the second half of the chapter confirms Applegate's specific observation about inter-war *Heimat* activists in Wilhelm Michel's Palatinate to the effect that 'nationalism could embrace their smaller worlds;

Germanness could encompass their diversity'.[227] Conversely, the concept of *Heimat* proves elastic enough in *Die Weltbühne* to enhance its authors' identification with the German national community. Nor did the profound emotional commitments required by such an understanding of the regional *Heimat* amount to unbridled idealism about its inherent characteristics. Apart from Applegate's discovery of provincial pride as a motor in the formation of national consciousness in the Weimar period, another concept that serves an important clarifying purpose is Shelley Baranowski's 'rural myth'. Whereas the East Prussian farm estate was held by its proprietors already to provide 'a sense of place, an identification with nature, indeed a *Heimat* that no other residence, no matter how attractive, could offer',[228] the *Weltbühne* writers rejected such right-wing mythologizing and the self-contained *Heimat* it implies in favour of a realistic sense of regional belonging that was embedded in a national tapestry. Instead of invoking the provincial community, in a manner typical of right-wing nationalists, as a bulwark against the manifold social and political freedoms associated with metropolitan mass society, these writers hoped to re-appropriate the regional *Heimat* as a site of liberation from which the nature of what it meant to be German could be redefined. To contribute to this redemptive endeavour was to promote regionalist patriotism.

---

227 Applegate, *A Nation of Provincials*, p. 13.
228 Baranowski, *The Sanctity of Rural Life*, p. 60.

CHAPTER 2

Internationalist Patriotism

In his treatise *Vers les Etats-Unis d'Europe* (1930) the French philosopher Bertrand de Jouvenel declared the pursuit of the national interest to be intrinsically incompatible with the spirit of international co-operation:

> Disons-le bien franchement: la conciliation du nationalisme et de l'internationalisme, c'est de la littérature. La verité, c'est qu'il faut choisir.
>
> Si l'on veut maintenir à son pays une pleine et entire souveraineté, alors les États-Unis d'Europe ne sont qu'un mot.[1]
>
> [The reconciliation of nationalism and internationalism, let's be frank, is a fairy tale. The truth is that we have to choose. If we wish to maintain full and complete sovereignty, a United States of Europe remains a dead letter.]

Jouvenel makes two implicit assumptions here: first, that love of country can only express itself as nationalism; and, second, that European internationalism inevitably strives towards the construction of a Continental superstate. Even as the German political climate soured either side of 1930, *Die Weltbühne* continued to carry articles that exposed how simplistic such a binary view was. Instead of presenting its readers with a straight choice between two ill-defined extremes, the journal repeatedly demonstrated that unreconstructed nationalism was far from the only option available to internationalists who also identified closely with Germany.

Arguably, the notion of a 'United States of Europe' did indeed attract attention in *Die Weltbühne*,[2] at least insofar as it can be elided with the movement for a Pan-European Union initiated by the Japanese-Austrian nobleman, Count Richard Coudenhove-Kalergi.[3] However, Glenda Sluga's authoritative

---

1 Bertrand de Jouvenel, *Vers les Etats-Unis d'Europe* (Paris: Librairie Valois, 1930), p. 201.
2 Ignaz Wrobel, 'Suomi-Finnland', *Die Weltbühne*, 21.2 (1925), 19–22 (p. 20); Werner Ackermann, 'Paneuropa – eine Gefahr!', *Die Weltbühne*, 22.2 (1926), 499–503.
3 Anita Prettenthaler-Ziegerhofer, 'Richard Nikolaus Coudenhove-Kalergi, Founder of the Pan-European Union, and the Birth of a New Europe', in *Europe in Crisis: Intellectuals and the European Idea, 1917-1957*, ed. by Mark Hewitson and Matthew D'Auria (New York: Berghahn, 2012), pp. 89–110.

recent volume on internationalism in the twentieth century relativizes the importance of pan-Europeanism by detailing the broad spectrum of ideas, institutions and ideologies associated with internationalism during the inter-war period.[4] In the first two chapters in particular Sluga demonstrates that internationalism, both before and after the First World War, was no easier than patriotism to reduce to a single, all-encompassing definition.[5] At the level of practical implementation, internationalists in peace societies, non-governmental organizations and multi-lateral diplomatic entities strove for concrete objectives, including mutual disarmament and the establishment of international courts of arbitration empowered to settle inter-state disputes and enshrine national sovereignty in the face of an invading force. At the same time, however, the term 'internationalism' also denoted a dawning sense of kinship across borders which Sluga calls an 'international sociability'.[6] This mindset was by turns pragmatic in its rejection of war as a means of solving disagreements and emotional in its readiness to see humanity as a single family.

By examining an assortment of articles that qualify by Sluga's measure as internationalist while simultaneously promoting a patriotic agenda, this chapter seeks to challenge the assumption of hostility between internationalist and patriotic casts of mind that has long hampered research into *Die Weltbühne*. The internationalist patriotism on display here takes three overarching forms, each of which commands its own section. In each section this thematic approach is further refined by means of subdivision into two variants or, in the case of the first section, three exemplars. The purpose is to do full justice to the multiplicity of modes of expression through which this internationally grounded love of country could be conveyed.

The first section compares the symbolic significance of France for three *Weltbühne* writers in turn, each of them writing in 1922. French revolutionary history meant that the country was typically seen in the journal as the birthplace and seat of Western democratic values. Their treatment of France is therefore a key indicator of the authors' hopes for the fledgling German democracy in the dramatically altered political landscape of post-war Europe. Each subsection duly considers the patriotic implications of the portrayal of France, addressing a series of contributions by Helene Keßler von Monbart, Felix Stössinger and Otto Flake that spanned six, seven and ten issues of *Die Weltbühne* respectively. United by their shared longing for what one stalwart columnist would later describe as the 'Augenblick, wo die Franzosen

---

4   Glenda Sluga, *Internationalism in the Age of Nationalism*, Pennsylvania Studies in Human Rights (Philadelphia, PA: University of Pennsylvania Press, 2013).
5   Glenda Sluga, 'The International Turn', in *Internationalism in the Age of Nationalism*, pp. 11–44; and 'Imagine Geneva, Between the Wars', in *Internationalism in the Age of Nationalism*, pp. 45–78.
6   Sluga, *Internationalism in the Age of Nationalism*, p. 61.

Deutschland zum ersten Mal wieder ohne militärische Schutzbrille ansehn',[7] these three writers nonetheless exhibit sufficiently nuanced perspectives on how Franco-German reconciliation might be effected as to justify separate consideration.

The second section turns away from France as an object of curiosity in *Die Weltbühne* to investigate the value system framing the internationalist patriotism of the journal. The language in which this was expressed is explicitly moralistic, furnishing the writers under discussion here with a rhetorical weapon with which to denounce militarism and advance the internationalist cause of diplomacy. Two distinct tendencies in this ethical discourse can be identified: messianism and maternalism. Putting the articles explored in Section 1 of this chapter into dialogue with others from different stages of the inter-war period reveals how these two ethical lodestars undergirded the continual calls by the journal for the Weimar Republic to repair its relations with its international neighbours.

The third section dissects the most pressing political cause of the internationalist patriotic lobby in *Die Weltbühne*: pacifism. This was deemed such a politically suspect position that many of its proponents, as the organization of this section shows, either felt compelled to emphasize the rational basis for disarmament or resorted to pathos to glamourize those who campaigned for a world without weapons. Whether columnists sought to present themselves as realists or martyrs, their passion for the survival of the German nation was a constant. Gesturing to, but ultimately moving beyond, Sandi E. Cooper's limited notion of patriotic pacifism,[8] the advocates of which stressed the right to self-defence, this final section therefore shines a light on a number of attempts to popularize peace work by making the patriotic case for the abstention of the Weimar Republic from armed conflict.

Taken as a whole, this chapter argues that *Die Weltbühne* laid the groundwork for a radical widening of the purview of patriotism in ways that its individual contributors may not have foreseen or even intended. In his monograph on the journal in the Weimar period, which includes short biographies of its three inter-war editors, Istvan Deak goes so far as to present the work of the second of these, Kurt Tucholsky, as a repudiation of patriotism,[9] thereby precluding even the nuance implicit in the tortured 'Hassliebe' for Germany with which it has become customary for critics to diagnose Tucholsky.[10] 'It was', argues Deak, 'his lack of German patriotism

---

7 Morus, 'Pariser Spritztour', *Die Weltbühne*, 23.1 (1927), 69–72 (p. 70).
8 Sandi E. Cooper, *Patriotic Pacifism: Waging War on War in Europe, 1815–1914* (New York: Oxford University Press, 1991).
9 Deak, *Weimar Germany's Left-Wing Intellectuals*, p. 42.
10 Enseling, *Die Weltbühne*, p. 140.

which permitted Tucholsky to be a true European'.[11] The following discussion exposes the fallacy of this opposition by demonstrating that national and international commitments were often yoked together in the pages of *Die Weltbühne*.

'Erzfreund' France: A Special Relationship?

The key reference point for the internationalist patriots of *Die Weltbühne* was France. Indeed, Istvan Deak dedicates an entire chapter of his book to the fundamentally friendly attitude the journal maintained towards France throughout the political vicissitudes of the post-war decade. This broadly pro-French stance did not preclude occasional criticism of bureaucratic overreach in Paris,[12] nor of the reticence of the country's leading republican politicians in the face of nationalist agitation.[13] Nonetheless, Deak is broadly accurate when he declares:

> The slogan of Franco-German reconciliation gave the *Weltbühne* writers a concrete program. They were to help close the terrible gap in understanding that separated the two countries, if not to unite French and Germans as 'two halves of one human soul' (Ernest Renan).[14]

Although Deak slightly overstates the ideological dependence of the journal on rapprochement between the two countries, the metonymic potency of France in left-wing intellectual circles at the time is well established.[15] It was onto France that *Weltbühne* columnists habitually projected their 'belief in an international community of Western nations as the only hope for peace and justice in Germany'.[16]

This admiration for France's commitment to freedom had a number of different objects. The *Weltbühne* writers, Deak summarizes:

> envied in the French their civil liberties, Latinity, *savoir vivre*, gaiety, and humanism; they admired the French for their artfulness in juxtaposing pedantry and disorder; they saw in France the mirror

---

11 Deak, *Weimar Germany's Left-Wing Intellectuals*, p. 45.
12 Robert Kuczynski, 'Wäre so etwas in Frankreich denkbar?', *Die Weltbühne*, 19.1 (1923), 493–94.
13 Ignaz Wrobel, 'Das nervöse Paris', *Die Weltbühne*, 21.1 (1925), 6–10 (p. 9).
14 Deak, *Weimar Germany's Left-Wing Intellectuals*, p. 89.
15 Markus Lang, 'Frankreich als Vorbild. Karl Loewenstein und die Grundlagen der Weimarer Demokratie', in *Deutsche Frankreich-Bücher aus der Zwischenkriegszeit*, ed. by Alfons Söllner (Baden-Baden: Nomos, 2011), pp. 101–24.
16 Deak, *Weimar Germany's Left-Wing Intellectuals*, p. 83.

of democracy, intelligence, anticonformism, good taste, artistic refinement, and progressive literature – in short, they admired the French for all that they felt the Germans lacked.[17]

Although the Weimar Republic was held to be deficient in these enlightened qualities, they were evoked not for the masochistic purposes of self-flagellation, but as a spur to Germany's collective conscience. The conviction of the journal that, to quote Deak again, 'Germany's greatest contributions could only be made within the mainstream of Western traditions' invites the interpretation that the latter was envisioned as a channel for German cultural achievements.[18] Indeed, Markus Lang's description of the mission of constitutional lawyer and later emigré Karl Loewenstein could also be applied to the work of certain *Weltbühne* columnists:

> In der Weimarer Republik hatte er sich als Brückenbauer zwischen Deutschland und den westlichen Demokratien verstanden. Er wollte seinem deutschen Publikum erst die 'Ideen von 1789' näher bringen und dann die Funktionsweise einer modernen Demokratie am praktischen Beispiel erläutern. So sollte Deutschland selbst seinen Platz unter eben jenen westlichen Demokratien finden.[19]

This image of Germany establishing itself as an equal partner in the democratic European landscape necessarily implies a patriotic interest in the project of rehabilitating the country's reputation in the wake of the First World War. Deak's own analysis of the internationalist slant of the journal, which also singles out France for special mention, is striking for the frequency of its references to patriotism. Although he stops short of characterizing the columnists of *Die Weltbühne* as patriots in their own right, he obliquely presents them as implicated in a nationwide struggle to define the contours of an acceptable form of patriotism. While pointing out that Weimar literary radicals objected on principle to 'philosophical patriotism',[20] which proudly emphasized Germany's undemocratic history, Deak creates the impression of a constituency of left-wing writers in search of a legitimate outlet for Germany's national energies.

This section scrutinizes the work of three authors whose work for *Die Weltbühne* complements Deak's one-dimensional portrayal of the attitude of the journal to France, thus showing that France was not only seen as an unimpeachable exemplar of Western democratic culture but also as

---

17 Deak, *Weimar Germany's Left-Wing Intellectuals*, p. 86.
18 Deak, *Weimar Germany's Left-Wing Intellectuals*, p. 83.
19 Lang, 'Frankreich als Vorbild', p. 121.
20 Deak, *Weimar Germany's Left-Wing Intellectuals*, p. 23.

an ambiguous cultural and political force pursuing its own agenda. These writers may all have considered the shape of Germany's relationship with France to determine its future, but what form this relationship should take was the subject of controversy. In the examples below, it is also instructive of the precise nature of the internationalism that informed each writer's patriotism.

Helene Keßler von Monbart: 'Wir und Ihr'

In this first case study the wider Franco-German relationship is refracted through the long-standing friendship between a French man and a German woman. The letter on which it is based was published in six instalments that appeared in *Die Weltbühne* under the title 'Wir und Ihr', evolving as the series developed into a meditation on the cultural affinity between the two nations. Its sporadically defiant tone only rarely corresponds, however, to the German inferiority complex one might expect from reading Deak's list of the qualities that were attributed to France in the journal. The letter writer was Helene Keßler von Monbart, the daughter of a Prussian officer of French extraction. Known elsewhere by the pseudonym Hans von Kahlenberg, under which she had forged a successful career as a novelist, Keßler had been born in Germany in 1870 but educated in France and England. In 1908, following her marriage to the forester Wilhelm Keßler, she moved to Switzerland, only returning to Germany after the First World War. The early months of 1922 saw the publication of her long-overdue response to an anonymous French correspondent who had fought on the Western Front during the First World War. The Frenchman had written to Keßler after Germany's surrender in 1918, only for the resentful recipient to ignore the letter. 'Wir und Ihr' attests to her attempt to rekindle the contact between the pair, while simultaneously refusing to concede any moral high ground to her friend's country.

Her later political reflections are at odds with the effusively sentimental tone of her personal recollections. As befits such an intimate exchange, Keßler does not attempt to establish any critical distance from her subject, instead recalling the arrival of her infant self in France as a natural coalescence of migrant and host culture. Her integration into French society is depicted as a thawing process during which all trace of her native environment had melted away under the influence of her new surroundings:

> Nur Gutes [...] hatt' ich in Frankreich erfahren! Seit ich, ein in altpreußischer Nüchternheit und Dürftigkeit erfrorenes Kind, in die farbige Buntheit, die warme und lachende Sonne Ihres Südens

getreten war. Meine [sic] Sprache Heimatlaut glaubte ich damals zu hören.²¹

These reminiscences are notable for their abundance of sensuous detail: touch, hearing and sight are all implicated. The carefree, tactile generosity of spirit Keßler claims to have found in her adoptive homeland stands in stark contrast to the cold, spartan rigour of her Prussian upbringing. Although it is tempered by the cautionary note of hindsight, Keßler's association of France with a personal *Heimat* unbound by geographical or political limitations suggests that she sees her German identity as a bureaucratic anomaly. It is, in fact, possible to infer from the above extract that Keßler understands *Heimat* in terms of crudely imagined hemispheres, with France and Germany representing opposite poles. According to this reading, an accident of birth has situated her in the wrong one.

In the second instalment Keßler goes still further, fondly recalling a pre-war age in which aristocrats from across Europe had apparently revelled in a post-national identity. Indeed, her memory of the social circle to which she and her French friend had belonged conjures a literal image of what Glenda Sluga calls 'international sociability':

> Sie erinnern sich, wie oft ich vor dem Kriege gesagt habe, daß wir eigentlich, viele von uns, die meisten einer bestimmten Oberschicht, seit Jahren schon gar nicht mehr Engländer, Russen, Deutsche, sondern Europäer waren. Wir neckten euch Franzosen mit einer gewissen Rückständigkeit. Zu zögernd, mißmutig nur, verließt Ihr dies über Alles geliebte Vaterland, die Gosse der rue du Bac, nach der Madame de Stäel in der Herrlichkeit von Coppet seufzte, den magischen Bezirk 'zwischen der Madeleine und der rue Drouot'. [...] Wir, hartgesottene und passionierte Reisende, lachten und neckten euch – Ihr seufztet und entzündetet eine neue Zigarette. Chinesen Europas, hinter eurer alten Mauer, die die modernen Himmelssöhne längst in Heuschreckenschwärmen durchbrochen und überflutet haben!²²

In Keßler's telling, European identity is a permanent substitute for, not a complement to, national affiliations. This phase of Keßler's life appears in retrospect to be a watershed in her personal development, as her spiritual homecoming to France gives way to her transformation into a transient

---

21 Helene Keßler von Monbart, 'Wir und Ihr. Briefe an einen französischen Freund', *Die Weltbühne*, 18.1 (1922), i, 36–40 (p. 36).
22 Helene Keßler, 'Wir und Ihr', *Die Weltbühne*, 18.1 (1922), ii, 64–68 (p. 64).

'Reisende': no longer an orienteer in search of co-ordinates, she has become a navigator without a destination.

Certainly, the younger Keßler's fluid sense of belonging points to her *Heimatgefühl* ceasing, as Elizabeth Boa and Rachel Palfreyman have it:

> to be conceived either as the place of origin or a utopian place of arrival, becoming instead a frame of mind: the commitment of citizens to the process of making a liveable social space. Man may be territorial, but the territory keeps changing.[23]

However, as the Gallic generalizations in the above passage indicate, this autonomous conception of identity is not without complications. Keßler's caricature of her laconic, chain-smoking French companions, whose intermittent sighs of ineffable melancholy betray an incurable homesickness, employs crass national stereotype even as she mocks the allegedly anachronistic insularity of the French exile. Admittedly, such inconsistencies seem lost on the author. When war was declared, Keßler recalls, the Frenchman had declared his German friend to be 'wie es auch kommen mag, von Gewalten verordnet, die außerhalb unsrer stehen – meine Schwester!'.[24] Ostensibly, this allusion to a cosmic kinship makes light of the friends' rival nationalities and Keßler is similarly inclined to present the friendship as a refutation of any idea of hereditary difference. Contrary to the divisive rhetoric of bellicose politicians, she insists, each of them combines French and German qualities in equal measure:

> [Die Freundschaft] wurde in einer Zeit scharfer Zuspitzung der nationalen Gegensätze geschlossen. (Immer bildeten ja diese Gegensätze, eingebildete oder vorhandene, die Trümpfe in der Hand aller gewerbsmäßiger Brett- und Glücksspieler Europas.) Ein ehrlicher Pakt zwischen der französischen Abstammung und Erziehung bei mir und Ihrem Hugenottenblut, dem Forscherdrang auf der Grundlage des menschenfreundlichen Lebenswerks Ihres edlen Vaters. [...] Sie hätten, dem ernsten Wesen, der Blondheit und Gründlichkeit nach, sehr wohl der Deutsche sein können. Sie, der Sie mein Vaterland aus Studentenjahren in Leipzig und Göttingen gut kannten und seine Sprache vollkommen beherrschen.[25]

Despite its anti-nationalist message, however, this passage rests on a paradox that is hidden in plain sight. According to Keßler's description she and her friend defy

---

23 Boa and Palfreyman, *Heimat – A German Dream*, p. 195.
24 Unnamed French friend, quoted in Keßler, 'Wir und Ihr', i, p. 38.
25 Keßler, 'Wir und Ihr', i, p. 36.

national stereotypes by displaying facets of the other culture which they have either inherited or internalized during spells of residence in that country. The inconvenient corollary to this claim, however, is that it assumes each nationality is defined by certain immutable qualities that cannot be dissociated from that particular culture, even if they are transferred to individual members of another nation. The Frenchman's disposition to thoroughness and fair hair, which give him the appearance of a German, therefore simultaneously undermine and reinforce essentialist notions of national identity.

The platonic friendship between the letter writers, in which their cultural particularities are at once preserved and resolved, proves to be a chaste foreshadowing of the fantasy into which Keßler's internationalist patriotism eventually coheres. She repeatedly urges the physical consummation on a grand scale of a mystical Franco-German bond that, once translated into the sex act, would alone be capable of preventing a reprisal of the First World War:

> Ich habe immer – Sie wissen, wie oft schon früher! – die Mischung des deutschen Mannes mit der französischen Frau empfohlen. Für meine Person glaube ich nicht, daß ich Frankreich wiedersehen könnte, ohne heftig zu leiden. Aber noch heute erblicke ich in der Allianz, in der unauflöslichen Blutmischung und Verknüpfung beider Volksstämme – man kann sie ja kaum Rassen nennen – die einzige Rettung und Zukunftshoffnung für Europa![26]

Systematic sexual intercourse between German men and French women is Keßler's panacea for geo-political instability on the European continent. For all that it is unaccountably prescriptive in gender terms and serves an international agenda, Keßler's interpretation of eugenist thinking[27] brings her into line with a wide range of progressive contemporaries whom Godela Weiss-Sussex describes as motivated not by racist prejudice but by 'an alarming reduction in the birth rate and the spread of what were then deemed

---

26 Keßler, 'Wir und Ihr', ii, p. 66.
27 For a discussion of how eugenist thinking morphed from relatively innocuous experiments in genetic improvement into a Nazi-led programme of mass sterilization and extermination, see Andreas Fahrmeir, *Citizenship: The Rise and Fall of a Modern Concept* (New Haven, CT: Yale University Press, 2007). Fahrmeir notes: 'From around 1900, the emerging science of genetics appeared to offer a solution [to the cost of maintaining public health]: favouring healthy "germ plasm" inherited from healthy parents and more remote ancestors. [...] After the First World War, massive loss of life initially led to a focus on population quantity and stricter laws against contraceptives and abortion. For many eugenicists, by contrast, the war had increased the chances of carriers of "defective germ plasm" to reproduce' (p. 161).

to be hereditary illnesses, such as syphilis, tuberculosis and alcoholism'.[28] By espousing strategic sexual union between select representatives of two nationalities, therefore, Keßler was merely widening the scope of a reformist interpretation of Darwinist evolutionary theory that sought not to eliminate the physically unhealthy, but to enhance overall racial hygiene by improving living and working standards for the sexually active sections of the population.[29]

The internationalism of Keßler's eugenist programme is overt, announcing itself in its architect's hope that Franco-German miscegenation will rescue the international community from fateful fracture. Early in the final instalment she asserts that the only salvation 'für Frankreich und die Welt' is a 'Bündnis' with Germany.[30] Any assumption that she thinks only of political concord is soon dispelled by the biologically charged language that follows:

> Sie lächeln über mich, die Psychologin von Beruf, die in diesem Moment des feilschenden Gezänkes Gesetze der Liebe zwischen den Todfeinden wünscht, weil sie Befruchtung, weil sie Fruchtbarkeit ist.
> Aber ich glaube, daß die Allianz ganz von selber aus der wirtschaftlichen Verquickung kommen muß, und daß sie kommen wird.
> Sie kommt ohne uns. Und wenn sie nicht kommt, ist es Europas Tod.
> Frankreich muß sich bewußt werden, daß sein, daß unser Erdteil der Zukunft zumarschiert.
> Oder es muß sterben.
> Es muß leiblich sterben ohne den Blutzuschuß der andern lebenskräftigern Nation.[31]

This passage is the prime example in the text of Keßler's fixation on fertility. In total, the letter contains no fewer than seven instances of words cognate with 'Frucht', of which 'Fruchtbarkeit' is the most common. More often than not, these references are plainly meant to be taken literally; indeed,

---

28   Godela Weiss-Sussex, 'The Monist Novel as Site of Female Agency: Grete Meisel-Hess' *Die Intellektuellen* (1911)', in *Biological Discourses: The Language of Science and Literature around 1900*, ed. by Robert Craig and Ina Linge, Cultural History and Literary Imagination, 27 (Oxford: Lang, 2017), pp. 111–33 (p. 113).
29   Ann Taylor Allen, *Feminism and Motherhood in Germany, 1800–1914* (New Brunswick, NJ: Rutgers University Press, 1991), p. 156; Deborah Holmes, '"… Die Menschheit verdient ein Massaker ohne Ende": The Warlike Pacifism of Grete Meisel-Hess', in *Pacifist and Anti-Militarist Writing in German, 1889–1928: From Bertha von Suttner to Erich Maria Remarque*, ed. by Andreas Kramer and Ritchie Robertson, London German Studies, 16 (Munich: Iudicium and London: Institute of Modern Languages Research, 2018), pp. 110–23.
30   Helene Keßler, 'Wir und Ihr', *Die Weltbühne*, 18.1 (1922), vi, 164–66 (p. 164).
31   Keßler, 'Wir und Ihr', vi, p. 164.

elsewhere in *Die Weltbühne* in the course of that year the word 'Frucht' appears four times in direct reference to childbirth.[32] The political world briefly intrudes here in the form of Keßler's prediction of 'wirtschaftliche Verquickung', but it is soon overshadowed by her graphic prophecy of France's biological deterioration without the injection of German blood into the French gene pool.

Keßler's literary work also bears the trace of these eugenist convictions. Published in 1901 under the pseudonym 'von Kahlenberg', the novel *Der Fremde* underlines Keßler's interest in genetic manipulation as a determining factor in the creation, or disruption, of crudely drawn socio-economic types, such as the physically robust bourgeoisie and the tubercular, sexually underpowered proletariat. Most pertinently, it also features a scene in which one dog pursues another through a crowd of spectators ahead of a public meeting of the Communist Party. The hereditary weaknesses of the bitch are emphasized in such a way as to invest the canine mating ritual with an allegorical significance worthy of the subtitle of the novel, '*Ein Gleichniss*': 'Der Riesenhund des Wirths trieb seine Allotria dazwischen mit einer ganz kleinen Hündin, einer proletarischen Mischung aller Rassen, die von jeder die Hässlichkeiten angenommen hatte'.[33] To read Keßler's prescriptions in 'Wir und Ihr' for the supposedly ailing France in the light of this passage, written over twenty years earlier, is to appreciate the raw physical implications of her biological rhetoric.

By casting Germany in 'Wir und Ihr' in the dubious role of saviour as inhabited by the landlord's hulking dog in *Der Fremde*, Keßler adds an ugly patriotic gloss to an image of consensual coitus between two nations that is now irrevocably marred by the intimation of physical force. In this, too, she was not alone: as well as being receptive to social engineering, other German left-wing writers were also capable of construing French territorial designs on Germany as analogous to the reproductive urge. In March 1923 Meridionalis, one of the longest-standing contributors to the journal, wrote an enthusiastic review[34] of a pamphlet by Ernst Bertram called *Rheingenius und Génie du Rhin*.[35] In the text Bertram, a fringe member of the circle around Stefan George, offers a polemical retort to a lecture series

---

32 Manfred Georg, 'Das Recht auf Abtreibung', *Die Weltbühne*, 18.1 (1922), 7–9 (p. 8); Bruno Manuel, 'Der Höhlenbewohner im Gefängnis', *Die Weltbühne*, 18.1 (1922), 127–28 (p. 127); Otto Flake, 'Die deutsche Problematik', *Die Weltbühne*, 18.2 (1922), 241–44 (p. 244); Alfred Polgar, 'Salzburger großes Welttheater', *Die Weltbühne*, 18.2 (1922), i, 310–14 (p. 312).
33 Hans von Kahlenberg, *Der Fremde. Ein Gleichniss* (Dresden: Reissner, 1901), p. 48 <https://www.gutenberg.org/files/36227/36227-h/36227-h.html> [accessed 15 September 2022].
34 Meridionalis, 'Deutsche und französische Propaganda', *Die Weltbühne*, 19.1 (1923), 291–94.
35 Ernst Bertram, *Rheingenius und Génie du Rhin* (Bonn: Cohen, 1922).

by the French author Maurice Barrès during which he had allegedly falsified history in order to justify the French claim to the left bank of the Rhine. In the afterword Bertram changes his line of attack to one of condescension, opining that the importance to France of the contested territory of Alsace derives from a desperate French impulse to avert their own extinction. Just as striking as Bertram's thesis, however, are the asymmetrical terms in which he expresses it:

> Es liegt in diesem Instinktstreben des französischen Volkes nichts, was uns beleidigen könnte. Wir fühlen, wie berechtigt es ist, und wir ehren in dem Streben Frankreichs nach der Rheingrenze demgemäß den Lebenswillen eines großen Volkes der europäischen Vergangenheit, sich durch deutsche Bluteinflößung, durch Verpflanzung deutscher Landschaften in den Leib des französischen Landes der europäischen Zukunft noch zu erhalten.[36]

This explanation of French foreign policy is accepted unreservedly by Meridionalis, who finishes his review by praising Bertram for articulating 'den unverkennbaren biologischen Niedergang der Rasse bei ungehemmtem Ausdehnungsdrang der Nation' in which early twentieth-century France was supposedly mired.[37] Bertram's image of the French body being inseminated by German landscapes echoes Keßler's with uncanny precision: the 'Blutzuschuß der andern lebenskräftigern Nation' simply re-appears in the guise of a 'deutsche Bluteinflößung'.[38] The gender roles assigned by Bertram to each country also match Keßler's ideal. In both cases France is ultimately cast as the submissive female partner dependent on a virile Germany for the perpetuation of its kind. Even though Bertram depicts France as making the sexual advances, it is the sought-after Germany which ends up fertilizing its pursuer as France reverts to a passive female role. In the process, Germany's sexual dominance is presented as a reflection of its greater vitality and therefore of its entitlement to heal a sickly Europe.

Keßler also contrives a more egalitarian metaphor for Franco-German reconciliation in the form of an image of two star-crossed lovers borrowed from a sixteenth-century ballad by the Swiss composer Ludwig Senfl. In 'Ach Elslein', a lovelorn man clings to the hope that a ship might be built to carry him across 'zwei tiefe Wasser' separating him from the eponymous Elslein.[39]

---

36 Bertram, *Rheingenius und Génie du Rhin*, p. 105.
37 Meridionalis, 'Deutsche und französische Propaganda', p. 294.
38 Keßler, 'Wir und Ihr', vi, p. 164.
39 Ludwig Senfl, 'Ach Elslein', in Hans Ott, *Der erst teil. Hundert vnd ainundzweintzig newe Lieder* (Nuremberg: Jheronimus Formschneyder, 1634), no. 37.

Transplanted into the strained environment of post-war Europe, the deep straits of Senfl's lyric become a diplomatic sea of hostility which France and Germany must bridge in order to bring peace to their continent:

> Die Seele eines Volkes ist unbesiegbar. Die Seele Frankreichs der Seele Deutschlands begegnend: das wäre der Friede, die Fruchtbarkeit.
> Wir haben davon geträumt. Selbst wenn eines Tages die unerbittliche Logik der Tatsachen die Widerwilligen und die Stumpfsinnigen in den toten Gleichschritt des Selbsterhaltungstriebes gezwungen hat, bleiben wir Liebende, die Liebenden des alten traurigen Volkslieds über das 'tiefe Wasser' hinüber.
> Liebende, deren Sehnsucht zugleich hoffnungslos und unsterblich ist.[40]

This whimsical passage is a reminder that the internationalist patriotism running through 'Wir und Ihr' is not only complicated by its author's continual migration between essentialism and a transcendental Europeanism that either minimizes the influence of national culture or seeks to overcome it altogether. As well as this friction there is also an insoluble tension between Keßler's desire for peace and the vehicle through which this is to be achieved. Even war has a place in her vision for a juster society, as proven by her impatient dismissal of the notion of war guilt:

> Wir finden auch als Volk den Aufstieg nicht, ohne die Ablösung von gestorbenen, von stumpf und brüchig gewordenen Bestandteilen, ohne Abstreifung der alten Haut.
> Es ist die schmerzhafte Gewalttätigkeit dieses Durchbruchs zu neuer Lebensgestaltung, die wir als Weltkrieg oder als Revolution erleiden.
> Möge man aufhören, uns Erwachsene mit dem Kinderstubenbegriff von Kriegs-Schuld und -Unschuld zu plagen![41]

Her desire to exonerate Germany of culpability for the outbreak of the First World War is masked here by Keßler's deliberate coining of the term 'war innocence', a sleight of hand that simultaneously implicates all parties to the fighting and relegates 'war guilt', through juxtaposition, to a similarly abstract realm of pointless conjecture. The larger implication of this cynicism, however, is that war is a necessary stage in the evolution of society about which it is inappropriate to harbour qualms of conscience; if the end is peace, Keßler hints, war is a legitimate means. The national bias is also hard to ignore: the possibility of redemptive war reinforces the atmosphere

---

40 Keßler, 'Wir und Ihr', vi, p. 166.
41 Helene Keßler, 'Wir und Ihr', *Die Weltbühne*, 18.1 (1922), iv, 113–16 (pp. 114–15).

of righteous violence first generated by the recurring images, both literal and figurative, of German sexual conquest.

Such loyalty to Germany eventually spills over into a rejection of the pan-European identity to which Keßler had laid claim. Although not a straightforward disavowal, this final confession marks an end point in the post-national journey on which she had supposedly embarked before the war:

> Ich möchte weinen. Auch das Briefschreiben tut mir weh. Ich fühle Heimweh nach Ihnen. Viel stärkeres, blutwarmes Weh um meine geschändete und gequälte Heimat.
> Sprechen Sie nicht mehr vom Weltbürgertum, vom Europäer!
> Ich bin deutsch heute. Und diese brennende und persönlichste Einzelerfahrung, das weiß ich, wird Sie nachdenklich stimmen. Weil sie die der Tausende und Hunderttausende ist im besetzten und abgesprengten Gebiet, die der Auswanderer, jener Amerika-Deutschen, die Briand sich nicht schämte zu loben.[42]

The *Heim* takes two distinct forms here: Keßler's longing for her friend, which is itself described as a highly concentrated form of *Heimweh*, surfaces first, only to be supplanted by a more powerful grief on behalf of her despoiled German *Heimat*. The intensely physical quality of this grief elevates it above the more abstract yearning she feels for her absent friend, leading her to make an unequivocal choice in favour of her national *Heimat*.

This choice appears to discount the possibility of hybrid identity that the two friends had once embodied. By describing the pain engendered by the military defeat of Germany and territorial losses as 'blutwarm', Keßler bars foreign nationals such as her French correspondent from her suffering. This departure from the aristocratic international with which she had still identified at the turn of the century is a belated sign of the times: Brent O. Peterson describes how, in the course of the nineteenth century, 'nationalism gradually and imperfectly undermined personal, caste, and dynastic loyalties, which had allowed their bearers considerable flexibility'.[43] An accelerated version of this process has evidently claimed the European pretensions harboured by Keßler and her fellow members of the pre-war *Oberschicht*. Keßler's emotional *Heimat* now appears to be impregnable for anyone without German blood in their veins, thereby reinforcing Peterson's claim that 'unlike

---

42 Keßler, 'Wir und Ihr', vi, p. 166.
43 Brent O. Peterson, *History, Fiction, and Germany: Writing the Nineteenth-Century Nation*, Kritik: German Literary Theory and Cultural Studies (Detroit, MI: Wayne University Press, 2005), p. 71.

the aristocracy, which was not so much a cohesive whole as a transnational continuum of gradations in title and pedigree [...] membership in the nation was increasingly based on race or blood'.[44] By replacing a *Heimatgefühl* based on mobility and freedom of association with one predicated on genetic exclusivity, Keßler ultimately subscribes to an immutable ethno-cultural identity over the fluid individualism of her younger years.

In 'Wir und Ihr' France is not depicted as a role model for post-war Germany to emulate. On the contrary, it is portrayed as a supplicant obliged to throw itself on the mercy of a resurgent Germany for its own survival. Indeed, Keßler's letter is unusual in its refusal to flatter France other than through the rose-tinted prism of childhood memory. Instead, Germany is to be the senior partner in the rekindled relationship; the humility with which France inspired most *Weltbühne* columnists is conspicuous by its absence from a series that calls for the forcible subjugation of Europe in general, and France in particular, to the benevolent leadership of Germany.

Felix Stössinger: 'Was ist uns Frankreich?'

Over the same period that saw the publication of 'Wir und Ihr', *Die Weltbühne* ran a seven-part essay by Felix Stössinger under the title 'Was ist uns Frankreich?'. Its Prague-born author, who grew up in Vienna, became a fixture of German political journalism after moving to the country in 1914. As well as serving between 1918 and 1922 as an editor of *Freiheit*, the official organ of the Berlin branch of the Independent Social Democratic Party, from 1916 he belonged to the editorial team at the controversial Social-Democrat journal *Die sozialistischen Monatshefte – Internationale Revue des Sozialismus*. Until its demise in the summer of 1919 Stössinger also led the propaganda department for the short-lived revolutionary Vollzugsrat des Arbeiter- und Soldatenrates Groß-Berlin.

Alf Enseling draws attention to one facet of Stössinger's thinking when he claims that he saw 'in der Verständigungspolitik zwischen Deutschland und Frankreich vornehmlich einen Schlag gegen die Balance-of-power-Politik der Engländer'.[45] Proof of this wariness of the intentions of the British Empire can be found in the very first instalment,[46] but Enseling's cynical understanding of Stössinger's attraction to France profoundly underestimates its sincerity. Indeed, 'Was ist uns Frankreich?' is characterized by a deference towards its subject almost entirely absent from Helene Keßler von Monbart's letter.

---

44 Peterson, *History, Fiction, and Germany*, p. 71.
45 Enseling, *Die Weltbühne*, p. 80.
46 Felix Stössinger, 'Was ist uns Frankreich?', *Die Weltbühne*, 18.1 (1922), i, 397–400 (p. 400).

Stössinger's intervention eulogizes France's politically progressive traditions and suggests that German public life could learn from its neighbour's liberal example. His overriding concern is the passivity of the German literary class, which he accuses of refusing to involve itself in current affairs. By contrast, he insists, the French writer lives:

> in beneidenswerter Einheit von Wort und Tat. Bei ihm sind nicht Wort und Welt durch Abgründe der Ohnmacht oder des Zweifels getrennt. Ich wüßte keinen Fall, daß ein großer französischer Dichter von sozialer Gesinnung durch sein Leben als Mensch Lügen gestraft würde. Das Verhältnis zwischen Kunst und Leben ist in Frankreich ebenso rein wie in Deutschland trübe, rein bis in die Abgründe der Selbstaufopferung hinab.[47]

In Stössinger's view, literature and politics should be inseparable: his ideal is the activist author whose public commitments are an extension of his or her authorial sympathies. In exonerating socially alert French authors from hypocrisy, he alludes to a photo of Leo Tolstoy in tennis whites that undermines the Russian's widely circulated contempt for 'Nichtstuer, die sich in eigens dazu angefertigten Hosen bemühen, einen Ball über ein Netz zu werfen, damit er in bestimmte Rasenvierecke falle'.[48] Whereas Stössinger's typical French writer would never compromise himself as did Tolstoy, German authors are held to be so reticent on social matters as to make any fear of hypocrisy seem a luxury.

It is no exaggeration to say that France is everything Stössinger wishes Germany were. France, he declares, is none other than 'das Mutterland des Sozialismus und des Pazifismus. Der Blutzeuge aller kontinentalen Republiken', adding: 'Unser Ideal: Gerechtigkeit und Lebensglück der Vielen mehr als die Schönheit des Einzelnen – das war und ist ja Frankreichs Ideal!'.[49] In the third and fourth instalments he makes this argument concrete by contrasting a notable figure from French culture with a German of similar fame and repute. In the first instance he compares Voltaire's posthumous stature with that of Frederick II, otherwise known as Frederick the Great, preferring to overlook their friendship and emphasize Voltaire's campaigning work. Voltaire had indeed confronted religious persecution by taking up an array of *causes célèbres* in opposition to the virulently Catholic French monarchy. As far as Stössinger is concerned, therefore, the esteem in which the memory of the French philosopher and the Prussian king is held in their

---

47 Felix Stössinger, 'Was ist uns Frankreich?', *Die Weltbühne*, 18.1 (1922), iii, 440–42 (p. 440).
48 Stössinger, 'Was ist uns Frankreich?', iii, p. 440.
49 Stössinger, 'Was ist uns Frankreich?', i, p. 398.

respective countries casts a harsh light on the contradictory values of the French and German peoples:

> In Deutschland wird einem Voltaire, den man gern mißgünstig einen Affen nennt, Friedrich der Zweite entgegengestellt, das heißt: einem Helden der Freiheit ein Despot! Welche Gesinnung! Man spricht von einem Zeitalter Friedrichs des Zweiten und meint: das erobernde und vertragsbrüchige Preußen, das Lessing, Klopstock, Winckelmann, Claudius verachtet haben. Man spricht vom Zeitalter Voltaires und meint: die Erhebung der Welt zur menschlichen Würde.[50]

For Stössinger's purposes Friedrich and Voltaire are not complex characters but personifications of two polar opposites: tyranny and unbridled freedom of expression. His compatriots' tendency to refer to the eighteenth century by the name of its dominant statesman, as opposed to that of an outspoken intellectual, consequently strikes him as symptomatic of a reactionary national character which glorifies despotism and mocks dissent. The pointed enumeration of famous German poets and intellectuals who had despised Frederick's Prussia points, however, to the existence of a different historical narrative if Germans can be persuaded to reassess their priorities.

In the following instalment Stössinger dampens any optimism that this reference to Lessing and his contemporaries might have generated by reminding his readers that none of them compares in profile to the politically conformist Johann Wolfgang von Goethe. Stössinger pointedly juxtaposes Goethe with Victor Hugo, whose flight from the forces of President Charles-Louis Napoléon Bonaparte after the latter's successful coup d'état in 1851 he presents as a gesture of republican heroism. Whereas Hugo's legacy can apparently be discerned in a universal French scepticism of authority in general and autocratic rule in particular, Goethe's status as lifelong advisor and friend to Karl August, Duke of Saxe-Weimar-Eisenach, is depicted in terms reminiscent of Original Sin:

> Es gibt Schicksalsstunden eines Volkes, wo es heilsamer ist, daß der größte Dichter des Landes ein verbannter Republikaner war, als ein Minister, der zwar die halbe Hofgesellschaft duzen durfte und Prinzen auf seinen Knieen schaukelte, aber doch nicht die Macht hatte, dem Volk auch nur die kleinste Erleichterung zu verschaffen.[51]

Goethe is thus depicted as compromised by association with his royal patron, as well as by the perceived absence from his work of any insurrectionary impulse. The ramifications of this complacency can be felt, Stössinger avers,

---

50 Stössinger, 'Was ist uns Frankreich?', iii, p. 442.
51 Felix Stössinger, 'Was ist uns Frankreich?', *Die Weltbühne*, 18.1 (1922), iv, 474–75 (p. 475).

in Germany's 'Schicksalsstunden', those decisive moments in their national history in which Germans have proved to be more disposed to inaction than rebellion. He does not trouble to name any, but his words can be read as much as a warning as they can an allusion to past omissions. The national poet's reticence is thus depicted as a curse under the spell of which his descendants are fated to make the same mistake over and again.

Neither frustration over Germany's lukewarm embrace of the democratic idea and its attendant political struggle, nor admiration for the strength of these traditions in France was confined to *Die Weltbühne*. Indeed, both Stössinger's criticism of Goethe and his lionization of Voltaire echo Heinrich Mann's unflattering juxtaposition of Goethe with Voltaire from his essay 'Voltaire – Goethe' (1910), published in 1919 as part of the collection *Macht und Mensch*.[52] The first treatise in the volume, 'Geist und Tat', pre-empts Stössinger's assertion that French writers lived 'in beneidenswerter Einheit von Wort und Tat', not least in Mann's dry observation that the French intellect is 'nicht das lustige Gespenst, das wir kennen – und drunten trottet plump das Leben weiter'.[53] In 'Voltaire – Goethe' Mann develops the theme by contrasting the latter's political apathy to the former's pugilistic nature:

> Goethe haßt, was unharmonisch ist, was durch Einseitigkeit des Geistes, der Leidenschaft, durch unversöhnlichen Sturm und Düsterkeit das Gleichgewicht der Natur stört. […] Goethe hat zur Menschheit die ferne, hohe Liebe eines Gottes zu seiner Schöpfung; Voltaire kämpft für sie im Staub. Er ist einseitig und will nicht anders sein. […] Er haßt alles Herkömmliche, unbewußt Gewordene, das sich dem Gedanken, der Kritik entziehen möchte. Er fragt nicht nach dem Willen der Natur und ihrer Tochter, der Überlieferung […]. […] Wie hoch und weise Goethe vom feierlichen Turm seiner Erkenntnisse über ihn hinsieht![54]

Whereas Mann's portrayal of Voltaire evokes a street fighter, Goethe resembles a sage cocooned in an ivory tower. Mann's sympathies clearly lie with the Frenchman, whose hatred of convention is portrayed as a more courageous and honourable stance than Goethe's loathing of disorder. Indeed, even the latter's professorial pose is an illusion. Just as Stössinger casts Germany in the role of a student with 'viel zu lernen',[55] Mann clearly considers France to be a model for the permeation of German literature by the spirit of sedition.

---

52 Heinrich Mann, 'Voltaire – Goethe', in *Macht und Mensch* (Leipzig: Wolff, 1919), pp. 12–19.
53 Heinrich Mann, 'Geist und Tat', in *Macht und Mensch*, pp. 1–9 (p. 3).
54 Heinrich Mann, 'Voltaire – Goethe', p. 13.
55 Stössinger, 'Was ist uns Frankreich?', i, p. 399.

Mann and Stössinger also agree on the root cause of the political impoverishment of German literature: self-absorption. The individualism that Mann calls 'die deutsche Überschätzung des Einzelfalles'[56] reappears in Stössinger's reflections as 'ein Genie der Musik, der Lyrik und des dramatischen Chaos'.[57] This image of unchecked aestheticism highlights a fundamental tension between the subversive liberties taken by French writers and the splendid isolation that supposedly typified their German counterparts. Whereas Mann associates French writers with iconoclasm, he suspects their German counterparts of indulging an apolitical 'Selbstkultus',[58] or even of harbouring reactionary views.[59] Similarly, Stössinger claims that his compatriots' tendency to introspection translates into a peculiarly German conservatism in social matters, thereby vindicating Thomas Mann's equation of German culture with an anti-democratic 'erhaltendem, aufhaltendem, sozialem Instinkt'.[60] Developing Heinrich Mann's description of France as 'das Volk, das die erhaltenden Lügen verachtet',[61] however, Stössinger argues that the reactionary instinct diagnosed by the younger Mann brother is counterproductive:

> Der [französische] Dichter ist der Sprecher, der Helfer, der Exponent der ganzen Nation. Frankreich ist kein Land des Individualismus, sondern strenger Gesellschaftsformen. Auch das vollkommenste Individuum hat keinen höhern Ehrgeiz, als dem Lande, dem Volke, der Menschheit zu dienen. [...] Den deutschen Dichter dagegen hat der Mangel an einer politischen und kulturellen Einheit durchweg zum Individualisten gemacht, zu diesem psychischen Produkt des Partikularismus. Dabei ist Großes herausgekommen, aber in den Organismus der Nation sind die Säfte, die Geniegröße genährt haben, nicht zurückgekehrt.[62]

The reader is encouraged to see the nation as a vulnerable living body to which the individual must minister for fear that its strength be depleted. Stössinger suggests that Germany has a delicate constitution which requires constant attention through the airing of republican ideas in its literature, all the more so because of its psychological disunity. German writers, he implies,

---

56 Heinrich Mann, 'Geist und Tat', p. 9.
57 Felix Stössinger, 'Was ist uns Frankreich?', *Die Weltbühne*, 18.1 (1922), vi, 522–23 (p. 523).
58 Heinrich Mann, 'Geist und Tat', p. 9.
59 Heinrich Mann, 'Geist und Tat'; 'Voltaire – Goethe'.
60 Thomas Mann, '"Gegen Recht und Wahrheit"', in *Betrachtungen eines Unpolitischen* (Berlin: Fischer, 1918), pp. 121–202 (p. 150).
61 Heinrich Mann, 'Geist und Tat', p. 4.
62 Stössinger, 'Was ist uns Frankreich?', vi, p. 522.

should set aside their vanity and dedicate their work to making their country a more humane place in which to live.

In the preceding instalment Stössinger reaches back into history again to show how much French artists have been prepared to sacrifice for the national cause. Citing the involvement of Paul Verlaine and Arthur Rimbaud in the Paris Commune as evidence of French writers' attraction to political activism, Stössinger then turns his attention to the plastic arts. In repeatedly demanding the destruction of a statue of Napoleon which had stood in the Place Vendôme until it was finally torn down by Commune forces, the painter Gustave Courbet is credited with having endorsed an act so uncompromisingly progressive that it would be unimaginable in Germany:

> Die ermbarmungslose Vernichtung von Kunstwerken einer überwundenen Gesellschaftsepoche ist überhaupt für den revolutionären Geist Frankreichs kennzeichnend. Niemals stellte sich das Volk schützend vor Denkmäler eines verhaßten Systems, weil es 'Kunstwerke' seien. Bei uns getraut man sich nicht einmal an die Sieges-Allee. [...] Die Franzosen haben ihre gesellschaftlichen Ideen zu allen Zeiten in der Kunst ausgedrückt und aus der Kunst wieder empfangen. Das politische und politisierende Volk hat stets den politischen Gedanken eines Kunstwerks mit Leidenschaft begriffen. [...] Wer kann leugnen, daß in solchen Zerstörungen ein schöpferischer Wille waltet, größer als unser konservierender, historischer Geist?[63]

Stössinger's breathless celebration of politically symbolic acts of 'Vernichtung' is testament to his indifference to national monuments; he even hints at his position in the post-war debate over the future of the royal statues that had adorned the Siegesallee since 1901 on the orders of Kaiser Wilhelm II.[64] This passage also blurs the borders between intellectuals and the wider population. The will to self-preservation of the German literary class and the intercessions of French writers on behalf of their republic are subtly rendered representative of two conflicting national predispositions. Whereas the French are said to be attuned to the political symbolism of any work of art, the Germans are found wanting in the social conscience necessary to perceive and act upon such connections. Only if more German writers condescend to make contributions to political debates, Stössinger argues, will their callow democracy ever mature into one of which republicans can be proud.

---

63 Felix Stössinger, 'Was ist uns Frankreich?', *Die Weltbühne*, 18.1 (1922), v, 496–98 (p. 496).
64 Dina Gusejnova, *European Elites and Ideas of Empire, 1917–1957*, New Studies in European History (Cambridge: Cambridge University Press, 2016), p. 100.

The answer to the question posed in the title to the series 'Was ist uns Frankreich?' seems clear: France is an example that Germany must follow if it is to fulfil its democratic potential. The final instalment ends with the same untraceable citation from an unnamed poem with which the series begins: 'Mein Bruder Frankreich, laß uns Erzfreund werden!'.[65] This is then followed by a reproduction of a manifesto signed by the French and German leagues for human rights, respectively the 'Ligue des droits de l'homme' and the recently re-named 'Deutsche Liga für Menschenrechte', that addresses 'die Demokratien Deutschlands und Frankreichs!' and implores them to patch up their differences.[66] Whatever these two appeals may suggest, however, the relationship between the two in 'Was ist uns Frankreich?' is not one of equals. Indeed, although Stössinger shares with Helene Keßler von Monbart the desire for a Franco-German 'Bündnis',[67] he believes that it is Germany which would be saved by such a rapprochement. Keßler, on the other hand, holds France to be doomed to extinction without German intervention. Whereas Keßler's patriotism resides largely in her belief that Germany already occupies the pinnacle of European civilization, Stössinger's is founded on a diametrically opposed view of Germany's cultural development. His unflattering comparisons with France reflect a desire for Germany to confront its current democratic deficit and thereby to become a juster society.

In stark contrast to Keßler, who urges the French to acknowledge their existential dependence on German vitality, Stössinger argues that Germans must seek to emulate their French counterparts in order to build a vigorous democracy. It is the alleged discrepancy between the acute social conscience of the French author and the self-regarding abstraction of his German counterpart that lays bare the shortcomings of wider German society in 'Was ist uns Frankreich?'. Stössinger's reading of history is, therefore, a study in a humble internationalist patriotism that does not seek any special distinction for Germany. Instead, it is France that lights the way as the seat of an all-encompassing republican internationalism in which there nonetheless remains no greater honour than to serve one's own country.

Otto Flake: 'Deutsche Reden'

The longest of the three series discussed in this section is 'Deutsche Reden', in which Otto Flake ties Germany's survival as a sovereign nation

65 Felix Stössinger, 'Was ist uns Frankreich?', *Die Weltbühne*, 18.1 (1922), vii, 544–46 (p. 546).
66 Französische Liga für Menschenrechte und die Deutsche Liga für Menschenrechte (Bund Neues Vaterland), 'Für eine Verständigung mit Frankreich!', *Die Weltbühne*, 18.1 (1922), 547–48 (p. 547).
67 Keßler, 'Wir und Ihr', vi, p. 164; Stössinger, 'Was ist uns Frankreich?', vii, p. 545.

to its compliance with French demands. As well as promoting classically internationalist causes such as pacifism, mutual disarmament and multilateral diplomacy, Flake grudgingly supports the provisional presence of French troops on German soil. The last position in particular would have been inadmissible in right-wing circles. According to Istvan Deak:

> only the small reviews of the left-wing intellectuals and of the revisionist Social Democratic opposition insisted that resistance on the Ruhr was national suicide and that reconciliation with France was mandatory, be it in the presence of the French army of occupation.[68]

As this book repeatedly shows, the importance of abiding by the post-war treaties and of not antagonizing the French occupiers whenever this failed was indeed paramount for *Die Weltbühne* throughout the first half of the Weimar period. However, this section will demonstrate that the inflammatory rhetoric in which Flake couches such arguments in 'Deutsche Reden' was a more frequent feature of the journal's largely pacific commentary on foreign affairs than has previously been acknowledged.

The title of this series, with its deliberate echo of Fichte's *Reden an die deutsche Nation* of 1807, raises the temperature instantly. In the seventh of his lectures Fichte had evoked an infinite German empire consisting of all the freedom-loving peoples of the earth. The spirit of freedom, Fichte proclaims, 'wo es auch geboren sei, und in welcher Sprache es rede, ist unsers Geschlechts, es gehört uns an, und es wird sich zu uns tun'.[69] In this context it hardly seems hyperbolic for Joseph Jurt to declare: 'Für Fichte war nicht mehr die französische, sondern die deutsche Nation die menschheitlich führende'.[70] In this key particular Flake diverges from Fichte. For all that he describes the philosopher in the first instalment as 'ein deutsches Ereignis, recht eigentlich de[n] Mann, der die Deutschen auf den Weg zur Nation führte',[71] in the sixth he declares Germany to be ill-suited to the status of a Great Power on the grounds that it has never managed to overcome its geographical disadvantage: 'Von jeher war die deutsche Geschichte die Geschichte dieses Versuches und seines Scheiterns: es wird nie gelingen, nie wird es ein deutsches Imperium geben'.[72] In this respect, the 'Deutsche Reden' represent a decisive break with the politics of force that had characterized Germany's approach to international relations under the *Kaiserreich*.

---

68 Deak, *Weimar Germany's Left-Wing Intellectuals*, p. 90.
69 Fichte, *Reden an die deutsche Nation*, p. 238.
70 Jurt, *Sprache, Literatur und Nationale Identität*, p. 188.
71 Otto Flake, 'Deutsche Reden', *Die Weltbühne*, 18.1 (1922), i, 337–40 (p. 338).
72 Otto Flake, 'Deutsche Reden', *Die Weltbühne*, 18.1 (1922), vi, 519–22 (p. 520).

The intemperate language of Flake's 'Reden' is explicitly calculated to win nationalist readers over to the democratic cause. Flake's re-definition of Germany's role on the world stage arrives packaged in terms with which some of his own colleagues would arguably have been uneasy, but he makes no apology for this:

> Die Deutschen haben trotz Allem, was gegen sie gesagt werden kann und muß, die Witterung dafür, daß die vitalen Ideen nicht bloß rationalistisch fundamentiert sein wollen, und die Nationalisten verraten ihre Herkunft von einem philosophischen, von einem wesentlichen Volk, wenn sie statt banaler Vernunftgründe Impulse geben.
>
> Man kann von ihnen lernen. Man kann sie nur mit ihren eignen Waffen schlagen. Man muß mit deutschen Methoden zu ihnen reden und, wie sie, vitale Spannungen erzeugen. Die Vereinsdemokratie vermag das nicht, dazu gehören andre Intelligenzen.[73]

Flake's mollifying admission that his nationalist adversaries have remained true to their 'philosophical' roots indicates his susceptibility to the same 'philosophical patriotism' from which, as mentioned in the introduction to this chapter, his *Weltbühne* colleagues habitually distanced themselves.[74] In spite of his disparaging reference to 'Vereinsdemokratie', by which he presumably means party politics itself, he does not share the anti-democratic animus of such patriotism. 'German methods', with their emphasis on emotional appeal over rational argument, are part of a long game whose aim is to embed democracy in the national psyche and thus to secure Germany's place in the international community.

However, this conciliatory strategy is initially concealed beneath Flake's protestations to the contrary. Persuading the German *Bürgertum* to rise to the demands of democratic citizenship, he insists, has nothing to do with diplomacy: 'Es geschieht nicht um des Eindrucks auf das Ausland willen, sondern um der deutschen Sache selbst willen, wenn ich sage, daß es nötig sei, von der Verzweiflung über das bürgerliche Denken zur Offensive überzugehn, von der Duldung zum Angriff'.[75] In fact, Flake's ultimate message is that the German national interest is served precisely by making a good impression on the country's French creditors, but he clearly imagines his immediate audience to be a domestic one and therefore denigrates the French even as he calls for their demands to be granted.

---

73 Otto Flake, 'Deutsche Reden', *Die Weltbühne*, 18.1 (1922), v, 467–70 (p. 470).
74 Deak, *Weimar Germany's Left-Wing Intellectuals*, p. 23.
75 Flake, 'Deutsche Reden', i, p. 339.

Flake does not exercise any restraint in his verbal onslaught. To the extent that the French occupation of the left bank of the Rhine is presented as a necessary evil, the evil is racial in nature. The French Army's colonial regiments are made to serve as collateral damage in what can be seen, in the absence of shared political aspirations, as a rhetorical charm offensive geared towards right-wing readers:

> Wir haben keine Sympathie für französische Offiziere, keine für Besetzungen, keine für Negergarnisonen, es geht uns einfach um die Sache. Die harte französische Hand – ich spreche nur von der Entwaffnungskontrolle – gehört zu den Dingen, die das Böse oder Selbstsüchtige wollen und das Gute oder Allgemeinnützliche schaffen.[76]

The recipients of Flake's off-hand racism are the troops recruited by the French Third Republic from their colonies in West and North Africa, first to fight on European battlefields during the First World War and then to assist in the occupation of the Rhineland in the aftermath of the conflict. As alluded to in this passage, their duties included the inspection of German military installations on behalf of the Military Inter-Allied Commission of Control.

Germans of all political affiliations found the experience of being supervised by Africans especially humiliating, as an article by Wilhelm Michel published a year after Flake's makes clear. In 'Die deutsche Krankheit', the title of which refers to German militarism and not the presence of African soldiers on German soil, Michel characterizes the latter as an imposition that no ethnic German, regardless of his or her patriotic stance, could be expected to welcome: 'Man braucht kein Chauvin zu sein, um von Herzen zu begreifen und zu billigen, daß unsre Arbeiter nicht unter der Aufsicht von Afrikanern fronen wollen.'[77] Michel's colonialist outlook is equally evident in his disparagement of his compatriots' militaristic attitudes, which he fears will culminate in Nietzsche being misrepresented 'als militärfrommen Kegelbruder und treuherzigen Wadelstrumpf-Indianer'.[78]

The ultimate target of such racial slurs, though, was the French state that had, so the argument ran, stooped so low as to hire African soldiers to oppress their fellow Europeans. In her work on the discourse of 'Black Horror', or 'Black Shame', which arose in Germany towards the end of 1919 and rapidly accumulated prominent sympathizers across the political spectrum

---

76 Otto Flake, 'Deutsche Reden', *Die Weltbühne*, 18.1 (1922), iii, 413–16 (p. 414).
77 Wilhelm Michel, 'Die deutsche Krankheit', *Die Weltbühne*, 19.1 (1923), 321–24 (p. 323).
78 Michel, 'Die deutsche Krankheit', p. 323.

in Britain, France and the United States, Iris Wigger argues that such racist scaremongering was manipulated in part 'to discredit France internationally, to put pressure on the French government and to achieve an alleviation of the hardships associated with the Allied occupation'.[79] Wigger has even shown that the perceived threat posed by the African soldiers, which centred on unfounded accusations of rampant sexual violence against German women, was intermittently framed by Germans as 'a French attempt to spoil their race by degeneration and diseases imported by coloured troops'.[80] This claim, a reversal of Keßler's to the effect that French expansionism was motivated by the desire to incorporate German blood into their national gene pool,[81] shows the proximity in German minds between the supposed sexual incontinence of the African soldiery and the insidious cunning of their French neighbours. In the above quotation from 'Deutsche Reden', France accordingly appears as a Mephistophelian entity bent on 'das Böse', the punishment of Germany, but ultimately more likely to bring about 'das Gute', general disarmament.[82]

Otto Flake was far from the only *Weltbühne* writer to insinuate that France was acting in bad faith, or at least with excessive force, by imposing sanctions on Germany in the name of European stability. Indeed, even his incendiary choice of words was echoed elsewhere in the journal. The most striking example of this is his borrowing of the figure of Shylock from Shakespeare's *Merchant of Venice*:

> Man muss, ohne Zwang und Reflexion, das Gestern verlassen können, den Schatten, die Erinnerungen, die Werte des Gestern. Der 'Feindbund', das war; daß die Franzosen, wie Shylock, auf ihrem Pfund Fleisch bestehn, ist nicht das Wesentliche, daß die Andern Schwierigkeiten mit dem Pazifismus haben, darf die eigne Mattheit nicht rechtfertigen.[83]

The most notorious use of the phrase 'Shylock peace' was arguably by the spokesman for the right-wing Deutschnationale Volkspartei (DNVP), Arthur Graf von Posadowsky-Wehner, who had described the Treaty of Versailles thus upon its imposition in 1919.[84] It is therefore all the more surprising that variations on this expression, with its inevitable anti-Semitic

---

79 Iris Wigger, *The 'Black Horror on the Rhine': Intersections of Race, Nation, Gender and Class in 1920s Germany* (London: Palgrave Macmillan, 2017), pp. 1–12 (p. 3).
80 Wigger, *The 'Black Horror on the Rhine'*, p. 85.
81 Keßler, 'Wir und Ihr', vi, p. 164.
82 Flake, 'Deutsche Reden', iii, p. 414.
83 Flake, 'Deutsche Reden', iii, p. 415.
84 Robert Gerwarth, *November 1918: The German Revolution*, Making of the Modern World (Oxford: Oxford University Press, 2020), p. 194.

overtones, should have made their way into a *Weltbühne* leader entitled 'Was ist das rechte Mittel?' at the height of the Ruhr Crisis in February 1923.[85] Used ironically by Heinrich Ströbel in an article in 1920 stressing the need for German nationalists to cease antagonizing their French opposite numbers by exaggerating the latter's malign intentions,[86] the figure of Shylock was not, with the exception of Flake's piece, subsequently mentioned other than in theatrical contexts until the aforementioned editorial. In this instance, however, the Venetian merchant is evoked four times, including twice in conjunction with a knife.[87] This is not least interesting because the author, who is not named, argues passionately for every effort to be made towards satisfying the French debt. 'Deutsche Reden', then, would not be the last *Weltbühne* article to argue for the obligation to pay reparations to be met while demonizing France as a depraved usurer.

The Ruhr Crisis threw the rationale behind Flake's grudgingly pro-reparations position into sharp relief in the pages of *Die Weltbühne*. In 'Die deutsche Krankheit', which was published five weeks after 'Was ist das rechte Mittel?', Wilhelm Michel does not only amplify Flake's racism, as discussed above, but also draws the ultimate consequence for the future of the German nation in the face of ongoing recalcitrance vis-à-vis French demands. Evoking the right-wing refrain 'Sieg oder ehrenvoller Untergang; lieber in Ehre sterben als in Schande leben', Michel retorts that, taken to its logical conclusion, this battle cry can only bring about the end of German sovereignty: 'Ich bin Deutscher und schwärme nicht für den ehrenvollen Untergang meines Volkes, sondern für dessen Leben und Gedeihen. Wenn ich Frankreich einen aussichtsvollen Krieg erklären könnte, würde ich es tun, um eine deutsch-französische Allianz herbeizuführen'.[88] The mutually beneficial Franco-German conflict that Michel imagines is not a realistic hope but a drily humorous hypothesis designed to highlight the ruinous impact of any actual war that could arise if Germany were to provoke France by contravening the post-war settlement. At this point Michel unfolds an apocalyptic vision of mass starvation, the division of Germany's remaining territory into colonies and the enslavement of the entire population. The brutal subjugation of Germany at the hands of France, Belgium, England, Poland and Czechoslovakia is an extravagant extension of the metaphorical 'harte[n] französische[n] Hand' described by Flake, whereby France could, in Michel's words, 'endlich unterm einmütigen Applaus des ganzen Planeten

---

85 [Anon.], 'Was ist das rechte Mittel?', *Die Weltbühne*, 19.1 (1923), 173–75.
86 Heinrich Ströbel, 'Denkt an das Ende!', *Die Weltbühne*, 16.1 (1920), 225–29 (p. 225).
87 [Anon.], 'Was ist das rechte Mittel?', p. 173.
88 Michel, 'Die deutsche Krankheit', pp. 322–23.

das Reich zertrampeln'.[89] Although this prophecy sounds melodramatic to modern ears, the possibility of another war in which Germany would disintegrate as an independent nation was taken with the utmost seriousness by *Weltbühne* columnists. Not for nothing did the article by Heinrich Ströbel mentioned above end on the warning 'Denkt an das Ende!';[90] while the plethora of pacifist articles published in the journal, a selection of which are considered in the final section of this chapter, point to the perceived immediacy of this threat.

In its view of France 'Deutsche Reden' occupies an intermediate position between 'Wir und Ihr' and 'Was ist uns Frankreich?'. Flake evinces little of the regard for the democratic traditions of France that inspires Felix Stössinger's eulogies, while remaining steadfastly aloof from any intimation of an emotional affinity with French culture comparable to that professed by Helene Keßler von Monbart. However, his recognition of France's position of military and economic power over Germany also inures Flake to the quasi-nationalist suggestibility which leads Keßler to believe in a mystical illusion of German greatness that relegates France in an imagined biological hierarchy of European nations. The result is a pragmatic call for the German state to accommodate temporary French interference in its own affairs in order to contribute to the emergence of a pacifist Continental order in which the Weimar Republic can play a constructive role.

*

This section addresses the view, articulated by Istvan Deak in the introduction, that France served *Weltbühne* columnists as an aspirational role model for the salutary transformation of their own country into a democracy along interchangeable Western European lines. Close inspection of three authors shows that this perception of France certainly existed, as in the case of Felix Stössinger, but that the journal was also home both to ethnically infused assertions of German supremacy, such as those promoted by Helene Keßler von Monbart, and to a welter of cynical assessments, of which Otto Flake's 'Deutsche Reden' is the archetype, of France as an ominous neighbour whom Germany had no choice but to placate if it was to survive and flourish. Reconciliation with France in the German national interest was unquestionably a key preoccupation of internationalist patriotism in *Die Weltbühne*. Whether Germany was the senior partner, a supplicant or simply a grudging participant in this rapprochement was a matter for individual writers.

89 Michel, 'Die deutsche Krankheit', p. 324.
90 Ströbel, 'Denkt an das Ende!', p. 229.

Moral Disarmament

The fact that the example of France loomed so large in the internationalist rhetoric of the *Weltbühne* does not in itself reveal anything about the language deployed by the journal in its quest to restore Germany to polite European society. The following section breaks new ground by identifying a consistently ethical overtone in the weekly's impassioned appeals for Germany to adopt a conciliatory attitude towards an international community loath to take the country's republican volte-face at face value. In the process it will become clear that this moral animus enabled *Die Weltbühne* to articulate a moderate patriotic vision that sought both radically to re-imagine Germany's role on the world stage and to cleanse public life in the country of what some columnists considered to be its ingrained tendency towards violence. The primary focus will be on the featured writer's choice of words as he or she strove to justify internationalist objectives in patriotic terms.

Several critics have remarked upon the fact that *Die Weltbühne* was a journal with a pronounced sense of moral mission, but none has substantiated this statement by means of close textual analysis, nor made any meaningful attempt to link it to the cultivation of a new patriotic idiom. Thus to Ian King, the most recent scholar to make this observation, it serves merely as a mitigatory afterthought to a comment on the journal's relatively low circulation figures: as he points out, *Die Weltbühne* never sold more than sixteen thousand copies during the Weimar period, 'galt aber vielen Lesern als moralischer Maßstab'.[91] For his part, Makiko Takemoto, in his dissertation on the approach of the journal to foreign policy, contents himself with reproducing Harry Pross's accurate description of the journal as:

> eine moralische Zeitschrift, denen ähnlich, die im achtzehnten Jahrhundert aus dem Geist der Aufklärung redigiert werden. Sie war eine gestrenge 'Tadlerin', weil ihr Herausgeber überzeugt war, man könne den 'verseuchten Geist' eines Landes nur dann bekämpfen, wenn man sein Geschick teile.[92]

In this extract Pross cites the reasoning of *Weltbühne* editor Carl von Ossietzky for declining to go into exile when sentenced to jail for high

---

91 Ian King, '"Das Bürgertum erliegt der Wucht...": Tucholsky zwischen Bürgertum und Arbeiterbewegung', in *Kurt Tucholsky und der Weltbühne-Kreis zwischen Bürgertum und Arbeiterbewegung*, ed. by Ian King, Schriftenreihe der Kurt Tucholsky-Gesellschaft, 11 (Leipzig: Ille & Riemer, 2016), pp. 25–47 (p. 30).

92 Makiko Takemoto, *Die Außenpolitik und der Pazifismus der Weimarer Intellektuellen im Umkreis der Zeitschriften der Weltbühne und des Tage-Buchs in der Zeit 1926-1933* (Hiroshima: Carl von Ossietzky Universität Oldenburg, 2007), pp. 4-5; Pross, *Literatur und Politik*, pp. 108–09.

treason following the publication in the journal of Walter Kreiser's article 'Windiges aus der deutschen Luftfahrt', which had drawn renewed attention to the complicity of the civilian airline Lufthansa in the illicit restocking of the German Air Force.[93] Weeks before this article was printed, Ossietzky, who had taken over from Kurt Tucholsky in 1926, wrote an admiring tribute to the French investigative journalist Albert Londres which contrasted the climate of relative press freedom in France to the ethical taboos allegedly still stifling the German print media.[94] Ossietzky's frustration with the self-censorship supposedly at work in German newsrooms suggests that he saw the potential for journalism to serve a radical moral purpose.

Asserting that 'jeder heitere, unabhängige, autoritätenverachtende Mensch' is 'ein Stück Revolution',[95] Ossietzky imagines the impact that the mooted publication of Londres's work in German translation might have on a German readership unaccustomed to encountering such unflinching reportage in those newspapers it deemed socially respectable:

> Es muß den deutschen Leser nachdenklich stimmen, mit welcher Offenherzigkeit dieser Mitarbeiter gutbürgerlicher pariser Blätter das heilige Geld, die heilige Kirche, den heiligen Staat behandeln darf. Seine Bücher wimmeln von politischen und religiösen Blasphemien. Wird drüben das Talent noch immer als eine überparteiliche Köstlichkeit betrachtet? Man könnte in Deutschland viel von diesem freien, anmutigen Kopfe lernen, dessen Bücher, wie ich höre, bald deutsch erscheinen sollen. Sie könnten alles in allem unsre Zeitungsleser ermuntern, an ihre lieben Journale höhere Ansprüche zu stellen.[96]

The heresies of the eponymous 'laughing reporter', whose satirical attitude is a deliberate echo of the self-styled 'rasender Reporter' and occasional *Weltbühne* contributor Egon Erwin Kisch, include campaigns against forced labour in overseas penal colonies and lethal working conditions on railroad construction sites in France's African territories. They are, therefore, both morally transgressive in their indictment of institutions that a German reader might have thought untouchable and morally righteous in their exposure of colonialist outrages. It is this combination of irreverence and campaigning zeal that Ossietzky evidently wishes his journal to embody.

Istvan Deak is thus far the only critic to engage with this moral vocation on anything other than a superficial level. In a chapter of his aforementioned

---

93 Jäger, 'Windiges aus der deutschen Luftfahrt', p. 407.
94 Carl von Ossietzky, 'Der lachende Reporter', *Die Weltbühne*, 25.1 (1929), 274–75 (pp. 274–75).
95 Ossietzky, 'Der lachende Reporter'.
96 Ossietzky, 'Der lachende Reporter', p. 275.

book entitled 'For a Humane Society', he explicitly acknowledges the ethical impetus of many of the campaigns waged in *Die Weltbühne*, identifying reform of the court system, the legalization of abortion and the protection of artistic freedoms as three matters on which writers from Kurt Tucholsky to Manfred Georg directly challenged the moral assumptions of both the legislature and its judicial arm. With one eye trained firmly on *Die Weltbühne*, he even goes so far as to say that 'the German intellectual ferment in the first years of the twentieth century was above all a revolt against conventional morality'.[97]

The journal's most moralistic writers knew that any international charm offensive would founder if Germans refused to embrace republican principles at home. Germany therefore had to prove that it had turned its back on militarism once and for all in order to deliver on the redemptive promise of the more grandiloquent columnists in *Die Weltbühne*. It is in this introspective spirit that Otto Flake calls in 'Deutsche Reden' for a 'moralische Offensive' that would reclaim the German nation from the forces of nationalism and forge 'ein neues Deutschtum'.[98] It is, he suggests, incumbent upon 'Geistigen, die sich als das Gewissen der Nation fühlen' to persuade their compatriots to internalize the democratic idea at the individual level.[99] For Flake, the final success of the moral campaign by the *Weltbühne* depended on triumph in this first skirmish.

As this rallying cry suggests, Flake was aware that Germany could only improve its image abroad by resetting its moral compass domestically. Indeed, he believed the moral deficit in the German people to be so grave that such fundamental political questions as the choice between privatization and nationalization receded in importance behind the basic commitment to democratic governance:.

> Politik ist in letzter Instanz ein moralisches Geschehnis. Ob das Branntweinbrennen besser Staatsmonopol ist oder der Privatindustrie überlassen bleibt, das heißt mir noch nicht Politik. Aber wie gewählt wird, wie gerichtet wird, wie erzogen wird: das ist Sache der Politik.
>
> Der Deutsche erweist sich als der Mensch, der diesen Zusammenhang nicht sieht. Er ist unpolitisch, weil er kein unmittelbares, heißes Verhältnis zum Moralischen mehr hat. Er ist in fünfzig Jahren zum Verräter an den menschlichen Werten geworden.[100]

---

97 Deak, *Weimar Germany's Left-Wing Intellectuals*, p. 129.
98 Flake, 'Deutsche Reden', i, p. 340.
99 Flake, 'Deutsche Reden', i, p. 340.
100 Flake, 'Deutsche Reden', i, pp. 337–38.

Forty-eight years of imperial rule had resulted, Flake argues, in moral self-abandonment. Not only had the 'human' values of autonomy, agency and human dignity supposedly guaranteed by participatory democracy been among the first casualties of the *Kaiserreich*, but they remained dormant at the time of writing in a nation of enfranchised subjects that had not yet made the mental adjustment necessary to exploit its electoral power.

In the fourth instalment Flake duly accuses the Weimar state of fostering a culture of latent militarism that is immoral in its duplicity. The warning signs are to be found, he writes, in the incongruities tolerated by the Republic. One such is the ceremonial gathering of decommissioned soldiers at a Potsdam barracks to mark the fortieth birthday of the erstwhile Crown Prince Wilhelm; another is the reluctance of those in power to remove busts and paintings of members of the overthrown monarchy from public buildings: 'Das ist, als beginne Einer, der sich von seiner Frau geschieden hat, alle Zimmer mit ihren Photographien zu behängen und einen beredten Kultus mit ihrem Andenken zu treiben. Es gibt Unsauberkeiten, die ein klarer Mensch nicht tut'.[101] This analogy between a divorcee's ongoing obsession with his former wife and the republican state's tolerance for imperial nostalgia works on two levels. On one hand, the behaviour of the Weimar Republic is shown to be inconsistent with its own founding principles and therefore illogical. On the other, Flake's image of sinister private perversions suggests that the political leadership consciously pursue a double life in which public appearances and secret loyalties do not match. In the process, 'sauber' takes on both its conventional meanings at once: coherent and clean.

Whereas Flake at this point still held out a measure of hope for his compatriots' redemption, commenting that the acquisition of morality and intellect ought to be 'das ABC für Deutsche, an dem sie, ewige Pubertätsmenschen, studieren mögen',[102] the assassination of Walter Rathenau condemned Germany to moral oblivion in his eyes.[103] In the opening remarks to the eighth instalment, Flake scathingly compares public condemnation of Walther Rathenau's assassination (24 June 1922) to the short-lived outcry over the fatal shooting of Matthias Erzberger (26 August 1921), the government minister who had signed the Armistice, by the same

---

101 Otto Flake, 'Deutsche Reden', *Die Weltbühne*, 18.1 (1922), iv, 437–40 (p. 437).
102 Flake, 'Deutsche Reden', iv, p. 438.
103 The column 'Nach dem Mord' appeared twelve days after the then Foreign Minister Walter Rathenau was assassinated by members of the far-right terror group Organisation Consul. Two months prior to Rathenau's murder Germany had officially renounced its territorial and financial claims against Russia by signing the Treaty of Rapallo (16 April 1922), which Rathenau had negotiated.

group the previous year. The reluctance to protect republican values at a symbolic level scorned by Flake in the fourth instalment thus becomes fatal in the eighth, as he lambasts the Weimar political class for lacking the courage to prevent murderous nationalists from being radicalized:

> Ich persönlich bin so weit, selbst die politische Auflösung Deutschlands zu wünschen, falls seine moralische Vereinheitlichung aussichtslos wird. Man wird es satt, unter Kastraten zu leben, denn man kann nicht unter ihnen wirken. Ein Volk, das kein politisches Temperament hat, hat kein Recht auf politische Existenz, es hindert die Welt.[104]

Flake's withering reference to the apathetic 'Kastraten' of the political mainstream, who had been incapable of defending Rathenau and other left-wing figures against right-wing violence, reinforces his aforementioned belief that most individual Germans are stuck in a state of arrested development. For all that the final instalment of 'Deutsche Reden' bears the defiant title 'Durchgreifen, Republik!',[105] Flake clearly believes the Weimar state and the democratic idea it represents to be teetering on the brink for want of moral courage.

Moral dissolution was by this point a staple concern of *Die Weltbühne*. In 1919 two authors characterized the immorality of the German people, which was invariably attributed to militant xenophobia, as a deadly disease. In February Richard Witting assumed the pseudonym Georg Metzler to issue an eighteen-page indictment of Germany's culpability for starting the First World War.[106] Early in his inquiry Witting cites the since disproved epidemiological findings of Max von Pettenkofer that the cholera virus only thrives if the soil in the surrounding area contains a certain amount of moisture.[107] Witting's point is that the wider European environment had to be primed for war in order for the German government to find the excuse it needed to spark one, but he prefers to stress the decisive existence of German

---

104 Otto Flake, 'Deutsche Reden', *Die Weltbühne*, 18. 2 (1922), viii, 1–3 (p. 3).
105 Otto Flake, 'Deutsche Reden', *Die Weltbühne*, 18. 2 (1922), x, 129–31.
106 Georg Metzler [Richard Witting], 'Die Schuld am Kriege', *Die Weltbühne*, 15.1 (1919), 163–81.
107 In 1849, in the face of a second epidemic in the space of twenty years, the Bavarian government summoned Max von Pettenkofer to join a commission tasked with researching cholera. Pettenkofer's recommendation that a sewage system be built in Munich to prevent future outbreaks proved judicious, but his claim that the condition of the soil was the decisive factor in the germination and spread of the disease was eventually refuted by Robert Koch (1884), prompting Pettenkofer to swallow a vial of cholera bacteria in front of Koch's students in an attempt to prove that a healthy constitution could withstand its effects. He survived.

ill will, which he refers to alternately as a 'Bazillus',[108] or a 'Kriegsbazillus'.[109] This metaphor was, perhaps fittingly, to prove contagious. In November of the same year Ferdinand Nübell argues in an article entitled 'Die Valuta der Moral' that *Die Weltbühne* was among a small minority of newspapers that had made it their mission to reveal the 'grauenhafte Korruption' in German public life, before declaring: 'Die Unmoral ist Gemeingut des Volkes geworden'.[110] The link between Witting and Nübell is most apparent, however, in the latter's description of this all-pervading moral turpitude as a 'Pestbazillus' whose effect on Weimar society is analogous to that of bowel cancer on the stricken human body.[111]

For Witting, the readiness of the German people to attribute responsibility for their defeat to the home front is no less a live moral issue than their retrospective apportioning of blame for the outbreak of the conflict. In a comparatively short article called 'Die verruchte Lüge', published in the second issue of the year, he lays the groundwork for his voluminous report into German war guilt the following month.[112] In this piece he chastises his compatriots for believing the right-wing claim that the German people had been forced by foreign aggressors into a war that it would have won outright were it not for the machinations 'vaterlandsfeindlicher Schurken in der Heimat'.[113] His gullible fellow Germans are portrayed as deficient in moral fibre:

> Um diese, in jedem einzelnen erlogenen Behauptungen zu glauben, dazu gehört nicht bloß ein erheblicher Mangel an sittlichem Gefühl, an Fähigkeit zur Selbstprüfung und Selbstkritik, sondern ein Maß von Einfalt, die nur ein seit ein hundert Jahren im Knechtssinn und Kadavergehorsam erzogenes Volk aufzubringen vermag.[114]

Nor was Witting alone in accusing his compatriots of an abdication of moral responsibility in connection with the war. In May Alsatian writer Victor Eschbach would echo the claim by the Lorrainian politician Hermann Wendel in a recent issue that the wartime conduct of the German Army had expunged any residual pro-German sentiment in Alsace-Lorraine.[115] Reiterating the fact that German troops in the region were seen as oppressors

---

108 Metzler, 'Die Schuld am Kriege', p. 166.
109 Metzler, 'Die Schuld am Kriege', p. 169.
110 Ferdinand Nübell, 'Die Valuta der Moral', *Die Weltbühne*, 15.2 (1919), 571–73 (p. 571).
111 Nübell, 'Die Valuta der Moral', p. 572.
112 Georg Metzler, 'Die verruchte Lüge', *Die Weltbühne*, 15.1 (1919), 34–37.
113 Metzler, 'Die verruchte Lüge', p. 34.
114 Metzler, 'Die verruchte Lüge', p. 34.
115 Hermann Wendel, 'Elsaß-Lothringen', *Die Weltbühne*, 15.1 (1919), 339–41.

and their French counterparts as providential liberators, Eschbach laments the fact that so many Germans in the embryonic Weimar Republic had allowed themselves to be persuaded that the opposite was true:

> Der Zusammenbruch Deutschlands ist nicht nur ein militärischer, politischer und wirtschaftlicher: er ist vor allem auch ein moralischer und intellektueller. [...] [D]aß das deutsche Volk, daß vor allem die gesamte deutsche Bildung, Publikum wie Presse, mit ganz verschwindenden Ausnahmen, nach wie vor belogen und betrogen sein will und den krassesten Schwindel aus unberufenstem Munde kritiklos und freudig entgegennimmt: das läßt die Mentalität dieses Volkes als hoffnungslos erscheinen.[116]

Eschbach's despair is confined to the supposed incorrigibility of the Germans, but wider-ranging conclusions were already a commonplace in the postwar *Weltbühne*. In 'Die verruchte Lüge' Witting depicts the international community in a state of perplexity 'vor dieser deutschen Mentalität'.[117] Unless Germany shows contrition and accepts its defeat, he predicts, the world will throw 'einen geistigen und wirtschaftlichen Schützengraben rings um Deutschland' such as to make Germany 'endgültig und für immer zum Helotenvolk in der Welt'.[118] The dread image of Germany as a vassal state corresponds to the apocalyptic tone of many *Weltbühne* articles at this time, which foretold their country's economic, territorial or moral annihilation if it remained steadfast in its avowal of the righteousness of the German war effort.

The notion that the exhibition of moral integrity was alone capable of averting Germany's 'Untergang' found a particularly vociferous proponent in the leader-writer Heinrich Ströbel, who was the author of some eighty-seven articles in the space of eighteen months. An article in late February 1920 demanded the removal from office of then Minister of Finance Matthias Erzberger, whom Ströbel describes, in English, as being afflicted by 'moral insanity'.[119] Ströbel argues that the government had to sack Erzberger, who had become embroiled in a corruption scandal, 'da die wirtschaftliche und gesellschaftliche Gesundung in dieser Zeit der allgemeinen Verwahrlosung fast mehr noch von der moralischen Wiedergenesung als von oekonomischen Heilmitteln abhängt'.[120] According to Ströbel, the good that the tainted Erzberger's perceived talent as a minister would do his country if he were

---

116 Victor Eschbach, 'Elsaß-Lothringen in Berlin', *Die Weltbühne*, 15.1 (1919), 495–99 (pp. 498–99).
117 Metzler, 'Die verruchte Lüge', p. 36.
118 Metzler, 'Die verruchte Lüge', p. 36.
119 Heinrich Ströbel, 'Tollhäuslerei und Erzbergerei', *Die Weltbühne*, 16.1 (1920), 257–61 (p. 259).
120 Ströbel, 'Tollhäuslerei und Erzbergerei', p. 259.

allowed to remain in post is surpassed by the moral dividends his dismissal would reap for Germany on the international stage.

Ströbel's concern for Germany's moral standing abroad was soon amplified and made concrete by Meridionalis, who responded to a French journalist's confession that he had invented a string of German atrocities during the war by proposing the creation of a parliamentary commission whose responsibility would be to restore Germany's good name in the wider world.[121] Deploying the same expression as had Ferdinand Nübell the previous year, Meridionalis demands to know what the new Foreign Minister, Walter Simons, intends to do, 'um jenes epochale Eingeständnis zur Hebung unsrer moralischen – und damit auch unsrer materiellen – Valuta zu verwerten.'[122] Meridionalis warns that German exports will suffer until Germany has freed itself from stigma, claiming that knives from Sheffield will be preferred to those from Solingen on the international market for as long as the Weimar political leadership fails to capitalize on this opportunity to exonerate their country from the worst charges made against it. Until a commission for moral currency is set up to complement the existing one charged with reviving the German *Deutschmark*, he predicts, the German will be seen as 'ein höchstens zweitklassiges Wesen [...], dem man keine Hand reichen solle, geschweige, daß man mit ihm Geschäfte machen dürfe.'[123] Germany's international isolation once again reveals itself to be the worst fear of *Weltbühne* writers in the early years of the Weimar Republic.

This section demonstrates precisely how a noteworthy contingent of these writers believed an internally reformed Germany might proceed to impose itself on the world stage. There were two principal ways in which the journal believed their country could express a quietly unshakeable moral authority over the bruised post-war Continent: messianism and maternalism.

Messianic Morality

As Istvan Deak explains, *Die Weltbühne* was a consistent proponent of the reassuring idea of *Macht in Ohnmacht*, according to which defeat in the war and the disarmament that this had brought in its train had bestowed upon Germany a moral authority peculiar to it as an effectively defenceless nation:

> For the moment Germany was in a unique position, for she alone of all the great powers had achieved the precondition for a peaceful

---

121 Meridionalis, 'Auch eine Wiederherstellungskommission', *Die Weltbühne*, 16.2 (1920), 380–81.
122 Meridionalis, 'Auch eine Wiederherstellungskommission', p. 380.
123 Meridionalis, 'Auch eine Wiederherstellungskommission', p. 381.

foreign policy: almost complete disarmament and the inability to defend herself. Free from all resentment and from revanchist hysteria, unarmed Germany could, if she wished, take the lead in international diplomacy.[124]

As we have already seen in the first section of this chapter, contributors to *Die Weltbühne* often saw it as their task to dislodge the hold of revanchism on the minds of many Germans. To this end they advocated the pursuit of global soft power as an alternative to military conquest. Pacifism, rather than militarism, was to be the field in which Germany would distinguish itself.

In 'Deutsche Reden' Otto Flake asserts that history has anointed Germany as the herald of the future. The way in which he singles out his country and elevates it to an unsolicited position of primacy closely resembles Deak's explanation of the thesis of *Macht in Ohnmacht*:

> Die Deutschen sehen die Geburtsschmerzen, unter denen die Zukunftsidee geboren wird, aber an die Idee glauben sie nicht. Die Idee ist so stark, daß sie trotz der schlechten Aufnahme Deutschland zu ihrer ersten Heimat wählen wird, denn Deutschland ist durch den Krieg zum Prototyp des unimperialistischen, von der Politik befreiten Landes geworden.[125]

For the Germans to overcome their scepticism of the pacifist 'Zukunftsidee', however, they must first undergo a process of 'moralische[n] Abrüstung',[126] thereby becoming, as Deak puts it, 'free from all resentment and from revanchist hysteria'. Only then, Flake cautions, can the inchoate German Republic hope to turn its chastening recent history to its advantage.

The formulation 'moralische Abrüstung' finds an uncanny echo in Benjamin Ziemann's work on republican patriotism in the Weimar era from 2013.[127] The phrase 'cultural demobilisation' is among the most frequently recurring concepts in Ziemann's book, which explores the pacifist campaigning of veterans' organizations such as the *Reichsbanner*.[128] By

---

124 Deak, *Weimar Germany's Left-Wing Intellectuals*, p. 83.
125 Flake, 'Deutsche Reden', vi, p. 521.
126 Flake, 'Deutsche Reden', i, p. 339.
127 Benjamin Ziemann, *Contested Commemorations*.
128 The *Reichsbanner Schwarz-Rot-Gold* was an association of republican war veterans founded in 1924 with the aim of defending parliamentary democracy through both its press and the military-style demonstrations at which its members disavowed war and eulogized the republican idea. The main impulse for the formation of the *Reichsbanner* came from SPD politician Otto Hörsing, who represented its interests in the Reichstag, but it was also designed as an organized counterweight to right-wing paramilitary groups such as the *Sturmabteilung* (SA).

this Ziemann means the efforts expended by republican ex-servicemen to dismantle their compatriots' residual wartime prejudice and establish in its place a store of fellow feeling for their democratic counterparts in France and other formerly Allied nations. As Ziemann shows, these efforts were far from being purely altruistic, but were intended partly to clear the way for Germany's metamorphosis into a stable, trusted force on the European stage:

> In the eyes of republican war veterans, support for internationalism and reconciliation with France in memory of the horrors of war did not imply an outright rejection of patriotism. [...] In July 1929, Erich Roßmann, head of the Reichsbund [der Kriegsbeschädigten und Kriegsteilnehmer], spoke at the annual gathering of the Union fédérale in Brest. He rejected the revanchist notion that love for one's fatherland would necessarily imply deep-felt enmity towards other countries. The congress rose to a storm of applause when he explained his vision with the words: 'We do not want to get rid of the nations and the love of one's own fatherland; rather, we want to place them like gems in the central sun of mankind so that they can fully develop their gloss and their richness in colour and shape'.[129]

Such purple prose as Roßmann's would hardly have passed muster with the famously demanding Siegfried Jacobsohn, but the pages of the *Weltbühne* nonetheless bear witness to the seismic shift in patriotic discourse generated by the traumatic experience of the First World War and traced by Ziemann. Since mass sacrifice on the battlefield evidently did not guarantee victory, patriotism could no longer be equated unproblematically with military conquest. 'Cultural demobilisation', or moral disarmament, promised a different route to national redemption.

In a leader article written in the summer of 1921, the Social Democrat Karl Rothammer, whose work is considered at length in the final chapter, explicitly promotes 'Macht in Ohnmacht' as a means 'dem deutschen Volke zu jener Weltwirkung zu verhelfen, von der Ludendorff geträumt hat'.[130] Rothammer, who wrote the bulk of the journal's leaders in 1921, begins 'Deutschland als Weltmacht' by distancing himself from any wish for Germany to save the world, only immediately to qualify this position:

> Wenn dennoch von einer Weltaufgabe Deutschlands, von einer neuen Art deutscher Weltmacht gesprochen werden soll, so kann dies nur auf der Grundlage dessen geschehen, was zur Zeit ist: auf der Grundlage deutscher Ohnmacht, auf der Grundlage eines

---

129 Ziemann, *Contested Commemorations*, p. 159.
130 Karl Rothammer, 'Deutschland als Weltmacht', *Die Weltbühne*, 17.2 (1921), 55–56 (p. 55).

entwaffneten, entmilitarisierten Deutschlands. Und dies, ohne daß man paradox zu sein wünscht.[131]

This reading of Germany's place in the world attests partly to its author's pragmatism. Not unlike Flake, after all, Rothammer believes the war to have been a foregone conclusion and its outcome definitively to have disqualified Germany from any pretension to military power. It is, however, also an inherently moral vision founded on a belief in Germany's destiny to lead the world out of a condition of perpetual warfare and into a future of mutual understanding.

The strength of this conviction means that Rothammer is not necessarily a reliable witness. At the end of the article he reflects on a recent speech by Joseph Wirth in which the Chancellor had addressed the challenges of running a country without the ability to defend itself and urged progressive Europeans to consider reducing military expenditure to a bare minimum in the interests of peace, stability, welfare and reconstruction. Rothammer liberally paraphrases Wirth's sentiments thus: 'Der deutsche Reichskanzler hat recht: hier wurzelt Deutschlands kommende Weltmacht!'.[132] This is a misrepresentation of Wirth's statement, which contained no claim of German exceptionalism.

Two weeks after the publication of 'Deutschland als Weltmacht' Rothammer reaffirmed his bullish confidence in the salutary effects of Germany's disarmament in an article simply called 'Vorteile der Ohnmacht'.[133] In his closing remarks he casts his mind back to the hubris of 1914 and declares: 'Glitzernde Romantik hat uns gefällt. Kahle Ohnmacht kann uns wieder erhöhen'.[134] This image of Germany's rise from the moral nadir of the First World War dates at least as far back as August 1919, when an article by then leader-writer Heinrich Ströbel appeared under the optimistic title 'Das neue Reich'.[135] The eponymous 'Reich' Ströbel craves is a 'Reich der Kultur' that owes its legitimacy to the collapse of the bellicose *Kaiserreich*.[136] This rebirth, too, is figured as an ascent to unassailable heights: 'Daß Deutschland auf neuen Wegen zur Höhe streben müsse, geht in keinen echten preußischen Kommißschädel'.[137]

The moral undertone of the idea of 'Macht in Ohnmacht' as manifested in the hands of Flake, Rothammer and Ströbel comes to the surface in 'Wir und Ihr'. Helene Keßler von Monbart infuses her own prophecy

---

131 Rothammer, 'Deutschland als Weltmacht', p. 55.
132 Rothammer, 'Deutschland als Weltmacht', p. 56.
133 Karl Rothammer, 'Vorteile der Ohnmacht', *Die Weltbühne*, 17.2 (1921), 83–84.
134 Rothammer, 'Vorteile der Ohnmacht', p. 84.
135 Heinrich Ströbel, 'Das neue Reich', *Die Weltbühne*, 15. 2 (1919), 149–54.
136 Ströbel, 'Das neue Reich', p. 149.
137 Ströbel, 'Das neue Reich', p. 149.

with a messianic quality that is merely implied in the secular iterations mentioned above: 'Heute glaube ich an Deutschlands Erholung. Mehr noch an Deutschlands gute Botschaft, eine deutsche Wiedererneuerung der Welt. Ich sehe vor ihm einen unendlich großen geschichtlichen Auftrag: die Umgestaltung des Wirtschaftslebens im Sinne des Sozialismus'.[138] Defeat in the war has, Keßler proclaims, granted Germany a divine mandate to craft a future of mutually assured peace. What form this future would take is left tantalizingly open, but Flake offers one answer several months later in the seventh instalment of 'Deutsche Reden', naming the Holy Roman Empire as his chosen model for a German-centric concert of European nationhood.

Averring that that empire had 'keinen andern Sinn [...] als durch Zusammenfassung des zivilisierten Abendlands den letzten und höchsten Gedanken zu verwirklichen: Friede und Recht',[139] Flake claims that this yearning was even behind the language used during the peace talks at the end of the First World War:

> Während der Friedensverhandlungen verstanden die Franzosen nicht, daß die Deutschen Reich statt Republik sagen wollten, und die Deutschen wußten nicht, warum sie an jenem Wort festhielten. Wir beginnen es wieder zu verstehen: mit dem 'Reich' ist nicht das Bismarckische, sondern das Hohenstaufische gemeint – die Idee des Hohenstaufischen, die zeitgemäß modifizierte Idee.[140]

Whereas Felix Stössinger, in 'Was ist uns Frankreich?', credits Napoleonic France with being the first regime to aspire to realize 'de[n] durch die Einheit Europas verewigte[n] Friede[n]',[141] Flake traces this ideal back to the entity that he calls, with deliberate patriotic emphasis, 'Heiliges römisches Reich deutscher Nation'.[142] Hope of a new German empire bound together by a historic mission is relatively widespread among political essays published in 1922, though it is striking how frequently authors lit not upon the Holy Roman Empire but Ancient Greece when looking for a historical prototype. Thus in the pamphlet discussed in the first chapter the *Weltbühne* columnist Wilhelm Michel describes Germany, as 'dazu bestimmt, das Erbe von Indien, Hellas und Rom anzutreten';[143] while in the aforementioned tract *Rheingenius oder Génie du Rhin* Ernst Bertram wills his country 'die griechische Idee

---

138 Keßler, 'Wir und Ihr', i, p. 40.
139 Otto Flake, 'Deutsche Reden', *Die Weltbühne*, 18.1 (1922), vii, 567–70 (p. 569).
140 Flake, 'Deutsche Reden', vii, p. 570.
141 Stössinger, 'Was ist uns Frankreich?', i, p. 400.
142 Flake, 'Deutsche Reden', vii, p. 569.
143 Michel, *Verrat am Deutschtum*, p. 22.

der europäischen Gemeinschaft über die Hochflut der gegenwärtigen europäischen Balkan-Barbarei hinüberzuretten'.[144]

For all that Flake takes pains to distinguish between the *Kaiserreich* and the mediaeval *Reich* of the Hohenstaufen and stays clear of the nostalgia for classical Greece displayed by some of his contemporaries, his engagement with the notion of the German imperium is no less liable to Ernst Toller's later reservations about the use by left-wing pacifists of nationalist vocabulary and images than Rothammer's musings on 'deutsche Weltmacht' or Keßler's foretelling of a 'deutsche Wiedererneuerung der Welt'. In her essay on the left-wing appropriation of right-wing rhetoric as diagnosed by Toller in a speech entitled 'Das Versagen des Pazifismus in Deutschland', Lisa Marie Anderson singles out for special attention the recurring image in Toller's writing of a conceptual bridge 'auf der die Unseren zum geistigen Feinde übergingen'.[145] By adopting conservative language in an attempt to broaden their appeal, Toller argues, leftist writers ended up merely amplifying the world view that they had intended to challenge.[146] As the author of fifty-nine articles for *Die Weltbühne*, Toller can be considered a dissenting voice from within the journal's own stable, even though the speech was delivered in 1935.[147]

His concerns were not unfounded: war also appealed to right-wing commentators as a source of moral credit, albeit generally one based on physical valour of the sort that might conceivably secure victory. In his essay 'Politik' (1917) Thomas Mann eschews speculation about the hidden blessings of defeat to offer a moral nationalism that, in traditional fashion, adduces the ongoing exploits in the field of the German Army as proof of his nation's moral superiority:

> Eines Tages wird [die Welt] sehend werden; und wie der Krieg nun enden möge, – eine deutsche Niederlage in irgendwelchem moralischen Sinn kann er längst nicht mehr bringen. Welche Marktschreierei hätte für das Recht dieses Volkes, teilzuhaben an der Verwaltung der Erde, mächtiger werben können, als seine Leistung von heute?[148]

---

144 Bertram, *Rheingenius und Génie du Rhin*, p. 49.
145 Lisa Marie Anderson, 'The Meaning of Failure and the Failure of Meaning: Ernst Toller on Pacifist Language and Literature in Interwar Germany', in *Pacifist and Anti-Militarist Writing in German*, ed. by Kramer and Robertson, pp. 136–48 (p. 144); Ernst Toller, 'Das Versagen des Pazifismus', in *Sämtliche Werke. Kritische Ausgabe*, ed. by D. Distl and others (Göttingen: Wallstein, 2015), IV.1, *Publizistik und Reden*, pp. 336–41.
146 The phrase Toller uses in the speech, which was only ever delivered in English translation in 1935, is: 'Aber diese Konzessionen [...] bauten die geistigen Brücken auf denen seine [des Pazifisten] Anhänger verwirrt ins feindliche Lager hinüberwechselten' ('Das Versagen des Pazifismus', p. 339).
147 Holly, *Die Weltbühne 1918–1933*, pp. 39–41.
148 Thomas Mann, 'Politik', in *Betrachtungen eines Unpolitischen*, pp. 203–371 (p. 329).

Unlike the writers discussed above, to whom losing the war provides Germany with an unprecedented historical opportunity to lead by the power of its example, Mann manifestly does not consider military defeat automatically to redound to Germany's moral glorification. Nonetheless, Ernst Toller might have reflected that prophesying the 'deutsche Wiedererneuerung der Welt', as Keßler had done, was outwardly little different from believing in Germany's hard-earned right to share in the 'Verwaltung der Erde'.

Nor was Toller the only *Weltbühne* writer to recognize the danger of indulging in platitudinous moral rhetoric. Indeed, Mann's pre-emptive claim of moral victory is a case study in a phenomenon illuminated with customary dry wit by Kurt Tucholsky eleven years later. In 1928 *Die Weltbühne* published Tucholsky's scathing review of Hans Grimm's recently published book *Die dreizehn Briefe aus Deutsch-Südwest-Afrika* (1928).[149] Operating under the pseudonym of the reliably acerbic Ignaz Wrobel, Tucholsky derides moral rhetoric as a desperate form of escapism from an unpalatable reality. His contempt for Grimm's crudely nationalistic storytelling prompts him to observe that Germans almost invariably take refuge in a specious morality when their superiority complex collides with incontrovertible evidence of their vulnerability:

> Der Deutsche beginnt, wie alle Welt, mit wirtschaftlichen Erwägungen, eine durchaus gesunde und rationale Methode. Greift die nicht durch – aber nur dann – : dann wird er moralisch. Vielleicht tun das alle Menschen, aber der Deutsche hat es in dieser Fähigkeit zu einer Meisterschaft gebracht, die ihresgleichen sucht. Wenn man auf den deutschen 'Geist' dieser Sorte trifft, so kann man in neunundneunzig Fällen von hundert darauf schwören, daß dem Herrn Geist-Inhaber etwas fortgeschwommen ist, wofür er sich zu trösten sucht. Der Geist ist in Deutschland immer die letzte Rettung nach den Niederlagen – sie gehen auf den Geist, wie andre auf den Abort. Als Sieger brauchen sie ihn nicht.
>
> Diese Art Deutscher hat nie unrecht, er geht nie in sich, er kommt nie auf den Gedanken, daß auch er vielleicht jemandem Unrecht getan haben könne – er siegt, und wenn er nicht siegt, dann borgt er sich einen Sieg, und den findet er immer in dem, was er 'Staatsraison' oder 'Gesinnung' oder 'Innenleben' oder 'vaterländische Religiosität' oder sonst dergleichen nennt.[150]

The only domain in which Tucholsky is prepared to declare Germany peerless is an imaginary world championship of self-pity. His suspicion

---

149 Ignaz Wrobel, 'Grimms Märchen', *Die Weltbühne*, 24.2 (1928), 353–60.
150 Wrobel, 'Grimms Märchen', pp. 355–56.

that such sanctimoniousness is merely a comforting delusion could just as well be applied to left-wing proclamations of Germany's uncompromised moral sanctity. There is a key difference, however. Whereas Mann insists that Germany's strength in adversity has earned it the right aggressively to control less morally endowed nations, the messianic moralists of *Die Weltbühne* wish their country instead to cajole those less fortunate than themselves into following their non-violent example.

Maternal Morality

Proponents of messianic morality in *Die Weltbühne* may have stressed the need for Germans to topple the war hero from his pedestal, but there was one conventional moral reference point which the journal did not wish to relinquish: the mother. The preoccupation of a small but prolific group of *Weltbühne* writers with the maternal principle, an imagined spirit of peace and constructive dialogue radically opposed to the military solution, is demonstrably a product of its time. In the wake of a war that had fractured the European map and exacted a heavy human price, the journal frequently called for an end to militarism and the dawning of a new pacifist age under the sign of an idealized mother figure.

Such optimism about the decisive contribution that mothers could make to the cause of peace flourished in close proximity to a more litigious view according to which mothers were directly culpable for the outbreak of the First World War and all subsequent spates of violence. The argument ran that militaristic culture was an indictment of a maternal dereliction of duty on a generational scale, since men could not be held responsible for obeying their naturally aggressive instincts. These writers maintained that, if the pre-ordained role of mothers was to keep these morbid passions in check, they had failed. In Germany, according to one sensational contribution discussed below, the void had been filled by a vigilante paramilitarism that put vast swathes of the nation's population in mortal danger.

This catastrophism was the exception to the eulogizing rule. Indeed, it was the pacifist philosopher Friedrich Wilhelm Foerster, himself an occasional contributor to *Die Weltbühne*, who provided one of the clearest articulations of a positive maternal feminism for which Germany might serve as standard-bearer. The reissue in 1922 of Foerster's disquisition on political ethics from 1918 contains a passage that clearly bears the hallmarks of the recent conflict. Its author is concerned with securing the ethical legacy of the war, with little importance ascribed to universal suffrage. Having acknowledged the prerogative of parents and teachers to discourage aggressive impulses in the children under their supervision,[151] Foerster urges German women to avail themselves of 'das höchste "Frauenstimmrecht"'.[152] Of greater importance than exercising their new-found right to vote in elections, Foerster suggests, is the improving influence that German women can bring to bear on their male contemporaries:

> Wieviel Kunst des Roten Kreuzes kann man in der richtigen Behandlung eines erkrankten Selbstgefühls, wieviel barmherzige Schwesternkunst in der Heilung von Männerkonflikten und von gestörten menschlichen Beziehungen betätigen! Die Frau glaubt heute, ihre Mission sei vollbracht, wenn sie die Wunden verbindet, die die Männer geschlagen haben – ihre größte Mission aber besteht darin, das Wundenschlagen überhaupt zu verhüten und geradezu eine heilige Wissenschaft aus der Kunst der Friedensbewahrung und Friedensstiftung in allen Lebensverhältnissen zu machen.[153]

The women of the world are expected to nurse society back to health by taking on a mediating role between belligerent male representatives of different nations and, in more intimate circles, by placating the damaged individual male ego. Foerster's evocation of the Red Cross is indicative of the international dimension of this task. It is no coincidence, however, that Foerster's exalted religious language should so closely resemble the messianic rhetoric of those voices in the *Weltbühne* which wished Germany in particular to impose itself on the European stage as a moral force.

According to the same author in an earlier treatise, the 'mission' to spread the 'holy science' of peace assigned to women above is none other than Germany's historical calling. Foerster, who shares with several *Weltbühne* writers discussed earlier a nostalgia for the Holy Roman Empire, even describes Germany as a providential force in the quest for world peace:

> Das Land der europäischen Mitte allein kann in dieser Krisis die Aufgaben lösen, jene geistige Grundlegung und jene religiös-sittliche Vertiefung der Weltorganisation zu vollbringen, durch die allein der Starrkrampf der Völker-Selbstbehauptung gelöst wird. So paradox es klingt: gerade weil Deutschland dieser Aufgabe noch so fern zu stehen scheint, gerade darum steht es ihr so nahe. Das Bewußtsein

---

151 Friedrich Wilhelm Foerster, *Politische Ethik und Politische Pädagogik, mit besonderer Berücksichtigung der kommenden deutschen Aufgaben* (Munich: Reinhardt, 1922), p. 463; 4th, rev. edn of 'Die staatsbürgerliche Erziehung in der Monarchie' (1918).
152 Foerster, *Politische Ethik*, p. 468.
153 Foerster, *Politische Ethik*, p. 468.

> dieser neuen und zugleich so alten Mission steht unverkennbar dicht vor dem Durchbruch, es sind nur noch wenige Hemmungen zu überwinden, die es dem deutschen Volke zurzeit noch verwehren, die ganze Aussichtslosigkeit und Verderblichkeit seines Nationalismus bis auf den Grund zu erkennen; ist das erst geschehen, so wird die wahre deutsche Natur unaufhaltsam herausbrechen und wird, vertieft durch erschütterndes Leid und schwer erlebten Irrtum, von neuem die Mittlerin der Welteinigung werden.[154]

This passage is a deeply ambivalent one. On one hand, Germany is destined to soothe nationalist tensions by uniting the peoples of the world in the cause of peace. On the other, in order for Germany to fulfil this destiny it will have to give full vent to its national character. This eruption of messianic energy is described in terms suggestive of a swollen river bursting its banks, somewhat obscuring Foerster's peaceable pretensions behind the ominous intimation of a natural disaster.

The problem faced by certain pacifists writing in *Die Weltbühne* was that this paradox, as Foerster himself calls it, often appeared insuperable. Indeed, it was in order to bridge the gap between the unifying German ideal summoned by internationalist patriots such as Wilhelm Michel and the more turbulent androcentric reality that these writers encouraged the cultivation of feminine, and most especially maternal, qualities over a stereotypically choleric masculinity. Such realism was, of course, itself informed by an essentialist understanding of sex that effectively blamed Germany's recent history on an excess of testosterone. In 'Wir und Ihr', Helene Keßler von Monbart even draws on pseudo-meteorology to validate her maternalist agenda, blaming Germany's intemperate climate for the predominance of a restless masculinity:

> In diesem Lande der überall offenen Grenzen, der verwischten Linien und Farben, des Nebels, des Drucks und der Enge werden wenig blutvolle, ganz in sich ruhende und gefestigte Persönlichkeiten geboren. Erst die Leistung gemeiniglich macht hier den Mann, die Stellung. [...] Er ist von Kindheit an in die fortwährende Heldenpose gezwungen, die den typischen Repräsentanten Neudeutschlands trotz alledem zur tragischen Figur macht.[155]

It is against this backdrop of vainglorious posturing and sensitive male pride that Keßler issues the impassioned plea, manifestly intended for

---

154 Friedrich Wilhelm Foerster, *Mein Kampf gegen das militaristische und nationalistische Deutschland. Gesichtspunkte zur deutschen Selbsterkenntnis und zum Aufbau eines neuen Deutschland* (Stuttgart: Friede durch Recht, 1920), pp. 260–61.
155 Helene Keßler von Monbart, 'Wir und Ihr', *Die Weltbühne*, 18.1 (1922), v, 142–44 (pp. 142–43).

European ears: 'Wir brauchen Priester, wir brauchen Lehrer, wir brauchen vor allen Dingen Mütter heute! Gendarmen, Maschinengewehre, Tanks und Besatzungstruppen sind Werkzeuge der Zerstörung'.[156] In judging war to be a watershed moment after which a concerted European effort of moral instruction could not be deferred any longer, Keßler echoes the appeals of female activists across interbellum Europe who wished to spread the edifying message of maternalism across national borders.

Ingrid Sharp has explored the ways in which women from different countries, including Germany, lobbied international organizations such as the League of Nations to instil pacifist principles in the Continent's schoolchildren. The Bund Deutscher Frauenvereine was among those groups which 'directed their campaign against the encouragement of militaristic masculinity in boys' education, suggesting that they were interested in creating conditions for a sustainable peace as well as simply regulating disputes between nations'.[157] The global purview of some of these movements left a mark on contemporary literature. One intriguing study of the role of mothers in Expressionist drama either side of the First World War summarizes the maternal mission as nothing less than 'die Erneuerung des Menschen', a humanitarian vocation that would cure mankind of its fatal attraction to the military solution.[158] In Jean Wotschke's analysis, this renewal does not refer only to the literal act of giving birth, but also to a morally improving force supposedly peculiar to the love of a mother for her child and capable of bringing about 'the betterment of mankind'.[159]

As this example shows, the patriotic motivation behind political internationalism was not always immediately obvious. Nonetheless, maternalist pacifism was mostly inseparable from the German national context in the columns of *Die Weltbühne*. This applied both to political commentary and to less focussed moral ruminations. Thus Manfred Georg, in an article from 1922 arguing for the right of women to have their pregnancies terminated, suggested the formation of an all-female parliamentary body with an exclusive mandate both to update Section 218 of the Criminal Code, which outlawed abortion, and to veto Germany's involvement in any future military conflict. The effect of Georg's so-called 'Kammer der Mütter' would

---

156 Keßler, 'Wir und Ihr', i, p. 38.
157 Ingrid Sharp, Judit Acsády and Nikolai Vukov, 'Internationalism, Pacifism, Transnationalism: Women's Movements and the Building of a Sustainable Peace in the Post-War World', in *Women Activists between War and Peace: Europe, 1918–1923*, ed. by Ingrid Sharp and Matthew Stibbe (London: Bloomsbury Academic, 2017), pp. 77–122.
158 Jean Wotschke, *From the Home Fires to the Battlefield: Mothers in German Expressionist Drama*, Studies in Modern German Literature, 85 (New York: Lang, 1998).
159 Wotschke, *From the Home Fires to the Battlefield*, p. 187.

be clear and tangible: 'Die glückliche "Republik der Mütter" erlebt keinen Krieg mehr'.[160]

As well as such practical, if probably unrealistic, policy suggestions as this, Georg contributed a more whimsical reflection on female virtue rooted in his own wartime experience. In a short article that appeared in the journal in early 1929 he recalls working in a makeshift field hospital in Flanders in 1915. His reminiscences revolve around the redemptive figure of his resident landlady, whose bedroom on the top floor of the monastery had been requisitioned for German medics. Georg and two of his colleagues came to see their hostess, who was a cleaner at the local poultry market, as a surrogate mother. With the exception of one from Hanover who became her lover, this anonymous Belgian treated her lodgers with the tenderness she might otherwise have bestowed upon her fallen son: 'Wir andern drei waren ihre Söhne. Ihr eigner, echter, lag drüben als belgischer Poilu, bei Menin. Sie strich dem Hannoveraner über die Stirn: "Ihr habt es alle nicht gewollt, meine Kinder, ich weiß es"'.[161] The refusal of the grieving Flemish woman to blame this particular group of Germans for the circumstances leading to the death of her son and her readiness instead to accord them victim status correspond to a widespread equation of motherhood and absolution in post-war reflections in word and image.[162] Mothers were vested with an inexhaustible capacity for forgiveness that elevated them above the partisan fray, with no exceptions made on grounds of wartime allegiance.

At the same time as highlighting her immunity to nation-based prejudice, however, Georg elides his landlady with a specific spirit of *Heimat* that partly explains her power over the traumatized German men in her care. Georg recalls their daily return to their top-floor living quarters from the typhoid ward as an ascent from an infernal realm: 'Wir waren zwischen Zwanzig und Dreißig. Sie gab uns Zigaretten und Schnaps. Wenn wir von den Toten herauftaumelten, glänzte diese Frau von Vierzig mit den gesunden Zähnen und im Kranz ihres Flachshaars wie Heimat'.[163] The image of physical health which the landlady represents is a living rebuttal of the scenes of death and infirmity on the floor below. Nonetheless, her approaching middle age implicitly separates her from Georg and the others, such that her physical

---

160 Georg, 'Das Recht auf Abtreibung', p. 9.
161 Manfred Georg, 'Das Herz im Feldwebel', *Die Weltbühne*, 25.1 (1929), 272–73 (pp. 272–73).
162 Anjeana K. Hans, 'Grief Reserved for the Mother: Käthe Kollwitz's *Krieg* Cycle and Gender in the Weimar Republic', in *Käthe Kollwitz and the Women of War: Femininity, Identity and Art in Germany during World Wars I and II*, ed. by Claire C. Whitner (New Haven, CT: Yale University Press, 2016), pp. 124–34 (p. 130).
163 Georg, 'Das Herz im Feldwebel', p. 273.

robustness serves each of them as a vivid reminder of an intact homeland, or *Heimat*, of reassuringly motherly proportions.

Given that much recent scholarship on the idea of *Heimat* has drawn out its links with nostalgia for a lost infant realm of maternal oversight, it is fitting that Georg should enjoy a filial relationship with his hostess. Indeed, Alon Confino argues that *Heimat* and motherhood are inseparable. Whereas the twin labels of *Vaterland* and *Nation* 'brought to mind Germany's borders, territorial integrity, political system or military',[164] Confino observes, *Heimat* had long been imagined as a female realm free of discord: 'Without male political protagonists, *Heimat* also lacked political faculties, such as making war'.[165] Georg's guardian angel, who placates an over-zealous *Feldwebel* initially bent on punishing her for illicitly supplying the orderlies with spirits, embodies this non-violent principle while inspiring a distinctively German sentimentality in her young tenants.

In the first instalment of 'Wir und Ihr', Helene Keßler von Monbart also casts her mind back to a wartime encounter with a foreign mother figure whose cameo role belies her wider significance. As news broke of Germany's surrender in November 1918, Keßler recalls, it fell to her washerwoman to console her. The latter is described as 'eine ungebildete Frau',[166] but her natural gift for compassion makes education redundant: 'Sie nahm mich in die Arme, gegen ihr ehrliches und mütterlich warmes Herz'.[167] This gesture is almost all we know of Keßler's comforter, but for one other significant detail: she is Italian. As a representative of the Allied nations, the wordless washerwoman comes to represent a vision of magnanimous femininity characterized by an undiscriminating kindness available to all, regardless of origin. Even if Keßler had not specifically identified the nameless washerwoman as 'mütterlich', the warmth of her heart might have invited comparison with 'die warme und lachende Sonne' of Southern Europe which had, as discussed in the first section of this chapter, transmitted a *Heimatgefühl* to the young Keßler.[168] Radiating across borders in a time of war, the washerwoman's homely empathy defies expectations of tribal animosity, adhering instead to that branch of pre-war maternalist feminism represented by Henriette Goldschmidt, which held that 'women's maternal ethic should lead them to reject "one-sided nationalism" and stand for international reconciliation'.[169]

---

164 Confino, 'The Nation as a Local Metaphor', p. 73.
165 Confino, 'The Nation as a Local Metaphor', p. 75.
166 Keßler, 'Wir und Ihr', i, p. 39.
167 Keßler, 'Wir und Ihr', i, p. 39.
168 Keßler, 'Wir und Ihr', ii, p. 36.
169 Taylor Allen, *Feminism and Motherhood in Germany*, p. 102.

However, Confino's division between a worldly, masculine *Vaterland* and a fairytale, feminine *Heimat* proves a little too neat adequately to describe Helene Keßler von Monbart's complex and developing relationship with Germany. As her train crosses the Swiss border into Germany in the immediate aftermath of the First World War, Keßler is overcome by a patriotic epiphany under the impression of which she re-imagines her beleaguered country not as a muscular Fatherland but as a hardy mother:

> Niemals kann ich Ihnen ausdrücken, was ich empfand. In tausend Schmerzen unter Mutterwehen geboren – den Begriff Vaterland. Ich, heimatlos, Weltwanderer, hatte endlich ein Vaterland! Mit der Hand hätte ich über den sanften Sammet der Felder streichen mögen, mich in die Baumgruppen bergen, ehrfurchtsvoll den alten Burgen auf der Höhe mich neigen mögen!
> Mutter der Schmerzen! Schmerzensvolle Mutter! – das war mir Deutschland. Nichts vom Vater in diesem ersten Erklingen, kein Kampf oder Zorn.
> Mutter! Arme Mutter![170]

The by now familiar triangular nexus of association connecting *Heimat*, motherhood and redemption remains intact in this passage. Nonetheless, Keßler's 'Mutter der Schmerzen' is too multi-faceted a figure not to strain at the confines of such a reading. Ostensibly she is a pitiful victim, helpless in the face of paternal rage and worthy of a name that echoes the *mater dolorosa* of Christian iconography. Far from being a passive observer of events, however, Mother Germany acts as guardian to her wayward children, while also drawing on bitter experience to become an ethical compass in a post-conflict era of international reconciliation.

Presided over as it is by a 'Mutter der Schmerzen', Keßler's newfound *Heimat* can no more provide her with an illusion of childhood innocence than it can truly satisfy any 'Verlangen nach Geborgenheit, nach einem Ruheraum, einer überschaubaren, heilen Welt'.[171] Faced with the German landscape outside the train window, the bewildered Keßler regresses instantly to childhood. Just as her desire to reach out and caress the fields she passes resembles that of an infant on its first outing in nature, her subsequent impulse to take refuge among the trees evokes a child burying itself in its mother's skirts. Nonetheless, the simultaneous presence of man-made fortresses on

---

170 Keßler, 'Wir und Ihr', ii, p. 66.
171 Marita Krauss, 'Heimat – Begriff und Erfahrung', in *Heimat, liebe Heimat. Exil und Innere Emigration (1933–1945)*, ed. by Hermann Haarmann (Berlin: Bostelmann & Siebenhaar, 2004), pp. 11–29 (p. 14).

the hill, before which Keßler has a curious urge to genuflect, ensures that this is no flight from reality. The grown woman's wish to hide herself in the folds of the cloak worn by her 'Mutter der Schmerzen' recalls Käthe Kollwitz's post-war sculptural work, in which mothers were increasingly portrayed as the guardians of the young against a military establishment intent upon conscripting them. As Henriëtte Kets de Vries points out in an essay on the aesthetic evolution of Kollwitz's pacifism:

> [I]mages that recall the *Schutzmantelmadonna* (sheltering-cloak Madonna or Virgin of Mercy) recur in several of her later works. Kollwitz appropriates this popular Renaissance theme, recasting it as a secular motif. For example, in lieu of a literal, physical cloak, Kollwitz instead echoes Renaissance iconography in her positioning of oversized arms and hands that take over the function as the signifiers for the corresponding emotion.[172]

Although Keßler's Mother Germany is introduced in terms that align her closely with the stricken *mater dolorosa*, the foliage into which the returning exile wishes to lose herself exercises precisely the same protective function as that exercised by the arms and hands of Kollwitz's secularized *Schutzmantelmadonna*. Nor does this connection remain speculative. In Keßler's memory, the dawning of her patriotism is immediately followed by a flashback to the last Sunday before World War I. Passing through a farming village in Lower Saxony, she had apparently been struck by the strong hands of the women relaxing in front of their houses.

This recollection is the key to understanding the pro-active impetus of Keßler's 'Mutter der Schmerzen'. Admiring 'die breiten knochigen Arbeitshände mit den stark hervortretenden Adern – Männerhände auch der Frauen, auf die Knie gelegt', she adds: 'Nur die Stadtdame, die Müßiggängerin, liebt die geschäftige Spielerei der stickenden oder häkelnden Nadel'.[173] The reader knows that this contrast between the labouring countrywomen and their idle city-dwelling counterparts has not saved their sons from their fate. Indeed, through the refrain 'Die Ernte reifte', with its foreshadowing of Käthe Kollwitz's choice of title for her pacifist etching 'Saatfrüchte sollen nicht vermahlen werden',[174] Keßler uses dramatic irony to chastise the resting fieldworkers for failing to foresee the danger. However, she does not depict the women as meek accessories to the human harvest. Oblivious though they

---

172 Henriëtte Kets de Vries, 'Mothers' Arms: Käthe Kollwitz's Women and War', in *Käthe Kollwitz and the Women of War*, ed. by Whitner, pp. 10–19 (p. 16).
173 Keßler, 'Wir und Ihr', ii, p. 67.
174 Kets de Vries, 'Mothers' Arms', p. 18.

are to the approaching slaughter, there appears to be a latent constructive power in these pre-war mothers.

Here, too, Käthe Kollwitz's maternal idiom is a revealing point of comparison. Sharp recognizes in the sculptor's later work, which dispensed with both revolutionary imagery and sacrificial motifs, the realization 'that the duty of age was to protect the young from the consequences of their own uncompromising will'.[175] Kollwitz gave expression to this conviction in a series of carvings in which disillusioned mothers intervene to prevent the abduction of more children for the next war effort. By depicting mothers as human shields planting themselves between their progeny and the press gang, the grieving Kollwitz casts her fellow mothers 'not solely as passive victims or mourners, but rather as potential forces for cultural change'.[176]

In 'Wir und Ihr' the nature of this transformative power lies in the radical potential of empathy to pre-empt future wars. As Keßler turns her gaze back to the present, the malnourished state of the boys in her carriage elicits an outpouring of compassion that washes away her instinctive resentment on behalf of Germany's ransacked youth. In this fleeting moment Keßler travels the path from vengefulness to saintly forgiveness upon which she wishes Germany to embark:

> Wenn ich denke, daß ein Knabe zehn Jahre alt, ist er sicherlich vierzehn; die Zwölfjährigen würde man für achtjährig halten. Überall erscheinen die Knaben kümmerlicher als die Mädchen. Mark der Nation! In ihrer Keimkraft getroffen! Eine würgende, gallige Bitterkeit steigt mir hoch. Weggeschwemmt in überwallendem, warm flutendem Mitleid.[177]

There is already a telling precedent in 'Wir und Ihr' for human understanding triumphing over nationalist revanchism against the odds: the warm motherliness of Keßler's Italian washerwoman, trained on her German employer, can be seen as just such an act of empathy across national divides. No deductive skills are necessary, however, to grasp that 'Mitleid' is a mature female quality in Keßler's lexicon. Referring not only to herself but to women in general, she tells her friend at the end of the first instalment: 'Dies Mitleid scheint mir die beste Frucht eines Erlebens von fünfzig Jahren'.[178] Not unlike the bereaved Kollwitz, Keßler hopes to translate such individual humanity into a national, and even a global, movement. If the accumulated wisdom

---

175 Ingrid Sharp, 'Käthe Kollwitz's Witness to War: Gender, Authority and Reception', in *Women in German Yearbook*, 27 (2011), 87–107 (p. 96).
176 Hans, 'Grief Reserved for the Mother', p. 133.
177 Keßler, 'Wir und Ihr', ii, p. 67.
178 Keßler, 'Wir und Ihr', i, p. 40.

of German motherhood can be concentrated into the redeeming national figurehead of the 'Mutter der Schmerzen', Germany can fulfil the sacred peace mission that Foerster foretells.

Given the weight of expectation on their shoulders, it is perhaps not surprising that mothers were vulnerable to losing their position at the summit of this moral hierarchy. Several scholars have noted that the flip side of ascribing such spiritual power to mothers was a tendency to blame them for the struggles of pacifism to gain traction.[179] *Die Weltbühne* was not entirely free of this trend. In August 1925 a lengthy first-hand exposé of life in the outlawed paramilitary units of the so-called *Schwarze Reichswehr* appeared anonymously under the title 'Die vaterländischen Verbände. Erlebnisse und Erfahrungen'.[180] The piece, written by the former Freikorps officer Carl Mertens, revealed the illicit regime of 'Fememorde', whereby renegade members of the Freikorps were added to secret hit lists and assassinated, thereby forcing a police investigation and securing *Die Weltbühne* what has been called its most important 'konkreten politischen Erfolg'.[181]

Mertens's pacifist conversion is borne along by a rather baroque patriotism that occasionally gives the impression of having simply transferred its object from the parade ground to the domestic sphere. Thus, in a sonorous appeal to the patriotism of those readers inclined to downplay the threat of paramilitary troops, Mertens proclaims on the first page: 'Noch heute schaufeln die gleichen Kräfte am Grabe des deutschen Volkes!'.[182] He sustains this operatic pitch over the subsequent eighteen pages, making the article a curious blend of feverish patriotism and emphatic anti-militarism. For the purposes of this study, however, the interest of Mertens's revelations lies mainly in the sometimes fiercely puritanical language with which he both denounces the disingenuous patriotic pretensions of the militiamen and excoriates the mothers who had permitted their sons to join up.

Mertens does not spare himself this moral inquisition, confessing early on that his principal motivation for writing 'Die Vaterländischen Verbände' is 'mich reinzuwaschen von der – wenn auch unbewußten – Schuld'.[183] The words 'Pflicht', 'Schuld' and 'Sühne' all make repeat appearances in

---

179 Ingrid Sharp, 'Blaming the Women: Women's "Responsibility" for the First World War', in *The Women's Movement in Wartime: International Perspectives, 1914–19*, ed. by Alison Fell and Ingrid Sharp (London: Palgrave Macmillan, 2007), pp. 67–87; Taylor Allen, *Feminism and Motherhood in Germany*, p. 2.
180 [Anon.] [Carl Mertens], 'Die vaterländischen Verbände. Erlebnisse und Erfahrungen', *Die Weltbühne*, 21.2 (1925), 239–58.
181 Greis and Oswalt, 'Die Geschichte der Zeitschrift', p. 18.
182 [Mertens], 'Die vaterländischen Verbände', p. 239.
183 [Mertens], 'Die vaterländischen Verbände', p. 239.

the piece, the overwrought register of which frequently spills over into unbridled verbal assaults on his former associates. Branding them 'Rohlinge, [...] verwegene Egoisten und perverse Schweine, denen jedes Gefühl für Sittlichkeit abhandengekommen ist',[184] Mertens paints a vivid picture of a horde of animalistic traitors indulging a sadistic blood lust in the name of national honour. The third target for his moral condemnation, however, are the fighters' parents, whose vicarious pleasure in their children's violent escapades he details in a section entitled 'Die Schuld der Eltern'.[185] Immorality breeds immorality, too: parental negligence, portrayed here as a sin of omission, brings in its train '[den] Verfall der deutschen Jugend'.[186]

Their complicity does not prevent Mertens from trying to enlist parents and teachers in the task of inoculating children against the glamour of armed combat:

> Ich widme meine Schrift allen Vätern und Müttern, namentlich aber den Erziehern der Jugend, den Lehrern und Lehrerinnen an den höhern Lehranstalten, die mit Stolz auf die schwarzweißrote Kokarde an den Mützen ihrer Zöglinge blicken. Mögen sie ihre Verantwortung erkennen![187]

Even allowing for his particular animus against bourgeois parents, however, these encouraging words soon ring hollow. Over the next two-and-a-half pages Mertens relates several anecdotes to prove the culpability of mothers and fathers for the radicalization of their children, breaking off only to vent his frustration in a string of heated rhetorical questions. Tellingly, all three of these lamentations are directed at mothers in particular:

> Diese Sorte Eltern will dressierte Mordbuben aus ihren Kindern machen. Ists nicht eine Schande, daß deutsche Mütter sich über ihre Kinder freuen, weil sie in schmucken Uniformen häßliche Großschnauzenlieder singen und mit leuchtenden Augen von bluttriefenden Plänen gegen das schaffende Volk reden? Haben sie die grauenhafte Tränenflut des Weltkriegs vergessen? Denken sie nicht mehr an die Gräber ihrer Gatten und Ältesten in fremder Erde?[188]

This indictment rapidly shifts from the shared responsibility of 'parents' in general to the particular moral aberration that Mertens feels maternal support for the *Schwarze Reichswehr* to be. These mothers, he suggests, have

---

184 [Mertens], 'Die vaterländischen Verbände', p. 244.
185 [Mertens], 'Die vaterländischen Verbände', pp. 239–43.
186 [Mertens], 'Die vaterländischen Verbände', p. 244.
187 [Mertens], 'Die vaterländischen Verbände', p. 244.
188 [Mertens], 'Die vaterländischen Verbände', p. 241.

forgotten themselves, let alone the deaths of their menfolk in the First World War, when they should be exploiting their natural moral authority to prevent another global conflagration.

As hinted at above, blaming the actions of a generation of men on the inaction of their mothers was the misogynistic corollary to the positive thesis of maternalist morality advanced by writers such as Helene Keßler von Monbart and Manfred Georg. Catherine Smale has shown that these logical contortions were even internalized by certain female poets of the period, for whom the First World War marked a generational failure of mothering.[189] For his part, Mertens does not merely amplify the idea, discussed in greater depth by Ingrid Sharp in her essay 'Blame The Women', that:

> women were supposed to have a civilising effect on men, to provide a moral influence and teach them the softer virtues of empathy, love, pity and forgiveness to compensate for innate male inadequacies in these areas and ensure that they were fully socialised.[190]

By reproaching bereaved mothers for indulging their surviving sons' blood lust, he effectively holds them responsible for the consequences.

For Mertens the most outrageous of these consequences is an obscene distortion of the national interest. A country in which mothers are attracted to violence cannot help but become one in which even brutality towards one's compatriots can be reconciled with the patriotic conscience. Mertens finds it intolerable that the same vigilantes who are prepared to fire on unarmed workers should be allowed to besmirch Germany's intangible national assets by claiming 'daß sie die heiligsten Güter der Nation zu hüten und die Tradition des hehren Deutschtums, dem Treue, Reinheit und Vaterlandsliebe Alles sind, zu bewahren hätten'.[191] It is presented as a grotesque double standard for these troops to declare themselves the anointed protectors of a sacred German national inheritance while sporadically turning on their own people. Echoing the warnings of national decline prevalent in *Die Weltbühne* at the beginning of the decade, Mertens depicts the illegal regiments as harbingers of Germany's doom: 'Je mächtiger sie werden, umso schneller steuert das deutsche Volk seinem Untergang, seinem kulturellen Ende zu'.[192] Both the apocalyptic warnings of Carl Mertens and the vaulting optimism of Helene Keßler von Monbart revolve around the decisive importance each ascribes

---

189 Catherine Smale, '"Auf uns sinken die Toten": Anti-War Sentiment in Expressionist Women's Writing from the First World War', in *Pacifist and Anti-Militarist Writing in German*, ed. by Kramer and Robertson, pp. 77–92 (p. 91).
190 Sharp, 'Blaming the Women', p. 67.
191 [Mertens], 'Die vaterländischen Verbände', p. 244.
192 [Mertens], 'Die vaterländischen Verbände', p. 258.

to the moral influence of mothers, but whereas Keßler dreams of a pacified world recast in Germany's domesticated image, Mertens fears his country's descent into oblivion for want of the maternal touch.

*

It is primarily through the prism of language that this section examines the notion of moral disarmament as expressed by Otto Flake. In the earliest days of the Republic a clutch of feverish leader articles stressed the existential need for Germans to sever themselves from the moral value system they had inhabited under the *Kaiserreich*. Once it had made the ethically charged case for the adoption of republican principles within the German population, the journal swiftly cast its gaze beyond the country's borders in the hope of coaxing the Weimar Republic onto the path of absolution and soft power. Whether it assumed a messianic or a maternalist form, the moral disarmament that *Die Weltbühne* demanded of the German nation implied the substitution of pacifism for aggression in its relationship with the post-war world. Stripped of any means of defending itself, Germany had little choice but to redefine its place in the international community, casting itself as a force for reconciliation in a world disinclined to disarm in its turn until the Weimar Republic had made a clean rhetorical break with its imperial predecessor. The pursuit of 'Macht in Ohnmacht' was not driven by an effusion of benevolence towards the Republic's European neighbours, but by the ardent desire to secure the future of Germany as a sovereign state. Engineering Germany's retreat from a psychological war-footing was therefore an unimpeachably patriotic cause.

Material Disarmament

This chapter now turns in its final section to the repeated calls by the journal for actual disarmament. This section overlaps in some of its conclusions with Sandi Cooper's exhaustive and influential book *Patriotic Pacifism: Waging War on War in Europe, 1815–1914*, but ultimately goes beyond Cooper's thesis by refuting its inherent assumption of hostility between pacifism and patriotism as guiding principles for political action. While Cooper's work highlights the intermittent legitimacy of military self-defence in pacifist circles in the century leading up to the First World War, it repeatedly implies that the pacifist world view tended in these instances simply to give way under the pressure of threatened foreign invasion to a crudely understood patriotic impulse of self-preservation.[193] What this suggestion does not

---

193 Cooper, 'Arms Control: The Dilemma of Patriotic Pacifism', in *Patriotic Pacifism*, pp. 116–39.

allow for is the possibility of synthesis between these two belief systems. In the febrile climate of post-war Europe *Die Weltbühne* was situated at the intersection of pacifism and patriotism, a point of ideological confluence at which pragmatism and passion mingled to sometimes surprising effect.

The contributions discussed here do not call into question the broadly conditional nature of European pacifism in the nineteenth and early twentieth centuries, for which Martin Ceadel devises the neologism 'pacificism'[194] in reference to the widespread acceptance of a country's right to protect itself against any infringement of its sovereignty.[195] Instead of taking issue with this characterization of orthodox European pacifism, whose debt to Cooper's coinage of 'patriotic pacifism' Ceadel explicitly acknowledges,[196] these articles encourage us to reassess the precise relationship between pacifism and patriotism by showing that the latter did not necessarily come at the expense of the former. The example of *Die Weltbühne* shows that the relative failure of absolutist, unconditional pacifism to garner support in mainland Europe, attributed by both the above scholars to the reluctance of countries with contiguous borders to divest themselves of their military arsenals,[197] did not automatically disqualify 'pacificist' writers from employing patriotic arguments to further their particular cause.

This section therefore considers how *Weltbühne* columnists at once distanced themselves from idealism and claimed a unique stake in the German national interest, thereby revising Cooper's definition of 'patriotic pacifism' to accommodate an understanding of pacifism that deliberately emphasizes its national bias, instead of ignoring or animadverting against it. If, as Martin Ceadel has claimed, the inter-war European peace movement reached 'a peak of support even higher than at the end of the 1840s and beginning of the 1850s', this plainly did not only happen in spite of patriotism, but also in alliance with it.[198]

Pragmatic Pacifism

Pacifist columnists writing in *Die Weltbühne* frequently presented themselves as pragmatists, in opposition to the allegedly deluded nationalists who had sworn revenge on Germany's wartime conquerors. The reason is easy to grasp: pacifists had themselves long been discredited as naïve idealists with

---

194 Martin Ceadel, 'Three Degrees of European Opposition to War: Anti-Militarism, Pacificism, and Pacifism in the Nineteenth and Early Twentieth Centuries', in *Pacifist and Anti-Militarist Writing in German*, ed. by Kramer and Robertson, pp. 14–30 (p. 20).
195 Ceadel, 'Three Degrees of European Opposition to War', p. 22.
196 Ceadel, 'Three Degrees of European Opposition to War', pp. 22–23.
197 Cooper, *Patriotic Pacifism*, p. 141; Ceadel, 'Three Degrees of European Opposition to War', pp. 19–20.
198 Ceadel, 'Three Degrees of European Opposition to War', p. 24.

little or no understanding of political realities. In order for their ideas to gain traction, these writers therefore felt compelled to try to turn the tables on their militarist adversaries. This was no easy task. Erich Dombrowski, who would co-found the *Frankfurter Allgemeine Zeitung* in 1949, neatly sums up in two *Weltbühne* articles what he regarded as the default historical view of pacifists in Germany. The first, published in the spring of 1919, was the fifty-seventh instalment of a long-running series of biographies written by Dombrowski under the name of the Early Modern satirist Johannes Fischart. Praising the unwavering pacifism of lawyer and recently appointed Democratic Member of the Weimar Assembly Walther Schücking, who would become the first German judge to be called to the International Court of Permanent Justice in the Hague in 1931, Dombrowski remembers the First World War as a time during which, to quote Sandi Cooper, 'rare was the pacifist in a belligerent nation who did not rally round the flag'.[199] This makes Schücking's refusal to compromise on his non-violent principles all the more noteworthy to Dombrowski:

> Wer sich früher offen als Pazifist bekannte, war in den Augen aller anständigen und korrekten Menschen vom Typ der Täglichen Rundschau und der Deutschen Tageszeitung ein Utopist, ein Schwärmer, ein unklarer Kopf, ein Reichsfeind, ein Mensch, der kein Gefühl furs Nationale hatte, ein Subjekt, das sicherlich jüdisch-international sei.[200]

Especially striking here is the contradictory nature of the accusations that apparently assailed pacifists before and during the war: some scorned their innocence, while others pandered to anti-Semitic conspiracy theories by imputing omnipotent malice to them. In a later instalment about the veteran activist Ludwig Quidde, Dombrowski again portrays the pacifist as the victim of suspicion and condescension in equal measure: 'Ein Pazifist war noch bis vor kurzem in Deutschland ein widerliches Gemisch von Idiot, internationalem Freimaurer und Landesverräter'.[201] Common to both descriptions is the assumption of naïvety, corruption and treachery, all of which were also charges routinely levelled at the French pacifist movement in the early years of the twentieth century.[202]

---

199 Cooper, *Patriotic Pacifism*, p. 140.
200 Johannes Fischart, 'Politiker und Publizisten: Walther Adrian Schücking', *Die Weltbühne*, 15.1 (1919), lvii, 406–10 (p. 407).
201 Johannes Fischart, 'Politiker und Publizisten: Ludwig Quidde', *Die Weltbühne*, 15.2 (1919), lxxiii, 218–23 (p. 220).
202 Cooper, *Patriotic Pacifism*, p. 167.

After the war, however, pacifists evidently sensed their opportunity to seize the initiative. At the end of the first article, Dombrowski presents Schücking as a redeeming figure who had, not unlike Job, survived a series of tests with his faith still intact:

> Nun, da der Krieg zu Ende ging, da selbst die höchsten Militärs, als sie nicht mehr ein noch aus wußten, nach einem Verständigungsfrieden schrieen, war Schückings Zeit, in ganz großem Rahmen zu wirken, endlich gekommen. Er hatte die letzte der vielen Leidensstationen passiert. Jetzt war sein Tag angebrochen. Das Fegefeuer lag hinter ihm.[203]

Dombrowski's biblically charged certainty that the pacifist idea had been vindicated by the sobering experience of war is supported by the election of both Schücking and Quidde to the inaugural Weimar parliament as delegates of the DDP.

The guarded optimism generated by the entry of the anti-war lobby into the political mainstream was no fleeting phenomenon. In early 1920 Austrian pacifist and Nobel Peace Prize laureate Alfred Hermann Fried declared his solidarity with Georg Friedrich Nicolai, whom he suspected of having been ejected from his lecturing post at the University of Berlin because of his outspoken pacifism. Nicolai's plight in the Weimar Republic bears more than a passing resemblance to that of the similarly forthright Schücking in the *Kaiserreich*, with the latter having found himself increasingly marginalized in his capacity as Professor of Constitutional and International Law at the University of Marburg. In spite of these echoes, Fried recalls the hope inspired in Allied countries during the war by a vocal minority of pacifist Germans who had spoken out against the notorious October Manifesto. In response to the Manifesto, in which a group of ninety-three high-profile German intellectuals including Gerhart Hauptmann, Adolf von Harnack and Max Liebermann unconditionally endorsed the German war effort, Nicolai had himself issued a plea for international reconciliation entitled 'Aufruf an die Europäer'.

Attributing patriotic motives to Nicolai and his fellow dissenters, Fried prophesies that their day will come:

> Und dennoch gab es draußen noch einige Hoffnung. Sie lenkte sich auf die wenigen Männer in Deutschland, die ihren Patriotismus anders verstanden als die Übrigen, die den Mut aufbrachten, ihre Überzeugung der riesigen Maschine entgegenzustellen, und die mit ihrer Kritik nicht zurückhielten. Es gab solche Männer. Der Tag wird

---

203 Fischart, 'Walther Adrian Schücking', p. 410.

kommen, wo das deutsche Volk ihnen Denkmäler setzen wird. Heute und gestern errichtete es ihnen, verblendet, Scheiterhaufen.[204]

For all that Fried's evocation of the conventional mediaeval punishment for witches and heretics casts a barbaric shadow over Dombrowski's declaration that the pacifists' day is already 'angebrochen', his vision of future glorification for pacifists reinforces his colleagues' teleological confidence in the righteousness of the cause.

This belief in the underappreciated patriotism driving German pacifists is grounded in a conviction that the national interest in the Weimar era was best served not by delusory self-aggrandizement, but by unsparing realism. Thus Fried indicts 'die deutsche Wissenschaft' in the shape of the signatories to the October Manifesto for inadvertently harming their country: 'Indem sie in die Vaterlandsliebe exzediert, hat sie in Wirklichkeit dem Vaterland den denkbar schlechtesten Dienst erwiesen'.[205] Germany was still counting the cost of this chauvinism, he argues, in the determinations of the Treaty of Versailles, which owed its severity to the impression of irredeemable bellicosity created by the Manifesto. Whereas the intellectuals had failed to foresee the impact of their inflammatory words at the outset of war, there was no longer any excuse for such incitement in the stark post-war reality into which the Weimar Republic had been born.

In the final issue of 1919, published on Christmas Day, Fried's article 'Weihnachtspazifismus' adopts the prosaic language of rationality to take issue directly with the distortion of pacifism by its opponents. The title refers to his suspicion that the extravagant festival of peace enacted every Christmas in the form of shop-window displays and carol services was an elaborate ploy devised by the state to suggest that a world without war was a fantasy to be indulged no more than once a year. 'Indem [ein Friedenskult] das Selbstverständliche zum Unvernünftigen stempelte', Fried maintains, Germans learnt to regard peace on earth as an illusory hope.[206] Weimar citizens were thus being conditioned to welcome a future war that would, in fact, threaten the existence of Germany as a sovereign nation state.

In Fried's telling, lucidity is the exclusive property of the very pacifists who routinely stand accused of intellectual impairment, whereas the war propagandists embedded in the school system are recast as malign bewitchers of the nation's youth:

---

204 Alfred Hermann Fried, 'Der Fall Nicolai in seiner internationalen Bedeutung', *Die Weltbühne*, 16.1 (1920), 389–92 (p. 391).
205 Fried, 'Der Fall Nicolai', p. 390.
206 Alfred Hermann Fried, 'Weihnachtspazifismus', *Die Weltbühne*, 15.2 (1919), 781–84 (p. 783).

> Die Macht- und Gewaltpsychose, die der Kriegerstaat erzeugte, durch die allein er leben konnte, umnebelten den als Rekrutenmaterial vorgemerkten Bürger von dem Augenblick an, wo er seine Umwelt mit tastenden Händen und naiven Augen wahrzunehmen begann. Schon in der Kinderstube baute die Kaserne vor und in der Schule hatte sie ihre wichtigen Vorposten aufgestellt.[207]

The idea that militaristic ideology had infiltrated pre-war educational establishments and clouded the minds of impressionable schoolchildren was axiomatic for *Die Weltbühne*, with Walter Mehring reflecting almost two years later: 'Der Militarismus nahm seinen Leuten das Denken ab, begleitete sie vom Schuleintritt bis zur Altersgrenze des Landsturms'.[208] According to this reading, the probability of conflict escalating into total war had been withheld from a generation that might have been saved annihilation by exposure to the unsentimental insights of the pacifist movement. It is against the backdrop of the First World War that Fried ends 'Weihnachtspazifismus' with a warning that could serve as the slogan for pragmatic pacifism. Appealing to the hindsight of his readers, he urges: 'Pazifismus ist Realpolitik geworden, das Brot des Zeitalters'.[209]

This identification of pacifism with infallible reason was the central plank in the strategy of the journal to destigmatize the peace movement. In 1921 former army captain Willy Meyer argued in an article entitled 'Berufssoldat und Pazifismus' that multilateral disarmament would be a triumph of common sense over emotional confusion:

> Es gibt eine erstaunliche Anzahl Menschen, die in angesehenen Stellungen und einflußreichen Aemtern sitzen und immer noch nicht wissen, daß der Pazifismus im Grunde nichts andres als die heutige Völkerbundsbewegung ist, die anstelle der zwischenstaatlichen Anarchie den bindenden Vertrag, die Institution des Rechts setzen will. [...] Aber zur Durchführung der weltumspannenden Organisationsaufgabe brauchen wir keine Engel, sondern nur Menschen mit klaren Köpfen und mit Herzen, die auf der richtigen Stelle sitzen.[210]

Meyer's characterization of pacifism as a pragmatic policy objective supported by a robust legal framework, as opposed to the unattainable dream of an eccentric minority, is typical of many articles published in *Die Weltbühne* in the immediate aftermath of the war that sought to portray mutually assured

---

207 Fried, 'Weihnachtspazifismus', p. 782.
208 Mehring, 'Die welsche Grenze', p. 306.
209 Fried, 'Weihnachtspazifismus', p. 784.
210 Willy Meyer, 'Berufssoldat und Pazifismus', *Die Weltbühne*, 17.1 (1921), 271–73 (p. 272).

peace not only as a realistic prospect, but also as the only viable aspiration in a modern world of economically interdependent and heavily armed states.[211] The pacifist cause, for which the League of Nations often served these authors as a synonym, was thereby depicted as the proper preserve of ordinary rational thinkers and not of an earth-bound host of angels with a preternatural gift for human kindness.

Over eleven years later, however, the struggle to liberate pacifism from popular associations with unbalanced ideological zeal had evidently not yet been won. This is exemplified in the journal's account of the trial for defamation to which its editor, Carl von Ossietzky, was subjected in 1932 for publishing Kurt Tucholsky's famous statement 'Soldaten sind Mörder' the previous year.[212] The defence mounted by the journalist and lawyer Rudolf Olden had apparently emphasized his client's commitment to the unvarnished truth over any particular pacifist animus: 'Er zeigte, daß es hier gar nicht um Pazifismus gehe sondern um das Recht, richtig zu denken und logisch zu sprechen.'[213] Even allowing for their understandable wish to amplify the justification for Ossietzky's acquittal, which centred on the objective fact that numerous writers throughout history had equated soldiers with murderers without being prosecuted for it, it is striking that the anonymous author of this report should decline the opportunity to defend Ossietzky's case on purely pacifist grounds, instead underlining the unimpeachable cogency on which it was supposedly predicated.

In the last ever issue of *Die Weltbühne* to appear on German soil, published on 7 March 1933, Kurt Hiller made one last unavailing attempt to prove the rational basis for pacifist foreign policy. In 'Heroismus und Pazifismus', which Horst H. W. Müller claims was 'doubtless' the reason for the Nazis' ban on *Die Weltbühne* that same day,[214] Hiller pleads for the substitution of armed diplomacy by an impartial system of supra-national arbitration. His desire to see this architecture of conflict resolution enshrined in law leads him to compare the involvement of international courts in inter-state disputes to the well-established use of civil law suits to settle disagreements between individual citizens:

---

211 Lothar Persius, 'Die Kriegsschuld der Rechtssozialisten', *Die Weltbühne*, 15.2 (1919), 789–92; Ströbel, 'Tollhäuslerei und Erzbergerei'; Heinrich Ströbel, 'Spaa', *Die Weltbühne*, 16.2 (1920), 33–36.
212 [Anon.], 'Ein guter Tag für die Justiz', *Die Weltbühne*, 28.2 (1932), 5–8. For Tucholsky's statement see Wrobel, 'Der bewachte Kriegsschauplatz', p. 192.
213 [Anon.], 'Ein guter Tag für die Justiz', p. 8.
214 Horst H. W. Müller, *Kurt Hiller*, Hamburger Bibliographien, 6 (Hamburg: Christians, 1969), p. 87.

> Längst gilt für die Einzelgeschöpfe im Staate, daß sie ihren Streit nicht gewaltsam austragen dürfen, nicht durch Kampf auf Leben und Tod, wie die Bestien; ihre Pflicht ist, sich an eine übergeordnete, ihrerseits mit der Pflicht zur Objektivität und zu gerechtem Urteil ausgestattete Instanz zu wenden, deren Entscheidung sie sich in ihrem wohlverstandenen eignen Interesse zu beugen haben: an das Gericht.[215]

If the alternative were a bestial fight to the death, Hiller suggests, few countries would deny the ultimate wisdom of recourse to a neutral arbiter. His image of a brawl between two individuals as an analogy for disagreement between nations is strikingly similar to that conjured over a decade earlier by the pacifist philosopher Friedrich Wilhelm Foerster in his treatise on political ethics:

> Ganz gewiß gibt es eine Altersstufe, auf der das Raufen physisches Bedürfnis ist, auch steckt in Knabenprügeleien oft viel verborgene Ethik – aber doch wohl eine Ethik, die dringend der allmählichen Veredelung und Läuterung und der wachsenden Anpassung an die immer schwierigeren Aufgaben eines hochentwickelten Gemeinschaftslebens bedarf.[216]

In the hands of Hiller and Foerster respectively, the inadmissibility of violence emerges as a fundamental tenet of civil society whose legitimacy in a complex world of competing interests has long been deemed beyond question. Their wish is for this pacifist principle to be transplanted into an international sphere in which national claim and counter-claim are destined repeatedly to collide, necessitating a bloodless means of mediation.

Hiller's legalistic interpretation of international relations crystallizes into an image that evokes classical representations of Lady Justice:

> Was in unsrer nationalen Erziehung fehlt, das ist die Wage [sic], die riesige Wage, inmitten allen Volkes errichtet, auf der die nationalen Werte gegeneinander abgewogen werden. Sie fehlt, weil, von Afterphilosophen genährt, das herrscht, was Immanuel Kant genannt hat: 'Misologie, das heißt Haß der Vernunft'.[217]

Hiller thus applies to international relations Kant's observation in the *Grundlegung zur Metaphysik der Sitten* that the quest for egotistical happiness through the implementation of reason leads to 'ein[em] gewisse[n] Grad von *Misologie*, d.i. Haß der Vernunft' when an individual realizes the scale

---

215 Kurt Hiller, 'Heroismus und Pazifismus', *Die Weltbühne*, 29.1 (1933), 349–55 (p. 350).
216 Foerster, *Politische Ethik und Politische Pädagogik*, p. 463.
217 Hiller, 'Heroismus und Pazifismus', p. 352.

of the social responsibilities that their relative happiness compels them to discharge.[218] This manipulation of Kantian thought, coupled with a passing swipe at the pseudo-philosophy of his revanchist adversaries, serves to portray militarized aggression as a breakdown in wisdom and pacifism as the only logically tenable attitude in a constellation of modern states among which contention is inevitable. Hiller's last word in *Die Weltbühne* is, therefore, to suggest that the traditional equation of pacifism with mental instability has been inverted by the course of history.

Passionate Pacifism

Weltbühne columnists did not by any means content themselves with mounting rational arguments for pacifism. In order to alter the public perception of pacifism summed up by Erich Dombrowski at the beginning of the previous section, they knew it would not be enough to correct the prevailing view that they were fantasists: they would also have to allay suspicions of treasonous intent. In 1925 Kurt Tucholsky lamented the absence of memorials to pacifist martyrs, contrasting this shortfall with the abundance of poignant statues in honour of the war dead. On a visit to the site of a massacre carried out during the French revolutionary Terror, Tucholsky is moved to reflect upon the ominous politicization of war memorials:

> Racheschwurhände erheben sich aus deutschem Marmor, Fackeln lodern, steinerne Handgranate werden abgezogen ... Hic ceciderunt?
> Hätten wir Pazifisten Märtyrer unsrer Sache so aufgebahrt, mit einem so niemals verlöschenden Gedächtnis, mit einer solchen Stärke unnachgiebiger und nie verzehrender Kraft, Grausen aufbewahrend, Mordtaten für die Jahrzehnte stempelnd, sinnliche Eindrücke mit der Moral so geschickt vermischend wie die katholische Kirche, die eine ungeheure sittliche Kraft sein könnte, befolgte sie ihre Evangelien –: es sähe anders um unsre Sache aus.[219]

By tweaking the traditional epitaph 'Hier sind sie gefallen' into a question, Tucholsky appears to insinuate that the covert role of war memorials is to stir the dead soldiers' descendants to avenge their ancestors. It is possible, though, that the ghosts whom Tucholsky seems to imagine rising balefully from their graves to incite their successors are, in fact, pacifists inspired by righteous

---

218 Immanuel Kant, *Groundwork of the Metaphysics of Morals: A German-English Edition*, ed. and trans. by Mary Gregor and Jens Timmermann, Cambridge Texts in the History of Philosophy (Cambridge: Cambridge University Press, 2011), p. 18.
219 Ignaz Wrobel, 'Märtyrer', *Die Weltbühne*, 21.2 (1925), 325–28.

indignation to haunt the architects of modern wars. Be that as it may, the alternative type of statuary Tucholsky has in mind in the next paragraph is clearly intended to combine the celebratory quality of a *Denkmal* with the admonitory sobriety of a *Mahnmal*. The individual glorification inherent in the notion of martyrdom is to be complemented by reproachful inscriptions on behalf of the unredeemed pacifist cause. The vindicating *Denkmäler* for which Alfred Fried had longed in his rehabilitation of Friedrich Nicolai are thus reconfigured here as a prerequisite for the triumph of the pacifist cause.

The anti-war movement is called upon to grasp the importance of self-promotion. The following year Tucholsky baldly details the lengths to which he had gone to avoid active combat during the First World War in an article entitled 'Wo waren Sie im Kriege, Herr –?'.[220] In answer to the recurring question about their war record, Tucholsky writes, 'drehen sich [viele Pazifisten]. Sie winden sich. Sie reden sich aus. Sie wollen ihren ethischen Standpunkt nicht verlassen, wollen aber auch nicht zugeben, feige gewesen zu sein'.[221] For Tucholsky this diffidence derives from a misplaced sense of guilt towards one's country. Instead of allowing nationalists to dictate whether they could consider themselves loyal Germans, pacifists, he insists, should challenge the former's right to define the national interest:

> Und das ist die einzige Antwort, die an die Sachwalter des falschen Kollektivwahns zu erteilen ist:
>
> Ihr interessiert uns nicht. Wir erkennen die Pflichten nicht an, die Ihr uns auflegt – möglich, daß es Gebote gibt, die unser Blut und das unsrer Kinder fordern: der Patriotismus, der Kampf für diesen Staat gehören nicht dazu. Wenn sich der Russe in die Rote Armee einreihen läßt, so kämpft er für seine Idee – Ihr wirtschaftet für die Ideenlosigkeit, für ein Vaterland, das es nicht mehr gibt.[222]

As in the earlier article, Tucholsky stresses the need for pacifists to go on the offensive in order to defend their convictions and, by extension, their patriotic credentials. Patriotism itself, which he disavows, is seemingly inseparable in his mind from support for the flawed Weimar state in its present form and the imperial regime that had preceded it. However, by speculating about a religiously charged national cause for which it would, in fact, be worth spilling the blood 'unserer Kinder', Tucholsky leaves tantalizingly open the possibility of patriotic identification with the German nation. Insofar as it does not rule out taking up arms if the cause is right, Tucholsky's pacifism can arguably

---

220 Ignaz Wrobel, 'Wo waren Sie im Kriege, Herr –?', *Die Weltbühne*, 22.1 (1926), 489–92.
221 Wrobel, 'Wo waren Sie im Kriege, Herr –?', p. 490.
222 Wrobel, 'Wo waren Sie im Kriege, Herr –?', p. 490.

be classified as belonging to the variety defined by Martin Ceadel in the introduction to this section, but his sympathy for the soldiers of the Russian Red Army implies that self-sacrifice on the battlefield should not be considered the ultimate expression of patriotic dedication. Tucholsky already speaks on behalf of a German collective bound together by a common pacifist faith. Evidently, it is only the sanctification of violence, and not the notion of making a solemn commitment to one's national community, that is alien to him.

All the same, this passage indicates an apparent contradiction in its author's allegiances that warrants a brief explanation. Tucholsky never overcame his unease with the term 'patriotism', while continually professing his affection for Germany. This tension was inextricably linked to his fierce pacifism. In 1932 he offers a characteristic repudiation of patriotism in the name of a vaguely formulated pacifism.[223] The article, which bears the uncompromising title 'Krieg gleich Mord', recalls those by Dombrowski and Fried in that it is an intercession on behalf of a publicly ostracized individual pacifist. The object of Tucholsky's sympathy is Hein Herbers, who edited the feuilleton pages of the pacifist weekly *Das Andere Deutschland* alongside his day job as a secondary-school teacher. The piece begins with a typically contemptuous dismissal of patriotic rhetoric that conflates all such language with the intemperate outbursts of the increasingly influential Nazi Party. According to Tucholsky, Herbers's public opposition to war is inimical to any profession of patriotic devotion:

> Das ist ein altes Rezept; es wird aber viel zu wenig befolgt. Im Gegenteil: wenn Hitler die blödsinnigsten patriotischen Parole ausgibt, dann verteidigen sie sich noch auf der andern Seite; statt ihn auszulachen, wollen sie sich an Patriotismus weder von ihm noch von einem andern übertreffen lassen. Grade darin aber siegt er – und mit Recht. Man lasse ihn mit seiner Staatenvergötzung allein, lache ihn aus und gehe zur Tagesordnung über.[224]

Six years after 'Wo waren Sie im Kriege, Herr -?', in which he likens accusing pacifists of insufficient patriotism to reproaching a vegetarian for the fact 'daß er auf einem Schlachtfest gekniffen habe',[225] Tucholsky reprises the notion that pacifists have no stake in patriotism. Even engaging in such debates is portrayed as beneath them.

However, the unspoken purpose of 'Krieg gleich Mord' is manifestly to defend the loyalty to his nation of Herbers, whose journalist activism had put his teaching career at risk. Crediting Herbers with acting out of 'einer

---

223 Peter Panter, 'Krieg gleich Mord', *Die Weltbühne*, 28.1 (1932), 588–90.
224 Panter, 'Krieg gleich Mord', p. 588.
225 Wrobel, 'Wo waren Sie im Kriege, Herr -?', p. 489.

heißen Liebe zu Deutschland',[226] Tucholsky declares his solidarity with the outspoken teacher against the restless school authorities in terms that undermine the monopolization of patriotism by apologists for war: 'Weder eine Schulbehörde noch sonst eine Behörde hat das Recht, für Deutschland zu sprechen. Deutschland sind auch wir. Wems nicht paßt, der sehe nicht hin'.[227] This passage, with its echoes of the same author's defiant line in his essay 'Heimat' (1929), can be read as a rallying cry to his fellow pacifists to carve out membership in a German national community that is more capacious than their bellicose compatriots would readily concede. Similarly, in 'Heimat' Tucholsky had distanced himself from the then German state while refusing to relinquish his claim on either the German *Heimat* or the nation to which it belonged. Indeed, resisting conservative efforts to 'lease' the entire country in the name of nationalism, Tucholsky even reminds readers: 'Wir sind auch noch da'.[228] In light of these almost interchangeable statements, Tucholsky's well-documented aversion to patriotism should not be taken at face value, as certain critics mentioned in the introduction to this chapter have done, nor should the lack of a less ideologically freighted term to describe his complex feelings for Germany be taken as proof that they did not exist. Tucholsky believed that, by actively making a virtue out of their pacifist principles, left-wing Germans had it in their power to make visible a patriotic movement that celebrated a different kind of national service.

As demonstrated in the first half of this section, such individual tributes as Tucholsky pays to Herbers were a tried-and-tested formula for rendering the pacifist cause sympathetic in the pages of *Die Weltbühne*. Indeed, the aforementioned 'Ein guter Tag für Justiz', published in the same year as 'Krieg gleich Mord', deploys an unusual amount of pathos to describe Carl von Ossietzky's performance in the courthouse. Ossietzky, who was already serving time for treason after publishing Walter Kreiser's revelations about the Russian manœuvres of the *Schwarze Reichswehr*, had knowingly risked the extension of his jail term by protesting his innocence instead of pleading guilty. That he had done so in defiance of the military establishment only enhances his dignity in the eyes of his observer:

> So wenig wir Personenkultus treiben wollen, so sei doch konstatiert, daß die Widerstandskraft, die er zeigt, vorbildlich ist. Bismarck hat beklagt, wir hätten zu wenig Zivilcourage. Was Ossietzky leistet, geht längst darüber hinaus, es ist nicht mehr Zivilcourage, nicht Zivilmut, es ist Ziviltapferkeit.[229]

226 Panter, 'Krieg gleich Mord', p. 589.
227 Panter, 'Krieg gleich Mord', p. 590.
228 Tucholsky, 'Heimat', p. 230.
229 [Anon.], 'Ein guter Tag für die Justiz', pp. 6–7.

For all his professed aversion to hero worship, this writer elevates Ossietzky to the status of a remote, indomitable icon. His history of authorizing anti-war publications may make him a figurehead for the universal pacifist cause, but the mention of Bismarck anchors the editor's convictions in a reliably German context. If Ossietzky's unbowed bearing does not resonate with his nationalist opponents, *Die Weltbühne* suggests, the fault does not lie with his lack of national feeling but with his critics' inability to recognize heroism in any form other than physical courage: 'Wenn einer so steht, unbewegt, unbesorgt um sich – denkwürdig, daß die Anhänger des Vulgärheroismus gar keine Anerkennung dafür empfinden'.[230]

Nor were the journal's pacifist writers above self-mythologizing. In 1925 Hellmut von Gerlach, the author of 127 articles for *Die Weltbühne*, answered the charge of inertia levelled at him and his colleagues by pacifist sympathizers. Casting his mind back to the imperial government's relentless legal campaign against pacifists during the First World War, Gerlach paints a picture of a beleaguered minority of German pacifists straining valiantly against oppression by an all-powerful state: 'Uns Pazifisten ist manchmal von befreundeter Seite vorgeworfen worden, wir hätten während des Krieges zu wenig getan. Mir scheint, wir haben unter Übernahme nicht ganz unerheblicher persönlicher Risiken getan, was wir tun konnten, ohne illegal zu werden'.[231] These reflections on the difficulty of working under an imperial regime intent on criminalizing pacifist organizations such as the *Deutsche Friedensgesellschaft*, the *Bund Neues Vaterland* or the *Zentralstelle Völkerrecht* create the impression of a group of insurgents under siege.

Gerlach, who co-founded the last of these organizations alongside Ludwig Quidde, clearly regards such tireless peace work as the definition of patriotism. In the last line he revives a familiar metaphor to describe the embattled pacifists' efforts to rescue Germany from militarist forces: 'Die Herren Militärs gestatteten keinem Deutschen, den von ihnen in den Abgrund kutschierten Karren aufzuhalten'.[232] With this choice of words Gerlach embellishes Richard Witting's warning in the aforementioned 'Die Schuld am Kriege' that paranoia about the intentions of the erstwhile Allied powers threatened 'unser armes Volk in den Abgrund zu schleudern'.[233] The image of a warlike Germany tumbling into an abyss without the judicious intervention of its pacifists also echoes the words of the lawyer Richard Grelling, whose exclusion from the government-appointed committee

---

230 [Anon.], 'Ein guter Tag für die Justiz', p. 7.
231 Hellmut von Gerlach, 'Erinnerungen an die Große Zeit. Die geschundenen Pazifisten', *Die Weltbühne*, 21.2 (1925), xvii, 901–06 (p. 905).
232 Gerlach, 'Erinnerungen an die Große Zeit', p. 906.
233 Metzler [Witting], 'Die Schuld am Kriege', p. 163.

for establishing responsibility for the war had made him a *cause célèbre* and led to the publication of an article in his defence by the journal's then leader-writer Heinrich Ströbel in early 1920.²³⁴ At the time of Ströbel's piece Grelling had already written an open letter to *Die Weltbühne* condemning his exclusion from the panel.²³⁵ In the epilogue to his exhaustive dossier *J'accuse* (1915), in which he had found Germany guilty of causing the First World War, Grelling had sought to pre-empt the insinuations of treachery which he believed publication of the book would prompt by portraying his work as a despairing attempt to save his country from itself.²³⁶ Ströbel quotes him thus: 'Ein treuer Sohn Germanias, sah' ich die geblendete Mutter dem Abgrunde zutaumeln und springe hinzu, sie vor dem tödlichen Sturz zu bewahren'.²³⁷ Ströbel even prefaces this citation with a tribute to Grelling's anti-war stance that reunites pragmatism and passion, the twin themes of this section, by emphasizing the link between the lawyer's clarity of vision and his patriotic devotion: 'Grellings Kampf gegen den deutschen Militarismus, gegen die Kriegslüge und den deutschen Siegeswahnsinn war darum die verdienstvollste Tat eines wirklichen, eines sehenden Patrioten'.²³⁸

The salient characteristic of the pacifist in *Die Weltbühne* is, in fact, his readiness to put his country before himself, a trait ascribed by the journal to most of the individuals who appear in this section. In 'Heroismus und Pazifismus' Kurt Hiller ascribes a higher order of heroism to those prepared to risk censure for their pacifist convictions than to those who die in battle. Casting the choice between warmongering and resistance as a choice between the pursuit of private gratification and selfless labour on behalf of an authentic national interest, Hiller ridicules the idea that the act of waging war could ever be synonymous with protecting the national honour. In reference

---

234 Heinrich Ströbel, 'Die Untersuchungsposse', *Die Weltbühne*, 16.1 (1920), 33–37.
235 Richard Grelling, 'Brief an den Herausgeber', *Die Weltbühne*, 15.2 (1919), 754.
236 Grelling's choice of title deliberately evokes Émile Zola's open letter of the same name, published in the Parisian newspaper *L'Aurore* on 13 January 1898, in which the novelist had accused the French government of anti-Semitism in its conviction of army officer Captain Alfred Dreyfus on charges of espionage four years earlier. Dreyfus, who was banished to the penal colony on Devil's Island off French Guyana, was eventually exonerated in 1906; the case would go down in history as an egregious miscarriage of justice. Grelling therefore seeks to portray Germany's refusal to admit responsibility for the outbreak of the First World War as a gross misrepresentation of the evidence.
237 Richard Grelling, *J'accuse*, in Ströbel, 'Die Untersuchungsposse', p. 34. The original quotation actually reads: 'Ein treuer Sohn Germania's seh' ich die geblendete Mutter dem Abgrunde zutaumeln und springe hinzu, sie vor dem tötlichen Sturz zu bewahren' (Richard Grelling, *J'accuse! von einem Deutschen*, 2nd edn (Lausanne: Payot, 1919 [1915]), p. 308). Ströbel has inadvertently substituted the praeterite ('sah') for Grelling's present-tense form ('seh').
238 Ströbel, 'Die Untersuchungsposse', p. 34.

to US president Herbert Hoover's announcement the previous year that the average annual global expenditure on arms was seventy per cent higher than before the war, he demands:

> Wem dient das; wofür diese phantastischen Ausgaben? Für den Schutz von Menschen? Wer wagt, so zu lügen? – Für die Interessen der Rüstungsindustrie! Für die Habsucht von Petroleumgroßaktionären! Für den Ehrgeiz skrupelloser politischer Romantiker! Für den geheimen Sexualkitzel von Quallüstlingen, die zu verlogen und feige sind, ihren Trieb direkt aber privat und an Einverstandenen abzureagieren! Für die sogenannte Ehre der Nation!
> Ich sage: die sogenannte. Denn ich leugne weder Ehre noch Nation. Freilich, die echte Ehre der Nation fordert andres als den Mord. Sie fordert Solidarität im Erfüllen der ewigen Aufgabe des schöpferischen Geistes. Sie fordert Humanität.[239]

Hiller unleashes the full force of his indignation in this passage, exposing the hypocrisy of those war profiteers who conceal their pursuit of personal gain and pleasure beneath patriotic platitudes. This he regards as an offence against national honour. Recalling Carl Mertens's description of far-right paramilitaries as 'perverse Schweine', Hiller compares the effect of war on its sponsors to the sexual frisson experienced by voyeuristic fetishists.[240] The secret ecstasies of Hiller's 'Quallüstlingen', by whom he presumably means sadistic military leaders, even revive Otto Flake's image of closet militarists in the Weimar era fashioning metaphorical shrines to the imperial regime while feigning commitment to republicanism.[241] The effect of shining a light on the thinly-veiled egotism of the nationalist Right is to cast the patriotic integrity of the pacifist lobby into even sharper relief.

Hiller was far from the first *Weltbühne* writer, then, to portray the military as a bestial institution. Indeed, in his aforementioned response to Walter Rathenau's assassination Otto Flake had warned that 'die Bestie Militarismus' had not been brought to heel, before urging: 'Bestien muss man totschlagen'.[242] Later in the same year Tucholsky apprehensively imagined a nationalist coup d'état in which extremist 'Hunde' would symbolically ignite the Weimar flag.[243] Where Hiller was highly unusual among *Weltbühne* columnists, however, was in his uninhibited approach to words and registers

---

239 Hiller, 'Heroismus und Pazifismus', p. 352.
240 [Mertens], 'Die vaterländischen Verbände', p. 244.
241 Flake, 'Deutsche Reden', iv, p. 437.
242 Flake, 'Deutsche Reden', viii, p. 3.
243 Kurt Tucholsky, 'Was wäre, wenn…?', *Die Weltbühne*, 18.1 (1922), 615–20 (p. 615).

conventionally associated with right-wing nationalism. Thus he feels no compunction either about coming to the defence of Germany's 'national honour', as above, or about legitimizing the notion of treason.[244]

Nor did Hiller's conversance with traditional patriotic rhetoric manifest itself only in attacks on militant nationalists, but also in an affirmative desire to embrace his national inheritance:

> Die Nationen sind eine gegebene Tatsache und übrigens eine liebenswerte. Ähnlich wie die Tierarten; ähnlich wie die Blumen. Nation und Natur hängen nicht bloß sprachlich aufs innigste zusammen. Deshalb ist Frivolität gegenüber dem Nationalen eine Lästerung der Natur und, daß die Nationen verschwinden mögen, ein unfrommer Wunsch.[245]

What is merely implicit in this early passage becomes explicit in the penultimate paragraph of 'Heroismus und Pazifismus', as the holy sanctity of every sovereign nation reveals itself to be the guiding principle behind Kurt Hiller's patriotic pacifism: 'Die reine Idee des Völkerfriedens ist der reinen Idee der Nation nicht entgegengesetzt, sondern klingt mit ihr zusammen in herrlichster Harmonie. Kein furchtbarerer Schade für die Nation als der Krieg; kein nationaleres Handeln als: ihn verhüten und verhindern!'.[246] This plea for peace in the national interest expresses the same patriotically internationalist wish as that which impels 'Heimat', the essay in which Kurt Tucholsky's satirical anthology *Deutschland, Deutschland über alles* culminates. Here Tucholsky, whose conflicted attitude to patriotism has been considered at length in this section, finally offers a clear and unambiguous route out of the bind in which his vehemence had left him: 'Nein, Deutschland steht nicht über allem and ist nicht über allem – niemals. Aber *mit* allen soll es sein, unser Land'.[247]

*

This section illustrates the extent to which the pacifist cause increasingly became a compact vehicle for the articulation of a broader internationalist patriotism in the journal. By calling for a world without war, the *Weltbühne* columnists discussed here amply fulfilled the basic requirement for internationalism contained within the definition put forth by Glenda Sluga in the introduction to this chapter. Their justification for this stance was

244 Hiller, 'Heroismus und Pazifismus', p. 354.
245 Hiller, 'Heroismus und Pazifismus', p. 350.
246 Hiller, 'Heroismus und Pazifismus', p. 355
247 Tucholsky, 'Heimat', p. 230.

unabashedly patriotic, however, with two clear tendencies emerging in this assessment of the journal's pacifism. The first of these was a pragmatic recognition of the complex demands of the post-war era and of Germany's particular geo-political vulnerability, the dramatic ramifications of which are explored in still greater detail in the middle section of this chapter. The second is a gradual escalation in the language used by *Weltbühne* writers as they built on their understanding of the mortal peril in which Germany supposedly found itself to make the strength of the individual Weimar German's pacifist convictions the litmus test of their patriotic passion. In the pages of *Die Weltbühne*, then, German pacifism at this time was frequently patriotic, even if German patriotism outside its confines was only infrequently pacifist.

Conclusion

This chapter ranges widely across the inter-war period to reveal the unceasing desire of the *Weltbühne* to re-situate and consolidate the rightful place of the Weimar Republic in a radically changed post-war world without renouncing its keen and sometimes mystical interest in Germany's perceived historical destiny. The Germans were to discard the belligerent approach to international relations that had not only carried them into war in the first place but now threatened to unleash another one. In so doing, they would finally redeem their innate flair for peace-keeping and thereby achieve an unassailable position of moral supremacy over their European neighbours that would accomplish Germany's national *raison d'être* and bring a multilateral wave of disarmament in its wake.

The first section analyses serialized contributions by three different authors to explore the competing emotions inspired in the *Weltbühne* stable by Germany's most influential neighbour, France. This conflict is embodied in the person of Helene Keßler von Monbart, whereas Felix Stössinger's unreserved admiration for French democratic traditions and Otto Flake's wariness of France's superior force are symptomatic of less nuanced, but more widespread, views of the country that Stössinger, perhaps in spite of himself, twice calls Germany's 'Erzfreund'. The central part of the chapter pans out from the Franco-German relationship and travels both backwards and forwards in time from 1922 to explain the role of moral rhetoric in articulating the vision of the journal for Germany's future as a democratic republic. Although the writers discussed in the first section all make an appearance, these articles are chiefly concerned with outlining a bold new mission for Germany that would see it emerge from the shadow of France and galvanize the world to follow its own imagined ethical example. The final section concentrates on the pacifist cause, arguing that the internationalist patriotism on show in *Die Weltbühne* crystallizes in sustained efforts by stalwart contributors such as Kurt Hiller and Kurt Tucholsky to save future generations of Germans from slaughter on the battlefield. Forging a world without war out of the smouldering embers of 1918 is seen at one and the same time as a global humanitarian imperative and as an urgent pre-requisite for national self-preservation.

In summary, the internationalist patriotic discourse that courses through *Die Weltbühne* from the end of the First World War right up to the rise to power of the National Socialists repeatedly stresses the allied necessities of Germany's moral and material disarmament, both of which resonate in the lengthy discussions of France foregrounded in this chapter. Germany was to be the progenitor and prime beneficiary of a new age in which national prestige would be redefined according to the desire and ability of a country to foster international dialogue and understanding. Shepherding in this imminent European era of peace and prosperity was to be Germany's peculiar distinction.

CHAPTER 3

Socialist Patriotism

To many left-wing commentators in the *Weltbühne* stable patriotism served as a convenient umbrella term for the multitude of right-wing agendas they wished to discredit. However, this chapter seeks to show that, in spite of their protestations to the contrary, a considerable number of the journal's columnists exhibited a solicitous attitude towards their country that was no less patriotic for being avowedly anti-nationalist. As outlined in the introduction to this study, the sentiments expressed towards Germany in *Die Weltbühne* demand that the conventional understanding of patriotism as the glorification of the nation at the expense of others be widened to encompass the defence of one's country against one's domestic political adversaries. At issue in this internal struggle was the question of how best to pursue the German national interest, a matter in which most of the commentators in the journal claimed to have as great a stake as their right-wing opponents.

The role of Socialism in this mission was clear. In most, though not all, articles under investigation in this chapter, Socialism appears as the only viable guarantor of German democracy, which is in turn routinely portrayed as the only political system capable of saving Germany from self-destruction. The return to power of military or dynastic elites, or the outbreak of a violent civil war between armed adherents of irreconcilable political ideologies, was feared as a certain harbinger of the nation's ruin. In this context, Socialism was not advocated only for the immediate socio-economic benefits it was thought singularly capable of bringing. Indeed, with relatively few exceptions, the democratic transformation of Weimar Germany into a genuinely Socialist society was promoted as the single means of saving the country from ostracism beyond its borders and fragmentation within them.

This shared belief in the salutary power of Socialism did not preclude friction between its proponents. Socialism, as the previous chapter shows to be true of internationalism, defies any attempt at straightforward definition. Contributions to *Die Weltbühne* in the inter-war period encompassed almost the whole gamut of left-wing political thought in circulation, while largely retaining a cool distance from the mantras of violent revolution issuing from Communist quarters in both the press and wider society. These strains could certainly be heard, however, and it would be disingenuous to examine the contribution of the journal to the emergence of a left-wing patriotic narrative without acknowledging that pleas for democratic social reform were, especially in the immediate aftermath of the Kaiser abdicating, sometimes forced to compete with equally vociferous demands for the forcible overthrow of the democratic Republic. A third way consisted in the marriage of revolutionary ideas with a republican *Staatsform*.

Insofar as its output can be assigned a political orientation, *Die Weltbühne* increasingly sought to carve out a niche for itself between the gradualist reform agenda of the Sozialdemokratische Partei (SPD) and the anti-democratic revolutionary rhetoric of the Kommunistische Partei (KPD) by articulating a broad-based national interest unencumbered by party dogma. While many authors positioned themselves in relation to one or other of these supposedly polarized institutions, it would, therefore, be too simplistic to reduce this chapter to a straightforward comparison of the approach to German patriotism of the KPD with that of the SPD. Instead, many of the articles under discussion freely borrow rhetoric from one party and basic principles from another, without fully subscribing to any single agenda. In these cases, their authors' sense of national belonging supersedes any sense of party-political loyalty.

The diversity of left-wing opinion accommodated by *Die Weltbühne* is underlined by Weimar-era contributor Axel Eggebrecht, who recalls: 'Es konnte durchaus folgendes geschehen. Im gleichen Heft wie der polemische Beitrag eines Nicht-Marxisten war der Aufsatz eines Kommunisten zu lesen'.[1] Scrutiny of *Die Weltbühne* thus exposes deep and multifarious fractures on the left flank of German politics during the Weimar years. Key to the present investigation is the fact that these disputes, in spite of their often doctrinal appearance, were not necessarily parochial in nature. Though the question of how much patriotic loyalty a Socialist owed to Germany's fledgling democracy was far from the only one to exercise leftist factions, it infiltrated numerous other debates, lending them an urgency that enabled what might otherwise have been relegated to the status of internecine squabbles to transcend their sectarian origins and, in theory at least, command the attention of a wider audience. Frequently Socialist contributors claimed a special interest in their compatriots' well-being and strove to present their ideology as inherently German.

This chapter, first, analyses a selection of articles that promote a range of revolutionary solutions to Germany's perceived ills before, second, examining a number of pieces advancing a more moderate understanding of Socialist

---

1   Axel Eggebrecht, *Das Drama der Republik* (Königstein/Taunus: Athenäum, 1979), p. 4.

patriotism. The first of these two sections, which is itself divided into two parts, concentrates predominantly on the years immediately following the First World War. This focus reflects the greater currency in the post-war period of revolutionary rhetoric, which declined in value as the middle of the decade approached and the prospect of extremist forces seizing the reins of political power in Germany came to seem ever more remote. The second section takes a failed right-wing revolt, the Kapp Putsch of 1920,[2] as its point of departure and follows the journal's turn away from political radicalism over the course of the first half of the ensuing decade, exploring the reaction of the journal to a string of incidents of civil unrest over the next few years. What does not change during this period of transition is the visibility in the pages of *Die Weltbühne* of the German national interest.

For a Socialist Revolution

The call for revolution, often to be heard in *Die Weltbühne* during the Weimar years, was not necessarily synonymous with support for the KPD, which had effectively been founded on 30 December 1918 in the course of the national conference of Rosa Luxemburg's Spartacus League.[3] Nor did it always imply hostility towards democracy, though the system of parliamentary representation itself was often regarded by the more radical of these commentators as a short-term means to a long-term end predicated on a version of direct democracy. Indeed, the dilemma of whether revolution or gradual reform was the best strategy for shielding Germany from being

---

2   This coup owes its name to the monarchist civil servant Wolfgang Kapp, who was even installed as head of state in its immediate aftermath, but it was made possible by the military force at the disposal of General Walther von Lüttwitz and the strategic advice of General Ludendorff. After a march on Berlin prompted by the impending dissolution of the Marine-Brigade Ehrhardt and various Freikorps regiments, the uprising succeeded in briefly deposing the democratically elected government, which promptly fled to Stuttgart. Among the triggers for the putsch was the drastic reduction in size of the German army imposed by the Treaty of Versailles.
3   Eric D. Weitz, *Creating German Communism, 1890–1990: From Popular Protests to Socialist State* (Princeton, NJ: Princeton University Press, 1997), p. 93. Taking its name from the rebel Roman slave, the *Spartakusgruppe* was launched as the 'Gruppe Internationale' on the 4 August 1914 by anti-war members of the SPD around Rosa Luxemburg, Clara Zetkin and Karl Liebknecht. Underpinned from the beginning by Marxist ideology, the faction adopted its revolutionary name in 1916 and substituted 'Bund' for 'Gruppe' during the November Revolution 1918, whereupon it also emerged from the shadow of the Unabhängige Sozialistische Partei Deutschlands and briefly operated as an independent movement seeking to overthrow the capitalist system and erect a 'dictatorship of the proletariat' in its place.

hijacked by right-wing forces drove a perennial debate in the pages of the journal that did little to dispel the ambiguity surrounding what revolution would actually mean. No matter whether *Weltbühne* writers were advocating for revolution or reform, however, they frequently sought to enhance the appeal of their particular Socialist modus operandi by presenting it as the only tenable patriotic choice for Germans of either a right- or a left-wing persuasion.

Indeed, the failure of the journal always to articulate the precise political implications of revolutionary rhetoric recedes behind the patriotic resonance with which it was often invested. Kurt Tucholsky, the most prolific contributor to the journal by a distance, frequently evoked revolution as a temperamental shift demanding the wholesale replacement of lingering reactionary beliefs and habits with progressive values and practices calculated to instil a collectivist republican ethos in future generations of Germans. His article 'Kapp-Lüttwitz', in which he calls for the de-Prussification of the army, the dismantling of military courts and the abolition of neighbourhood militias, culminates in the provocative wish that the right-wing Kapp Putsch might prompt republican politicians to transform the *Novemberrevolution* into a movement worthy of the name: 'Wir haben keine Revolution gehabt. Macht eine'.[4] One of the intangible changes in collective mentality which Tucholsky entrusts to the revolution is a reassessment of what had conventionally been considered the ultimate patriotic duty. The revolution, he argues, would entail 'Aufklärung darüber, daß der Offizier, genau wie jeder andre Staatsbürger, den Gesetzen unterworfen ist, daß Hochverräter nicht immer Ballonmützen und rote Schlipse tragen, und daß rohe Gewalt auch dann zu verachten ist, wenn sie sich militärisch kostümiert'.[5] Tucholsky's deployment of the legal concept of high treason against the self-appointed guardians of the national interest among the officer class reveals a concern for the German nation palpable in his subsequent appeal for avowedly nationalistic teachers to be driven out of the republican school system. The choice between cultivating or thwarting republican principles thereby becomes not simply a political decision but a matter of patriotic loyalty.

By the same token, the demand that the Weimar government discharge its duty of care to its citizens shifted much of the burden of patriotic loyalty from the destitute of Germany onto the government charged with their protection. One pre-condition for the espousal of wholehearted patriotism by those of a leftist disposition was the transformation of the Weimar Republic into a genuine welfare state. In his aforementioned report from

---

4 Ignaz Wrobel, 'Kapp-Lüttwitz', *Die Weltbühne*, 16.1 (1920), 357–63 (p. 363).
5 Wrobel, 'Kapp-Lüttwitz', p. 362.

the workers' colonies of the Ruhrgebiet in 1928, Erik Reger, an author of socially critical novels and intermittent contributor to the journal, submits the refrain from Hoffmann von Fallersleben's sentimental poem 'Mein Vaterland' – 'was ich bin und was ich habe | dank ich dir, mein Vaterland' – to a sarcastic re-working that draws attention to the insufficiency of Weimar state support: 'Das soziale Problem ist in diesem Lande durch Wohlfahrt gelöst. Wohlfahrt von der Wiege bis zum Grabe; was ich bin und was ich habe, dank ich dir, mein Vaterland'.[6] Reger's adaptation of the 'treue Liebe bis zum Grabe' pledged to his Fatherland by von Fallersleben's narrator amounts to a charge of hypocrisy against the welfare state whose promise of 'cradle to the grave' support for its citizens already rings hollow. The context for Reger's pastiche is the unsubtle pressure exerted by intrusive industrial employers on their resident workers to procreate while paying them less than a subsistence wage. Whereas Tucholsky and others sought to protect German schoolchildren against nationalist indoctrination, the nation's young are depicted here as literally dying of paternal neglect. Until this changed, the working class and its sympathizers could hardly be expected to celebrate the status quo.

Over a decade before revolution brought the imperial edifice toppling to earth, Clara Zetkin had sketched the contours of a progressive patriotism with which Leftists could identify. In a piece published in 1907 in *Die Gleichheit*, the SPD-run journal she edited between 1891 and her break with the party in 1917, Zetkin firmly distances such patriotic commitment from that extolled by those classes who profited by the *Kaiserreich*. Entitled 'Unser Patriotismus', the article mobilizes a bullish Socialist subversiveness against the staid and self-serving patriotism of the upper classes. Zetkin describes proletarian revolt as an intrinsically patriotic cause aiming at the liberation of the Fatherland:

> Der Patriotismus der Bourgeoisie und der Aristokratie ist reaktionär .... [...] Der Patriotismus des Proletariats ist dagegen revolutionär. Er will nicht erhalten, er muß umwälzen. Seine Aufgabe ist es, die schädigenden und schändenden Bande der Klassenherrschaft zu sprengen, deren Gefangener das Vaterland ist. Jenseits der zerschmetterten bürgerlichen Ordnung winkt dem Proletariat das freie Vaterland.[7]

Read with the benefit of hindsight and alongside Wrobel's scepticism that a revolution worthy of the name had actually taken place, Zetkin's depiction

---

6   Reger, 'Ruhrprovinz', p. 921; August Heinrich Hoffmann von Fallersleben, 'Mein Vaterland', in *Unpolitische Lieder*, 2 vols (Hamburg: Hoffmann und Campe, 1840), I, 165.
7   Clara Zetkin, 'Unser Patriotismus', in *Die Gleichheit*, 27 May 1907, 1–2 (p. 2).

of the bourgeoisie and the nobility as the jailers of the Fatherland raises the spectre of an insidious class tyranny capable of surviving such technicalities as the transition to republican democracy. Certainly, it provides a prototype for the accusation, frequently levelled in the *Weltbühne* in the early years of the Republic, that the working classes were still being cheated of their rightful national inheritance.

In post-war Germany, however, the proletariat had ceased to be the sole focus of emancipatory Socialist rhetoric, with the writers of *Die Weltbühne* even exhibiting a tendency to include themselves and their fellow intellectuals in the masses of the disenfranchised. Zetkin herself, by this time a prominent Communist member of the Reichstag, eventually acknowledged the broader class basis of Socialist patriotism in a provocative speech to her fellow representatives. Claiming to speak on behalf of 'alle diejenigen, die mit der Arbeit ihrer Hand oder ihres Hirns das materielle und das kulturelle Erbe der Gesellschaft mehren, ohne dass sie fremde Arbeitskraft ausbeuten', she effectively turned the charge of treason on the arch-capitalists.[8] This interpretation of 'das schaffende Volk', a phrase encountered in Carl Mertens's 'Die vaterländischen Verbände' in the previous chapter, anchors left-wing publications such as *Die Weltbühne* firmly in a third estate, whose overwhelming numerical advantage stood in inverse proportion to its ability to influence and profit from transactions carried out in its name. For the journal, too, the removal of class privilege from German society was not only a Socialist imperative, but an opportunity to free the concept of patriotism itself from nationalist monopoly in open ideological combat.

Needless to say, this task sometimes proved to be a delicate tightrope walk. The case of Alphons Steiniger shows that, under the gradual influence of events, ideological absolutism could eventually prevail over patriotism. Steiniger, who had written his first article for *Die Weltbühne* in 1923 and eventually became political editor before ending his association with the journal in 1928, wrote a considerable number of leader articles over a two-year period from early 1924 onwards that sought to isolate the nationalist parties and expose their retrograde aims. In a flurry of early activity he elaborated his vision for a streamlined German party-political landscape inhabited exclusively by three blocs: the Monarchists, the pro-republican Democrats and the Communists, who were supposedly in favour of a state modelled on the Soviet workers' councils.[9] Steiniger's own sympathies were

---

8   Clara Zetkin, 'Gegen Poincaré und Cuno' (Rede im deutschen Reichstag, 312. Sitzung, 7. März 1923), in *Verhandlungen des Reichstags, 1. Wahlperiode 1920*, CCCLVIII (Berlin: Norddeutsche Buchdruckerei und Verlags-Anstalt, 1923), 9989–96 (p. 9992).
9   Alphons Steiniger, 'Parteien-Abbau!', *Die Weltbühne*, 20.1 (1924), 31–32 (p. 32).

reserved for the republican system at this time, though this is sometimes concealed by the unrestrained radicalism of his rhetoric.

The undercurrent of patriotic concern in his work is a constant. Thus, in one leader in 1924 he speculates about the possibility of defusing the latently violent stand-off between Germany's rival parties by appealing to an innocent sense of national belonging supposedly common to all. Writing a week after the dissolution of the Reichstag on 13 March of that year, he casts a wary eye forward to May's elections, which he feared would trigger a bloody civil war. For the sake of Germany's future he implores candidates not to incite violence against their opponents:

> Ich beschwöre um des Aufbaus willen, den Alle wünschen (Jeder in einem andern Zeichen, und ich bin tolerant genug, auch Hakenkreuz und Sowjetstern noch als deutsche Zeichen hinzunehmen), um der Steigerung deutscher Lebensfähigkeit willen beschwöre ich Alle, die nicht im extremsten Radikalismus dem Exlex-Zustand zusteuern, ihre persönlichen Reizbarkeiten zurückzustellen und einen Friedenspakt zu schließen, der diese Wahlen ohne Blutvergießen hingehen läßt. Ist so ganz unmöglich, eine Gemeinschaft der Anständigen, der Beherrschten, der im besten Sinne Nationalen aufzubringen?[10]

Steiniger is evidently all too aware that the term 'national', here nominalized as 'National', has become tainted by association with nationalism, but he demonstrates a momentary desire to rehabilitate it as a benignly progressive marker of identity. In the event, though, the cautious optimism that had led him to enfold Soviet Communism and the swastika-clad ultra-nationalist right into a temporary compact of the 'im besten Sinne Nationalen' did not survive the year.

By June Steiniger had become convinced that the minimum voting age of twenty-five that had prevailed during the *Kaiserreich* should be restored in order to protect Germany from the extremist inclinations of the newly enfranchised youth. In an access of magnanimity he suggests that the change be made only on a temporary basis, 'denn die Hoffnung bleibt, daß nach der Generation der Hitlerknaben und der kommunistischen Hundertschaftler ein Geschlecht ernsterer deutscher Männlichkeit heraufkommt, dem der Eintritt in die Staatsgemeinde nicht verweigert werden könnte'.[11] The muscular patriotism that Steiniger clearly craves from the German electorate, and on which he wishes to make entry into 'den deutschen Kampfplatz' contingent,

---

10 Alphons Steiniger, 'Wahlkampf ohne Bürgerkrieg', *Die Weltbühne*, 20.1 (1924), 355–56 (p. 356).
11 Alphons Steiniger, 'Die unmündigen Wähler', *Die Weltbühne*, 20.1 (1924), 871–73 (p. 873).

is no longer to be found at either end of the political spectrum.¹² In a further sign of his increasing ideological inflexibility, Steiniger became even more obdurate in his waxing hostility towards extremism in September. In the leader spot for its thirty-seventh issue of the year, *Die Weltbühne* published his open letter to the KPD. Styling himself a constructive critic of Communism, Steiniger accuses the party leaders of having only a tenuous grip on reality, scathingly describing Moscow as a city 'deren kulturelle, wirtschaftliche und geistige Beziehung zu Süd-, Nord- und Westdeutschland unerklärlich, zu Ostdeutschland mindestens fraglich ist'.¹³

Two years after this abrupt expulsion of the hard Left from the patriotic community, however, Steiniger performs a brazen about-turn.¹⁴ Writing almost exactly two years after his missive to the KPD, Steiniger acknowledges the Soviet Union as a surrogate parent on the grounds that Germany has never shown itself to be capable of taking care of its own:

> Wir aber, Roter Block oder Deutsche Linke oder sonstwie geheißen, wir Revolutionäre: Sozialisten aus der SPD, Unorganisierte, Kommunisten, linke Pazifisten und Kampfjugend – wir werden die andre Front bilden. Washington gegen Moskau – mag traurig sein, daß auf die Fahnen von 1848 die Sonne nicht mehr scheinen will, daß Deutschland, die Heimat, nie recht politischer Inhalt geworden ist. Mag alles schmerzlich und bitter sein! Wir aber hungern […]!¹⁵

This passage charts, in miniature, the gradual extinction of a moderate German nationalism born in the pro-democratic upheavals of 1848. Conversely, the article as a whole, in which Steiniger declares his unstinting allegiance to the revolutionary cause, records an unwelcome feeling of national homelessness which its author had long resisted in his journalism. A little over midway through the life span of the Republic the journal's political editor thus confirms the emotional disinheritance felt by many revolutionary Germans. His reluctant conclusion that national loyalty is an anachronism in an age supposedly defined by two competing doctrines reflects a patriotic disillusionment that sees no alternative but to prioritize the prosaic benefits of a universal political ideology over the emotional claim of one's national *Heimat*.

In the context of the wider *Weltbühne*, Steiniger's break with Germany is an anomaly that serves only to highlight the potential dangers inherent in

---

12 Steiniger, 'Die unmündigen Wähler', p. 873.
13 Alphons Steiniger, 'An die deutschen Kommunisten', *Die Weltbühne*, 20.2 (1924), 369–72 (p. 372).
14 Alphons Steiniger, 'Republikanische Union', *Die Weltbühne*, 22.2 (1926), 446–48.
15 Steiniger, 'Republikanische Union', p. 448.

pursuing uncompromisingly radical political solutions to what some would regard as their logical conclusion, divorced from any purpose other than their own implementation. His subordination of the national interest to the ideological imperative of the Communist International in the above passage does not reflect an anti-national turn in the broader editorial line. To the extent that his writing can be deemed representative of the enduring patriotic preoccupations of the journal, it is in the pronouncedly retrospective vein of its revolutionary rhetoric. As will now be seen, *Weltbühne* radicals were more likely to mobilize sentimentalism than visionary idealism in order to make the patriotic case for revolution.

Gazing into the Past or Staring into the Future?

For all its finality, Alphons Steiniger's crisis of patriotic conviction is instructive in its terms of expression. Although he did so forlornly, he was not alone in instinctively casting his gaze backwards into nineteenth-century German history in search of revolutionary inspiration. In the first issue of 1919 a poem by Kurt Tucholsky, alias Kaspar Hauser, appeared beneath the title 'Achtundvierzig'. Lamenting the rise of the belligerent *Kaiserreich* in the place of a democratic federal Germany, Tucholsky urges his compatriots to ensure that the defeat of the revolution seventy years ago not be in vain:

> Wofür, mein Gott, hat die Freiheit geblutet?
> Wofür wurden Männer und Mädchen geknutet?
> Spartacus! Deutsche! So öffnet die Augen!
> Sie warten, euch Blut aus den Augen zu saugen –
> Der Feind steht rechts![16]

Tucholsky's readiness to address the German populace *en masse* as Spartacus while warning them to heed the lessons of the past ties the revolutionary demands of the Weimar-era Germans to those of their forefathers. This claim of continuity between the two generations builds on the subtle message conveyed in the third stanza, which relates in the past tense the betrayal by the bourgeoisie of the Revolution of 1848 before switching almost imperceptibly into the present tense:

> Die Krone gleißte. Die Bürger krochen.
> Die treusten deutschen Herzen pochen
> im Proletariat.[17]

---

16 Kaspar Hauser, 'Achtundvierzig', *Die Weltbühne*, 15.1 (1919), 20.
17 Hauser, 'Achtundvierzig', p. 20.

Tucholsky's sleight of hand resides in his use of a verb, 'pochen', the third person plural present tense of which is an echo of the imperfect form of 'kriechen' in the same conjugation. The German working class as a historical entity are thus portrayed as having remained true to the original revolution until the present day.

In the same issue the leader-writer for the journal in the first two months of 1919, Ludwig Jurisch, endeavours to anchor the ongoing revolution in a lengthy German tradition of Socialist idealism stretching even further back than 1848. Jurisch's lodestar is Heinrich Heine, after whom, he asserts 'jede deutsche Stadt jetzt eine Straße nennen müßte'.[18] Writing in 1833, Heine had, in fact, presented the republican idea as a revolutionary aspiration, as opposed to the bourgeois construct that some Weimar-era observers perceived it to be.[19] In his first column Jurisch unequivocally announces his own radical intentions in an opening gambit that ends on the opening line from Heine's poem 'Doktrin' (1844), thus bridging the seventy-five year gap between the poet's contemporaries and his own:

> Der Artikel an dieser Stelle wird fortan allwöchentlich, wieder von ein und derselben Feder niedergeschrieben, politische Ereignisse zergliedern und revolutionäre Forderungen verfechten, kulturelle Angelegenheiten fördern und menschliche Dinge menschlich betrachten. Eine Feder taugt in stürmischen Zeiten nur als Ersatz für eine Flinte, und unmittelbarste Wirkung zu erwecken, ist auch der Sinn dieser Artikel. Schlage die Trommel und fürchte dich nicht![20]

The radicalism of this manifesto statement marks it out as a product of the immediately post-war *Weltbühne*, though the tendency to apostrophize the readership remained a feature throughout the Weimar period. Nor should Jurisch's modern variation on the adage of the pen and the sword be dismissed as mere cliché. In the next paragraph he iterates his intention 'die Revolution vorwärts[zu]treiben, mit Zuruf, wenn es ausreicht, *mit Ruten, wenn es nicht vom Fleck geht*, mit Skorpionen, wenn nichts andres verfängt',[21] before urging his fellow revolutionaries 'sich von der alten revolutionären Weisheit durchdringen [zu] lassen, daß, um Omelettes zu backen, Eier zerschlagen werden müssen'.[22] Jurisch's apparent desire for his figures of speech to be

---

18 Ludwig Jurisch, 'Ansage', *Die Weltbühne*, 15.1 (1919), 1–3 (p. 2).
19 Heinrich Heine, *Zur Geschichte der Religion und Philosophie in Deutschland* (Frankfurt a.M.: Insel, 1966), p. 200; 1st edn in *Der Salon*, 4 vols (Hamburg: Hoffmann und Campe, 1835), II, 1–284.
20 Jurisch, 'Ansage', p. 1.
21 Jurisch, 'Ansage', p. 1. Italics mine.
22 Jurisch, 'Ansage', p. 1.

interpreted literally is underlined by the relish with which he extends the metaphor: 'Und nach der langen, grauen Zeit der Rationierung: Jedem ein Ei! wollen wir jetzt wirklich ein goldgelbes, schmackhaftes, appetitlich duftendes Omelette, einen wahren Staatseierkuchen backen'.[23] The citation of this hackneyed truism about breaking eggs, which Jurisch acknowledges to be well-worn, confirms the debt owed by modern German revolutionaries to their oratorical and rhetorical progenitors in the radical tradition, among whom Heine clearly occupies prime position for Jurisch.

After quoting Heine a second time and at length, Jurisch concludes by finding revolutionary potential in Germany's pre-national history. To this extent he pre-empts the next two *Weltbühne* authors examined in this section, though in his version of events it is the resilience the masses have always demonstrated in defeat, as opposed to their courage in rising up against their oppressors, that proves their heroic credentials. Having conceded that the revolution could prove an arduous process, Jurisch nonetheless declares that his compatriots are uniquely qualified to finish the task:

> Aber das deutsche Volk, das die Zerrüttung des Dreißigjährigen Krieges, die Erniedrigung der napoleonischen Herrschaft, das Elend der Kleinstaaterei, ja, sogar siebenundvierzig Jahre die Lüge des bismärckischen Reichs ertragen hat, ohne moralisch zu Grunde zu gehn – dieses Volk ist unverwüstlich, und welches Chaos auch noch kommen mag: ein Kosmos wird ihm noch entsteigen. Darum Kopfhänger bei Seite, Schwarzseher aus dem Weg!
> Schlage die Trommel und fürchte dich nicht![24]

The repetition of Heine's exhortation to 'beat the drum' anchors Jurisch's piece firmly in a specifically German radical tradition, even if, in political terms, the homogenous German people whose fortitude Jurisch takes as inspiration for the successful prosecution of the revolutionary cause is self-evidently a figment of his imagination arising from an anachronistic reading of history. Not for the last time in the history of the journal, Jurisch constructs an exceptionalist national narrative upon tenuous historical foundations. Unlike proponents of right-wing nationalism, however, these articles foreground popular protest movements from history in the hope of generating enough momentum for Weimar Germany to fulfil its revolutionary destiny.

The evocation of momentous staging posts from Germany's revolutionary past also enabled *Weltbühne* writers to imbue their radical words with a reliably patriotic spirit, as well as undermining nationalist commentators' attempts

---

23 Jurisch, 'Ansage', p. 1.
24 Jurisch, 'Ansage', p. 3.

to write progressive movements out of the national story. In the fourth issue of 1921 the pacifist Otto Lehmann-Rußbüldt evokes a state of indignity apparently common to the bulk of the German population in an outpouring of patriotic defiance. Echoing Clara Zetkin's division of society into the exploiters and the exploited, he lambasts the 'angeblich schöpferischen, in Wahrheit aber schröpferischen' industrialists of the Ruhrgebiet before calling on Germany's near-inexhaustible army of producers to rise up in the name of their country:

> Grade, weil ich mich als Deutschen fühle, grade, weil ich das Deutschtum von je her als Mannestum und Unabhängigkeit verstanden habe – grade deshalb, sage ich, daß wir alle, die wir tätig sind als Bauern, Handwerker, Arbeiter jeder Art den Nebel des deutschnationalen Riesenschwindels von der Untertänigkeit des Bürgers zerhauen und uns endlich die Rechte nehmen müssen, derentwegen unsre Väter in die Freiheitskämpfe zogen, derentwegen sie 1848 kämpften, derentwegen sie glaubten, vor sechs Jahren den Kampf mit der ganzen Welt aufnehmen zu sollen.[25]

Lehmann-Rußbüldt's equation of Germanness with manly self-sufficiency applies pressure on any reader answering to the intentionally all-encompassing description 'Arbeiter jeder Art' to fight for his inalienable rights or be suspected of indifference to the patriotic cause. Through his almost theatrical repetition of 'derentwegen' he places the overcoming of nationalism in a long tradition of heroic armed uprisings beginning with the expulsion of Napoleon and taking in the failed democratic Revolution of 1848, as well as Germany's apparently misconceived entry into the First World War.

A clear line can be traced from Lehmann-Rußbüldt's pugilistic rallying cry 'den Nebel des deutschnationalen Riesenschwindels von der Untertänigkeit des Bürgers [zu] zerhauen' back to the uncompromising language of Clara Zetkin's 'Unser Patriotismus' fourteen years earlier. At the same time as highlighting the proletariat's sense of national displacement, Zetkin suggests that the intolerable fact of their oppression become the basis for a patriotic movement that would create a country with which the working classes could identify:

> Das Proletariat muß sich sein Vaterland erst erobern. Nicht im Kampfe gegen eine fremde Nationalität oder Rasse, die seine 'heiligsten Güter' bedroht, wohl aber im Kampfe gegen die besitzenden, ausbeutenden

---

25 Otto Lehmann-Rußbüldt, 'Die undeutsche Demokratie', *Die Weltbühne*, 17.1 (1921), 91–94 (p. 94).

und herrschenden Klassen, die ihm rauben, was das Geburtsland zum Vaterland macht.²⁶

It is hardly surprising that pre-war Socialist orators should have presented the proletariat as the victims of a capitalist conspiracy to defraud them of their birthright: a sense of kinship with the country of their birth. The fact that such forceful language was still deemed necessary after the revolution had come to pass, however, proves that regime-change had changed little in the minds of many republican commentators.

Ten years after Lehmann-Rußbüldt's broadside, and presumably under the influence of a fractious decade, Hanns-Erich Kaminski delivered the negative corollary to this flattering historiography. In an article entitled 'Der deutsche Sumpf' (1931) Kaminski adduces the sixteenth-century Peasants' Revolt,²⁷ the Revolution of 1848 and the exclusion of Austria from the North German Confederation (1866), among other flashpoints, as proof for his view of German history as a chain of compromise and festering discord.²⁸ In 1921, however, Lehmann-Rußbüldt chooses to emphasize and take heart from the emancipatory will that prompted these conflagrations. Although he subsequently describes his ancestral idols as 'Revolutionäre, in keinem Sinne aber Patrioten',²⁹ his declaration of affinity with purportedly German qualities suggests that his disapproval of patriotism is merely a semantic one.

Another iteration of this revisionist ploy would arrive in 1923, when Rudolf Geldern called on film-makers to shoot historical films about such events as the Early Modern peasants' revolts or 1848 in order to highlight 'jene andre deutsche Vergangenheit, die es gibt trotz der in Deutschland üblichen Geschichtsschreibung'.³⁰ The alternative history which Geldern sketches is a perennial struggle between revolutionary and reactionary forces; yet the genre of the historical film is, he observes, the exclusive preserve of nationalist narratives that glorify military conquest, uphold aristocratic privilege and elicit anti-Semitic outbursts in the auditorium. In this incendiary atmosphere the cinema can all too easily become a cell of monarchist resistance within the Weimar Republic: 'Es ersteht uns vor Augen

---

26 Zetkin, 'Unser Patriotismus', p. 75.
27 Starting in 1524 and continuing in fits and starts until its decisive quashing in 1526, the *Deutscher Bauernkrieg* was a geographically dispersed wave of armed uprisings against feudal oppression (including by the Catholic Church, a major landowner); it was also influenced by Protestant tenets and the writings of Martin Luther. It has been estimated that the violent unrest across Thuringia, Saxony, parts of Southern Germany, Alsace, the Tirol and Switzerland claimed between 70,000 and 75,000 lives on all sides.
28 Hanns-Erich Kaminski, 'Der deutsche Sumpf', *Die Weltbühne*, 27.2 (1931), 366–68.
29 Lehmann-Rußbüldt, 'Die undeutsche Demokratie', p. 92.
30 Rudolf Geldern, 'Der historische Film', *Die Weltbühne*, 19.2 (1923), 297–98 (p. 297).

unser heimliches Kaiserreich'.³¹ The article concludes with a wry citation of the 'Heckerlied' (1848),³² a student anthem dedicated to the exiled revolutionary Friedrich Hecker, whose 'dream of the German republic' survived his flight to North America in September 1848. Geldern's mischievous insinuation that the post-war German state will remain a republic in name only without a historically grounded revolutionary counter-narrative suggests that he considers 'the German republic' to be the glorious culmination of this neglected revolutionary history. Weimar is evidently no more than a step in the right direction.

Alongside these nostalgic exhortations to revolution *Die Weltbühne* also played host to pleas for German Socialism to start afresh. In an article published in early 1919 Franz Varssovius focusses on a different medium from that later addressed by Rudolf Geldern: song.³³ The challenge of implanting the revolution into a popular consciousness still in thrall to delusions of imperial grandeur is the same in both articles. Each acknowledges the obstinate appeal of nationalist narratives, with Varssovius even conceding some anthems are 'schön und bewundernswert, und es ist in ihnen der besiegte und leblose Geist jener Geistlosigkeiten so eingeschlossen wie das zweitausend Jahre alte, seit unendlich langer Zeit krepierte Insekt in einem edlen Stück Bernstein'.³⁴ For his part, Geldern emphasizes 'den entscheidenden Wert des Imponderabile. Stärker denn alles Andre wurzelt im Volk die Legende'.³⁵ The difference between the two resides in their fundamental attitude to the past. Whereas Geldern urges producers to refresh the Germans' memory of various revolutionary episodes in the nation's history, Varssovius overcomes the palpable tension between his admiration of existing patriotic lyrics and wariness of their reactionary undercurrents by suggesting that his fellow revolutionaries make a clean break with them. He therefore proposes a competition to write a modern 'Deutsches Freiheitslied',³⁶ described

---

31 Geldern, 'Der historische Film', p. 297.
32 The 'Heckerlied' features the refrain: 'Er hängt an keinem Baume; | er hängt an keinem Strick; | Er hängt nur an dem Traume; | Der deutschen Republik'. It commemorates the failed plan of Friedrich Hecker, a qualified lawyer and popular orator, to occupy Karlsruhe and overthrow the government of Grand Duke Leopold I of Baden. Hecker fled to Switzerland and thence to the United States of America, where he became an officer in a German regiment fighting on the side of the Union in the American Civil War of 1861–65.
33 Franz Varssovius, 'Gefährliche Lieder', *Die Weltbühne*, 15.1 (1919), 151–54.
34 Varssovius, 'Gefährliche Lieder', p. 152.
35 Geldern, 'Der historische Film', p. 298.
36 Varssovius, 'Gefährliche Lieder', p. 153. The Revolution of 1848 became the subject of many revolutionary songs, such as the aforementioned 'Heckerlied', but the title 'Deutsches Freiheitslied' echoes, intentionally or otherwise, a waltz composed by Johann Strauss the Younger during the revolutionary convulsions in Vienna. The piece had originally, and no less provocatively, been called *Barrikadenlieder* but was re-named a week after its première on 28 May 1848.

elsewhere in the piece as 'de[r] Hymnus eines befreiten Volkes auf sich selbst'.³⁷ Varssovius evidently wishes the German people to be liberated not only from the tyranny of the *Kaiserreich* but also from those of its trappings which remain embedded in popular culture.

By contrast, Geldern's comfort with his national heritage is plain from his casual citation from Hoffmann von Fallersleben's 'Das Lied der Deutschen' (1841) to emphasize the ubiquity of the historical film. These films are shown, he notes, 'von der Etsch bis an den Belt'.³⁸ For his part, Varssovius shows only a fleeting interest in rehabilitating von Fallersleben's poem from the charge of 'imperialistischen Größenwahns',³⁹ ultimately acknowledging that it has become a favourite of the Freikorps troops, 'die ausziehen, den Spartacus auszuräuchern – und in fürchterlichen Träumen hört man es wieder das ganze deutsche Land durchbrausen: wie Donnerhall … '.⁴⁰ Von Fallersleben's revolutionary credentials cannot save his words from Varssovius's condemnation as he seeks a new lyrical vehicle for an emancipated German patriotism.

This wariness of von Fallersleben's song was not shared by the Weimar political establishment: President Ebert declared it to be the new national anthem in August 1922, capitalizing on the pro-republican backlash to the assassination of Walter Rathenau earlier that summer. Nonetheless, Varssovius's resigned elision of 'Das Lied der Deutschen' with the overtly nationalist words of 'Die Wacht am Rhein' highlights the unintended connotations with which patriotic songs can all too easily become freighted.⁴¹ By comparing the resonance of von Fallersleben's song to 'Donnerhall', and thereby linking it to the more fervently nationalist 'Wacht am Rhein', he emphasizes its anti-French tenor and suppresses the pro-unification message that might otherwise have proved serviceable in a time of heightened political uncertainty. Varssovius's pessimism about the potential for reviving canonical

---

37 Varssovius, 'Gefährliche Lieder', p. 152.
38 Geldern, 'Der historische Film', p. 297; this quotation is taken from the first stanza of the song.
39 Varssovius, 'Gefährliche Lieder', p. 152. In 'Die undeutsche Demokratie' Lehmann-Rußbüldt also absolves Hoffmann von Fallersleben of the apparently weighty charge of being a 'patriot' (p. 92).
40 Varssovius, 'Gefährliche Lieder', p. 152.
41 Written by Max Schneckenburger in 1840 in response to the *Rheinkrise*, the same diplomatic conflagration that would prompt Hoffman von Fallersleben to write the comparatively pacific 'Das Lied der Deutschen', 'Die Wacht am Rhein' was a call to arms against French territorial ambitions on the left bank of the River Rhine featuring such verses as 'Solang ein Tropfen Blut noch glüht; | Noch eine Faust den Degen zieht; | Und noch ein Arm die Büchse spannt; | Betritt kein Feind hier deinen Strand' <https://www.dhm.de/mediathek/der-rhein-von-basel-bis-koblenz/deutsch-franzoesische-geschichte-am-rhein/wacht-am-rhein-liedtext/> [accessed 27 June 2024].

narratives is further underlined by the image of the Freikorps paramilitaries setting out to hunt down their Spartacist adversaries, surely a deliberately ironic play on the title of the Grimm fairy tale 'Das Märchen von einem, der auszog das Fürchten zu lernen'.[42] Germany's literary heritage, especially its stock of patriotic lyrics, appears tarnished by nationalist instrumentalization. Indeed, by casting the Freikorps as the heroes in a fable that would have been familiar to the *Weltbühne* readership, Varssovius arguably suggests that left-wing revolutionaries occupy a treasonous position in the popular imagination consistent with their disenfranchisement in the national songbook.

This symbolic deficit was not only felt on the far Left. As Manuela Achilles points out, in his posthumously published memoir Weimar Minister of Justice Gustav Radbruch of the SPD rues the fact that the prosaic work of democratic governance had not been supplemented with stirring patriotic ceremonials.[43] He argues that, having taken the lead in Germany's transition to republican democracy, his party's mistake was:

> daß sie zu ihrer nationalen Haltung nicht die entsprechend nationale Begleitmusik machte, vielmehr das national Notwendige stumm und mit zusammengekniffenen Lippen ausführte. Auch für die Nachkriegszeit galt noch das Wort in Karl Brögers Kriegsgedicht An das Vaterland: 'Immer schon haben wir eine Liebe zu dir gekannt / bloß wir haben sie nie mit einem Namen genannt'.[44]

The composition of an entirely new 'Deutsches Freiheitslied' is Varssovius's answer to the exclusion of the Socialists from the patriotic pantheon. His detached observation of the Germans' almost constitutional need to articulate their patriotism through song shows that he does not share this compulsion, yet he recognizes the necessity of catering for it. Indeed, Radbruch's hindsight seems less impressive when read alongside Varssovius's insight from early 1919:

> Im neuen Deutschland wie im alten werden die Menschen das Bedürfnis finden, sich zuweilen zusammenzufinden und denjenigen Gefühlen, die sie für Staat und Vaterland beseelen, einen lauten, auf

---

42 Jakob and Wilhelm Grimm, 'Das Märchen von einem, der auszog das Fürchten zu lernen', in *Grimms Märchen*, ed. by Heinz Rölleke, Suhrkamp BasisBibliothek (Frankfurt a.M.: Suhrkamp, 1998 [1812]), pp. 11–20.

43 Manuela Achilles, 'Reforming the Reich: Democratic Symbols and Rituals in the Weimar Republic', in *Weimar Publics/Weimar Subjects: Rethinking the Political Culture of Germany in the 1920s*, ed. by Kathleen Canning, Kerstin Barndt and Kristin McGuire, Spektrum: Publications of the German Studies Association, 2 (New York: Berghahn, 2010), pp. 175–91 (p. 175).

44 Gustav Radbruch, *Der innere Weg. Aufriß meines Lebens*, ed. by Lydia Radbruch (Stuttgart: Koehler, 1951), p. 177.

einige Entfernung vernehmbaren Ausdruck zu verleihen. Sie werden sich hierzu des Gesanges bedienen. Und da ihnen keine andern Lieder zur Verfügung stehen, so werden sie patriotische singen: auch Nichtpatrioten werden es [...].[45]

Varssovius's distaste for the world view that he calls 'patriotic' does not betoken an aversion to German nationhood as such, but only to those songs that serenade conventional national symbols, leave social hierarchies intact and endorse German expansionism while celebrating military force and demonizing other nations.

This recognition of the power of song has more than a faint echo of the *cri de cœur* of Heine's narrator upon crossing the German border after an absence of thirteen years at the beginning of the verse epic *Deutschland. Ein Wintermärchen*, first published in 1844.[46] Hearing 'das alte Entsagungslied' from a 'Harfenmädchen', the hero is moved by impatience to declare:

> Ein neues Lied, ein besseres Lied,
> O Freunde, will ich euch dichten!
> Wir wollen hier auf Erden schon
> Das Himmelreich errichten.[47]

The returning exile's suspicion of the reactionary implications of the harpist's lyrics, which defer the fulfilment of private hopes and dreams to a blissful afterlife, is a pithier iteration of Heine's mission statement in the essay *Zur Geschichte der Religion und Philosophie in Deutschland*, published ten years earlier. In this passage Heine claims that he and his fellow pantheistic thinkers are driven by a more powerful revolutionary impulse than that impelling those insurrectionaries driven by purely political considerations:

> Wir kämpfen nicht für die Menschenrechte des Volks, sondern für die Gottesrechte des Menschen. [...] Wir wollen keine Sansculotten sein, keine frugalen Bürger, keine wohlfeilen Präsidenten; wir stiften eine Demokratie gleichherrlicher, gleichheiliger, gleichbeseligter Götter. Ihr [Männer der Revolution] verlangt einfache Trachten, enthaltsame Sitten und ungewürzte Gemüse: wir hingegen verlangen Nektar und Ambrosia, Purpurmäntel, kostbare Wohlgerüche, Wollust und Pracht, lachenden Nymphentanz, Musik und Komödien.[48]

---

45 Varssovius, 'Gefährliche Lieder', p. 153
46 Heinrich Heine, *Deutschland. Ein Wintermärchen* (Stuttgart: Reclam, 1979); 1st edn Hamburg: Hoffmann und Campe, 1844.
47 Heine, *Deutschland. Ein Wintermärchen*, p. 10.
48 Heine, *Zur Geschichte der Religion und Philosophie in Deutschland*, pp. 124–25.

This very passage is, in fact, quoted approvingly by Jurisch in 'Ansage' to define an expansive Socialist ideal whose dimensions, he maintains, encompass 'eine neue Welt, ein[en] neue[n] Geist, ein[en] neue[n] Mensch[en]'.[49] Neither he nor Varssovius, who envisages a song capable of uniting all the people of the world, wish any more than had Heine to speak only to their compatriots. Nonetheless, the revolutionary Socialism of both men is impelled by the same desire first to save their fellow Germans from the pernicious influence of nationalism such as that which had motivated Heine's political writing.

Ritchie Robertson describes Heine's intentions thus:

> Unlike the German nationalists, who claimed that the Germans' deepest instincts were conservative, Heine […] preferred to think that the German people, deep down, were committed to freedom. His obvious course, therefore, was to adapt folk-poetry and folk-tales so as to bring out their latent revolutionary content, link it to the political programme of emancipation, and thus deprive the German nationalists of one of their most potent weapons.[50]

Heine's purported faith in his compatriots' rebellious instincts chimes with Lehmann-Rußbüldt's aforementioned belief that the German national character is defined by 'Mannestum und Unabhängigkeit'.[51] A common thread throughout the articles discussed thus far in this section, including the backward-looking ones considered first, is the tendency polemically to re-write German history as the tale of a repeatedly frustrated will to revolution, as opposed to an unbroken ascent to national greatness based on a shared German self-understanding. In this context, Varssovius's projection in 'Gefährliche Lieder' of a new patriotic narrative unencumbered by chauvinist resentment or grudges can also be seen as a radical contribution to the partially unwritten story of Germany's national development.

The Shock of the Old: A Case Study

As these examples show, the dividing line between forward- and backward-looking revolutionary blueprints in the early years of the Weimar-era *Weltbühne* was often blurred. Ultimately, attempts to establish a mutually productive relationship between radical Socialism and a distinctively German patriotism were wont to blend both approaches, drawing on national traditions in order to legitimize a thoroughgoing revolution of German society and its place in the world. Among the most controversial of

---

49 Jurisch, 'Ansage', p. 2.
50 Ritchie Robertson, *Heine*, Jewish Thinkers (London: Weidenfeld & Nicolson, 1988), p. 27.
51 Lehmann-Rußbüldt, 'Die undeutsche Demokratie', p. 94.

these efforts was a thirty-five-part series beginning in November 1919 called 'Das alte Heer', which featured a plethora of biographical articles concerning prominent members of the Imperial German Army, as well as essays on different aspects of military life under the old regime. Its anonymous author, a veteran soldier who wrote under the byline of 'Ein Stabsoffizier', was a Communist sympathizer with a marked propensity for invoking German cultural icons in support of his revolutionary vision. Consequently, 'Das alte Heer' is a rare document of unabashedly Communist patriotism that welds internationalist radicalism onto a conventional tableau of inspirational German ancestors. As such, it merits extended consideration.

Admittedly, some of the officer's sentiments are predictable in a career soldier. Engaged in a running feud over the legacy of the wartime *Wehrmacht* with Kurt Tucholsky, whose own retrospective series had begun in January 1919,[52] the officer also drew dissenting reactions in the pages of *Die Weltbühne* from disillusioned servicemen keen to challenge any narrative that threatened retrospectively to glorify the war effort in which they had actively participated. An especially striking example of this is 'Die Sage von den gefallenen Aktiven', attributed simply to an anonymous army captain.[53] This article, written by a veteran of the Western Front, casts doubt on the veracity of the claim made by the Stabsoffizier in the fourteenth instalment of 'Das alte Heer' that eighty-three per cent of the German officer class had died in the fighting.[54] Nor was the weighty charge of revisionism levelled only in one direction: 'Offizierstypen' was itself a riposte to the most recent iteration of Tucholsky's 'Militaria' series, which had allegedly underestimated the bravery of the German officer class.[55]

In spite of these ructions, undue fixation on the contentiousness of the series risks giving rise to the impression that its author was bent on defending the honour of the Imperial Army against any charge that might be directed against it. In fact, far from being an apologist for his colleagues' typically reactionary political instincts, the officer exhibits a patriotism that is emphatically subversive in nature, culminating in a peculiarly ambiguous stand-alone piece that weds the language of militant nationalism to a yearning for worldwide Communist revolution. In exposing the critical misapprehension that 'Das alte Heer' constitutes the self-exculpatory counterpoint to Tucholsky's anti-militarism, the following case study therefore draws attention to the idiosyncratic patriotism of its subject.

---

52 Ignaz Wrobel, 'Militaria. Offizier und Mann', *Die Weltbühne*, 15.1 (1919), i, 38–41.
53 Ein Hauptmann, 'Die Sage von den gefallenen Aktiven', *Die Weltbühne*, 16.1 (1920), 266–69.
54 Ein Stabsoffizier, 'Das alte Heer. Offizierstypen', *Die Weltbühne*, 16.1 (1920), xiv, 174–79.
55 Ignaz Wrobel, 'Militaria', *Die Weltbühne*, 16.1 (1920), 106–14.

For all that he is quick to defend the active soldiery against blanket charges of hedonism, heartlessness or cowardice, the officer does not paint a uniformly flattering picture of his profession, repeatedly excoriating the reckless posturing of Kaiser Wilhelm II in the capacity of Commander-in-Chief,[56] while reserving uniquely stinging criticism for the intra-mural school system of the Army, with its sadistic, ignorant teaching body.[57] This does not stop him drawing on the language of outright nationalist aggression in his flattering appraisal of the German war effort. Thus, in February 1920, he utters the hope:

> daß das deutsche Volk Stolz lernt, Stolz auf sich selbst und damit auch auf seine Armee. Es war doch immerhin eine Leistung, vier Jahre lang gegen die ganze Welt Krieg zu führen. Ich sehe in der Tatsache, daß wir Deutschen dieser Riesenleistung fähig waren, [...] den Beweis, daß wir doch ein Herrenvolk sind.[58]

The image of an isolated Germany being forced against its will to defend itself against a numerically vastly superior adversary and resisting against all the odds for four years was a common feature of heroic nationalist narratives at this time. Not content merely with amplifying this version of events, the officer even extrapolates from it Germany's right to the status of a Great Power. As we see in the second chapter, contributors to *Die Weltbühne* generally evinced little interest in Germany dominating its European neighbours through force of arms, preferring to imagine a Weimar Republic endowed with unassailable moral authority to one founded on military conquest.

However, the jingoist overtones of the above passage should not distract from the true object of the officer's solicitude: the beleaguered individual soldier. Castigating the bellicose approach of Kaiser Wilhelm II to foreign affairs, he presents the humble private as the undeserving victim of the Emperor's fatefully naïve political manoeuvres:

> Seine katastrophale Außenpolitik brachte es fertig, daß die ganze Welt gegen das deutsche Heer zum Kampfe antrat, und daß die Gräber unsrer Soldaten in drei Erdteilen verstreut sind – dieser feldgrauen deutschen Männer, über deren tieftragischen Kampf ein süddeutscher Fürst das gute Wort sprach: 'Von dem deutschen Soldaten kann man eigentlich nur mit Tränen in den Augen reden'.[59]

---

56 Ein Stabsoffizier, 'Das alte Heer. Die Waffengattungen', *Die Weltbühne*, 15.2 (1919), iv, 654–69.
57 Ein Stabsoffizier, 'Das alte Heer. Das Kadettenkorps', *Die Weltbühne*, 16.1 (1920), xiii, 139–44.
58 Ein Stabsoffizier, 'Das alte Heer. Offizierstypen', p. 178.
59 Ein Stabsoffizier, 'Das alte Heer. Die Waffengattungen', pp. 658–59.

For all that this passage displays deference to a robustly martial masculine ideal embodied in the field-grey colours of the German troops, it also regards its representatives with a sentimental pity at odds with the emotionally restrained model of manliness that George Mosse claims was especially pronounced in first-hand accounts of the First World War: 'Passions had to be kept under control; a true man did not cry out in pain nor did he shed a tear even for fallen comrades'.[60] The officer's endorsement of the reportedly lachrymose demeanour of King Wilhelm II of Württemberg as he bade farewell to one of his regiments in August 1914 therefore presents a dual challenge: to the legend of the so-called *Augusterlebnis* that had supposedly united Germans across the political spectrum in pro-war patriotic fervour;[61] and to the hyper-masculine national role model embodied by the stoical soldier. As a result, this epitaph to Germany's fallen soldiers ultimately resists the temptation to lionize the dead or romanticize the German war mission.

Even allowing for this criticism, the officer's denunciation of Germany's war-time leaders cannot compare in its ferocity to Tucholsky's 'Militaria' series, written in the characteristically combative guise of Ignaz Wrobel. For the latter, as he avows in the first instalment, the war must represent a salutary caesura in German history after which German manhood will rise up in a new form:

> Nur durch völlige Abkehrung von dieser schmählichen Epoche kommen wir wieder zur Ordnung. Spartacus ist es nicht; der Offizier, der sein eignes Volk als Mittel zum Zweck ansah, ist es auch nicht – was wird es denn sein am Ende?
> Der aufrechte Deutsche.[62]

At the superficial level this ambiguous image of an upright German hardly signifies a departure from the conventional military ideal of physical rectitude that Tucholsky held in contempt. Indeed, ten years later Tucholsky himself would use a scathing book review to ridicule the way in which nationalist author Arnolt Bronnen depicts the self-anointed 'freedom fighters' of the Freikorps in his recently released novel *O.S.* (1929). The reader learns that Bronnen repeatedly equips his heroes, who have marched on Upper Silesia

---

60 George L. Mosse, *The Image of Man: The Creation of Modern Masculinity*, Studies in the History of Sexuality (Oxford: Oxford University Press, 1996), p. 111.
61 This phrase is particularly popular among historians to describe a supposedly near-unanimous spirit of enthusiasm among German civilians for the war upon its outbreak. War broke out on 28 July 1914, when Austria declared war on Serbia; Germany entered it on 1 August by declaring war on Russia. The accuracy of the phrase is keenly contested.
62 Wrobel, 'Militaria. Offizier und Mann', i, p. 41.

to 'liberate' the formerly German territory from Poland, with a brisk bearing and curt manner of speaking. Tucholsky's verdict is unrestrained:

> Es gibt in diesen deutschen Büchern ein Wort, das nie fehlt, weil es so recht zeigt, wie sich die Verfasser einen deutschen Mann vorstellen. Es ist das Wort 'kurz'. 'Herr Pfarrer Ulitzka gab ihm kurz zur Antwort' ... die Fakultäten, die so schöne Preisaufgaben stellen, sollten einmal als Thema geben: 'Kurz und Knapp in ihrer Beziehung zum patriotischen Schundroman des zwanzigsten Jahrhunderts.' Denn dies ist ein deutsches Ideal: jemand kurz anzufahren; nehmen Sie herrisch, dergleichen hebt immer.[63]

It is hard to imagine the author of these lines elevating an imagined 'upright German' to the status of national role model. However, in the sixth column of the 'Militaria' series, Tucholsky presents the alternative: the self-abasing German whose subservience towards his superiors co-exists with a predilection '[andere Deutsche] mit Füßen zu treten' that is frequently presented, both here and elsewhere in Tucholsky's œuvre, as his sole motivation for seeking promotion.[64] Nor is this mutually beneficial arrangement, according to which every German is entitled to tyrannize those directly below him in the chain of command, confined to the barracks. Thus Tucholsky describes the prize for the demilitarization of German society as nothing less than 'die Freiheit des Deutschen',[65] while his final word in his debate with the Stabsoffizier labels civilians in senior positions throughout the country 'Offiziere in derber Karikatur' labouring under the misconception that 'nicht der Mann zum Mann, der Deutsche zum Deutschen stehe sondern der Herr zum Kerl'.[66] Tucholsky pictures a nationwide struggle for liberation that is patriotic in its devotion to the idea of a dormant German essence but reliant upon individual enlightenment for its realization.

Tucholsky's rejection of the Spartacist movement, presumably because of its inherent emphasis on a sense of collective responsibility hostile to individual self-expression, allows the Stabsoffizier to position himself, in a later article to be discussed in more detail, to the left of his adversary on the political spectrum. The selflessness enforced by army discipline is portrayed as the perfect complement to the Communist idea, the German exponents of which, the KPD, had issued from the Spartacist League two years previously:

> Uns schreckt der Kommunismus nicht. Soldaten und Mönche sind im Grunde die besten Kommunisten, und ein armer Teufel, der bereit ist,

---

63 Wrobel, 'Ein besserer Herr', p. 955.
64 Ignaz Wrobel, 'Militaria. "Unser Militär"', *Die Weltbühne*, 15.1 (1919), vi, 201–05 (p. 205).
65 Wrobel, 'Militaria. "Unser Militär"', p. 203.
66 Ignaz Wrobel, 'Schlußwort', *Die Weltbühne*, 16.1 (1920), 219–20 (p. 220).

sein bißchen Leben an eine große Sache zu setzen, steht uns Soldaten menschlich unendlich viel näher als die sattgefressenen Nutznießer des gegenwärtigen Zustands.[67]

The suggestion that no individual should hesitate to subordinate his fate to the common cause is incompatible with Tucholsky's rehabilitation of the individual's right to dignity and self-respect, all the more so in view of the officer's praise for the hypothetical 'arme[n] Teufel' who is prepared to make the ultimate sacrifice. The pair's disagreement over whether to save Germany from the bottom up through an epiphanic process of awakening, or from the top down by means of mass mobilization, therefore points to the multiplicity of forms that revolutionary patriotism could assume.

What unites both is their hope that all Germans will come to see one another as equals and consign the hierarchical spirit permeating German society to the past. By way of conclusion to '"Unser Militär"' Tucholsky appeals to his fellow Germans to acknowledge their common duty to one another as members of one national community:

> Und mit derselben Macht und mit derselben Faust wie die bunten Burschen, aber getrieben von strömendem Herzblut, ringen wir um die schlafenden Seelen Deutschlands. Land! Es gibt Höheres, als vor der Geliebten mit einem Rang zu prunken! Land! Wir Deutsche sind Brüder, und ein Knopf ist ein Knopf und ein Achselstück ein Achselstück.[68]

The 'bunten Burschen' condescended to here are presumably the flag-bearing *Burschenschaften*, whose loyalty to the imperial colours morphed into open anti-republicanism following Germany's signature of the post-war treaties. Speaking on behalf of an unspecified collective that shares his convictions, Tucholsky claims that he and his allies can match the physical force of the nationalist groups while mustering deeper reserves of 'Herzblut', a metaphor for personal integrity and common decency. In the face of paramilitary fervour, this bottomless well of humble virtues is to be instrumental in rousing from its slumber a patriotic spirit of egalitarianism capable of seeing martial regalia for the intrinsically worthless attire that they are. Tucholsky's repetition of the remonstrance 'Land!' elevates the German nation above the petty self-importance of many of its citizens, whose quest for validation has led them to forego their responsibility to the national family of which they are a part. Tokens of distinction in both military and civilian life are thus seen as a barrier to authentic patriotic consciousness.

---

67 Ein Stabsoffizier, 'Der neue Krieg', *Die Weltbühne*, 16.2 (1920), 638–40 (pp. 639–40).
68 Wrobel, '"Unser Militär"', p. 205.

As Dieter Langewiesche explains, there already existed in many European countries a long-standing precedent for projecting the image of a national community of equals in which political power would no longer be vested in hereditary authority. Tracing the birth of such egalitarian nationalism back to the late eighteenth century, Langewiesche claims that the profusion of principalities within the territory that would eventually become Germany rendered the new patriotic ideal even more destabilizing there than in Revolutionary France. Unlike its neighbour, Germany was not yet a unified country, meaning that the proposition of a centralized state founded on democratic principles mounted a double challenge to the privilege of the ruling potentates:

> Wer sich zur modernen Idee der Nation bekannte, richtete eine Kampfansage an die überlieferte Ständegesellschaft mit ihrem dichten Geflecht an Privilegien und Ausgrenzungen. Auch wo ein gemeinsamer Staat bereits bestand, wie in Frankreich, wirkte die Idee der Nation als ein egalitärer Zukunftsentwurf. Er versprach jedermann – Frauen wurden noch nicht in das Egalitätsversprechen einbezogen – politische und rechtliche Gleichberechtigung. [...] Deshalb war das Zukunftsmodell 'Nation' eine potentiell revolutionäre Kraft.[69]

For all that Weimar Germany was a single nation state under one constitution, its claim to being a genuine democracy was often presented as a sham by commentators such as Tucholsky. In his writing, therefore, the post-war Republic often resembles a blank canvas not dissimilar to that which the pre-unification patchwork of dynasties had represented for his idealistic nineteenth-century forebears. Until the Germans had divested themselves of their native obsequiousness and tendency to torment their juniors, he suggests, the long shadow of imperial presumption would continue to hang over the 'Egalitätsversprechen' of republicanism.

The emphasis placed by Tucholsky on the need for Germans to treat their compatriots with humanity is, as we shall see in due course, also discernible in the magnanimous Communism espoused by the officer. Indeed, the author of 'Das alte Heer' goes further, imagining the triumph of humanity as an unprecedented pledge of fealty to a set of values transcending narrow class-based, or even national, affiliations. In 'Militaria', on the other hand, the longed-for dawn of a spirit of humanity generally lacks such universal dimensions. Thus the call for a 'neue, uralte Menschlichkeit' that brings the sixth instalment of the latter series to a close coheres in a later article into a vision of a battle for hearts and minds that would stop at Germany's borders.[70]

---

69 Dieter Langewiesche, *Nation, Nationalismus, Nationalstaat in Deutschland und Europa*, Beck'sche Reihe, 1399 (Munich: Beck, 2000), p. 192.
70 Wrobel, '"Unser Militär"', p. 205.

At the end of a lengthy riposte to his critics, published to coincide with the anniversary of the outbreak of the First World War five years previously, Tucholsky announces a potential turning point in attitudes following the belated withdrawal of the *Baltikumer* from Latvia: 'Wir werden dafür zu sorgen haben, daß ohne zerschlagene Fensterscheiben und ohne politische Morde in den Köpfen unsrer Volksgenossen eine geistige Revolution entsteht, wie sie bisher gefehlt hat'.[71] Distancing himself from the tactics of violent overthrow, Tucholsky instead calls for a bloodless coup in which an endemic culture of deference before authority would be swept away.

Tucholsky's desire to furnish his patriotism with fundamentally human attributes reaches its climax in his closing remarks. Reviling the officer class as 'menschenunwürdig' thrice in the space of a single paragraph, he rings its death knell in the final paragraph: 'Wir bekämpfen nicht den einzelnen Offizier. Wir bekämpfen sein Ideal und seine Welt und bitten alle Gleichgesinnten, an ihrer Zerstörung mitzuhelfen. Nur sie kann uns eine neue, reinere Heimat geben'.[72] This knowing evocation of a national 'Heimat', the diverse and frequently retrograde connotations of which are explored in detail in the first chapter, harnesses a vernacular idea of Germanness to a new and emerging socio-political reality that was imagined as dispensing with the idolatry of the imperial age in favour of a more collegiate national identity still in a state of flux. *Heimat* itself thereby becomes malleable. Describing it as more amenable to re-appropriation than the concept of 'Vaterland', Alon Confino even goes so far as to assert that *Heimat* lent itself more readily to relatively radical Leftists than to the professed internationalists of the Social Democratic Party:

> Socialists saw Heimat as a particularly suitable idea for imagining the nation precisely because it was apolitical: while it disarmed socialists by excluding classes, it at the same time disarmed antisocialists by eliminating the very weapons with which they attacked socialism, namely militarism and authoritarianism, thus allowing socialists to embrace the nation without condoning antisocialist ideas.[73]

In Confino's understanding, the inviting void of political meaning contained within the term *Heimat*, acknowledged by Tucholsky himself in 1929,[74] was

---

71 Ignaz Wrobel, 'Militaria (Zur Erinnerung an den Ersten August 1914)', *Die Weltbühne*, 15.2 (1919), 190–99 (p. 199). The officially decommissioned soldiers mobilized in support of the Kapp Putsch (1920) were known as *Baltikumer* because of their unsanctioned reign of terror in Latvia and Lithuania since the end of the First World War.
72 Wrobel, 'Zur Erinnerung an den Ersten August 1914', p. 199.
73 Confino, 'The Nation as a Local Metaphor', p. 77.
74 Wrobel, 'Ein besserer Herr', p. 957.

not supposed to remain empty for long. Similarly, by imagining the German *Heimat* as an aggressively demilitarized zone purged of its last vestiges of military influence by a constituency of 'Gleichgesinnten', in 'Militaria' Tucholsky seeks to muster an inherently political insurgency against the nationalist factions.

Although his series does not signal a *tabula rasa* of all traditional objects of national pride, the anonymous war veteran's embrace of Communism reflects the future-facing orientation of his patriotism. Admittedly, he is not above revanchism: he twice lends credence to the *Dolchstoßlegende*, according to which the German Army had remained undefeated in the field only to have the Armistice foisted upon them by shady domestic forces, blaming first the home front and then the Ministry of War for the German defeat.[75] At the same time, however, he demands that Germany immerse itself in the prevailing political current of the post-war period: Communism. In the seventh instalment of 'Das alte Heer', a largely unsympathetic verdict on General Hindenburg's character and career at the head of the wartime General Staff, the officer identifies hostility to Communism as the future president's great failing:

> Die große Bewegung der Zeit: der Sozialismus war seinem Wesen fremd. Ihn in den Dienst seiner Sache einzuspannen, weiterzukämpfen, und sei es unter der roten Fahne des Proletariats gegen den Kapitalismus der Welt bis zum Siege: das lag ihm nicht und konnte ihm garnicht liegen. Friedrich der Große wäre in diesem Krieg Kommunist geworden und hätte sein Volk in Arbeiter und Soldaten eingeteilt. Hindenburg stand hilflos vor der neuen Zeit, deren Notschrei nach einem großen Führer er nicht begriff. Für die Zukunft ist nichts mehr von ihm zu erwarten.[76]

The officer's utilitarian attitude to Socialism, hinted at in his disappointment that Hindenburg had been unwilling 'ihn in den Dienst seiner Sache einzuspannen', resurfaces in the following instalment on Ludendorff, who is described as having been disinclined 'die Gedanken des Sozialismus zu verstehen und *für seine Zwecke zu verwenden*'.[77] This choice of words, which reappears in his final declaration of support for worldwide revolution,[78] raises

---

75 Respectively: Ein Stabsoffizier, 'Das alte Heer. Ludendorff', *Die Weltbühne*, 15.2 (1919), viii, 785–89; and Ein Stabsoffizier, 'Das alte Heer. Das Offiziercorps im Kriege', *Die Weltbühne*, 16.1 (1920), x, 38–42.
76 Ein Stabsoffizier, 'Das alte Heer. Hindenburg', *Die Weltbühne*, 15.2 (1919), vii, 759–63 (p. 763).
77 Ein Stabsoffizier, 'Ludendorff', p. 788. My italics.
78 Ein Stabsoffizier, 'Der neue Krieg', p. 638.

the legitimate question of what purpose Socialism was supposed to serve beyond its own realization. The answer may lie in the glorification of the German nation: the officer's highly debatable assertion that Friedrich II of Prussia, were he to have been transplanted into the twentieth century, would have espoused the Communist ideology in order to win the war on behalf of a global proletariat does at least suggest that the neglect of Socialist ideas is not only an abandonment of political principles, but a patriotic betrayal.

The war that Hindenburg and Ludendorff should have waged would, according to the officer, have transcended national loyalties. Germany's imagined position at the vanguard of this global revolutionary battle therefore appears calculated to assuage patriotic German qualms about joining such a conflict, for all that the officer evidently holds out little hope of persuading the Weimar leadership to join forces with the Russian regime against the irredeemably capitalistic Anglosphere:

> Vielleicht überlegen sich aber die Führer der verschiedenen sozialistischen Parteigruppen einmal – wenn der Bruderkrieg ihnen dazu Zeit läßt –, was aus der Sache des Sozialismus hätte werden können, wenn die Ebert und Haase sich offen mit Rußland verbündet und den Krieg des Proletariats gegen den Kapitalismus weitergeführt hätten bis zum Ende, bis zur Errichtung des großen Reichs auf sozialistischer Grundlage von Sibirien bis Frankreich. Das wäre für Deutschland eine weltgeschichtliche Aufgabe gewesen: den Bolschewismus zu durchgeistigen, die Russen mit Offizieren, Ingenieuren und Soldaten zu unterstützen und in dem großen kontinentalen Weltreich ein Gegengewicht gegen die angelsächsischen Imperien zu schaffen.[79]

In spite of the post-national implications of a Continental empire predicated on Communist principles, this passage hints at the infiltration of the Russian sphere by salutary German influence. Germany's role is, or would have been, to permeate Bolshevism with its *Geist*, as well as to provide additional manpower in order to establish a Communist Europe as a force capable of withstanding the dual empires of the United States and the United Kingdom. If Russia is the centre of gravity for the liberation struggle of the international proletariat, Germany constitutes its indispensable seat of power in Western Europe.

In the first issue of the *Weltbühne* in 1920 the officer duly ridicules the suggestion by a monarchist colonel, Oberst Bauer, made in an interview with an American newspaper, that Crown Prince Wilhelm of Prussia ascend his father's empty throne and restore the Hohenzollern monarchy. The officer

---

[79] Ein Stabsoffizier, 'Das alte Heer. Der Generalstab im Kriege', *Die Weltbühne*, 16.1 (1920), xii, 101–06 (p. 106).

clearly finds the Prince repugnant on a personal level, but what ultimately disqualifies the latter from power is his umbilical connection to the old order. What Germany needs, the officer repeats, is a strong leader imbued with the radical spirit of the new age. This is the call that Hindenburg had supposedly failed to heed:

> Und die Revolution! Wo ist ein Mirabeau, ein Danton, ein Lafayette, wo ist der geniale Fanatiker von gigantischem Wollen, mit einer Feuerseele, mit großem Herzen und reinen Händen, der es versteht, die bezwingende Form zu finden für den einzigen schöpferischen Gedanken dieser Tage: für den Kommunismus als geistige Bewegung! Vielleicht kommt er noch, vielleicht ersteht ein Mann stärker als Luther, der uns die zweite Reformation bringt und wieder einmal anknüpft bei Christus selbst, dem Vater der kommunistischen Idee.[80]

The image of Germany's salvation by a messianic revolutionary is a classic example of the Führer-discourse illuminated by Thomas Mergel in his essay on the Weimar electorate's strained relationship with the concept of representative democracy.[81] According to Mergel there was nothing uniquely right-wing in this craving for an exceptional leader capable of rising above the petty doctrinal squabbles and moral compromise associated in the popular German imagination with party politics. Common to autocratic fantasies across the ideological spectrum was the conviction that:

> the Führer was a nonconformist, a bolt from the blue, and the very essence of irrationality. This discourse of irregularity and unpredictability was in no way restricted to the political Right, but was widely shared by all sides. [...] Whether Left or Right, all sides in Weimar politics contended with the phenomenon of a charismatic leader who could overcome the political paralysis of the republic. Yet, the appearance of the Führer was not amenable to planning; he would simply emerge.[82]

The single-mindedness and indomitable will that would enable the imagined Führer to override the sclerosis of the parliamentary system manifests itself in the officer's prophecy of a man capable of contriving a 'bezwingende Form' for the Communist idea, while the former's irrationality is mirrored by the fanatical genius of the latter. A further point in common is the

---

80 Ein Stabsoffizier, 'Das alte Heer. Der Kronprinz', *Die Weltbühne*, 16.1 (1920), ix, 12–16 (p. 16).
81 Thomas Mergel, 'High Expectations – Deep Disappointment: Structures of the Public Perception of Politics in the Weimar Republic', in *Weimar Publics/Weimar Subjects*, ed. by Canning, Barndt and McGuire, pp. 192–210.
82 Mergel, 'High Expectations – Deep Disappointment', pp. 198–99.

organic nature of their apparition: whereas Mergel's subject is expected to materialize without warning, the officer envisions the Communist redeemer arising seemingly from nowhere, with the verb 'erstehen' echoing Christ's 'Auferstehung'. Finally, the officer's decision to equip the revolutionary leader with a large heart and clean hands offers up an uncanny echo of a column in the *Deutsche Allgemeine Zeitung* (*DAZ*) from 1924, cited by Mergel, that urges Reichstag deputies to discharge their duties with 'reine[n] Hände[n] und reine[n] Herze[n]!'.[83] Evidently, left-wing commentators such as the Stabsoffizier were just as likely as their counterparts on the right to vest in an individual of brilliance the same hopes that others, such as the leader-writers of the *DAZ*, were inclined to place in the sum of the Republic's democratic representatives.

Having first invoked Friedrich II of Prussia to reproach Hindenburg for his deficient political instinct, the officer reaches back once again into Germany's national pantheon in search of the elusive figure on whom Germany's Communist saviour might model himself: Martin Luther. In his history of German thought, written in 1833, Heinrich Heine had also foretold the coming of a great redeemer in whom Luther's emancipatory legacy would live on:

> In der Trübnis der Gegenwart schauen wir hinauf nach ihren tröstenden Standbildern, und sie nicken eine glänzende Verheißung. Ja, kommen wird auch der dritte Mann, der da vollbringt, was Luther begonnen, was Lessing fortgesetzt, und dessen das deutsche Vaterland so sehr bedarf, – der dritte Befreier![84]

Leaving aside Heine's eulogy of Gotthold Ephraim Lessing, there is a striking similarity between these two passages. In both cases Luther's defiance of papal authority is the historical reference point without which the liberation of Germany from present-day tyranny is inconceivable. For both his admirers, however, the sixteenth-century monk is no more than a point of departure, the invocation of whom is meant to inspire their contemporaries to emulate and elaborate on his deeds instead of conjuring the image of a golden age that must be restored. In the case of the officer, Luther's modern successor is to go even further by unlocking the Communist potential of Christ's teachings.

As Rida Vaquas explains in a recent discussion of SPD theorist Karl Kautsky's religious writings published in the Marxist journal *Cosmonaut*, there was already a clear precedent for harnessing the Protestant tradition to the Socialist movement. Of the fashion within the Social-Democratic

---

83 'Wie muß der neue Reichstag beschaffen sein?', *Deutsche Allgemeine Zeitung*, 1 January 1924, pp. 5–6 (p. 6).
84 Heine, *Zur Geschichte der Religion und Philosophie in Deutschland*, p. 141.

movement at the turn of the twentieth century for authoring pointedly political texts on Christian themes, Vaquas writes:

> Most of these publications are underpinned by a form of Protestant secularism: in which the medieval church is represented as a dominant institution within society rather than a 'central system of practices, meanings and values', a medium through which all social life was conducted. Rosa Luxemburg wrote that the Counter-Reformation was a part of what 'shattered the beginnings of a new human culture', which brought those in German lands back under the yoke of an oppressive church. Radical religious movements are recurrently praised insofar as they are a struggle against the papacy, identified as exploiter and ruler analogous to modern states.[85]

The last line of this passage suggests that it was largely the symbolic power of Lutheran revolt that led to its being cherished by left-wing radicals in imperial Germany, but the heralding by the Stabsoffizier of Christ's Second Coming hints at the presence in his patriotism of a genuinely pious devotion. Heine's longing for the German Fatherland to be liberated by a saviour of Luther's proportions and progressive credentials, a foreshadowing of Luxemburg's depiction of Germany labouring under a foreign clerical yoke that could easily be construed as a proto-capitalist behemoth, becomes explicitly religious in tone in the officer's hands.

The architect of this second Reformation therefore has a curious brief, consisting simultaneously of founding a bold new faith and of reinvigorating society's flagging interest in implicitly outdated biblical teachings. However, the reforming mission acquires coherence, as well as its necessarily German characteristics, through the integration of a Goethean maxim. Thus the principle of brotherly love contained within Christ's injunction in the Book of Matthew (Matthew 22.39) and the moral refrain from Goethe's poem 'Das Göttliche' (1783) are united in the image of a temple inscribed with both instructions and symbolizing a new era infused with German *Geist*:

> Merkt denn Niemand, daß die alten Religionen überlebt und leer geworden sind, daß die Zeit dürstet nach einem neuen Glauben, nach einer Weltanschauung, die einen Schritt vorwärts bringt, die Christus mit Goethe verbindet, und deren Tempel für Alle offen sind und die beiden Inschriften tragen: 'Liebe deinen Nächsten wie dich selbst!' und 'Edel sei der Mensch, hilfreich und gut!'.[86]

---

85 Rida Vaquas, '"Saint Francis of Assisi" by Karl Kautsky', *Cosmonaut*, 29 July 2019 <https://cosmonautmag.com/2019/07/saint-francis-of-assisi-by-karl-kautsky/> [accessed 12 April 2022].
86 Ein Stabsoffizier, 'Der Kronprinz', p. 16.

The elevation of 'Das Göttliche' to the status of a religious commandment may offer a clue as to what the officer has in mind when he assigns to Germany, in a later instalment cited above, the responsibility 'den Bolschewismus zu durchgeistigen'.[87] The poem begins by attributing to humankind a capacity for conscious benevolence that is unique among the species of Earth and equips its members theoretically to match the heavenly deities in virtue. However, the emphasis soon shifts from simply doing good to identifying evil and punishing it accordingly, another innate ability which supposedly sets humanity apart from the other inhabitants of the planet. This change in tone, which culminates in a paean to social responsibility and justice, adds rigour to Christ's message of common decency. Despite its foundations in Christianity and Communism, the edifice of the officer's all-encompassing world faith evidently requires the insertion of a German keystone so as not to cave in.

The need to fabricate revolutionary patriotism from a carefully calibrated blend of national and international values is a constant in the officer's writing. In October 1920 an article entitled 'Der neue Krieg' was published under the pseudonym 'Ein Stabsoffizier'; in it the author appears to retract his earlier support for a German-Russian military alliance against the capitalist countries on the grounds that war would leave Germany fighting for its very survival.[88] However, when a Communist named Wilhelm Markstahler responded to this piece with an open letter in favour of taking up arms against the allegedly exploitative nations of the West,[89] the officer abruptly reverted to his original position and held out the possibility of a final battle that would settle the course of human history once and for all in favour of Communism.[90] He admits that any such conflict would have to be pitched to the war-weary German people in explicitly patriotic terms, conjoining the Socialist ideology with the national interest in a manner rarely attempted until then:

> Was hat bisher alle diese Leute, die nach vielen Tausenden zählen, abgehalten, Sozialdemokraten oder Kommunisten zu werden? Doch nur die engstirnige Unduldsamkeit der sozialistischen Parteien gegen Alles, was irgendwie nach Bürgertum riecht, und die Betonung des internationalen Gedankens auf Kosten des nationalen. Wenn jetzt eine

---

87 Ein Stabsoffizier, 'Das alte Heer. Der Generalstab im Kriege', p. 106.
88 Ein Stabsoffizier, 'Der neue Krieg', *Die Weltbühne*, 16.2 (1920), 446–50. For the avoidance of confusion, this is not the same article as the aforementioned one of the same name, which appears in the next sentence with its complete citation reinstated for the sake of clarity.
89 Wilhelm Markstahler, 'Der neue Krieg I. Brief an den Stabsoffizier', *Die Weltbühne*, 16.2 (1920), 510–13.
90 Ein Stabsoffizier, 'Der neue Krieg', *Die Weltbühne* (16.2, 1920), 638–40.

> sozialistische Gruppe ihre Ziele etwas weiter steckt, etwa den Weg zur Internationale über Potsdam wählt und es versteht, die nationale Idee für ihre Zwecke einzuspannen, so erobert sie sich damit sicherlich abertausende von Anhängern aus der unübersehbaren Schar Derjenigen, die politisch nicht allzu viel nachdenken, und die durch die wirtschaftliche Not der Zeit so wie so zu Proletariern werden, aber auf keinen Fall die nationale Idee aufgeben wollen.[91]

The Germans whom the officer regards as ripe for conversion belong to the increasingly impoverished middle classes, whose obstinate attachment to their own Germanness continues to breed suspicion of a Socialist movement to which they might be drawn if its leaders were only to appeal to their patriotism as well as their pecuniary self-interest. The officer has changed his emphasis since 'Das alte Heer' reached its conclusion in the summer of the same year: whereas Socialism had been presented as a means to an unspecified patriotic end in his articles on Hindenburg and Ludendorff, it is now the national idea that serves the Socialist cause. As before, the impression created by this open cynicism is one of ambivalence concerning the author's true priorities.

However, the officer's desire for the Socialists even to pay lip service to 'the national idea' instantly sets him apart from other left-wing sympathizers of the post-war period. This distinctiveness is even more marked when compared with other ex-servicemen, given that these contributors had once taken up arms on behalf of their nation. Lothar Persius, who had served as an officer in the Imperial Navy before resigning in 1908, had made a second career for himself as a pacifist journalist. In the last issue of 1919 Persius wrote a favourable review of a pamphlet by the journal's then leader-writer and member of the anti-war Unabhängige Sozialdemokratische Partei (USPD) Heinrich Ströbel entitled 'Die Kriegsschuld der Rechtssozialisten'. Persius's review echoes Ströbel's frustration with the pro-war stance of the majority SPD, which both men attribute to an excess of nationalism in the party ranks. Finally, Persius calls on the party to steer a course away from nationalism:

> Weite Kreise, viele Männer, die es sich als Hauptaufgabe gesetzt haben, dem Kriege den Krieg zu erklären, sehnen sich danach, ihre Kräfte einer politischen Partei zu leihen, von der sie erwarten dürfen, daß sie ihre ganze Energie aufrichtig in den Dienst der Friedensarbeit, in den Dienst für den Völkerbund stellt. Man wird mir erwidern: das tut ja die Sozialdemokratische Partei! Aber kann ein Sozialdemokrat darüber im Zweifel sein, daß der unglückselige Streit in der Partei unzählige Deutsche abhält, sich ihr anzuschließen? Sobald die

---

91 Stabsoffizier, 'Der neue Krieg', p. 639.

Mehrheitssozialisten dem Militarismus und Nationalismus entsagt haben, sobald die Unabhängigen einen scharfen Trennungsstrich gegen links gezogen haben, müßte die Streitaxt begrabt werden können. Dann könnte die Sozialdemokratische Partei die Idealpartei sein für das gesamte Proletariat, soweit es politisch erwachsen ist, für das Proletariat, das heut unermeßlich stark ist, da eine gewaltige Menge Intellektueller dazu gehören.[92]

The content and beseeching tone of Persius's conclusion pre-empts to a remarkable degree the message of the Stabsoffizier to the Socialist movement the following year. Both believe that an inestimably large number of Germans, which the officer describes as an 'unübersehbare Schar' and Persius as 'unzählig', are waiting for their cue to join the Socialist movement but are 'abgehalten' by insuperable reservations. However, their remedies are diametrically opposed. Whereas Persius wants the SPD to distance itself from nationalism in order to win round the pacifist section of the population, the officer calls on the Socialist movement to appeal to the patriotic sentiments of middle-class Germans in order to dispel their lingering doubts about voting for a left-wing party. Both men long for world peace and endorse the notion of the Völkerbund, or League of Nations, to this end; but Persius's belief that the SPD would make its pacifist pretensions more credible by foreswearing nationalism is at odds with the officer's conviction that the left wing could render pacifism more palatable precisely by presenting it as a national cause.

This friction is reflected in the two authors' apparently conflicting uses of the term 'Krieg dem Kriege', which Persius seems to deploy in a strictly metaphorical sense. As becomes immediately apparent in 'Der neue Krieg', what the officer has in mind is no mere war of words designed to discredit war once and for all, but rather an actual battle that would prompt him 'meinen Stahlhelm vom Boden [zu] holen und mich bei meinem alten Regiment oder sonstwo [zu] melden'.[93] His subsequent claim 'Und so denken Tausende' is immediately undermined by Willy Meyer, a former regimental captain and veteran of the First World War, whose later defence of conditional pacifism is touched upon in the second chapter.[94] In a rejoinder to 'Der neue Krieg' published on the same page, Meyer becomes the latest ex-serviceman to greet the thought of a second world war with horror and plead for the enlargement of the Völkerbund to include Germany in its stead.[95] Even Meyer cannot resist the temptation to mythologize his own compatriots, paraphrasing

---

92 Persius, 'Die Kriegsschuld der Rechtssozialisten', p. 792.
93 Ein Stabsoffizier, 'Der neue Krieg', p. 639
94 Meyer, 'Berufssoldat und Pazifismus'.
95 Willy Meyer, 'Ergänzung', *Die Weltbühne*, 16.2 (1920), 640–42.

English historian Norman Angell's assertion in his recent critique of the Treaty of Versailles, 'daß ein so großes, intelligentes, willensstarkes Volk wie das deutsche sich nicht zu langsamem Hungertod verurteilen lassen werde'.[96] However, the possibility of Germany waging a retaliatory war instils fear in him, while the Stabsoffizier evidently regards the prospect with relish.

It should be noted that the suggestively post-national idea of declaring war on war, which the officer clearly imagines as a transcendentally ideological conflict between a capitalist West and a Communist East reaching beyond the oriental fringe of Europe, does not necessarily leave much room for the protection of specifically national interests. In his study of radicalism on the Left and Right in inter-war Germany, Timothy S. Brown identifies opposition to so-called 'imperialist war' as a theme beloved of KPD propagandists in the Weimar period,[97] before reproducing an undated KPD flier bearing the legend 'Krieg dem imperialistischen Kriege!' in a later discussion of the open rhetorical warfare between the Communist and Nazi parties.[98] The fact that the poster also declares in block capitals 'SCHÜTZT DIE SOWJETUNION' demonstrates the proximity of such slogans to political movements that were at best indifferent to the German national interest. Indeed, Brown himself deduces from the loudly professed allegiance of the KPD to the USSR the party's purely cynical relationship with such potentially patriotic concerns as the purportedly imperialistic and widely despised Treaty of Versailles.

However, the profession by the Stabsoffizier of national feeling is no charade. His liberal use of patriotic language and tropes alone, from an embattled and besmirched *Heimat* through blood-sucking foreign forces to the Rhine as a military and emotional frontier, gives the lie to Brown's default scepticism of the sincerity of radical left-wing patriotism. The officer imagines Germany's war veterans flocking to a Communist leader at the helm of a national dictatorship of the proletariat who issued the following call to arms:

> Soldaten der Reichswehr und der alten Armee! Noch einmal ruft die schwer bedrängte Heimat euch zu den Waffen, zum letzten Kriege, zum Kampf um den Weltfrieden und für den Völkerbund aller befreiten

---

96 Meyer, 'Ergänzung', p. 641; Norman Angell, *The Peace Treaty and the Economic Chaos of Europe* (London: Swarthmore, 1919). Angell had written that 'a moment's reflection should convince us that a racially and nationally cohesive block of 70 millions with a gift for discipline and organisation, surrounded by smaller States, most of whom are in bitter conflict with one another, cannot be condemned to slow starvation. Somehow, somewhen, they would find a means of breaking out of their prison' (pp. 79–80).

97 Timothy S. Brown, *Weimar Radicals: Nazis and Communists Between Authenticity and Performance*, Monographs in German History, 28 (New York: Berghahn, 2016), p. 25.

98 Brown, *Weimar Radicals*, p. 100.

> Nationen Asiens und Europas. Unsre deutsche Heimat ist befleckt durch fremde Besatzungen kapitalistischer Regierungen, die unserm Volk das Blut aussaugen und die stolze sieggewohnte deutsche Nation für immer versklaven wollen. Wir wollen arbeiten – aber für uns selbst, für unsre Frauen und Kinder, nicht für einige fremde Ausbeuter und Großkapitalisten. Vier Jahre habt ihr einer Welt in Waffen widerstanden und waret das erste Heer der Welt. Noch einmal zum letzten Kampf soll die alte Waffenherrlichkeit erstehen, noch einmal sollen die alten Fahnen und Standarten im Winde flattern dem Rheine zu und hoch über allen die rote Fahne der Völkerbefreiung, der Völkerversöhnung und des Weltfriedens.[99]

This fantasy of Communist patriotism sets off a number of echoes that largely drown out the patent eccentricity of summoning Germany's defeated and diminished Armed Forces out of retirement to wage another world war in the name of a lasting peace. The first derives from the officer's use of the term 'Heimat', the initial evocation of which is clearly intended to create a siege mentality. The second reference to 'Heimat' is loaded with ethnic tension: German soil is contaminated by the presence of Allied troops, to whom the author even ascribes vampiric characteristics. The contrast between this horde of bloodthirsty invaders and the implicitly pure German people, whose unexceptionable wish is to protect their women and children, could hardly be starker.

It is no coincidence that this righteous characterization of a nation prey to an ethically indefensible attack from beyond the Rhine should share its moral certainty with certain eighteenth- and early-nineteenth-century dramatic representations of the *Hermannsschlacht* (Battle of Teutoburg Forest (9 AD)) explored by Hans Peter Herrmann in the first and last chapters of his volume on German proto-nationalism.[100] Herrmann argues that the hero of these plays, the Germanic tribesman Hermann, is cast as a man of unimpeachable rectitude, with Friedrich Gottlieb Klopstock's *Hermanns Schlacht* (1769) featuring a scene in which the eponymous warrior demands of a Roman prisoner who broaches the subject of just war: 'Ich bin, und

---

99 Stabsoffizier, 'Der neue Krieg', p. 639.
100 Hans Peter Herrmann, *Machtphantasie Deutschland. Nationalismus, Männlichkeit und Fremdenhaß im Vaterlandsdiskurs deutscher Schriftsteller des 18. Jahrhunderts*, suhrkamp taschenbuch wissenschaft, 1273 (Frankfurt a.M.: Suhrkamp, 1996). In the nineteenth century the wooded ridge on which the battle was fought was officially renamed from Osning to the Teutoburger Wald in memory of the clash, which Tacitus records as taking place in the valley of *Teutoburgiensis*. It lies in the north-eastern corner of modern-day North-Rhine-Westphalia. Tacitus's name for the victorious German chieftain and Roman citizen, Arminius, has proved less durable, often giving way in modern texts to 'Hermann'.

ich will sein [...] ein Krieger für die Freiheit meines Vaterlands; kennst du einen gerechteren?'.[101] Herrmann's interpretation of this exchange is hard to dispute: 'Der Krieger für die "Freiheit des Vaterlandes" ist eo ipso ein gerechter Krieger'.[102] The officer's imaginary address to the nation is similarly unequivocal in its moral judgement, depicting the capitalist governments as would-be slavers and the Germans as one of a multitude of unfree peoples driven to violence against their will by the intolerable fact of their oppression.

For his part, the officer's preoccupation with France is undisguised. Indeed, by way of proving the inevitability of intermittent Franco-German conflict he recalls in 'Der neue Krieg' a conversation with a French counterpart in the ruins of a Belgian village during the First World War: 'Wir einigten uns schließlich dahin, daß erst dann Ruhe sein würde, wenn eine Revision des Vertrages von Verdun, der das Reich Karls des Großen teilte, auf irgendeine Weise herbeigeführt würde'.[103] Fanciful though it may seem at first glance, the officer's exchange with the Frenchman is reminiscent of an incident reported by Heinrich Heine in the closing passages of *Zur Geschichte der Religion und Philosophie in Deutschland*. By way of a warning to his French readership not to underestimate some Germans' animosity towards them, Heine remarks:

> Was man eigentlich gegen euch vorbringt, habe ich nie begreifen können. Einst im Bierkeller zu Göttingen äußerte ein junger Altdeutscher, daß man Rache an den Franzosen nehmen müsse für Konradin von Staufen, den sie zu Neapel geköpft. Ihr habt das gewiß längst vergessen. Wir aber vergessen nichts.[104]

While the tone in which Heine relates this vignette shows that he does not condone the lone nationalist's vendetta, the anecdote suggests that the public execution in 1268 of the teenage Swabian Duke Konrad IV, the last male heir of the Hohenstaufen dynasty, at the hands of a rival French pretender to the Sicilian throne still rankled with nineteenth-century German nationalists. In this context, the conjuring by the Stabsoffizier of congenital resentment over the Treaty of Verdun (843), which distributed the Frankish Empire once ruled over by Charlemagne among his grandsons and first imposed borders between those territories which would later become France, Germany and Italy, no longer appears quite so implausible.

Given that the offending treaty was a mediaeval document, it may be stretching a point to construe modern France as a substitute in the officer's

---

101 Friedrich Gottlieb Klopstock, *Hermanns Schlacht. Ein Bardiet für die Schaubühne* (Hamburg: Cramer, 1769), p. 112.
102 Herrmann, *Machtphantasie Deutschland*, p. 46.
103 Stabsoffizier, 'Der neue Krieg', p. 638.
104 Heine, *Zur Geschichte der Religion und Philosophie in Deutschland*, p. 203.

mind for imperial Rome, but it is striking that the capitalist regimes which he dreams of expunging from the map are associated with the same vice as their Roman forebears in the eighteenth-century Hermann plays: love of money and the leverage it offers. Thus the demonic blood-sucking exploiters mentioned in the officer's imaginary call-to-arms closely resemble the Roman 'Händlervolk' in Johann Elias Schlegel's *Herrmann. Ein Trauerspiel* (1743), 'das sich die Welt mit Hilfe einer überlegenen Finanzkraft zu eigen macht und das Geldprinzip, die Begehrlichkeit nach dem Gold (wie die Begehrlichkeit nach fremden Leibern), weiter verbreitet'.[105] For twentieth-century officer and eighteenth-century playwright alike, the German national cause derives its legitimacy from the threat of subjugation by overbearing neighbours. Against this multi-generational backdrop, the officer's image of 'die alten Fahnen und Standarten' blowing towards the Rhine at the head of the German military convoy acquires an additional historical momentum.

As if to emphasize the unique wariness that France had long inspired in Germans of a patriotic disposition, Herrmann sums up the foreign threat in Heinrich von Kleist's *Die Hermannsschlacht. Ein Drama* (1808) as follows: '[D]ie fremdländische (römische, französische) Unterdrückung Deutschlands stellt sich dar nicht nur im Horizont von Gewalt und Sklaverei, sondern auch im Horizont von Kauf und Bereicherung'.[106] As a product of the Napoleonic era, Kleist's play is here interpreted as an allegorical comment on French presumption, an interpretation that is reinforced in a letter in which Kleist laments the subjugation of Europe by the French Emperor: 'Wir sind die unterjochten Völker der Römer. Das Ganze ist auf eine Ausplünderung von Europa abgesehen, um Frankreich reich zu machen'.[107] Whereas in Kleist's play Rome serves as a convenient substitute for a contemporary enemy, the officer feels no need of allegory in his broadsides against France. His description of a blameless Germany valiantly fighting for its life in the face of invasion by avaricious and amoral Western forces mirrors the stark moral dichotomy on which the Hermann plays rest. When the alternative is to succumb to a malicious army bent purely on accruing more wealth and power, patriotic resistance is an inescapable ethical imperative.

To the objective observer, the polyphony of cultural and historical resonances contained within the officer's call-to-arms generates an atmosphere of vengeful nationalism in which the red flag of the Communist International seems distinctly incongruous. In the closing paragraph of

---

105 Herrmann, *Machtphantasie Deutschland*, p. 54.
106 Herrmann, *Machtphantasie Deutschland*, p. 56.
107 Heinrich von Kleist, Letter to Ulrike von Kleist, 24 October 1806, in *Heinrichs von Kleist Briefe an seiner Schwester Ulrike*, ed. by A. Roberstein (Berlin: Schroeder, 1860), pp. 108–10 (p. 110).

the article, however, the officer reunites patriotism with internationalism in a religiously charged vision of a German political party of the poor. His country is not yet, he argues, in any fit state to fight the righteous war of liberation imagined earlier in the piece because it remains disunited:

> Zur Zeit also ist nur möglich, die Vorbereitungen für die Wiedergeburt Deutschlands zu treffen und die Idee zu finden, auf die sich der größte Teil des Volkes, vornehmlich die Jugend, einigen kann. Bringt uns der Kommunismus diesen neuen Glauben, der die Herzen begeistert und entflammt, der der Menschheit neue Ziele weist und sie aufwärts führt, so soll er willkommen sein. Mir schwebt eine Partei vor, die ihre Tore weit öffnet für Alle, die mühsälig und beladen sind, eine Partei der Armen, die die Menschenliebe predigt wie Franz von Assisi, die zwar von ihrer großen internationalen Mission nicht abzubringen ist, aber doch zunächst einmal an das eigne schwer geprüfte Volk denkt. Die Gründung dieser Partei wäre eine neue Reformation, für die die Zeit reif ist, nach der sie sich sehnt, die imstande wäre, Proletarier, Studenten und Soldaten als Jünger und Propheten zu sammeln.[108]

According to the officer's blueprint, Germany is to be remade on the basis of a new national idea propounded by the youth. At first glance, the clarity of this vision is obscured by its points of reference: the thirteenth-century friar Francis of Assisi and, as in the ninth instalment of 'Das alte Heer', Martin Luther as the father of the Protestant Reformation.[109] There would appear to be an inescapable incongruity in founding a party of national unity in the image of a canonized Catholic mystic, while simultaneously characterizing it as the next stage of a sober reformist tradition hostile to the idea of a visionary elect. In fact, however, the same Socialist tradition that repeatedly harked back to Luther's act of defiance as a source of inspiration for its own radical designs also exhibited a marked sympathy with the abstemious egalitarianism of Francis of Assisi, whom the aforementioned Karl Kautsky described in 1904 as a preacher of Communism.[110]

Francis's particular appeal to Kautsky resides in his veneration of work, which extended to ordering the members of his order to join together with woodcutters, fruit-pickers and bakers to earn their subsistence. The collectivist spirit of Francis's teachings is even presented as an early form of Protestantism that would, in the course of the Reformation, be rendered not invalid but simply surplus to requirements. It is, therefore, apt that a

---

108 Stabsoffizier, 'Der neue Krieg', p. 640.
109 Stabsoffizier, 'Das alte Heer. Der Kronprinz', p. 16.
110 Karl Kautsky, 'Der heilige Franz von Assisi. Ein Revisionist des mittelalterlichen Kommunismus', in *Die Neue Zeit*, 22.35 (1903/1904), 260-67 (p. 260).

pre-requisite for admission into the party of the poor proposed by the Stabsoffizier should be the quality of being 'mühsälig und beladen' (Matthew 11.28). Indeed, the defining characteristic of the political movement the officer has in mind is the capacity to work on behalf of the wider community. It is the national proportions of this community that lend an unabashedly patriotic flavour to the war veteran's flirtation with world peace. The hybrid faith around which the officer imagines his cross-class flock of believers uniting may be humanitarian Communism, but its main beneficiary, at least in the short term, is the embattled German nation.

*

A clear trail of sympathy leads from the internationalist patriots discussed in the previous chapter of this book to the revolutionary patriots of the early Weimar-era *Weltbühne* explored in this section. For all that their horizons are similarly expansive, however, their ideological allegiances do not necessarily overlap. The extravagantly idealistic Socialism of the Stabsoffizier, for instance, is but one strand of the journal's commitment to its cosmopolitan name. The unique status of the series 'Das alte Heer' resides in its unknown author's readiness to marry conventional German iconography such as the figure of Luther together with dramatic rhetoric about the coming of a Communist turn in world history, thereby absorbing into a single world view aspects of both the nostalgia and the radicalism highlighted earlier in the chapter. By intertwining the innate internationalism of the Communist movement with a dogged insistence on the German revolutionary's obligation to his home country, the officer does not only combine national and international prerogatives, but unites Socialism and patriotism as two sides of the same coin. The case study with which this section concludes thus exemplifies the simultaneously plangent and oracular tone struck by the boldest proponents of Socialist patriotism in *Die Weltbühne*.

For Reformist Socialism

As the Weimar period progressed and the post-revolutionary turbulence died down, reformism gradually prevailed over revolution in the pages of *Die Weltbühne*, permanently re-defining the nature of the journal's Socialist patriotism. Indeed, radical voices such as Ludwig Jurisch's became increasingly marginalized as the sense of possibility engendered by the abdication of the Kaiser diminished. The steady retreat of revolutionary rhetoric in *Die Weltbühne* in the three years following the Armistice reflects the relative alacrity with which the journal adapted to the rapidly moving political landscape. This adaptability could express itself in unequivocal pronouncements that accorded transient phenomena greater historical or contemporary importance than they necessarily possessed in the final analysis. Nonetheless, the purpose and effect of such sweeping judgements, which promoted rather simplistic narratives founded on generalizations, was to call time on those forms of radicalism the journal deemed too impatient, and instead to endorse a gradualist transformation of German society that apparently could not fail to bear fruit if given space to grow. As the Weimar Republic advanced in years, *Weltbühne* writers reluctantly came to see Germany's path to political enlightenment as long and circuitous.

The leader column of *Die Weltbühne* is a faithful barometer of the journal's shifting stance in the aftermath of war. By the time it ceased to be the exclusive property of one writer in 1922, the column had divested itself of the agitative style peculiar to Jurisch in exchange for a more moderate, consistent view of the political climate in which the fledgling Republic would thrive. After Heinrich Ströbel's succession had led to a softening in tone, the decisive break was made in November 1920 with the arrival of Karl Rothammer, an avowed Social-Democrat who scorned insurrection as a vehicle for social change. Although a believer in the masses' fundamental right to revolt, Rothammer was a staunch critic of the KPD and their seditious tactics until the end of his tenure in October 1921.

In an otherwise volatile climate Rothammer's leaders describe a largely moderate course that distances *Die Weltbühne* from the revolutionary elements of the left-wing movement while repudiating reactionary right-wing agitation with still greater force. Both extremes are portrayed as misrepresenting a German national interest crying out for a grassroots overhaul of the national economy and body politic under the sign of reformist Socialism. This caution was allied with a potent patriotic rhetoric exemplified in an editorial from March 1921. Looking ahead to the Prussian state elections later that month, Rothammer declares with a rhetorical flourish: 'Fest steht nur, wie die Wacht am Rhein: der Block der Sozialdemokratie als Hüter der Volksfreiheit und der gesunden Entwicklung des deutschen Wirtschaftslebens'.[111] By linking social democracy to an image of armed resistance against foreign onslaught, Rothammer invests the gradualist objectives of the SPD with an aura of robust patriotic heroism, thereby elevating the patriotic credentials of electorally-mandated reformism above those of extremist revolution.

Rothammer's arrival marks the culmination of a sobering in the journal's editorial policy that Alf Enseling mistakenly traces back to the mid-Twenties.

---

111 Karl Rothammer, 'Die Preußenwahlen', *Die Weltbühne*, 17.1 (1921), 237–39 (p. 239).

In reference to the five-year period between the Dawes Plan of 1924 and the global economic crisis of 1929,[112] popularly known in the Anglosphere as the 'Golden Years', Enseling asserts: 'In den Jahren der Konsolidierung erachtete die "Weltbühne" es als ihre vornehmste Aufgabe, das sich festigende Gefüge der Republik durch die Einigung und Stützung aller linken Elemente abzusichern und auszubauen.'[113] In fact, the Weltbühne did not wait until the revised reparations package had been signed before throwing its weight behind the Weimar state; it had maintained an unwaveringly pro-republican line since the beginning of the decade. As we shall see in the first part of this section, the seminal event in the development of an expressly patriotic left-wing narrative in the journal was the Kapp Putsch of March 1920. The suppression of this right-wing uprising was swiftly exploited by Die Weltbühne to construct a legend of moderate left-wing patriotic activism in which Socialist civilians figured as the saviours of German democracy from self-serving nationalist forces.

Nor was 'Putschismus', as contributors often disparagingly called the belief in seizing power by force, associated solely with the right wing. Indeed, as Eric D. Weitz notes, the German Revolution had:

> established the precedent of armed political struggle in Germany. In four of the first five years of the Republic, the KPD sought to found a Socialist system through military means: the (misnamed) Spartacist Uprising of 1919, the Ruhr conflict that followed the Kapp-Putsch in 1920, the so-called March Action of 1921, and the uprising of October 1923.[114]

In the second and third parts of this section the journal's view of ongoing unrest in the Ruhrgebiet and its response to the March Action are scrutinized, revealing the scathing Weltbühne view of left-wing radicalism as well as its counterpoint on the far Right.

The reformist writers discussed here were not indifferent to international politics, with Heinrich Ströbel routinely inveighing against Germany's perceived victimization under the Treaty of Versailles in general and the implementation of the Treaty by France in particular. Indeed, in the capacity of leader-writer Ströbel repeatedly employed the phrase

---

112 This was an economic aid package that stabilized the German currency through a significant loan and reduced the amount of annual war reparations that Germany would have to pay, thereby solving the Franco-Belgian occupation of the Ruhrgebiet known as the Ruhr Crisis. It earned its architect, the American Republican politician Charles Dawes, the Nobel Peace Prize in 1925.
113 Enseling, Die Weltbühne, p. 81.
114 Weitz, Creating German Communism, p. 196.

'Entente-Imperialismus' as shorthand for Allied rapacity vis-à-vis Germany.[115] However, the overcoming of the imperialist idea on a global scale soon receded in importance behind the campaign in the leader column against domestic extremism of all stripes. This section thus bears witness above all else to the attempts by the *Weltbühne* Socialists to win a patriotic struggle with the far Right and Left over how to define the German national interest, with the pursuit of the international Socialist cause relegated down the list of patriotic priorities.

The Kapp Putsch, 1920: Taking the Fight to the Right

From 1920 onwards republicanism became the left-wing patriotic cause of choice in *Die Weltbühne*. The role of the Kapp Putsch in this change cannot be overstated as it presented the journal with an irresistible example of the capacity of democracy to inspire an authentic cross-class solidarity in opposition to self-interested nationalism. The coup d'état around the monarchist civil servant Wolfgang Kapp saw the democratically elected government put to flight by a makeshift alliance of decommissioned soldiers and mercenaries. The aim was to restore an authoritarian state on the imperial model, albeit without the *Kaiser* as figurehead, but this was swiftly thwarted when the ousted SPD-run government endorsed a general strike of both blue- and white-collar labour unions.

The propaganda potential of the Putsch did not immediately dawn on all of the journal's writers. In an article published the following week, Kurt Tucholsky, in the guise of Ignaz Wrobel, claims that it might not have happened at all if the mistreatment of the regular soldier at the hands of the officer class during the First World War had occasioned a Socialist epiphany capable of permanently neutering the political influence of the military leaders who had engineered the Putsch. Their reticence allegedly rendered the high-circulation newspapers and political elite of the country culpable for the coup attempt: 'Das fürchterliche Leiden des deutschen Volkes im Kriege unter seinen eignen größenwahnsinnig gewordenen Landsleuten, das Leiden des gemeinen Soldaten – das wurde verschwiegen. (Töricht genug: hier ist der Keim einer ganz großen Volksbewegung, hier der Angelpunkt für eine wahre Demokratie.)'[116] The shared predicament of German privates between 1914 and 1918 could, Tucholsky reflects, have inspired a re-organization of national life along democratic lines. According to this reading, the Kapp

---

115 Heinrich Ströbel, 'Das baltische Komplott', *Die Weltbühne*, 15.2 (1919), 525–30 (p. 530); 'Tollhäuslerei und Erzbergerei', p. 257; 'Zwischen zwei Militarismen', *Die Weltbühne*, 16.1 (1920), 417–21 (p. 420).
116 Wrobel, 'Kapp-Lüttwitz', p. 360.

Putsch was quite simply an indictment of the Germans' failure to rout imperial privilege and usher in a new era of egalitarianism.

However, Heinrich Ströbel's leader in the same issue, portentously entitled 'Nach dem Putsch', claims the stifling of the Kapp Putsch as the historical moment at which German workers had indeed risen as one in defence of a common national asset: the democratic Republic. For Ströbel, therefore, the Putsch represents a blessing in disguise:

> Denn er hat erreicht, was alle Mahnungen zu politischer Vernunft bisher nicht vermochten: er hat das Proletariat zu einer Einheit zusammengeschweißt. Als die Baltikumer einrückten und Prätorianerfäuste sich um die Gurgel der Demokratie legten, da war alle faselnde Revolutionsromantik und aller dogmatische Sektenfanatismus mit einem Schlage zerstoben, und das Gebot des Augenblick: der einmütige Kampf gegen die Piraten der Republik trat machtvoll an die Stelle des Parteigezänks.[117]

In this operatically swelling passage, the journal's chief leader-writer paints a vivid picture of an instantaneous explosion of patriotic solidarity in which the entire working class had suddenly resolved to prioritize the salvation of German democracy over their doctrinal differences. Indeed, 'der Keim einer ganz großen Volksbewegung' longed for by Tucholsky announces itself in this alliance between the proletariat, the salaried classes and the Civil Service. Even the dynamism of Ströbel's language itself is suggestive of a clarifying national movement: tribal equivocations are dispersed 'mit einem Schlage' out of deference to the 'Gebot des Augenblick', which enforces 'Einmütigkeit' in its turn.

In the heat of the moment *Die Weltbühne* was not the only left-wing publication to capitalize on the Putsch in this way. In the immediate aftermath of the turmoil, the SPD's own organ, *Vorwärts*, had likewise credited the survival of the Republic to the workers' account and demanded that their intervention mark a watershed in the evolution of German republicanism: 'Die bürgerlichen Parteien werden einsehen müssen, daß gegen die Arbeiter, die die Republik gerettet haben, nicht regiert werden kann'.[118] A fortnight later *Die Weltbühne* published a contrary claim from the pen of the Stabsoffizier. Casting doubt on the efficacy of the general strike as a political tool, the officer insists that the resistance of certain divisions of the regular army was the decisive factor in the survival of the Republic, adding: 'Alle Politiker müssen sich aber bei dieser Gelegenheit darüber klar

---

117 Heinrich Ströbel, 'Nach dem Putsch', *Die Weltbühne*, 16.1 (1920), 353–56 (p. 355).
118 'Vorwärts in den Kampf!', *Vorwärts*, 22 March 1920, pp. 1–2 (p. 1).

werden, daß der Soldat, wo es hart auf hart kommt, doch stärker ist als der Arbeiter, wenn dieser auch die Betriebe beherrscht'.[119] In general, though, the journal was remarkable for its sustained attempts to translate the ruthless spontaneity and unspoken unity of purpose eulogized in Heinrich Ströbel's article into the plausible image of an organic popular will massed behind the Socialist idea.

This will was frequently vested in an entity known as 'das schaffende Volk'. This phrase, which we encounter in Carl Mertens's denunciation of illicit militarism in the previous chapter, served in these pages as an implicit judgement on the idle and exploitative upholders of a suspected conspiracy between military and business leaders at the expense of the German worker. As such, it was a formulation that combined sharp criticism of the capitalist system with a patriotic appeal to a German nationhood predicated on hard work. Martin Kley has demonstrated that the notion of work could be deployed in left-wing texts of the Weimar period either as a unifying force in the face of a common capitalist enemy or as a marker of exclusive professional identity that distinguished between factory workers and artisans or small business owners.[120] In Ströbel's usage, it is the former: a binding agent holding together a coalition of economically active Germans whose particular professional pursuits are subsumed into a single proletarian life force:

> Aber wenn das Proletariat sich nicht wieder von perfiden reaktionären Drahtziehern und von gewissenlosen Demagogen eines läppischen Phrasenradikalismus auseinander und gegeneinanderhetzen läßt, sondern seine Kraft auf erreichbare Ziele zu konzentrieren versteht, so wird, namentlich durch eine gemeinsame Wahlfront gegen rechts, die Arbeiter-Regierung, die Regierung der schaffenden Kräfte des Volkes, tatsächlich die Form werden, in der die Demokratie die Vollstreckerin der Revolution und der Hebel der Sozialisierung werden kann![121]

Ströbel's appeal to the proletariat and evocation of an 'Arbeiterregierung', with its inescapable echoes of the decentralized, proletarian-powered concept of the *Arbeiterrat*, indicates a blue-collar bias in his vision for a revitalized national community. To overstate this point, though, would be to obscure the unitarian message underpinning 'Nach dem Putsch'. Instead of promoting the revolutionary model of the *Arbeiterrat*, which Martin Jay

---

119 Ein Stabsoffizier, 'Das alte Heer. Soldat und Politik', *Die Weltbühne*, 16.1 (1920), xxi, 393–96 (p. 395).
120 Martin Kley, *Weimar and Work: Labor, Literature, and Industrial Modernity on the Weimar Left*, Studies on Themes and Motifs in Literature, 114 (New York: Lang, 2013).
121 Ströbel, 'Nach dem Putsch', p. 355–56.

describes as 'a new form of political *cum* economic organization in which local power and communal solidarity would restore power to the people – or at least the working class – rather than their representatives',[122] Ströbel imagines a government acting 'speziell als die Vertreterin aller arbeitenden Volksschichten'.[123]

In Ströbel's lexicon, 'das schaffende Volk',[124] otherwise known as 'die schaffenden Kräfte des Volkes',[125] is synonymous with a cross-class constituency of manual labourers, office workers and civil servants. It was, he stresses on several occasions, 'das schaffende Volk, die Arbeiter, Angestellten und Beamten' that had foiled the Kapp Putsch: 'An der Tatkraft der Arbeiter, Angestellten und Beamten allein zerschellte der Militärputsch'.[126] Ströbel's inclusive interpretation of the Socialist movement as one which embraces the middle classes and aspires to control the levers of central government instead of dispersing power among a multiplicity of councils lends the Socialist revolution of which he dreams an authentically nationwide dimension not impinged upon by class warfare.

This openness to fraternization between working and middle classes may not appear altogether surprising in a career Social Democrat. According to Timothy Brown, even Communism sometimes 'manipulated Marxist categories to include elements of the middle classes among the "oppressed", and by placing the nation – sometimes explicitly – at the forefront of the class struggle'.[127] Unconstrained by the hard Left's intermittent wariness of compromising itself with overt appeals to the middle classes, Ströbel has no compunction about allocating white-collar Germans a place in his re-imagined nation. Nonetheless, an article by Karl Kautsky published in the journal in early 1920 shows that this position could not be taken for granted at a time when the concept of the *Arbeiterrat* was evidently sweeping the rank and file of the SPD. Describing the 'Räte-Gedanke' as 'etwas ungemein Vages und Wechselndes' and as 'eine Löwenhaut, in der mancher Schnock der Schreiner Platz findet',[128] Kautsky singles out fellow USPD renegade Ströbel as one of the few prominent party members who had not succumbed. As the principal architect of the Erfurter Programm (1891), which had committed

---

122 Martin Jay, 'The Weimar Left: Theory and Practice', in *Weimar Thought: A Contested Legacy*, ed. by Gordon and McCormick, pp. 377–93 (p. 383).
123 Ströbel, 'Nach dem Putsch', p. 355.
124 Ströbel, 'Nach dem Putsch', p. 353.
125 Ströbel, 'Nach dem Putsch', p. 356.
126 Ströbel, 'Nach dem Putsch', p. 353.
127 Brown, *Weimar Radicals*, p. 46.
128 Karl Kautsky, 'Belagerungszustand und Unabhängige', *Die Weltbühne*, 16.1 (1920), 165–69 (p.167).

the SPD to a non-revolutionary, reformist course following the expiration of Bismarck's *Sozialistengesetz* the previous year, Kautsky was hardly likely to prove susceptible himself.

Inevitably, the fluidity of the concept of the *schaffendes Volk* in the Weimar era made it appealing to advocates of exclusionary ethno-nationalist narratives, as well as to proponents of affirmative patriotic visions. In the autumn of 1930 the phrase makes an appearance in the insurrectionary manifesto statements of the rebel *Sturmabteilung* (SA) leader Walter Stennes to denote the constituency in whose name he wished to found a rival paramilitary organization that would stay true to the purportedly revolutionary founding principles of the Nazi Party.[129] The malleability of the term only underscores the unifying patriotic power it was thought to possess. Indeed, Michael Mann has shown that, at least on the face of it, Fascist ideologues meant the same thing by it as veteran Social Democrats such as Ströbel: 'the workers of all classes' or, alternatively, 'the productive classes', as opposed to their 'unproductive' opposite numbers.[130] Predictably, as Timothy Brown points out, this crude distinction between dependent workers and their bosses was overlain with anti-Semitic connotations arising from the association between Jews and high finance; one Nazi theorist even labelled the latter 'raffendes Kapital', as against 'schaffendes Kapital'.[131] As the rhetorical focus for any movement with nationwide pretensions, however, *das schaffende Volk* proved unusually versatile.

This myth of a uniformly industrious people synonymous with the nation itself reappears more than three years after the Kapp Putsch in an article written by Hans von Zwehl against the backdrop of the Ruhr Crisis. In 'Von Ruhr und Rhein' von Zwehl casts his mind back to the Kapp Putsch, evoking a massed popular army analogous to the *schaffendes Volk* whose humble aim had been confined to 'defending' the Weimar Republic. Momentarily omitting to mention the failed *Ruhraufstand* that followed the quashing of the Putsch, von Zwehl takes pains to foreground the democratic impulse behind the industrial action:

> Einstmals, drei Jahre ists her, als die Musikkapelle des Diktators Kapp vor dem Café Josty militärische Weisen spielte, sahen wir diese Kumpels sich zu einer hunderttausendfältigen Armee zusammenballen, Menschen aller Parteien, Evangelische, Katholiken, Rote, Anarchisten, Hirsch-Dunckersche: sie wollten die Republik der Deutschen verteidigen.[132]

---

129 Brown, *Weimar Radicals*, p. 70.
130 Michael Mann, *Fascists* (Cambridge: Cambridge University Press, 2004), p. 7.
131 Brown, *Weimar Radicals*, p. 52.
132 Hans von Zwehl, 'Von Ruhr und Rhein', *Die Weltbühne*, 19.2 (1923), 503–06 (p. 503).

Just as Ströbel applauds the strikers for setting aside 'Parteigezänk' for the sake of the Republic, von Zwehl emphasizes the irrelevance of party allegiance. His choice of the word 'Kumpel' even implies that the patriotic cause had acted as a social leveller, dissolving confessional and class identities in such a way as to unite the participants in mutual recognition of their shared Germanness.

In von Zwehl's telling, this patriotic animus is directed not at some indeterminate revolutionary objective but at the maintenance of a status quo the basic republican tenets of which are held to be worth defending. The mounting by the working multitudes of an essentially conservative rearguard action in defence of national law and order leaves the right-wing rebels in the unaccustomed role of seditious traitors, while the workers are cast as national guardians or, in Ströbel's words, 'die Retter der alten Regierung, der Verfassung, der Demokratie'.[133] Von Zwehl's tantalizing evocation of a 'Republik der Deutschen' suggests a desire to infuse the republican idea with a peculiarly German quality and thereby lend it an unassailable popular legitimacy that it was widely thought still to lack four years after its inception. This rehabilitation of republicanism as a patriotic idea recalls Wilhelm Michel's demand, considered at greater length in the first chapter, for 'eine deutsche Demokratie und [...] unsre Republik', with which he hoped to burnish the patriotic credentials of his fellow left-wingers.[134] Running counter to the scholarship from the 1960s discussed in the introduction to this book,[135] these articles show that the Weimar Republic was not smothered in its infancy by the left-wing press, but instead found energetic support from otherwise measured columnists.

Trouble in the Ruhr, 1920–25: Asserting the Will of the People

With the democratic Republic established as a patriotic cause worthy of unanimous support, Die Weltbühne could turn its attention over the next five years to converting its extremist critics on Left and Right. The simmering tension in the Ruhrgebiet during the first half of the decade put the journal on a collision course with right-wing radicals swearing revenge on the French occupiers, as the German response to invasion became a matter of national life or death. The Ruhr Crisis, which was by no means the first incident on Germany's western border to derail Franco-German relations, began with the invasion of French and Belgian forces on 11 January 1923 and lasted until the final withdrawal of troops on 25 August 1925. By this time the journal had

---

133 Ströbel, 'Nach dem Putsch', p. 353.
134 Michel, 'Glaube an Deutschland', p. 537.
135 Golo Mann, *Deutsche Geschichte des 19. und 20. Jahrhunderts*; Enseling, *Die Weltbühne*.

begun to endorse a policy of appeasement and to warn readers of the risks of stoking Francophobia. Most commentators claimed that the true threat to German unity was not the invaders but those Germans who insisted on provoking them. If the French government saw fit to dispatch its army across the German border in order to take by force what it was owed in accordance with the post-war treaties, the Weimar regime was duty-bound to find a means of meeting their neighbours' demands and thus to bring about their withdrawal. Germany's survival as a sovereign state was deemed to be at stake.

In the first issue of 1921 leader-writer Karl Rothammer leaves little to the imagination in his take on the issue of reparations. Reproaching nationalists for their hypocrisy in urging a tough strategy on patriotic grounds, he calls for an end to such rhetoric so that Germany can be readmitted to the international community:

> Nur in Gestalt der Republik kommt Deutschland an den Tisch, an dem Weltpolitik gemacht wird. Reaktion; Gefasel von einer neuen Monarchie; Kloakenfluß aus Biergehirn; Germania-Tinte und Revanche-Schleim: dergleichen mehrt nur die Hindernisse, die wir an und für sich zu überwinden bereits Mühe genug haben.[136]

To illustrate the effect of right-wing nationalist rhetoric, Rothammer conjures the image of a viscous slurry of worthless waste matter stifling Germany and thwarting its rehabilitation in the eyes of its neighbours. As the article continues, the language becomes even more graphic:

> Für das kommende Jahr kann man deshalb dem deutschen Volke nichts Besseres wünschen, als daß allen seinen Adlerputzern und Hohenzollernbüstenabstäubern die Hände verdorren, aller reaktionären Agitation die Giftzähne ausgebrochen werden, alle kaiserlich und so gesonnenen Offiziere, Beamte, Lehrer und Professoren zum Teufel gehen. Nur aus der Leiche der Reaktion blüht Deutschland neues Leben, und erst, wenn es von dieser Leiche heißt: 'Völker der Welt, sie stinket schon', wird das Wunder der Auferstehung geschehen.[137]

Out of the rancid corpse of the reactionary Right, with its withered hands and toothless gums, a reinvigorated Germany will arise to preach the sustaining virtues of moderate social democracy. The virulence with which Rothammer meets the Francophobic venom of his political adversaries is, as the third and final subsection shows, a startling rhetorical feature of the anti-extremism of the journal.

---

136 Karl Rothammer, 'Reaktion und Weltpolitik', *Die Weltbühne*, 17.1 (1921), 1–2 (p. 2).
137 Rothammer, 'Reaktion und Weltpolitik', p. 2.

By advocating so trenchantly for an *Erfüllungspolitik* vis-à-vis the Allied powers, Rothammer pre-empts Clara Zetkin's perspective on treason, pronounced two years later in her aforementioned speech to the *Bundestag*. According to Zetkin, it was unjust to level the charge of treason at Communists who sought to unite the international proletariat across national borders because it was not them but the self-proclaimed patriots of the industrial class who were offering the Allies a pretext for invasion: 'Sie sind Landesverräter, die dem Ententeimperialismus das Tor zum Einfall in das Ruhrgebiet geöffnet haben'.[138] By this logic, industrialists who defied the Treaty of Versailles by refusing to countenance deliveries of goods could no more claim to have Germany's best interests at heart than those nationalistic newspaper columnists who had once authored, in Rothammer's words, 'Leitartikel, die der französischen und englischen Hetzpresse Material liefern'.[139] To Rothammer, as to Zetkin, such nationalist intriguers are no better than 'Hochverräter' who have forfeited their right to cast aspersions on leftist writers' patriotism.[140]

As Franco-German relations foundered, it was not only regular contributors, nor even necessarily professional journalists, who argued against the popular understanding of patriotism. In July 1923 a reader's letter offers first-hand testimony to the effects of the Ruhr Crisis on the industrial workforce and blames Germany's increasing impoverishment on the obstinacy of the German industrialists and the architects of the policy of passive resistance. Then editor of the *Weltbühne* Siegfried Jacobsohn had, he explains in a preface to the letter, reproduced the account in its entirety by way of a rejoinder to the claim made by the politician Graf Kuno von Westarp, a member of the Deutschnationale Volkspartei, in the right-wing *Kreuzzeitung* that the population of the Ruhr would welcome the opportunity to fight their French occupiers. Instead, the anonymous worker presents the settlement of Germany's outstanding debts as an authentic patriotic imperative:

> Wenn man für Verständigung ist, für Abbau des passiven Widerstandes, der ja keiner ist, dann ist man kein Miesmacher, sondern hat mehr Vaterlandsliebe im kleinen Finger als alle übrigen zusammengenommen in ihren hochqualifizierten Gehirnen, aus denen entweder nur Mist ausgebrütet wird oder ein hochlohnendes Geschäft. [...] Aber natürlich die Leute um Schlageter sind die wahren Patrioten und Cuno der Retter des Vaterlandes. Ich bin der Ansicht: wer es ehrlich mit Deutschland meint, ist für Verständigung,

---

138 Zetkin, 'Gegen Poincaré und Cuno', p. 995.
139 Rothammer, 'Reaktion und Weltpolitik', p. 2.
140 Rothammer, 'Reaktion und Weltpolitik', p. 1.

Abbau des passiven Widerstandes und Rückkehr zu einer ehrlichen Erfüllungspolitik, zu der wir wohl als Besiegte verpflichtet sind.[141]

Somewhat remarkably, Karl Rothammer's image of faecal matter issuing from the brains of nationalist commentators is reprised in this passage, reinforced by insinuations about the personal rapacity believed by the author to be motivating the brinkmanship of the capitalist class. Jacobsohn himself lends credence to these suspicions by adding a postscript to his letter to the effect that the industrial magnate Hugo Stinnes was earning 'unvergleichlich mehr' since re-orienting his coal business away from mining and towards the import market in the early stages of the Ruhr Crisis.[142]

The sarcastic reference to the veteran of the Kapp Putsch Albert Leo Schlageter, who had been executed by the French military for carrying out repeated acts of sabotage against cargo trains in the Ruhr, is one of several contemptuous allusions to the Freikorps fighter's terrorist tactics in the course of this letter. Schlageter's role as a scapegoat for the unnamed worker's ire confirms the gulf between those Germans intent on cultivating a siege mentality in the face of Allied invasion and those who wish permanently to relieve the 'Fatherland' of the foreign presence by agreeing to the invaders' demands. The juxtaposition of Schlageter and Chancellor Wilhelm Cuno, who had first ordered the Ruhr workers to walk out after French troops marched into the Ruhr less than two months into his tenure, renders the government complicit in a patriotic charade the sole interest of which is allegedly in maximizing the profits of the industrial elite.

The journal's patriotic opposition to passive and military resistance against the French invaders is exemplified by a trio of articles by Hans von Zwehl that appeared in three consecutive issues of *Die Weltbühne* published in the second half of November 1923. In the first of this sequence, 'Reisen im besetzten Gebiet', he relates an encounter with a bigoted haberdasher on a train.[143] When his fellow passenger opines that Germany is in need of a dictatorship to solve its financial ills, von Zwehl retorts that a dearth of political will is all that is stopping Germany from paying off its debts. His use of the subjunctive throughout his account of this exchange suggests von Zwehl's amused distance from some of his own more provocative statements, including his mischievous comparison of the modern Germans' predicament with their ancestors' reluctance to pay back Kriemhild's dowry

---

141 [Anon.], 'Antworten: "Wahrheitsfreund"', *Die Weltbühne*, 19.2 (1923), 106–08 (p. 108).
142 Siegfried Jacobsohn, '"Wahrheitsfreund"', *Die Weltbühne*, 19.2 (1923), 108.
143 Hans von Zwehl, 'Reisen im besetzten Gebiet', *Die Weltbühne*, 19.2 (1923), 476–79.

in the *Nibelungenlied*.¹⁴⁴ There is, however, a ring of conviction about the observation: 'Schon die alten Germanen ließen ihr ganzes Volk lieber zugrunde gehen, als daß sie die Siegfried-Bons bezahlten'.¹⁴⁵ For von Zwehl there is a danger of history repeating itself on the banks of the Rhine, as German recalcitrance in the face of foreign demands risks the country's obliteration.

The next article in the sequence, touched upon in the previous section, sees von Zwehl cast his mind back to the earlier French invasion in 1920 to remind readers of the dividends of not antagonizing the French. After the German government had dispatched *Reichswehr* and irregular troops into the demilitarized zone on the left bank of the Rhine to suppress the *Ruhraufstand*, the French regime responded in kind. Von Zwehl's impressionistic account in 'Von Rhein und Ruhr' exposes a latent revolutionary streak in Weimar Germany's industrial heartland that is entirely distinct from the nationalist backlash against the invaders. In fact, the workers' sobriety in mind and body is so much at odds with the inebriated thuggery of their nationalist compatriots that they come to represent a third party to this territorial dispute, whose relationship to the drunk German nationalists is no clearer than that to the tipsy French occupiers:

> Nationalismus, Betrunkenheit und Cabaret schwärmten von völkischer Wiedergeburt. Im Stadttheater hatte man den Tell gegeben. Noch auf der Straße prügelten sich die Leute ... Auch die Franzosen waren oft betrunken. Auf sie wirkte das Klima. Sie sagten noch öfter Je m'en fou [*sic*], als sie das ohnehin zu tun pflegen ... Gedrungen und prosaisch, langsam und angestrengt denkend gingen Arbeiter herum. Die Zukunft in ihnen hämmerte.¹⁴⁶

On the surface this passage invites an anti-French reading. The mention of Schiller's *Wilhelm Tell* (1804), a dramatic treatment of the life of the legendary Swiss national hero whose tyrannicide is said to have inspired his countryfolk to rebel against Habsburg rule, ostensibly ascribes to the French forces the role of irredeemable villain. Conversely, von Zwehl's implication that the workers of Dortmund identify with Tell outwardly casts them as

---

144 An easily accessible version of the *Nibelungenlied*, whose author and precise genesis are obscure, is the parallel text *Das Nibelungenlied. Mittelhochdeutsch/Neuhochdeutsch*, ed. by Ursula Schulze, trans. into New High German by Siegfried Grosse (Stuttgart: Reclam, 2013).
145 von Zwehl, 'Reisen im besetzten Gebiet', p. 478. The phrase 'Siegfried-Bons' is a reference to Kriemhild's dowry, which Hagen sunk in the Rhine after killing its rightful recipient, Siegfried, by means of a spear in the back (the source of the *Dolchstoßlegende*). Kriemhild demanded its restitution, but Hagen refused to divulge its whereabouts, choosing instead to die at Kriemhild's hand and take the secret with him to his grave.
146 von Zwehl, 'Von Ruhr und Rhein', p. 504.

the protagonists in a dormant movement of national liberation against a modern-day foreign oppressor.

However, this miniature *schaffendes Volk* does not harbour revolutionary intentions, still less nationalistic resentment. Whereas 'völkisch' agitation relies on excited rhetoric and promises of ethnic reincarnation, the workers are portrayed as methodically planning to emancipate their country from armed struggle and reshape it in their own image. The gradual politicization of the workers therefore appears as an organic process impervious to nationalist theatrics and destined to mature only at the historically opportune moment, a reading that accords with the orthodox Marxist belief that the workers' state would inevitably eventuate from the collapse of capitalism and the increasing desperation of the proletariat.[147] Indeed, for all that von Zwehl is critical of the lethargy he encounters among the working classes of Dortmund and Essen, 'wo sich das schon ganz westfälische und das proletarische Phlegma die Wage halten',[148] he is still more disapproving of the spontaneous frenzy that greets the French invasion: 'Plötzlich marschierten die Franzosen ein. Infanterie patrouillierte die Eisenbahnschienen ab. Der Aberglaube des passiven Widerstands ergriff die Industrie. Ein Tohuwabohu von Meinungen, Patriotismus, Gleichgültigkeit tobte sich aus'.[149] This snapshot of life under French occupation in 1920, which ended little over a month after it began, depicts the unceremonious collision of two nationalisms, with von Zwehl's idealized industrial workforce fulfilling a watching brief. The suddenness of the French invasion is replicated by the equally peremptory nature of the reactions it brings in train: 'Plötzlich war wieder Belagerungszustand. Oder Streik. Oder auch nur ein Auflauf'.[150] The German resistance is just as culpable for the prevailing state of nervous tension. Indeed, von Zwehl twice deploys the verb 'zucken' to convey the lack of any pre-meditated strategy behind the spasmodic demonstrations against the French presence.

Be it offensive or defensive, chauvinist activity is defined here by an ill-considered haste which affords little time for contemplation. This characterization resembles the *Weltbühne* view of revolutionary activity in general, trained here on the specifically right-wing insurgency against the French forces. Far from contradicting the stirringly patriotic spirit in which he had anointed the Weimar Republic 'die Republik der Deutschen', von Zwehl's wariness of intemperate 'Patriotismus' merely accords with his *Weltbühne* colleagues' misleading tendency to regard nationalism and patriotism as

---

147 William W. Hagen, *German History in Modern Times: Four Lives of the Nation* (Cambridge: Cambridge University Press, 2012), p. 163.
148 von Zwehl, 'Von Ruhr und Rhein', p. 504.
149 von Zwehl, 'Von Ruhr und Rhein', p. 503.
150 von Zwehl, 'Von Ruhr und Rhein', p. 504.

interchangeable labels for the same chauvinistic reflex. The crude identity politics and destructive energy powering chauvinism are antithetical to the patriotic project von Zwehl has in mind, which derives its momentum not from Francophobic agitation, but from working-class solidarity against capitalist exploitation.

For all that the deliberate mention of *Wilhelm Tell* creates an atmosphere of indigenous revolt, the workers' grievance is never assigned an exclusive human object. Instead, it is the cruel machinations of capitalism that linger constantly behind the undisguised violence carried out in the name of two rival nations. Thus the industrial machinery to which the freedom fighters of the Ruhrgebiet owe their livelihood is invested with an imperturbable rhythm to match the workers' ponderous progress through the streets of Dortmund. The workers' slowly dawning political consciousness is even likened to blows from a hammer, paving the way for an epoch-defining clash between two slow-moving but unstoppable forces: 'Die Zechen, die in Glut am Himmel standen, hielten einen kalten, gleichmäßigen Takt. Wenn siedende Dämpfe pfiffen, war es, als ob Wölfe in einer unbetretenen Finsternis heulten. Die Nacht lag schwer'.[151] The passing distraction of a few thousand French troops pales into insignificance in the shadow of this homemade nemesis, whose cold and metronomic exterior belies the white heat it generates. Momentary national animosities are put into perspective by the recurring nightmare of mineral extraction, as the workers' yearning for freedom chafes at the yoke of German industrial capitalism. In and of itself, the relentless output of the plants calls into question their owners' decision to obstruct the delivery of war reparations. With the factories still operating at a normal level, the enforcement of a curfew around the Herne steelworks gives the invasion in 1920, and the ongoing Ruhr Crisis in turn, the appearance of a stand-off that is, in more ways than one, manufactured.

The following week von Zwehl again warns his compatriots against overestimating the malice of the French government, remarking wryly that Kleist's dramatic adaptation of the theme of the 'Hermannsschlacht' remains popular because of its explicitly anti-French tenor, whereas Christian Grabbe's had supposedly been forgotten because it was merely written 'für seine Deutschen'.[152] Following his more radical predecessors in evoking Heinrich Heine, von Zwehl refuses to draw any parallels between Napoleon's troops and the modern-day French forces:

> Als Heinrich Heine ein junger Dichter war, sah er den Kaiser Napoleon durch die düsseldorfer Königsallee reiten, und er sah den

---

151 von Zwehl, 'Von Ruhr und Rhein', p. 504.
152 Hans von Zwehl, 'Köln, Coblenz, Düsseldorf', *Die Weltbühne*, 19.2 (1923), 533–35 (p. 533).

Siebenmeilenstiefelngedanken auf des französischen Herrschers Stirn. Heute ist die düsseldorfer Königsallee noch ebenso beschaffen und die französischen Pferde, die sich hier tummeln, auch; aber kein Siebenmeilenstiefelngedanke ist mehr vorhanden. Es würde auch kein deutscher Genius anwesend sein, der ihn groß und dichterisch anschauen könnte. Und in Ermanglung eines solchen Geistes treibt man seinen Kult mit den Reliquien des Herrn Schlageter.[153]

With this disparaging reference to Schlageter, von Zwehl distances himself from the so-called 'Schlageter line'. This posthumous cult of personality around the Freikorps fighter had been cynically encouraged by Karl Radek, an agent of the Russian Exekutivkomitee der Kommunistischen Internationale [Komintern], in an ultimately doomed effort to forge an alliance between the KPD and their nationalist adversaries that nonetheless signified a rare and short-lived moment of imbrication between extremists on the Right and Left.[154] The complexity of von Zwehl's own patriotism reveals itself in this article, which combines stern criticism of the allegedly half-hearted German Republic and its jeopardizers with a mystical appreciation, gestured to in passing, of an essential German nature embarked upon a perpetual and slightly masochistic quest for the 'Höhen des geistigen Leidens und Menschentums'.[155] Von Zwehl leaves no doubt, however, that he considers the worship of xenophobic violence to be a perversion of patriotism.

Xenophobic language was not, of course, unheard of in *Die Weltbühne*, even in those articles that counselled the adoption of an *Erfüllungspolitik*. A prime example of such a discrepancy between language and message is the last leader of 1923, entitled 'Ruhrkrieg und Pfalz'.[156] As noted in the first chapter of this book, Wilhelm Michel, the author of 'Ruhrkrieg und Pfalz', had already used a column in the journal earlier in the year to reject the notion that the pro-French separatist movement in his native Pfalz region would ever command enough popular support to threaten the territorial integrity of Weimar Germany.[157] He had since been proved wrong by the formation of the Rheinische Republik, but its subsequent dissolution after barely a month appears to have confirmed Michel in his convictions:

Einer der wenigen Punkte, über die in der ganzen Pfalz Einigkeit herrscht, ist die überall mit ruhiger Kälte konstatierte Tatsache, daß die Separatisten Lumpengesindel sind. Die Belege liegen zu

---

153 von Zwehl, 'Köln, Coblenz, Düsseldorf', p. 533.
154 Brown, 'Faces of Social Militarism in the Weimar Republic', in *Weimar Radicals*, pp. 15–41.
155 von Zwehl, 'Köln, Coblenz, Düsseldorf', p. 533.
156 Wilhelm Michel, 'Ruhrkrieg und Pfalz', *Die Weltbühne*, 19.2 (1923), 643–47.
157 Michel, 'Pfalz, Bayern, Deutschland'.

Dutzenden vor, Jeder kennt einen oder den andern von ihnen und weiß, daß er ein verdächtiges Subjekt ist.[158]

The remainder of the article reveals the curiously anachronistic overtones of the phrase 'verdächtiges Subjekt' to be in keeping with Michel's exalted evocations of an ancient national essence sealed in the German soil itself and impervious to the ransacking of the country's natural resources by its ethnically compromised French neighbour. The totem of Michel's patriotic rearguard action against French invasion is the German forest. Indeed, in making the ancient woodland of his childhood a leitmotif expressive of both national resilience and loss, Michel takes up von Zwehl's challenge to invest the German 'Laubwald' with more than just a tokenistic patriotic significance.[159] To recycle von Zwehl's phrase with regard to Kleist's drama, Michel's use of such national tropes in 'Ruhrkrieg und Pfalz' crosses the permeable border between affirmative patriotism and exclusionary nationalism by directing itself 'gegen die Franzosen',[160] as opposed to simply serving as a rallying point 'für seine Deutschen'.

Upon arrival in his home town, Michel first confesses that the presence of French staff at the railway station gives him 'einen kleinen Stich',[161] then abruptly pronounces the Pfalz 'ein besetztes, von den Fremden bis in alle Winkel durchdrungenes Land',[162] an observation lent an additional racist complexion by the reference in the next sentence to a sentry post guarded by French colonial troops as the 'Marokkanerwache'.[163] The melodramatic shift in tone lasts for the rest of the piece, as the trees surrounding Michel's family home are conscripted into a losing battle against the French woodcutters.

Michel's first invocation of his town's arboreal guardians is defiant. After a litany of disorientating incidents culminating in the revelation that the town post office has itself relocated, he attempts to revive his spirits by reminding himself that the natural landscape remains unspoilt even while the fabric of municipal life comes apart at the seams: 'Und während ich durch tiefsten Straßenkot meinem Heimathaus zustrebe, suche ich mich zu trösten mit dem Gedanken, daß trotz allem die Wälder noch droben stehen, stark und stolz, die kühlen Waldtäler, die kühnen Felsen und Burgen'.[164] In his desperation Michel imagines the woods arranged in military formation, ably assisted

---

158 Michel, 'Ruhrkrieg und Pfalz', p. 643.
159 von Zwehl, 'Reisen im besetzten Gebiet', p. 477.
160 von Zwehl, 'Köln, Coblenz, Düsseldorf', p. 533.
161 Michel, 'Ruhrkrieg und Pfalz', p. 643.
162 Michel, 'Ruhrkrieg und Pfalz', p. 644.
163 Michel, 'Ruhrkrieg und Pfalz', p. 644.
164 Michel, 'Ruhrkrieg und Pfalz', p. 644.

by formidable regiments of forts and impassable rock faces. It is tempting to consider the valleys under their protection as the dwelling place of an idealized Germanness, uncharted by and impenetrable to the occupiers. However, the futility of this illusion of rootedness is immediately made apparent by the fact that the very ground beneath Michel's feet has been rendered so uneven that he repeatedly stumbles on unexpected abrasions in the once familiar road surface. This, we are told, is also the fault of the Ruhr Crisis, which has comprehensively undermined the author's affinity with his place of origin.

It soon transpires that Michel's glorification of the woods is also the product of wishful thinking, as this putative seat of German resolve proves to be one of the principal targets of a French-led operation that he describes in terms suggestive of an obscenely large spiderweb ensnaring his Palatinate *Heimat*. Their decision to take by force what they are owed implicates the Allies in the desecration of a landscape that is both the emotional stay and the livelihood of so many villagers. Thus Michel's resentment at the reduction of the woods to the status of a commodity is combined with his recognition of its monetary value:

> Der Wald wird ausgestohlen. [...] Bei den Riesen-Holzversteigerungen, die gegenwärtig von den Franzosen abgehalten werden, handelt es sich um Abholzung ganzer Bezirke. Grade der Waldteil, in dem mein Heimatdorf liegt, wird auf das empfindlichste davon betroffen, aber die deutschen Händler, große wie kleine, stehen mangels ausreichender Zahlungsmittel machtlos daneben und müssen zusehen, wie belgische, französische, holländische Firmen ihnen ihren eignen Wald am Haus vorbeifahren.[165]

Alongside its allusions to the palpable economic cost of the destruction of the wood, this passage radiates righteous indignation at the seizure of a Palatinate birthright by people whose arguable legal entitlement to the timber will never outweigh the moral claim of the woodlanders themselves. The crowning humiliation of having to witness, if only vicariously, the precious cargo being paraded through the village on its way to the border is almost too much for Michel to bear, provoking him to exclaim 'Ruhrkrieg! Idiotismus!'.[166] For him, the incalculable damage which the experience of subjugation by a foreign power has wrought on the consciously German identity of the *Pfälzer* supersedes in importance the more easily quantifiable consequences of Allied sanctions: 'Man hat diese Ärmsten nicht nur wirtschaftlich vernichtet, sondern auch seelisch gebrochen und um den Glauben an das Deutschtum

---

165 Michel, 'Ruhrkrieg und Pfalz', p. 645.
166 Michel, 'Ruhrkrieg und Pfalz', p. 644.

gebracht'.[167] In Michel's telling, the cannibalized woods stand as much as a memorial to a bankrupted sense of German national pride as to an act of economic vandalism.

At the same time, Michel's answer to the question of culpability for the Ruhr Crisis exonerates his account of any charge of unalloyed chauvinism. Indeed, the persistent anti-French animus of 'Ruhrkrieg und Pfalz' is balanced at every turn by exasperation with the stubborn refusal of his compatriots to settle their debts of their own accord, which he believes not only to have occasioned the crisis in the first instance but now to be risking the extinction of German culture on the left bank of the Rhine. Even as he bids a bitter farewell to the woods, 'die ich nicht mehr sehen werde, die durch zweihundert, dreihundert, vierhundert Jahre sorglich gehegt worden sind, um jetzt dem Ruhrblödsinn zum Opfer zu fallen',[168] his expectation that the occupiers will not stop until they have eradicated the woods does not prevent him from apportioning a significant measure of blame to his own people. Whereas resisting Allied demands is presented as a reckless act of bravado that could jeopardize the German way of life in the Ruhrgebiet and beyond, acceding to these ultimata is none other than 'die einzige nationale Handlungsweise, die hier in Frage kommt'.[169] Compliance, not combat, is depicted as the patriotic choice for power-brokers in the Weimar Republic.

It cannot be overlooked that Michel repeatedly borrows from the nationalist lexicon to articulate his feelings. In the last paragraph the phrase 'Westland' appears a sum total of three times in reference to the occupied area that Michel wishes to return to sole German control. As Thomas Müller explains in his book on the symbolic import of Germany's western border, the phrase 'Westmark' had gained in currency in the latter half of the nineteenth century to denote a vast tract of land, stretching as far north as Belgium and as far south as Switzerland, on which segments of the German right wing harboured territorial designs. This loosely defined space, with its echoes of the East Prussian *Ostmark*, soon acquired different names, among them 'Westraum' and 'Westland'. Müller traces the different connotations that each term carried with it, concluding that 'Westland' generally denoted 'die Grenze im Sinne der völkischen Ideologie als eine spezifische, aus der Landschaft herauslesbare Synthese von Raum und Volk, als eine deutsche Teillandschaft also'.[170] Such a qualitatively German landscape presents itself

---

167 Michel, 'Ruhrkrieg und Pfalz', p. 645.
168 Michel, 'Ruhrkrieg und Pfalz', p. 646.
169 Michel, 'Ruhrkrieg und Pfalz', p. 647.
170 Thomas Müller, *Imaginierter Westen. Das Konzept des 'deutschen Westraums' im völkischen Diskurs zwischen Politischer Romantik und Nationalsozialismus* (Bielefeld: Transcript, 2009), p. 21.

in Michel's heroic image of the German forest, which itself inevitably awakens associations with the aforementioned first-century *Hermannsschlacht*. This legendary battle, in which the efforts by the Roman Empire to subject the length of the right bank of the Rhine to its rule were decisively repelled in the Forest of Osning by soldiers loyal to the Cherusci tribesman Hermann, has often been credited with the salvation of Germanic culture. For Michel, writing in 1923, the stakes are no smaller, although the geographical locus has shifted westwards across the Rhine.

Crucially, however, the modern-day incursion is not only different in that it is centred on the opposite bank of the Rhine: in Michel's telling, the threat to Germany's territorial integrity now comes predominantly from within. The appearance of French troops is merely the natural consequence of German provocation: 'Eindringlich ist zu sagen: Erhaltung des Lebens im besetzten Gebiet ist ohne weiteres identisch mit Erhaltung des Deutschtums! Jedes kindische Sichsperren gegen Lebensnotwendigkeiten des Westlandes unterhält die moralische Kraft und saugt automatisch neue fremde Elemente ins Land herein.'[171] This passage encapsulates Michel's attempt aggressively to reclaim patriotism from the nationalists by re-orienting the national interest towards self-preservation, as opposed to self-aggrandizement; there is no indication that his solicitude for the 'Westland' is expansionist in nature. Indeed, not only does the battle against French infiltration appear to be purely defensive, but its energies must be turned inward, against those Germans whose behaviour is exerting an irresistible magnetic attraction on the Allied forces. According to this understanding of events, Germany's ruling classes are, however inadvertently, acting in concert with their nominal enemy. The government's puerile retaliation against the occupiers, with its ruinous consequences for those who live near the western frontier, is therefore cast as the cardinal sin against which the patriotic conscience must rebel.

The March Action, 1921: Inoculating Germany against Extremism

In line with its disapproval of retaliatory tactics vis-à-vis France, *Die Weltbühne* remained steadfast throughout the Weimar period in its opposition to the use of force, be it in the sense of military expansionism,[172] domestic oppression,[173] or paramilitary repression of political debate. As this section shows, this injunction extended to left-wing radical tactics, reaching a rhetorical climax either side of the Komintern-inspired *Märzkämpfe*, or

---

171 Michel, 'Ruhrkrieg und Pfalz', p. 647.
172 Ludwig Lewinsohn, 'Die Kunst, ein Jude zu sein', *Die Weltbühne*, 21.2 (1925), 594–97 (p. 597).
173 Agathon, 'Mussolini, Seeckt und Südtirol', *Die Weltbühne*, 23.1 (1927), 933–37 (p. 937).

March Action. In March 1921 the March Action broke out in the industrial area known as Mitteldeutschland and centred on the towns of Halle, Leuna and Merseburg. Partly orchestrated by the Komintern and leading to almost two hundred deaths, this workers' uprising broke down inside two weeks after failing to generate meaningful support outside its base for its planned nationwide campaign of industrial action. The KPD declined in popularity as a result. This slump appeared to vindicate the more circumspect editorial line of *Die Weltbühne*, which henceforth rarely deviated far from Karl Kautsky's contempt for 'putschlüsterne Kommunisten [, die mit] bolschewistischen Lockungen stärkster Art [arbeiten]'.[174]

Dating back to the departure of Ludwig Jurisch as leader-writer, the fastidious distaste of the journal for the notion of 'Gewalt' was starkly illustrated by Heinrich Ströbel in an editorial from the summer of 1920 entitled 'Spaa'.[175] Characteristically, Ströbel raises the spectre of Allied imperialism running riot if the eponymous conference were to end in mutual recrimination.[176] He warns that the result would be a conflict between imperialism and Bolshevism: 'Kommunistische Fanatiker beglückwünschen sich und die Menschheit zu dieser Entwicklung; wir unsrerseits zögen es vor, wenn der Weg zu einer höheren Entwicklungsstufe der Gesellschaft nicht erst über Millionen neuer Leichen führen würde'.[177] The reference by the veteran Social Democrat to the gradual evolution of human society reflects his enduring adherence to the orthodox Marxism that his erstwhile SPD ally Karl Kautsky had built into the party programme in 1891, almost three decades before both men joined the breakaway USPD.[178] The lives of millions, he warns, depended on the Socialist movement placing its trust in reformism and forestalling any rush to revolution.

Ströbel's distaste for hard-left violence resounded long after his disappearance from the journal's pages later that year. In 1926 an article by Carl von Ossietzky, who would take over the editorship inside a year, laments the fact that the Communist Party-affiliated *Roter Frontkämpferbund* (RFB) had evinced no interest in converting their critics to the Communist cause

---

174 Kautsky, 'Belagerungszustand und Unabhängige', p. 169.
175 Ströbel, 'Spaa'.
176 The Belgian town of Spa played host to a conference from 5 to 16 July 1920 at which the Supreme War Council, comprising the Allied heads of government and appointed senior military officers, issued the fledgling Weimar government with a range of specific demands concerning disarmament, coal shipments and war reparations on the basis of the Treaty of Versailles (1919). The meeting marked the first time that German representatives had been invited to take part in multilateral discussions since the end of the war.
177 Ströbel, 'Spaa', p. 36.
178 Hagen, *German History in Modern Times*, p. 162.

through reasoned argument, preferring instead to mount shows of strength designed to intimidate opponents and passers-by alike:

> Nein, hier wird nicht mehr eine Idee demonstriert, sondern nur, daß Deutsche ohne Strammstehen und Beinschwenken noch immer nicht leben können. Die Parteien verschanzen ihre geistige Ohnmacht hinter Riesenschaustellungen von militarisierter Vereinsmeierei und organisiertem Willen zur Gewalttätigkeit. Neue Symptome alter Nationalleiden. An dem Tag, wo die Parteisoldaten verschwunden sind, wird Deutschland gesund sein.[179]

Although he does not suggest that the Communist Party is uniquely violent, Ossietzky's disapproval of the tactics of the RFB reflects a trend in *Die Weltbühne* for denouncing the pervasive *Kampfkultur* that has come to be regarded as a lasting hallmark of the far Left in the Weimar Republic. Distinguishing it from the policies of affirmative action pursued by Communist leaders in imperial Germany, Sabine Hake traces these carefully orchestrated displays of bravado back to the recent experience of war and subsequent internalization of its attitudes and body language.[180] Hake is not the first to argue that first-hand participation in the First World War left an indelible mark on its survivors' relationship to violence. In *Creating German Communism*, his study of German Communism in the century preceding the fall of the Berlin Wall, Eric D. Weitz claims that, far from inculcating a spirit of pacifism, the experience of war had not only normalized violence for a generation of combatants but created an appetite for it.[181] However, Dirk Schumann has since challenged what he calls the 'brutalization thesis', a phrase he explicitly derives from Eric Hobsbawm's description of the First World War as a 'machine for brutalizing the world'.[182] On the contrary, Schumann argues, the most violent excesses had largely abated by mid-1921 to give way to more ceremonial shows of force that produced relatively little bloodshed.[183]

No matter how pervasive this wartime mentality truly was, Hake is surely right that the martial manoeuvres of the Communist Left inevitably

---

179 Carl von Ossietzky, 'Rif und Riffe', *Die Weltbühne*, 22.2 (1926), 833–37 (p. 837).
180 Sabine Hake, 'Marxist Literary Theory and Communist Military Culture', in *The Proletarian Dream: Socialism, Culture, and Emotion in Germany 1863–1933*, Interdisciplinary German Cultural Studies, 23 (Berlin: De Gruyter, 2017), pp. 255–69.
181 Weitz, *Creating German Communism*, p. 200.
182 Eric Hobsbawm, *Age of Extremes: The Short Twentieth Century, 1914–1991* (London: Abacus, 1995 [1994]), p. 125.
183 Dirk Schumann, 'Political Violence, Contested Public Space, and Reasserted Masculinity in Weimar Germany', in *Weimar Publics/Weimar Subjects*, ed. by Canning, Barndt and McGuire, pp. 236–53.

brought about conflict with 'not only the democratic institutions of the Weimar Republic but also the SPD as the party of political defeatism and, in the heated rhetoric of the times, social fascism'.[184] William W. Hagen has also pointed out the historic rift between the pragmatism of an SPD party with aspirations to election and radical Communist rhetoric that called the legitimacy of the entire political system into question.[185] For its part, *Die Weltbühne* was almost as likely to disparage the policies of the SPD as those of the KPD, but its fundamental support for the principle of social democracy manifested itself in a disdain for the aggressive tactics of the Communist Party that was sometimes so vehement as to spill over, somewhat paradoxically, into incitement. In particular, the leader columns of Karl Rothammer around the time of the March Action attest to a sympathy for certain classist anathemas unleashed on the Communists by the SPD. Indeed, Rothammer's disparagement of the Communists could have been lifted from contemporary diatribes directed by the Social Democratic camp at the so-called 'Lumpenproletariat', that part of the working class deemed to be politically unenlightened on account of its dormant class consciousness. These outpourings were the by-product of what Michael Schwartz has called 'jene spezifisch eugenische Politik der deutschen Sozialdemokratie […], die sich faktisch wesentlich gegen das sozial, politisch und biologisch definierte "Anders-Sein" des "Lumpenproletariats" richtete'.[186]

The common denominator in most of the texts under discussion in this section is the patriotic idea of the *Volkskörper*; it is indeed no coincidence that Ossietzky should have chosen in his denunciation of the RFB to present militarism as a blight on the national constitution and its excision as a cure. It is, moreover, in this context that the arresting similarities between Social Democrat derision of the urban poor and Rothammer's scorn for Communist strategy must be understood. For proof of Karl Heinz Roth's characterization of the SPD's 'Aversion vor dem Mob' as one that turned 'das intellektuelle Zentrum der Sozialdemokratie in einen Hort sozialdarwinistischer Sanierungsutopien gegenüber der ausschweifenden und dreckigen Straße',[187] one need look no further than Rothammer, who reviles the politics of the street in terms strongly suggestive of contamination.

---

184 Hake, *The Proletarian Dream*, p. 260.
185 Hagen, *German History in Modern Times*, pp. 165–66.
186 Michael Schwartz, '"Proletarier" und "Lumpen". Sozialistische Ursprünge eugenischen Denkens', *Vierteljahrshefte für Zeitgeschichte*, 42 (1994), 537–70 (p. 538).
187 Karl Heinz Roth, 'Schein-Alternativen im Gesundheitswesen. Alfred Grotjahn (1869–1931) – Integrationsfigur etablierter Sozialmedizin und nationalsozialistischer Rassenhygiene', in *Erfassung zur Vernichtung. Von der Sozialhygiene zum 'Gesetz über Sterbehilfe'*, ed. by Karl Heinz Roth (Berlin: Gesundheit Berlin, 1984), pp. 31–56 (p. 39).

In Robert Heynen's analysis, evocations of a beleaguered *Volkskörper* in Weimar-era texts partly reflect male insecurities over the increasing influence of women in the public and professional spheres, but he points out that class prejudice also contributed.[188] To this end, Heynen recalls the characterization by the French psychologist Gustave Le Bon in 1898 of the crowd as 'feminised',[189] before stressing that bourgeois observers in the interwar period were inclined to define the working-class crowd in particular as 'an amorphous, unruly and dangerous threat to the health of the *Volkskörper*'.[190] Le Bon himself had, in fact, already established a connection between the collective mindset and illness by explaining the susceptibility of the crowd to political manipulation as a result of instant mental contagion.[191]

In Rothammer's first leader article, published in mid-November 1920, he portrays the Berlin-wide electricians' strike earlier that month as the result of just such a collective mania. Depicting the electricians as labouring under what he calls the 'Streikfetisch',[192] and echoing Ströbel's sentiments, Rothammer directly quotes Marx to the effect that the evolution of human society towards Socialism is pre-ordained and cannot be pre-empted. Although he would later mount a robust defence of the basic right to strike,[193] he argues here that the electricians' fundamental, and costly, misapprehension was to believe that they could force the downfall of a capitalist economy that was 'noch lange nicht fallreif' and therefore easily capable of overcoming short-term electrical outages in the capital.[194]

In the event, Rothammer pointedly observes, the lights happened to stay on in the high-class Hotel Esplanade, which belonged at that time to a business associate of the industrialist Hugo Stinnes, thus enabling the film society then in session to continue proceedings and demonstrating to Rothammer 'die ausschlaggebende Kräfteverteilung zwischen Kapitalismus

---

188 Robert Heynen, 'Degeneration: Gender, War, and the Politics of the Volkskörper', in *Degeneration and Revolution: Radical Cultural Politics and the Body in Weimar Germany*, Historical Materialism, 93 (Leiden: Brill, 2015), pp. 58–134.
189 Gustave Le Bon, *Psychologie des Foules* (Paris: Alcan, 1895), p. 24. Le Bon writes: 'On remarquera que, parmi les caractères spéciaux des foules, il en est plusieurs, tels que l'impulsivité, l'irritabilité, l'incapacité de raisonner, l'absence de jugement et d'esprit critique, l'exagération des sentiments, et d'autres encore, que l'on observe également chez les êtres appartenant à des formes inférieures d'évolution, tels que la femme, le sauvage et l'enfant'.
190 Heynen, *Degeneration and Revolution*, p. 71.
191 Le Bon, *Psychologie des Foules*, p. 28. The full quotation reads: 'La première suggestion formulée qui surgit s'impose immédiatement par contagion à tous les cerveaux, et aussitôt l'orientation s'établit'.
192 Karl Rothammer, 'Wedding und Esplanade', *Die Weltbühne*, 16.2 (1920), 569–70 (p. 569).
193 Karl Rothammer, 'Das Streikrecht der Beamten', *Die Weltbühne*, 16.2 (1920), 696–99.
194 Rothammer, 'Wedding und Esplanade', p. 570.

und Proletariat'.[195] Throughout the Weimar period Stinnes figures in *Die Weltbühne* as the incarnation of unscrupulous capitalism, as exemplified by a contribution in 1925 by Russian revolutionary Larissa Reissner, author of the German-language reportage *Hamburg auf den Barrikaden* (1923). Stinnes is named as a co-conspirator in the self-enrichment of the capitalist class in a lengthy piece designed to expose the hypocrisy of armaments manufacturers and their enablers in the coal and steel industries who claim to be motivated by patriotism but will, in fact, sell their goods to the highest bidder.[196] In this atmosphere it is small wonder that the cruel irony of the well-connected businessman's establishment being spared the power cut should provoke Rothammer into a tirade against class-based injustice:

> Zugegeben, daß hinter der Willkür der berliner Elektriker schamlos aufgescheuchter Instinkt für Gerechtigkeit sich reckte. Diese Männer wissen von dem Krepieren der Kinder, von dem Blutbrechen der Halbverhungerten, von den Skeletten in den berliner Elendsquartieren. Sie sehen die unzugängliche Herrschaftsbastion des alten Reichtums, die brutale Lebensgier des jungen. Wer will ihnen da verdenken, daß sie den Griff an die Kehle des Untiers wagen![197]

The principal target of Rothammer's metaphor-laden eloquence is the capitalist system, embodied here by a literal bastion of privilege in the form of the hotel formerly patronized by Kaiser Wilhelm II. Nonetheless, the politics of brute force is ultimately portrayed as reflecting badly on the Socialist movement as a whole: 'Zum zweiten Mal, zum hundertsten fällt der Ruhr-Schatten auf das deutsche Proletariat. Wieder einmal wird der Sozialismus, der beinah zur Weltanschauung reift, Bürgerschreck'.[198] Rothammer's sensitivity to the dim view of Socialism that strike action was wont to engender in middle-class observers acts as a brake on his outrage over the endemic inequality of German society.

In early 1921, having refrained from such rhetoric in his earliest columns, Rothammer obliquely welcomes the 'allgemeine Versachlichung, die, unbekümmert um nervöse Störungen, dauernd zunimmt' as an antidote to the ailments of the *Volkskörper*.[199] Approvingly, he notes a growing 'Wille[n] zur Realpolitik' in defiance both of reactionary obstruktionismus and of the Communist 'Katastrophen-Taktik'.[200] In an article largely devoted to ridiculing

---

195 Rothammer, 'Wedding und Esplanade', p. 569.
196 Larissa Reissner, 'Krupp und Essen', *Die Weltbühne*, 21.2 (1925), 729–34.
197 Rothammer, 'Wedding und Esplanade', p. 570.
198 Rothammer, 'Wedding und Esplanade', p. 570.
199 Karl Rothammer, 'Berlin-München-Paris', *Die Weltbühne*, 17.1 (1921), 89–91 (p. 90).
200 Rothammer, 'Berlin-München-Paris', p. 90.

the suggestion that a 'Bürgerblock' comprising Social Democrats and the right-wing parties might be the outcome of the Prussian elections, Rothammer's specifically male hypochondria fixates on the nationalist Right. Musing that such a coalition would have been theoretically possible in the previous legislature, he recalls: 'Aber die Demokraten fürchteten die deutschnationale Infektion. Können sie, falls sie nicht ihren letzten Rest Mannbarkeit opfern wollen, anders verfahren [...]?'.[201] The insinuation embedded within this rhetorical question is that proximity to nationalist politicians could corrode the masculinity of their Democratic coalition partners, which Rothammer renders not as 'Männlichkeit' but as the sexually freighted 'Mannbarkeit'. This careful choice of words dictates that it is not merely male pride but sexual function itself that is at stake. Rothammer thus bestows pernicious female characteristics upon the nationalists by casting them as a threat to their prospective coalition partners' basic ability to perform as male members of the species.

For the implicitly male *Volkskörper*, dispersed here among the actual bodies of a select few German men, an excess of nationalism has the potential to sap its life force. Entertaining nationalist ideology at such close quarters is portrayed as a threat to the virility of Social Democrat ministers. In Rothammer's vocabulary there is little functional difference between extremism and nervous excitement, the emasculating connotations of which are intended to override political loyalties and appeal directly to one's most intimate insecurities. Such language recurs in 'Preußenwahlen', the article with which the second half of this chapter began and in which Rothammer credits the SPD with enabling the Weimar Republic to withstand 'die vielen nervösen Erschütterungen' from Right and Left[202] and pronounces: 'Nervöse Leute sind immer schwache Leute'.[203]

Rothammer's preoccupation with the nervous system is typical of political journalism throughout the Weimar period, as Dirk Schumann's analysis of the two leading bourgeois newspapers in the Prussian state of Saxony shows.[204] The *Saale-Zeitung* diagnosed the *Märzkämpfe* as a symptom of the German people's 'Übernervosität als Folge des zerrüttenden Krieges', while eleven years later the *Magdeburgische Zeitung* warned of the possibility of the country lapsing into a state of 'Entnervung'.[205] Building on these findings,

---

201 Rothammer, 'Berlin-München-Paris', p. 90.
202 Rothammer, 'Die Preußenwahlen', p. 237.
203 Rothammer, 'Die Preußenwahlen', p. 238.
204 Schumann, 'Political Violence'.
205 [Anon.], 'Die roten Banden zersprengt', *Saale-Zeitung*, 2 April 1921, p. 1; *Magdeburgische Zeitung*, 1 January 1932. Both cited in Schumann, 'Political Violence', p. 249. Schumann gives no precise page references for the latter and the 1932 archive for the newspaper is not publicly accessible.

Schumann perceives a link in the journalistic imagination between nervous collapse and the salutary powers of 'Sachlichkeit' which mirrors that in Rothammer's mind. It is now a commonplace of Weimar scholarship to read the socio-cultural phenomenon known as 'Neue Sachlichkeit' partly as a function of male insecurity. Both in literature and in social intercourse more generally,[206] the performance of unflappable equanimity has come to be associated with the 'Resouveränisierungsstrategien' of a generation of German men that felt itself to be under attack from the forces of female emancipation.[207] Thus it is in the context of 'general male anxieties about a feminized public sphere in Weimar Germany' that Schumann writes:

> The shaky balance between emotionality and its rational control was also part of the debate about how to (re)construct the subject in response to the traumata of war and defeat. The concept of 'new objectivity' played a crucial role here. It combined cool detachment, expressed in its appreciation of technology, with cynicism, sadism and misogyny, apparent in its fascination with phenomena of violence, *Lustmord* in particular.[208]

The barely concealed violence of Rothammer's rhetoric, as well as his preoccupation with 'Sachlichkeit', accord with Schumann's analysis of 'New Objectivity' as a gendered mechanism of suppression. In an earlier section of the essay Schumann even shows how the language of 'Sachlichkeit' could reinforce the rhetoric of the 'Volkskörper', citing a contemporary article in the *Magdeburgische Zeitung* that characterized the Communist perpetrators of the *Ruhraufstand* in terms of which Rothammer might have approved. Thus the 'Übel am Volkskörper' represented by the revolutionaries calls for a 'scharfen operativen Eingriff',[209] without which the German nation risked succumbing to a degenerative disease such as that incubated by what Rothammer would eventually call the Communist 'Krankheitsherd'.[210]

---

206 David Midgley, *Writing Weimar: Critical Realism in German Literature, 1918–1933* (Oxford: Oxford University Press, 2000), p. 19; Änne Söll, *Der neue Mann. Männerporträts von Otto Dix, Christian Schad und Anton Räderscheidt 1914–1930* (Munich: Fink, 2016); Helmut Lethen, *Verhaltenslehren der Kälte. Lebensversuche zwischen den Kriegen* (Frankfurt a.M.: Suhrkamp, 1994). Söll describes the literary iteration of *Neue Sachlichkeit* as a means by which to subsume 'als "weiblich" verachtete Werte und Verhaltensmuster in ein "männliches" Kulturmodell' (p. 15); while Lethen summarizes it as an 'Ästhetik [...] der Faszination der "scharfen" Grenzziehung und klaren Kontur' (p. 133).
207 Söll, *Der neue Mann*, p. 231.
208 Schumann, 'Political Violence', p. 249.
209 *Magdeburgische Zeitung*, 22 March 1920, cited in Schumann, 'Political Violence', p. 246. Schumann again provides no page reference.
210 Karl Rothammer, 'Der Kommunistenputsch', *Die Weltbühne*, 17.1 (1921), 371–72 (p. 372).

Even at the time of the March Action the *Weltbühne* reader would probably already have been no stranger either to the idea of the *Volkskörper*, to which Rothammer repeatedly gestures without ever spelling it out, or to its articulation with the supposedly salutary attitude of 'Sachlichkeit'. In light of his well-documented sensitivity to cliché and superstition, it is somewhat surprising that Kurt Tucholsky should have elected to describe his own aforementioned series 'Militaria' (1919) as 'eine schmerzhafte, aber heilsame Operation am deutschen Volkskörper'.[211] That he did so, however, shows the breadth of appeal exercised by the term. Tucholsky perceives his country as a sickly patient in need of medical attention and momentarily appoints himself as the doctor whose role it is to administer the only available cure. This takes a familiar form: 'Es gibt eines und in ihm liegt das Heil der Welt und die Genesung dieses unglücklichen, verblendeten Landes. Und es heißt: Sachlichkeit'.[212] By claiming 'Sachlichkeit' as his guiding principle, Tucholsky seeks to fend off accusations of anti-German malevolence. Here as elsewhere, 'Sachlichkeit' is presented as an almost immanent quality of pragmatism impervious to corruption by partisan motive.

Published in the wake of the subduing of the *Märzkämpfe*, 'Der Kommunistenputsch' mobilizes the clear-sighted virtues of 'Sachlichkeit' against the self-destructive enthusiasm of revolt. In fact, Rothammer's conflicted stance on working-class unrest shows a remarkable degree of continuity with the ambivalence of his first leader. In its breathless enumeration of the injustices visited on the proletariat, the following passage closely resembles that in which Rothammer had partially exonerated the Berlin electricians' actions on the grounds of the years of hardship they had been forced to endure:

> Entmenscht durch vierjährigen Krieg, durch jahrhundertelange preußische Züchtung, von Kindesbeinen an bis zum Kriegervereinsgreisenalter ins Soldatenspiel verliebt, unterernährt, zur Raserei gebracht durch die Behandlung der Mörder aller ihrer revolutionären Führer, können sie eben nicht lassen, die Handgranate für wirksamer zu erachten als Recht und Freiheit.[213]

On one hand, Rothammer insists that the working classes are entitled to an acute sense of grievance over their low quality of life and restricted political freedoms. On the other, this bestialized proletariat is credited with responsibility for its actions, however limited by social conditioning and

---

211 Wrobel, '"Unser Militär"', p. 204.
212 Wrobel, '"Unser Militär"', p. 202.
213 Rothammer, 'Der Kommunistenputsch', p. 371.

recent experience of war, and thus denied the right to cite generations of repression and brutalization in mitigation. In Rothammer's view, the fact that no 'reaktionäre Hetze' has followed the March Action,[214] as it had the 1920 *Ruhraufstand*, does not vindicate the strikers. Instead, the German people themselves have merely begun to appreciate the virtues of circumspection over impetuous tribalism. This change in temperament, Rothammer adds for good measure, marks not a squandering of revolutionary opportunity but a 'Fortschritt zur Gesundung'.[215]

This article, the title of which establishes a degree of equivalence between the Communists and the protagonists of the Kapp Putsch the previous year, marks an escalation in Rothammer's deployment of the concept of the *Volkskörper*. 'Der Kommunistenputsch' is replete with metaphors of disease and contamination. Having begun in conciliatory fashion by describing revolution as 'ein natürliches Grundrecht der Mehrheit des Volks' and the hoisting of the red flag as a 'sittliche Pflicht',[216] Rothammer insists that any revolution be judged on its ability to enhance economic production and therefore to be classified 'im Buch der Menschheit und des Menschlichen als Wachstum und nicht als Verkrüpplung'.[217] His subsequent indictment of this particular attempt at revolution duly equates Communism with illness: 'Aaskäfer eines verfaulten Militarismus! Blutarme Degeneration mißbrauchter Muskelbravour!'.[218] This furious vilification of the leftist revolutionaries reaffirms the connection in Rothammer's thinking between revolutionary zeal and physical depletion, echoing both the pseudo-scientific language of the eugenics movement and a wider paranoia over the health of the national community characteristic of *Volkskörper* discourse.

As well as bearing traces of the misogynist and classist neuroses considered above, Rothammer's piece praises the SPD-led government for smothering 'den kommunistischen Krankheitsherd'[219] and its associated 'Ausbrüche der Hysterie'.[220] This reference to hysteria maps neatly onto a widely held scholarly belief that men across early-twentieth-century Germany were afflicted by a phobia of emasculation arising from a perceived loosening of patriarchal control in modern society. This could apparently manifest itself in a fraught monitoring of one's own physical and mental stability and an impulse to express such concerns in a medical register: everyone was

---

214 Rothammer, 'Der Kommunistenputsch', p. 371.
215 Rothammer, 'Der Kommunistenputsch', p. 371.
216 Rothammer, 'Der Kommunistenputsch', p. 371.
217 Rothammer, 'Der Kommunistenputsch', p. 371.
218 Rothammer, 'Der Kommunistenputsch', p. 371.
219 Rothammer, 'Der Kommunistenputsch', pp. 371–72.
220 Rothammer, 'Der Kommunistenputsch', p. 372.

potentially a patient. As George Mosse explains, men were now deemed especially vulnerable to ailments once considered the exclusive preserve of women:

> Hysteria had previously been confined to women as a sign of their tender nerves and barely controllable passions. Nervousness, after all, was the very opposite of the image of masculinity. Now, toward the end of the century, the words *nervous* and *nervousness*, which in Germany had been confined to some medical texts, became part of the general vocabulary. Hysteria, in turn, was considered the most serious disease of the nervous system, its symptoms being mental instability, bodily contortions, and abrupt movements.[221]

In 1886, Mosse adds, Sigmund Freud had even given a paper arguing *inter alia* that male hysteria was a routine occurrence. In this pathologically self-conscious climate Rothammer's heightened language would have struck the keen observer as a study in modern male panic. Even his response might now be described as 'textbook': the radical menace is to be treated with a show of manly self-possession and clinical efficiency that recalls Helmut Lethen's thesis of the hyper-masculine 'kalte Persona'.[222]

Nor is it any exaggeration to say that Lethen's argument that German men in the inter-war period dealt with the unsettling symptoms of modernity by affecting a sovereign indifference to their surroundings might have been designed for cases such as Rothammer. Culminating in the parenthetical phrase '(auszulöschen – nicht: niederzuschlagen)',[223] Rothammer's chillingly pedantic expression of satisfaction that the SPD administration had managed not only to stifle but to extinguish the 'kommunistischen Krankheitsherd' altogether is an exercise in such deliberate self-detachment. According to the leader-writer, the revolutionaries' implicitly feminine hysteria was ultimately 'kalt behandelt',[224] having first met with 'd[er] kühle[n] Abwehr' of a German working class unsympathetic to the thought of a nationwide Communist uprising.[225] After an inconclusive state election earlier in the year, Rothammer had similarly praised the SPD for 'remaining cool' amid widespread uncertainty.[226] In this respect, Rothammer's faith in emotional reserve as the only healthy political attitude is reminiscent of his predecessor Ströbel's witheringly sarcastic warning,

---

221 Mosse, *The Image of Man*, p. 83.
222 Lethen, *Verhaltenslehren der Kälte*.
223 Rothammer, 'Der Kommunistenputsch', p. 372.
224 Rothammer, 'Der Kommunistenputsch', p. 372.
225 Rothammer, 'Der Kommunistenputsch', p. 372.
226 Rothammer, 'Die Preußenwahlen', p. 238.

in a piece headed 'Vor dem neuen Putsch', against the 'Kriegspsychose' of the nationalists, 'der die Angehörigen der auserwählten deutschen Nation ja ebenso widerstandslos erliegen wie dem Tropenkoller'.[227] Ströbel's view of right-wing radicals as succumbing to a tropical fever hints at the same dichotomy between hot and cold as that which recurs in Rothammer's work. This symmetry is scarcely disturbed by the leader-writers' divergent attitudes to medical prescriptions: Rothammer's boundless enthusiasm for surgical interventions against extremism and Ströbel's fear for the end of the German nation 'wenn je Reaktion und Militarismus es mit einer Eisenbartkur versuchten!' belong to the same trend of imagining their country under a metaphorical knife.[228]

The *Volkskörper* discourse outlasted the March Action in the pages of *Die Weltbühne*. Late the following year, Wilhelm Michel condemned right-wing nationalism as an ideology 'der immer nur wütend oder hysterisch verängstigt die Oberfläche des nationalen Körpers abtastet'.[229] Succinctly characterizing this molestation of the *Volkskörper* by the professed patriots of the Right as a feminizing assault on the male nervous system, Michel adds in parentheses: 'Wer entlarvt uns endlich den ludendorffischen Kinnbackenkrampf als das, was er ist: als die deutsche Form der Nervenschwäche, als Nationalhysterie?'.[230] Michael Kane's claim that the personified modern Western state, to the extent that it was identified with an idealized male figure, 'was often described specifically in terms of its *virility* or criticized for its lack of it' does not augur well for any German *Volkskörper* hewn in Ludendorff's lockjawed image.[231] The excitable figure of Ludendorff is, after all, the antithesis of the 'kalte Persona' with which Rothammer wishes to overlay the national *Volkskörper*. Since the defining characteristic of the latter, 'Sachlichkeit', can only be transmitted by aggressive treatment, or 'Versachlichung',[232] it is small wonder that the suppression of popular revolt by the SPD party machine should apparently have taken place in an operating theatre, with the Socialist movement as the patient: 'Die Politik der Sachlichkeit hat erfolgreich operiert'.[233] Ultimately, the subtext of disease and answering medical intervention that runs throughout 'Der

---

227 Heinrich Ströbel, 'Vor dem neuen Putsch', *Die Weltbühne*, 16.1 (1920), 641–45 (p. 641).
228 Ströbel, 'Vor dem neuen Putsch', p. 645.
229 Michel, 'Glaube an Deutschland', p. 538.
230 Michel, 'Glaube an Deutschland', p. 538.
231 Michael Kane, *Modern Men: Mapping Masculinity in English and German Literature, 1880–1930* (London: Cassell, 1999), p. 112.
232 Rothammer, 'Der Kommunistenputsch', p. 371.
233 Rothammer, 'Der Kommunistenputsch', p. 372.

Kommunistenputsch' reflects Karl Rothammer's belief that radicalism is a dangerous contagion capable of bringing about the emasculation and destabilization of the German nation.

*

This section demonstrates the drastically different forms that reformist patriotism could assume in *Die Weltbühne*. By focussing on three separate incidents of domestic unrest in chronological order, it charts concrete changes in the editorial policy of the journal during the first half of the interwar decade. To some extent these shifts were clearly a function of events over which *Weltbühne* columnists had, at least in the first instance, no control. Thus, whereas the armed nationalist uprising around Wolfgang Kapp had supposedly rendered necessary a corresponding show of force from the republican workforce, the arrival of a superior military power on German soil appeared to dictate a more subtle response. The third and final section indicates, however, that the journal took an increasingly and intransigently intolerant line towards extremists of all political persuasions as the dust settled on the war and republican democracy struggled to consolidate its grip on German society. The protection of the German *Volkskörper* from antidemocratic currents becomes the paramount concern under the stewardship of the leader-writer Karl Rothammer, as the *Staatsform* that Hans von Zwehl would later call the 'Republik der Deutschen' morphs into a patriotic article of faith. Although the writers of *Die Weltbühne* are only rarely prepared to identify themselves as patriots, they frequently and explicitly challenge the right of their right-wing opponents to claim that label for themselves, instead proposing a patriotic counter-narrative according to which national self-preservation takes precedent over the headlong pursuit of world revolution and right-wing agitation amounts to national self-harm.

Conclusion

The Socialist patriotism of *Die Weltbühne* represents the journal's multifaceted attempt definitively to sever the bond that prevailed in the popular imagination between solicitude for Germany and the sensibilities and strategies of right-wing nationalism. All too aware of their own vulnerability to insinuations of indifference or hostility to the national community, a vociferous group of writers used an array of different rhetorical techniques to illustrate both their commitment to their homeland and the righteousness of their particular left-wing vision for its future. Ostensibly, the overcoming of militarism is the central concern of these articles, in which capitalism and armed violence are often regarded as inseparable threats to the survival of an independent Germany. However, the importance of militarism as such was partly symbolic, since it often constituted a code for reactionary politics as a whole. Vanquishing conservatism in all its forms was seen as synonymous with turning Germany's first parliamentary democracy into a republic in more than name only.

Long before the Weimar Constitution was ratified in August 1919, *Die Weltbühne* had swung unambiguously behind the German Revolution, which it still regarded as ongoing even after the inception of the Weimar Republic. This radical orientation was clearest in the appointment of Ludwig Jurisch as leader-writer in early 1919, but its legacy endured far into the following decade in the sometimes casually revolutionary rhetoric of prominent members of the *Weltbühne* stable. Nonetheless, the political implications of this by turns nostalgic and utopian language were not always clear and, in any case, the journal proved increasingly reluctant to amplify the subversive programmes of Right or Left, as the republican system laboured to gain a foothold in the unstable political landscape of post-war Germany. Thus the second half of this chapter traces the tempering of the demands by the journal amid the insurrectionary tremors that continued unabated right up to the so-called 'Golden Years' between 1924 and the Great Depression.

The conversion of *Die Weltbühne* from revolutionary tribune to weekly reformist manifesto in the course of the first half of the life span of the Weimar Republic did not signal that its writers had become any less forceful in their conviction that they were acting in Germany's best interests. Indeed, Karl Rothammer's record as chief leader-writer is merely the most abrasive example of the fervently patriotic rhetoric of which the journal was capable in its eagerness to dislodge the monopoly of the right-wing reaction on public professions of patriotic feeling. Such protestations did not shy away from invoking points of reference, be they the spiritual power of the German forest or the founding legend of the *Hermannsschlacht*, which had long served as touchstones for nationalist effusions. The difference resided in the desire of *Weltbühne* writers to press such imagery and narratives into the service of the democratic Socialist cause and shield Germany from the self-inflicted decline, or even dissolution, that otherwise beckoned. They believed that the fatal curse of capitalism could only be lifted if enough Germans pledged a solemn vow to the Republic that revolution had made possible.

CONCLUSION

This investigation proposes a bold expansion of the conventional understanding of patriotism on the basis of the close textual analysis of a left-wing weekly newspaper much more readily associated with its anti-nationalism than with its patriotism. It is, in fact, nothing less than the fundamental contention of this book that these two ideas are not mutually exclusive. Indeed, over the fifteen years of the Weimar Republic *Die Weltbühne* gave a platform not only to revelations about the secret re-arming of the *Reichswehr* or to sardonic correctives to national self-aggrandizement, but also to keen expressions of interest in the fate of the German nation. In drawing attention to this under-appreciated body of evidence, this study argues that the existence of an alternative patriotic idiom to the right-wing nationalist one has been unjustifiably disregarded in most studies of Weimar culture to date.

The introduction quotes Roger Chickering's definition of the *deutschnational* world view, which identifies paranoid aggression towards a vaguely defined host of enemies as the defining characteristic of this right-wing nationalist mindset. The patriotism of *Die Weltbühne* also defined itself in implacable opposition to a matrix of hostile cultural forces that threatened its vision for Germany's future, but these were only rarely to be found beyond Germany's borders. Whereas the *deutschnational* lobby in the form of the pre-war nationalist associations railed against nebulous foreign threats, the writers of *Die Weltbühne* turned their fire on the reactionary elements in post-war German society. These were allegedly rife not only in court rooms, lecture theatres and the newspaper offices of the Hugenberg publishing house, but deep within the German *Bürgertum*.[1] *Weltbühne* columnists,

---

1 The industrialist Alfred Hugenberg had capitalized on the collapse of the Scherl-Verlag in 1916 to take over its struggling titles and lay the foundations for what would become a sprawling media empire. Within the space of a few years the Hugenberg-Konzern controlled a significant number of influential right-wing newspapers in both metropolitan and provincial areas, among the most prominent of which was the *Berliner Lokal-Anzeiger*. The company, which acted as a press agency for over 1,500 newspapers nationwide by the end of the 1920s, also had a stake in the aforementioned *Saale Zeitung*.

most of whom themselves belonged to the *Bürgertum*, typically regarded this social stratum as a repository of nationalist prejudice and sometimes even as an incubator of class hatred. The journal therefore held that entrenched middle-class orthodoxies were incompatible with true German patriotism.

It is evident from the *Weltbühne* corpus alone that no one political orientation can claim a monopoly on patriotism. Love of one's country can, moreover, evidently take on a multiplicity of forms. Thus this exploration of *Die Weltbühne* scrutinizes three basic types of left-wing patriotism, each of which itself constitutes a broad category containing at least two derivative variants. This approach reveals a complex eco-system in which regionalism, internationalism and Socialism nourish, and occasionally compete with, one another. The soil from which these branches of left-wing thought draw their nutrients, however, is their exponents' critical solicitude for the well-being of the country in which they were intended to bear fruit.

The critical nature of the patriotism on display in the journal is demonstrably conditioned by the recent memory of the First World War. With the comforting illusion of Germany's military invincibility shattered and a new Continental order enshrined in the post-war treaties, *Weltbühne* columnists tailored their patriotism to a new reality in which delusions of grandeur were no longer tenable. Behind this shift was the conviction that the national interest now compelled a different set of values from that which had governed Germany's actions in 1914. Hubris was to give way to humility, blind self-belief to introspection and authoritarianism to individual political empowerment. Presenting themselves as the defenders of a new national interest did not mean that the *Weltbühne* writers abandoned the idea of rescuing or reanimating an ancient national inheritance. Instead, they simply adopted a selective approach to German history, giving precedence to instances of rebellion and non-conformism over the dominant narrative of civil obedience in the face of political repression. Martin Luther and Heinrich Heine were recurring figureheads around whom the journal strove to rally readers, with the former's confrontation of the Catholic Church and the latter's revolutionary verses held up as acts of courage befitting the more self-assured, less subservient national role model of which the German Left dreamt. Part of these *Weltbühne* writers' revisionist strategy was to discredit the notion of the *Kaiserreich* as a worthy object of nostalgia, instead casting it as a fateful aberration in the natural evolution of Germany. Embracing the republican turn in the German national story was, therefore, less a question of cutting ties with Germany's past than of rediscovering its radical pedigree.

Nor did the espousal of a new national interest imply the diminishment of Germany's status as a Great Power. On the contrary, *Die Weltbühne* repeatedly called on Germany to seek leadership status in the field of pacifist diplomacy, proving itself to be a staunch advocate for the thesis of *Macht in Ohnmacht*. This idea, which was explicitly and enthusiastically amplified in the journal in the immediate post-war period, presented a means by which Germany could turn its defeat in the First World War to its advantage, lighting the way to lasting peace for an international community reluctant to relinquish its weapons. Here, too, historical revisionism played a cameo role; some contributions even claimed that it was no less than Germany's pre-ordained destiny to show war-torn Europe the path to redemption. The *Weltbühne* stable hoped that Germany would seize the opportunity presented by mandatory disarmament and substitute the moral imperative for militarism as its guiding principle. Germany's pursuit of international pre-eminence would thus come not at the expense of its neighbours, but would exert an improving influence on any country in its orbit through the power of its example.

This study began by exposing a rich seam of long-form reflections on Germany's new-found status as a defeated and territorially depleted nation that revolve around a lost or endangered regional *Heimat*. Departing from attempts by Paul Krische, Joachim Klose and, in particular, Celia Applegate to reanimate the idea of *Heimat* as a locus for progressive politics, the early part of the book follows this vein of regionalist patriotism over a time span of ten years and a geographical area extending as far east as modern-day Latvia. By imagining their chosen *Heimat* as the seat of a future Socialist revolution or depicting it as a relic of a more humane age, Arnold Zweig and Kurt Tucholsky reclaimed the provincial German *Heimat* as a left-wing concern. At the same time, as hinted at by the more conventionally chauvinistic essay by Otto Flake with which the first half of the first chapter ends, this study of *Die Weltbühne* yields an array of sometimes contradictory answers to the tripartite 'German Question' posed by Erin Hochman concerning the rightful boundaries, form of government and membership for any German nation. For all that the journal generally stopped short of irredentism, it did not seek unduly to muzzle the frustrations of a minority of columnists such as Flake whose contempt for certain movements for national self-determination was palpable.

Since Germany's borders, populace and political organization had been redrawn, reduced and revolutionized within less than a year of the Armistice, it is hard not to read *Die Weltbühne* as a seismograph of the ensuing aftershocks. Accordingly, the first chapter distils a decade of tortured self-interrogation into a representative selection of poems, essays and pieces of whimsy to show that the post-war Treaties of Versailles and Saint-Germain-en-Laye had, in the pages of *Die Weltbühne* as elsewhere, thrown long-standing uncertainty over the rightful contours of Germany into sharper relief than ever before. However, the particular contribution of this chapter to our understanding of the response by the journal to this upheaval is, first, to examine the ensuing emotional tremors at the more tangible regional level and, second, to illuminate a pronounced tendency in *Die Weltbühne* to emphasize the self-inflicted nature of this turmoil. As acknowledged above, the journal was not immune to delusions of ethnic supremacy, with recurrent anti-Slav chauvinism clouding the otherwise clear picture of self-recrimination presented by the engagement of the journal with the concept of *Heimat*. Nonetheless, agitation against the perceived injustices of the post-war settlements occupied relatively little space in *Die Weltbühne* compared to moralistic laments that identified the threat to Germany's territorial integrity as issuing not from Allied rapacity, but from Germany's own pursuit of industrial might and military dominance.

The first chapter thus lays bare a tendency in most expressions of regionalist patriotism in the journal to blame the break-up of Germany on the crass nationalism cultivated by the *Kaiserreich* and the failed war to which it had led. In so doing, it anticipates the second chapter by showing the great extent to which *Weltbühne* writers found the root of Germany's international ostracism in their country's own intransigence. Situated at the heart of the monograph, the second chapter then argues that this premise prompted *Die Weltbühne* to elaborate a patriotic vision that exalted the virtues of international collaboration over conquest. A steady stream of *Weltbühne* articles from the beginning to the end of the Weimar Republic made both hard-headed and emotional pleas to the German people in general, and the authors' opposite numbers in the right-wing press in particular, to abandon their revanchist rhetoric for the sake of national survival. For its part, the journal regarded the Treaty of Versailles as an unreasonable diktat motivated by the Allied nations' fear and desire for retribution, but it calculated that most of its terms should be accepted in order to avert the possibility of occupation or even colonization by its Western European neighbours. In the realm of internationalist patriotism, then, the war and its aftermath once again set the tone for the journal's understanding of both the national interest and its country's moral responsibility for its own predicament. Indeed, imperial Germany's alleged culpability for the outbreak of war is a rare issue on which *Weltbühne* writers, with the notable exception of Helene Keßler von Monbart, were bound together by an almost unanimous consensus.

Chapter 2 represents the first in-depth inquiry into the journal's oft-remarked moral dimension, as well as an innovative attempt to link left-wing patriotism to morality in such a way as to counter George Kateb's assertion, quoted in the introduction, that patriotism is fundamentally amoral, or even immoral. Whether it is intended to serve as a vehicle for pacifism or for rapprochement with France, the internationalist patriotism of *Die Weltbühne* invariably manifested itself in an ethical crusade against the widely dispersed nationalist lobby in Germany. Its proponents struck out against those who showed no interest in Germany's international moral rehabilitation and continued to deny the wisdom of multilateral disarmament. Since the journal believed that Germany's only hope of world leadership lay in the domain of constructive dialogue, they claimed that those who vowed to avenge Germany's wartime humiliation on the battlefield were acting against the national interest. On occasion *Weltbühne* writers even accused right-wing agitators of being prepared deliberately to sacrifice Germany's future as a sovereign nation for the passing thrill of combat and an egotistical desire for personal glory.

The third and final chapter sheds light on the numerous ways in which *Die Weltbühne* presents Socialism as the only authentically patriotic political ideology. It thereby mounts a robust challenge to traditional scholarly assumptions of equivalence between Socialism and an implicitly rootless, or even anti-national, internationalism by demonstrating the former's debt in this case to patriotism. Socialism alone, the journal argued, could save Germany from civil war and dethrone the self-serving capitalist class which, even in peacetime, had carried on enriching itself at the expense of the proletarian masses. The journal's rejection of the use of force and its stubborn faith in the art of persuasion are two of the hallmarks of its patriotic programme; this chapter charts the growth of this non-violent stance out of the early Weimar climate of political extremism in which the journal had itself taken part. At the beginning of its post-war life, *Die Weltbühne* was a revolutionary paper steeped in the radical rhetoric of the time and frequently called on Germany to realize the revolutionary potential of the nineteenth-century emancipation movements. For veteran columnists such as Otto Lehmann-Rußbüldt, the so-called *Befreiungskriege* against Napoleon's forces were the first in a line of thwarted progressive uprisings that culminated in the failure of 1848. The unreservedly democratic impulse of such proto-nationalism remained an inspiration for those *Weltbühne* writers who suspected that the Weimar Republic would not fulfil their expectations. However, as the Republic was engulfed in attempts at an armed coup from both ends of the political spectrum in the early 1920s, the journal changed tack in an attempt to protect Germany's democratic gains from annihilation at the hands of extremists.

Not for the last time in its history, its conversion to social democracy prompted *Die Weltbühne* to manipulate the language of right-wing nationalism to endear republicanism to a supposedly sceptical German public. By portraying both Fascist and Communist insurrectionaries as threats to the German *Volkskörper*, the journal positioned itself as the guardian of a healthy, prosperous German nation. Socialism came to mean not only the redistribution of resources into public hands and the attendant destruction of monopoly capitalism, but the eradication from German public life of all institutions and mindsets that *Die Weltbühne* regarded as holdovers from the imperial era: the Army; monarchist factions within the Civil Service and the university teaching body; and, last but by no means least, the ingrained masochism of the much-maligned *Bürgertum*, with its slavish and unquestioning respect for established authority, shameless pursuit of personal advantage and total disregard for anyone outside their own professional circles. The latter symptom was an object of especial loathing for *Weltbühne* writers, chief among them Kurt Tucholsky, because of the utter lack of solidarity with their fellow German citizens it implied. This perceived middle-class animus against the proletariat was deemed to be an existential threat to the German nation, one which had to be vanquished not through class warfare but by reconciling Germany's estranged constituencies with one another. The journal's increasingly voluble antipathy towards extremism must therefore be seen as a reflection of its determination to expunge sectarian squabbles and internecine hatred from Weimar Germany. This is the main patriotic ingredient of its intermittently intemperate Socialism.

It would be disingenuous to overlook the fact that the left-wing patriotism of *Die Weltbühne* shared a handful of characteristics with its antithesis, right-wing nationalism. As hinted above, the most evident of these common traits were a weakness for national mythology, sporadic outbursts of racism and an affinity with the imperialist, or even Fascist, lexicon. Most such instances of crossover between left- and right-wing love of country, however, were superficial. In these cases, ostensible similarities are revealing not of retrograde nationalism masquerading as progressive patriotism, but of a poverty of language preventing the latter from being properly articulated. Attention has been drawn at several points in this book not only to the absence of an alternative to the word 'Patriotismus' itself, but also to the liability of words such as 'Reich' and 'Deutschtum' to be misunderstood by an audience unaccustomed to hearing them in a left-wing context. Indeed, it is only by dwelling on precisely how and why these terms are invoked that one can gain a full appreciation of how radical the engagement of the journal with patriotism was. By reinterpreting concepts long thought insolubly welded to the nationalist world view, *Die Weltbühne* undermined the popular consensus on how to define patriotism itself.

As a weekly publication specializing in long-form journalism, *Die Weltbühne* offered a more conducive forum for the elaboration of a nuanced patriotism than any of the thousands of daily newspapers available in the

Weimar Republic, many of which operated within the constraints of a particular political agenda and its accompanying phrasebook. Indeed, the national vision which emerges from this study of the journal is founded less in political doctrine as such than in a German cultural idealism compounded in equal parts of nostalgia and utopian optimism. The ideology of *Die Weltbühne* was of an unmistakeably left-wing hue, but it is not by chance that the three-part analysis undertaken in this volume should highlight a constellation of values which transcend narrow party loyalties: regionalism, internationalism and Socialism. The patriotic aspirations of the journal could hardly be satisfied by manifesto promises, nor even by the successful implementation of partisan political programmes, because these aspirations depended for their fulfilment on a unanimous and unequivocal commitment to improving life in the German nation as a whole.

The three chapters of this volume have deliberately isolated the principal characteristics of patriotism in *Die Weltbühne*: its self-critical energy, its moral fervour and its Socialist passion. To the writers of this journal Germany was an object not of blind devotion, but of watchful concern. Moreover, whereas German nationalists typically saw their country as an ethno-cultural artefact and themselves as its dutiful embalmers, the progressive patriots of *Die Weltbühne* largely perceived Germany as a changeable living organism made up of vulnerable human beings with a duty of care to one another. The influence of the contemporary political climate cannot be underestimated, with the unsparingly pragmatic outlook of the journal compelling it to counsel the adoption of a new national demeanour that would not antagonize the Weimar Republic's more powerful neighbours among the wartime Allies. Political expediency alone, however, is insufficient to explain the abomination expressed in *Die Weltbühne* of right-wing nationalism. Instead of constituting a merely reactive response to changed international circumstances, the body of work explored here presents an alternative vision for how the future of the German nation might unfold if an affirmative left-wing patriotism were to prevail.

Its writers' dogged prioritization of the national interest over factional self-interest, alongside their readiness to expose the perceived hypocrisy of the nationalist right wing in its prosecution of the former, ensures that *Die Weltbühne* remains highly relevant in the early-twenty-first century. In an era of resurgent nationalism on the European continent, the meaning of patriotism has once again become the subject of fierce debate. In the second decade of the new millennium, the left-wing response to the nationalist rhetoric of an emboldened right wing was initially encumbered by a palpable reluctance to be associated with patriotism. This reticence subsided somewhat when the nationalist Right began first to gain a foothold in public discourse and then to win power in some Central and Western European states, while the United Kingdom's protracted withdrawal from the European Union following the referendum of 2016 prompted a belated reckoning with the growing currency of isolationist narratives and exceptionalist myths within the world's largest trading bloc. The increasing normalization of nationalist rhetoric that these developments have brought in train has forced left-wing politicians to reappropriate, or at least re-engage with, the patriotic idea. However, sheer political self-preservation no more accounts for the general revival of left-wing interest in patriotism at the time of writing than did the threat of national extinction in the case of *Die Weltbühne* about a century ago. Instead, the gradual reincarnation of progressive patriotism today reaffirms the enduring emotional power of the national idea across the political spectrum. As the example of *Die Weltbühne* shows, the perennial struggle between Left and Right has always been in part a struggle over how best to serve the national interest.

BIBLIOGRAPHY

Articles from *Die Weltbühne*

[Anon.], 'Wie Oberschlesien verloren ging!', *Die Weltbühne*, 17.2 (1921), 441–45

[Anon.], 'Was ist das rechte Mittel?', *Die Weltbühne*, 19.1 (1923), 173–75

[Anon.], 'Antworten: "Wahrheitsfreund"', *Die Weltbühne*, 19.2 (1923), 106–08

[Anon.], 'Ein guter Tag für die Justiz', *Die Weltbühne*, 28.2 (1932), 5–8

Ackermann, Werner, 'Paneuropa – eine Gefahr!', *Die Weltbühne*, 22.2 (1926), 499–503

Agathon, 'Mussolini, Seeckt und Südtirol', *Die Weltbühne*, 23.1 (1927), 933–37

Eschbach, Victor, 'Elsaß-Lothringen in Berlin', *Die Weltbühne*, 15.1 (1919), 495–99

Fischart, Johannes [pseudonym], 'Politiker und Publizisten: Walther Adrian Schücking', *Die Weltbühne*, 15.1 (1919), lvii, 406–10

— 'Politiker und Publizisten: Ludwig Quidde', *Die Weltbühne*, 15.2 (1919), lxxiii, 218–23

Flake, Otto, 'Deutsche Reden', *Die Weltbühne*, 18.1 (1922), i, 337–40

— 'Deutsche Reden', *Die Weltbühne*, 18.1 (1922), iii, 413–16

— 'Deutsche Reden', *Die Weltbühne*, 18.1 (1922), iv, 437–40

— 'Deutsche Reden', *Die Weltbühne*, 18.1 (1922), v, 467–70

— 'Michel über Michel', *Die Weltbühne*, 18.1 (1922), 514

— 'Deutsche Reden', *Die Weltbühne*, 18.1 (1922), vi, 519–22

— 'Deutsche Reden', *Die Weltbühne*, 18.1 (1922), vii, 567–70

— 'Deutsche Reden', *Die Weltbühne*, 18.2 (1922), viii, 1–3

— 'Deutsche Reden', *Die Weltbühne*, 18.2 (1922), x, 129–31

— 'Die deutsche Problematik', *Die Weltbühne*, 18.2 (1922), 241–44

— 'Südsteiermark', *Die Weltbühne*, 21.2 (1925), 160–68

French and German Leagues for Human Rights, 'Für eine Verständigung mit Frankreich!', *Die Weltbühne*, 18.1 (1922), 547–48

Fried, Alfred Hermann, 'Weihnachtspazifismus', *Die Weltbühne*, 15.2 (1919), 781–84

— 'Der Fall Nicolai in seiner internationalen Bedeutung', *Die Weltbühne*, 16.1 (1920), 389–92

Geldern, Rudolf, 'Der historische Film', *Die Weltbühne*, 19.2 (1923), 297–98

Georg, Manfred, 'Das Recht auf Abtreibung', *Die Weltbühne*, 18.1 (1922), 7–9
— 'Das Herz im Feldwebel', *Die Weltbühne*, 25.1 (1929), 272–73
Gerlach, Hellmut von, 'Erinnerungen an die Große Zeit. Die geschundenen Pazifisten', *Die Weltbühne*, 21.2 (1925), xvii, 901–06
Glenk, Hans, 'Zurück zum Balkan', *Die Weltbühne*, 22.1 (1926), 88–95
Grelling, Richard, 'Brief an den Herausgeber', *Die Weltbühne*, 15.2 (1919), 754
Hauptmann, Ein, 'Die Sage von den gefallenen Aktiven', *Die Weltbühne*, 16.1 (1920), 266–69
Hauser, Kaspar, 'Kurländisches Landknechtslied', *Die Weltbühne*, 15.2 (1919), 486
— 'Achtundvierzig', *Die Weltbühne*, 15.1 (1919), 20
Hiller, Kurt, 'Heroismus und Pazifismus', Die Weltbühne, 29.1 (1933), 349–55
Jacobsohn, Siegfried, 'Wahrheitsfreund', *Die Weltbühne*, 19.2 (1923), 108
Jäger, Heinz [pseudonym], 'Windiges aus der deutschen Luftfahrt', *Die Weltbühne*, 25.1 (1929), 402–07
Jurisch, Ludwig, 'Ansage', *Die Weltbühne*, 15.1 (1919), 1–3
Kaminski, Hanns-Erich, 'Der deutsche Sumpf', *Die Weltbühne*, 27.2 (1931), 366–68
Kautsky, Karl, 'Belagerungszustand und Unabhängige', *Die Weltbühne*, 16.1 (1920), 165–69
Keßler von Monbart, Helene, 'Wir und Ihr. Briefe an einen französischen Freund', *Die Weltbühne*, 18.1 (1922), i, 36–40
— 'Wir und Ihr', *Die Weltbühne*, 18.1 (1922), ii, 64–68
— 'Wir und Ihr', *Die Weltbühne*, 18.1 (1922), iv, 113–16
— 'Wir und Ihr', *Die Weltbühne*, 18.1 (1922), v, 142–44
— 'Wir und Ihr', *Die Weltbühne*, 18.1 (1922), vi, 164–66
Kollenka, Walter, 'Die Deutschen in der Tschechoslowakei', *Die Weltbühne*, 16.1 (1920), 635–38
Kuczynski, Robert, 'Wäre so etwas in Frankreich denkbar?', *Die Weltbühne*, 19.1 (1923), 493–94
Lehmann-Rußbüldt, Otto, 'Die undeutsche Demokratie', *Die Weltbühne*, 17.1 (1921), 91–94
Lewinsohn, Ludwig, 'Die Kunst, ein Jude zu sein', *Die Weltbühne*, 21.2 (1925), 594–97
Manuel, Bruno, 'Der Höhlenbewohner im Gefängnis', *Die Weltbühne*, 18.1 (1922), 127–28
Markstahler, Wilhelm, 'Der neue Krieg I: Brief an den Stabsoffizier', *Die Weltbühne*, 16.2 (1920), 510–13

Mehring, Walter, 'Die welsche Grenze', *Die Weltbühne*, 17.2 (1921), 306–09
Meridionalis, 'Auch eine Wiederherstellungskommission', *Die Weltbühne*, 16.2 (1920), 380–81
— 'Deutsche und französische Propaganda', *Die Weltbühne*, 19.1 (1923), 291–94
Mertens, Carl, 'Die vaterländischen Verbände. Erlebnisse und Erfahrungen', *Die Weltbühne*, 21.2 (1925), 239–58
Metzler, Georg [Richard Witting], 'Die verruchte Lüge', *Die Weltbühne*, 15.1 (1919), 34–37
— 'Die Schuld am Kriege', *Die Weltbühne*, 15.1 (1919), 163–81
Meyer, Willy, 'Ergänzung', *Die Weltbühne*, 16.2 (1920), 640–42
— 'Berufssoldat und Pazifismus', *Die Weltbühne*, 17.1 (1921), 271–73
Michel, Wilhelm, 'Glaube an Deutschland', *Die Weltbühne*, 18.2 (1922), 537–38
— 'Die deutsche Krankheit', *Die Weltbühne*, 19.1 (1923), 321–24
— 'Reichsdämmerung', *Die Weltbühne*, 19.2 (1923), 397–400
— 'Pfalz, Bayern, Deutschland', *Die Weltbühne*, 19.2 (1923), 470–74
— 'Ruhrkrieg und Pfalz', *Die Weltbühne*, 19.2 (1923), 643–47
Morus, 'Pariser Spritztour', *Die Weltbühne*, 23.1 (1927), 69–72
Nübell, Ferdinand, 'Die Valuta der Moral', *Die Weltbühne*, 15.2 (1919), 571–73
Ossietzky, Carl von, 'Seeckt und Severing', *Die Weltbühne*, 22.2 (1926), 559–62
— 'Rif und Riffe', *Die Weltbühne*, 22.2 (1926), 833–37
— 'Der lachende Reporter', *Die Weltbühne*, 25.1 (1929), 274–75
— 'Rechenschaft', *Die Weltbühne*, 28.1 (1932), 689–709
Panter, Peter, 'Christian Wagner', *Die Weltbühne*, 15.1 (1919), 182–83
— 'Ein untergehendes Land', *Die Weltbühne*, 15.2 (1919), 11–14
— 'Frühlingsvormittag', *Die Weltbühne*, 19.1 (1923), 341–42
— 'Krieg gleich Mord', *Die Weltbühne*, 28.1 (1932), 588–90
Persius, Lothar, 'Die Kriegsschuld der Rechtssozialisten', *Die Weltbühne*, 15.2 (1919), 789–92
Polgar, Alfred, 'Salzburger großes Welttheater', *Die Weltbühne*, 18.2 (1922), i, 310–14
Reger, Erik, 'Ruhrprovinz', *Die Weltbühne*, 24.2 (1928), 918–24
Reimann, Hans, 'Heimat', *Die Weltbühne*, 22.1 (1926), 616
Reissner, Larissa, 'Krupp und Essen', *Die Weltbühne*, 21.2 (1925), 729–34
Rothammer, Karl, 'Wedding und Esplanade', *Die Weltbühne*, 16.2 (1920), 569–70
— 'Das Streikrecht der Beamten', *Die Weltbühne*, 16.2 (1920), 696–99
— 'Reaktion und Weltpolitik', *Die Weltbühne*, 17.1 (1921), 1–2

— 'Berlin-München-Paris', *Die Weltbühne*, 17.1 (1921), 89–91
— 'Die Preußenwahlen', *Die Weltbühne*, 17.1 (1921), 237–39
— 'London', *Die Weltbühne*, 17.1 (1921), 267–69
— 'Der Kommunistenputsch', *Die Weltbühne*, 17.1 (1921), 371–72
— 'Deutschland als Weltmacht', *Die Weltbühne*, 17.2 (1921), 55–56
— 'Vorteile der Ohnmacht' *Die Weltbühne*, 17.2 (1921), 83–84
Schwann, Hans, 'Friedrich Wilhelm Foerster', *Die Weltbühne*, 25.1 (1929), 813–17
Seehof, Arthur, 'Freiheitskampf in Mörs', *Die Weltbühne*, 25.2 (1929), 237–38
Siemsen, Hans, 'Ich liebe Deutschland', *Die Weltbühne*, 16.2 (1920), 740
Ein Stabsoffizier, 'Das alte Heer. Die Waffengattungen', *Die Weltbühne*, 15.2 (1919), iv, 654–69
— 'Das alte Heer. Hindenburg', *Die Weltbühne*, 15.2 (1919), vii, 759–63
— 'Das alte Heer. Ludendorff', *Die Weltbühne*, 15.2 (1919), viii, 785–89
— 'Das alte Heer. Der Kronprinz', *Die Weltbühne*, 16.1 (1920), ix, 12–16
— 'Das alte Heer. Das Offiziercorps im Kriege', *Die Weltbühne*, 16.1 (1920), x, 38–42
— 'Das alte Heer. Der Generalstab im Kriege', *Die Weltbühne*, 16.1 (1920), xii, 101–06
— 'Das alte Heer. Das Kadettenkorps', *Die Weltbühne*, 16.1 (1920), xiii, 139–44
— 'Das alte Heer. Offizierstypen', *Die Weltbühne*, 16.1 (1920), xiv, 174–79
— 'Das alte Heer. Soldat und Politik', *Die Weltbühne*, 16.1 (1920), xxi, 393–96
— 'Der neue Krieg', *Die Weltbühne*, 16.2 (1920), 446–50
— 'Der neue Krieg', *Die Weltbühne*, 16.2 (1920), 638–40
Steiniger, Alphons, 'Parteien-Abbau!', *Die Weltbühne*, 20.1 (1924), 31–32
— 'Wahlkampf ohne Bürgerkrieg', *Die Weltbühne*, 20.1 (1924), 355–56
— 'Die unmündigen Wähler', *Die Weltbühne*, 20.1 (1924), 871–73
— 'An die deutschen Kommunisten', *Die Weltbühne*, 20.2 (1924), 369–72
— 'Republikanische Union', *Die Weltbühne*, 22.2 (1926), 446–48
Stössinger, Felix, 'Was ist uns Frankreich?', *Die Weltbühne*, 18.1 (1922), i, 397–400
— 'Was ist uns Frankreich?', *Die Weltbühne*, 18.1 (1922), iii, 44–42
— 'Was ist uns Frankreich?', *Die Weltbühne*, 18.1 (1922), iv, 474–75
— 'Was ist uns Frankreich?', *Die Weltbühne*, 18.1 (1922), v, 496–98
— 'Was ist uns Frankreich?', *Die Weltbühne*, 18.1 (1922), vi, 522–23
— 'Was ist uns Frankreich?', *Die Weltbühne*, 18.1 (1922), vii, 544–46
Ströbel, Heinrich, 'Das neue Reich', *Die Weltbühne*, 15. 2 (1919), 149–54
— 'Das baltische Komplott', *Die Weltbühne*, 15.2 (1919), 525–30
— 'Alt-Preußen und Neu-Deutschland', *Die Weltbühne*, 15. 2 (1919), 777–81
— 'Die Untersuchungsposse', *Die Weltbühne*, 16.1 (1920), 33–37

— 'Denkt an das Ende!', *Die Weltbühne*, 16.1 (1920), 225-29
— 'Tollhäuslerei und Erzbergerei', *Die Weltbühne*, 16.1 (1920), 257-61
— 'Nach dem Putsch', *Die Weltbühne*, 16.1 (1920), 353-56
— 'Zwischen zwei Militarismen', *Die Weltbühne*, 16.1 (1920), 417-21
— 'Vor dem neuen Putsch', *Die Weltbühne*, 16.1 (1920), 641-45
— 'Spaa', *Die Weltbühne*, 16.2 (1920), 33-36
Tucholsky, Kurt, 'Was wäre, wenn…?', *Die Weltbühne*, 18.1 (1922), 615-20
— 'Die zufällige Republik', *Die Weltbühne*, 18.2 (1922), 25-30
— 'Fünfundzwanzig Jahre', *Die Weltbühne*, 26.2 (1930), 373-82
Varssovius, Franz, 'Gefährliche Lieder', *Die Weltbühne*, 15.1 (1919), 151-54
Voigt, Arno, 'Korfanty', *Die Weltbühne*, 17.1 (1921), 303-06
Warschauer, Frank, 'Die Heimat ist schön', *Die Weltbühne*, 19.1 (1923), 164
Wendel, Herman, 'Elsaß-Lothringen', *Die Weltbühne*, 15.1 (1919), 339-41
Wrobel, Ignaz, 'Militaria. Offizier und Mann', *Die Weltbühne*, 15.1 (1919), i, 38-41
— 'Militaria. "Unser Militär"', *Die Weltbühne*, 15.1 (1919), vi, 201-05
— 'Militaria (Zur Erinnerung an den Ersten August 1914)', *Die Weltbühne*, 15.2 (1919), 190-99
— 'Die baltischen Helden', *Die Weltbühne*, 15.2 (1919), 500-04
— 'Militaria', *Die Weltbühne*, 16.1 (1920), 106-14
— 'Schlußwort', *Die Weltbühne*, 16.1 (1920), 219-20
— 'Kapp-Lüttwitz', *Die Weltbühne*, 16.1 (1920), 357-63
— 'Das nervöse Paris', *Die Weltbühne*, 21.1 (1925), 6-10
— 'Suomi-Finnland', *Die Weltbühne*, 21.2 (1925), 19-22
— 'Märtyrer', *Die Weltbühne*, 21.2 (1925), 325-28
— 'Wo waren Sie im Kriege, Herr –?', *Die Weltbühne*, 22.1 (1926), 489-92
— 'Grimms Märchen', *Die Weltbühne*, 24.2 (1928), 353-60
— 'Ein besserer Herr', *Die Weltbühne*, 25.1 (1929), 953-60
— 'Der bewachte Kriegsschauplatz', *Die Weltbühne*, 27.2 (1931), 191-92
Zwehl, Hans von, 'Reisen im besetzten Gebiet', *Die Weltbühne*, 19.2 (1923), 476-79
— 'Von Ruhr und Rhein', *Die Weltbühne*, 19.2 (1923), 503-06
— 'Köln, Coblenz, Düsseldorf', *Die Weltbühne*, 19.2 (1923), 533-35
Zweig, Arnold, 'Oberschlesische Motive', *Die Weltbühne*, 17.1 (1921), 247-49

Other Primary Literature

[Anon.], 'Sollt ich einem Bauern dienen?', in *Sammlung Deutscher Volkslieder welche noch gegenwärtig im Munde des Volkes leben und in keiner der bisher erschienenen Sammlungen zu finden sind*, ed. by Wilibald Walter (Leipzig: Rein, 1841), pp. 13-16

[Anon.], 'Vorwärts in den Kampf!', *Vorwärts*, 22 March 1920, pp. 1–2

[Anon.], 'Die roten Banden zersprengt', *Saale-Zeitung*, 2nd April 1921, p. 1

[Anon.], 'Wie muß der neue Reichstag beschaffen sein?', *Deutsche Allgemeine Zeitung*, 1 January 1924, pp. 5–6 (p. 6)

Angell, Norman, *The Peace Treaty and the Economic Chaos of Europe* (London: Swarthmore, 1919)

Bertram, Ernst, *Rheingenius und Génie du Rhin* (Bonn: Cohen, 1922)

Fichte, Johann Gottlieb, *Reden an die deutsche Nation* (Berlin: Realschulbuchhandlung, 1808)

Foerster, Friedrich Wilhelm, *Mein Kampf gegen das militaristische und nationalistische Deutschland. Gesichtspunkte zur deutschen Selbsterkenntnis und zum Aufbau eines neuen Deutschland* (Stuttgart: Friede durch Recht, 1920)

— *Politische Ethik und Politische Pädagogik, mit besonderer Berücksichtigung der kommenden deutschen Aufgaben* (Munich: Reinhardt, 1922); 4th, rev. edn of 'Die staatsbürgerliche Erziehung in der Monarchie' (1918)

Grelling, Richard, *J'accuse! von einem Deutschen*, 2nd edn (Lausanne: Payot, 1919 [1915])

Grimm, Jakob, and Wilhelm, 'Das Märchen von einem, der auszog das Fürchten zu lernen', in *Grimms Märchen*, ed. by Heinz Rölleke, Suhrkamp BasisBibliothek (Frankfurt a.M.: Suhrkamp, 1998 [1812]), pp. 11–20

Heine, Heinrich, *Zur Geschichte der Religion und Philosophie in Deutschland* (Frankfurt a.M.: Insel, 1966); 1st edn in *Der Salon*, 4 vols (Hamburg: Hoffmann und Campe, 1835), II, 1–284

— *Deutschland. Ein Wintermärchen* (Stuttgart: Reclam, 1979); 1st edn Hamburg: Hoffmann und Campe, 1844

Hoffmann von Fallersleben, August Heinrich, 'Mein Vaterland', in *Unpolitische Lieder*, 2 vols (Hamburg: Hoffmann und Campe, 1840), I, 165

Hofmannsthal, Hugo von, 'Österreich im Spiegel seiner Dichtung', in *Gesammelte Werke in Einzelausgaben*, ed. by Herbert Steiner, 4 vols (Frankfurt a.M.: Fischer, 1950–55), *Prosa*, III (1952), 333–49

Jacob, Berthold, *Weltbürger Ossietzky. Ein Abriß seines Werkes* (Paris: Carrefour, 1937)

Jouvenel, Bertrand de, *Vers les Etats-Unis d'Europe* (Paris: Librairie Valois, 1930)

Jünger, Ernst, *In Stahlgewittern. Aus dem Tagebuch eines Stoßtruppführers* (Leisnig: Meier, 1920)

Kahlenberg, Hans von, *Der Fremde. Ein Gleichniss* (Dresden: Reissner, 1901) <https://www.gutenberg.org/files/36227/36227-h/36227-h.html> [accessed 15 September 2022]

Kant, Immanuel, *Groundwork of the Metaphysics of Morals: A German-English Edition*, ed. and trans. by Mary Gregor and Jens Timmermann, Cambridge Texts in the History of Philosophy (Cambridge: Cambridge University Press, 2011)

Kautsky, Karl, 'Der heilige Franz von Assisi. Ein Revisionist des Revisionist des mittelalterlichen Kommunismus', in *Die Neue Zeit*, 22.2 (1903–04), 260–67

Kleist, Heinrich von, Letter to Ulrike von Kleist, 24 October 1806, in *Heinrichs von Kleist Briefe an seiner Schwester Ulrike*, ed. by A. Roberstein (Berlin: Schroeder, 1860), pp. 108–10

Klopstock, Friedrich Gottlieb, *Hermanns Schlacht. Ein Bardiet für die Schaubühne* (Hamburg: Cramer, 1769)

Krische, Paul, *Heimat! Grundsätzliches zur Gemeinschaft von Scholle und Mensch* (Berlin: Paetel, 1918)

Mann, Heinrich, 'Geist und Tat', in *Macht und Mensch* (Leipzig: Wolff, 1919), pp. 1–9

— 'Voltaire – Goethe', in *Macht und Mensch* (Leipzig: Wolff, 1919), pp. 12–19

Mann, Thomas, 'Ossietzky zu Tode gemartert', *Deutsches Volksecho*, 14 May 1938, pp. 4–5

— '"Gegen Recht und Wahrheit"', in *Betrachtungen eines Unpolitischen* (Berlin: Fischer, 1918), pp. 121–202

— 'Politik', in *Betrachtungen eines Unpolitischen* (Frankfurt a.M.: Fischer, 1918), pp. 203–371

Michel, Wilhelm, *Verrat am Deutschtum. Eine Streitschrift zur Judenfrage* (Hanover: Steegemann, 1922)

Radbruch, Gustav, *Der innere Weg. Aufriß meines Lebens*, ed. by Lydia Radbruch (Stuttgart: Koehler, 1951)

Remarque, Erich Maria, *Im Westen nichts Neues* (Berlin: Propyläen, 1929)

Spranger, Eduard, *Der Bildungswert der Heimatkunde. Rede zur Eröffnungssitzung der Studiengemeinschaft für wissenschaftliche Heimatkunde* (Berlin: Hartmann, 1923)

Toller, Ernst, 'Das Versagen des Pazifismus', in *Sämtliche Werke. Kritische Ausgabe*, ed. by D. Distl and others (Göttingen: Wallstein, 2015), IV.I, *Publizistik und Reden*, pp. 336–41

Tucholsky, Kurt, 'Heimat', in *Deutschland, Deutschland über alles* (Berlin: Neuer Deutscher Verlag, 1929), pp. 226–31

— 'Starter, die Fahne – ! Ab mit 5 PS', in *Kurt Tucholsky: Panter, Tiger & Co*, ed. by Mary Gerold-Tucholsky, 2nd edn (Hamburg: Rowohlt, 1955 [1954]), pp. 8–10; originally published as 'Start', *Die Weltbühne*, 23.2 (1927), 964–66

Wagner, Christian, *Gedichte*, 2nd edn (Munich: Müller, 1913 [1913])

Zetkin, Clara, 'Unser Patriotismus', in *Die Gleichheit*, 27 May 1907, 1–2
— 'Gegen Poincaré und Cuno' (Rede im deutschen Reichstag, 312. Sitzung, 7. März 1923), in *Verhandlungen des Reichstags, 1. Wahlperiode 1920*, CCCLVIII (Berlin: Norddeutsche Buchdruckerei und Verlags-Anstalt, 1923), 9989–96

Secondary Literature

Achilles, Manuela, 'Reforming the Reich: Democratic Symbols and Rituals in the Weimar Republic', in *Weimar Publics/Weimar Subjects: Rethinking the Political Culture of Germany in the 1920s*, ed. by Kathleen Canning, Kerstin Barndt and Kristin McGuire, Spektrum: Publications of the German Studies Association, 2 (New York: Berghahn, 2010), pp. 175–91

Anderson, Lisa Marie, 'The Meaning of Failure and the Failure of Meaning: Ernst Toller on Pacifist Language and Literature in Interwar Germany', in *Pacifist and Anti-Militarist Writing in German, 1889–1928: From Bertha von Suttner to Erich Maria Remarque*, ed. by Andreas Kramer and Ritchie Robertson, London German Studies, 16 (Munich: Iudicium and London: Institute of Modern Languages Research, 2018), pp. 136–48

Applegate, Celia, *A Nation of Provincials: The German Idea of Heimat* (Berkeley, CA: University of California Press, 1990)

Baranowski, Shelley, *The Sanctity of Rural Life: Nobility, Protestantism, and Nazism in Weimar Prussia* (New York: Oxford University Press, 1995)

Bavaj, Riccardo, *Von links gegen Weimar. Linkes antiparlamentarisches Denken in der Weimarer Republik*, Politik- und Gesellschaftsgeschichte, 67 (Kempten: Dietz, 2005)

Blickle, Peter, *Heimat: A Critical Theory of the German Idea of Homeland*, Studies in German Literature, Linguistics, and Culture (Rochester, NY: Camden House, 2002)

Boa, Elizabeth, and Rachel Palfreyman, *Heimat – A German Dream: Regional Loyalties and National Identity in German Culture 1890–1990*, Oxford Studies in Modern European Culture (New York: Oxford University Press, 2000)

Brown, Timothy S., *Weimar Radicals: Nazis and Communists Between Authenticity and Performance*, Monographs in German History, 28 (New York: Berghahn, 2016)

Caldwell, Peter, 'Sovereignty, Constitutionalism, and the Myth of the State: Article Four of the Weimar Constitution', in *The Weimar Moment: Liberalism, Political Theology and Law*, ed. by Leonard V. Kaplan and Rudy Koshar, Graven Images (New York: Lexington, 2012), pp. 345–70

Ceadel, Martin, 'Three Degrees of European Opposition to War: Anti-Militarism, Pacificism, and Pacifism in the Nineteenth and Early Twentieth Centuries', in *Pacifist and Anti-Militarist Writing in German, 1889–1928: From Bertha von Suttner to Erich Maria Remarque*, ed. by Andreas Kramer and Ritchie Robertson, London German Studies, 16 (Munich: Iudicium and London: Institute of Modern Languages Research, 2018), pp. 14–30

Chickering, Roger, *We Men Who Feel Most German: Cultural Study of the Pan-German League 1886–1914* (Boston, MA: Allen & Unwin, 1984)

Confino, Alon, 'The Nation as a Local Metaphor: National Memory and the German Empire, 1871–1918', *History and Memory*, 1 (1993), 42–86

Cooper, Sandi E., *Patriotic Pacifism: Waging War on War in Europe, 1815–1914* (Oxford: Oxford University Press, 1991)

Davidson, G. W., and others (eds), *Chambers Concise 20th Century Dictionary* (Edinburgh: Chambers, 1986)

Deak, Istvan, *Weimar Germany's Left-Wing Intellectuals: A Political History of the 'Weltbühne' and Its Circle* (Berkeley, CA: University of California Press, 1968)

Eggebrecht, Axel, *Das Drama der Republik* (Königstein/Taunus: Athenäum, 1979)

Eigler, Friederike, *Heimat, Space, Narrative: Towards a Transnational Approach to Flight and Expulsion*, Studies in German Literature, Linguistics and Culture, 147 (Rochester, NY: Camden House, 2014)

Eksteins, Modris, *The Limits of Reason: The German Democratic Press and the Collapse of Weimar Democracy*, Oxford Historical Monographs (Oxford: Oxford University Press, 1975)

Enseling, Alf, *Die Weltbühne. Organ der intellektuellen Linken*, Studien zur Publizistik, 2 (Münster: Fahle, 1962)

Fahrmeir, Andreas, *Citizenship: The Rise and Fall of a Modern Concept* (New Haven, CT: Yale University Press, 2007)

Ferber, Christian, 'Für jedermann: Anmerkungen zu einer öffentlichen Einrichtung' (Vorwort), in *'Berliner Illustrirte Zeitung'. Zeitbild, Chronik, Moritat für jedermann, 1892–1945*, ed. by Christian Ferber (Berlin: Ullstein, 1982), pp. 5–10

Fischer, Conan, *The Ruhr Crisis, 1923–1924* (Oxford: Oxford University Press, 2003)

Föllmer, Moritz, 'The Problem of National Solidarity in Interwar Germany', *German History*, 23 (2005), 202–31

Galston, William, 'In Defense of a Reasonable Patriotism' <https://www.brookings.edu/research/in-defense-of-a-reasonable-patriotism/> [accessed 25 June 2020]

Gellner, Ernest, *Nations and Nationalism*, New Perspectives on the Past, 2nd edn (Ithaca, NY: Cornell University Press, 2008 [1983])

Gerwarth, Robert, *November 1918: The German Revolution*, Making of the Modern World (Oxford: Oxford University Press, 2020)

Gierlak, Maria, 'Deutsche Presse in Polen 1919–1939: Forschungstand, -postulate und -desiderate', in *Grenzdiskurse: Zeitungen deutschsprachiger Minderheiten und ihr Feuilleton in Mitteleuropa bis 1939*, ed. by Sibylle Schönborn (Essen: Klartext, 2009), pp. 67–80

Gordon, Peter E., 'German Idealism and German Liberalism in the 1920s: Remarks on Ernst Cassirer and the Historicity of Interpretation', in *The Weimar Moment: Liberalism, Political Theology and Law*, ed. by Leonard V. Kaplan and Rudy Koshar, Graven Images (New York: Lexington, 2012), pp. 337–44

Green, Abigail, *Fatherlands: State-Building and Nationhood in Nineteenth-Century Germany*, New Studies in European History (Cambridge: Cambridge University Press, 2001)

Greenberg, Udi, 'The Limits of Dictatorship and the Origins of Democracy: The Political Theory of Carl J. Friedrich from Weimar to the Cold War', in *The Weimar Moment: Liberalism, Political Theology and Law*, ed. by Leonard V. Kaplan and Rudy Koshar, Graven Images (New York: Lexington, 2012), pp. 443–64

Greis, Friedhelm, and Stefanie Oswalt, 'Die Geschichte der Zeitschrift', in *Aus Teutschland Deutschland machen. Ein politisches Lesebuch zur 'Weltbühne'*, ed. by Friedhelm Greis and Stefanie Oswalt (Berlin: Lukas, 2008), pp. 13–23

Grenville, Brian P., *Kurt Tucholsky: The Ironic Sentimentalist*, German Literature and Society, 1 (London, Wolff: 1981)

Grossmann, Kurt R., *Ossietzky. Ein deutscher Patriot* (Munich: Suhrkamp, 1963)

Großmann, Stefan, 'Zum Anfang', *Das Tage-Buch*, 10 January 1920, p. 1

Gusejnova, Dina, *European Elites and Ideas of Empire, 1917–1957*, New Studies in European History (Cambridge: Cambridge University Press, 2016)

Hagen, William W., *German History in Modern Times: Four Lives of the Nation* (Cambridge: Cambridge University Press, 2012)

Hake, Sabine, *The Proletarian Dream: Socialism, Culture, and Emotion in Germany 1863–1933*, Interdisciplinary German Cultural Studies, 23 (Berlin: De Gruyter, 2017) [DOI: 10.1515/9783110550863]

Hans, Anjeana K., 'Grief Reserved for the Mother: Käthe Kollwitz's *Krieg* Cycle and Gender in the Weimar Republic', in *Käthe Kollwitz and the Women of War: Femininity, Identity and Art in Germany during World*

Wars I and II, ed. by Claire C. Whitner (New Haven, CT: Yale University Press, 2016), pp. 124–34

Harrington, Austin, *German Cosmopolitan Social Thought and the Idea of the West: Voices from Weimar* (Cambridge: Cambridge University Press, 2016)

Hermand, Jost, and James Steakley, 'Preface', in *Heimat, Nation, Fatherland: The German Sense of Belonging*, German Life and Civilization, 22 (New York: Lang, 1996), pp. i–ix

Hermand, Jost, and James Steakley (eds), *Heimat, Nation, Fatherland: The German Sense of Belonging*, German Life and Civilization, 22 (New York: Lang, 1996)

Herrmann, Hans Peter, *Machtphantasie Deutschland. Nationalismus, Männlichkeit und Fremdenhaß im Vaterlandsdiskurs deutscher Schriftsteller des 18. Jahrhunderts*, suhrkamp taschenbuch wissenschaft, 1273 (Frankfurt a.M.: Suhrkamp, 1996)

Hewitson, Mark, 'Inventing Europe and Reinventing the Nation-State in a New World Order', in *Europe in Crisis: Intellectuals and the European Idea, 1917–1957*, ed. by Mark Hewitson and Matthew D'Auria (New York: Berghahn, 2012), pp. 63–81

Heynen, Robert, *Degeneration and Revolution: Radical Cultural Politics and the Body in Weimar Germany*, Historical Materialism, 93 (Leiden: Brill, 2015)

Hobsbawm, Eric, *Age of Extremes: The Short Twentieth Century, 1914–1991* (London: Abacus, 1995 [1994])

Hochman, Erin R., *Imagining a Greater Germany: Republican Nationalism and the Idea of Anschluss* (Ithaca, NY: Cornell University Press, 2016)

Holly, Elmar E., *Die Weltbühne 1918–1933. Ein Register sämtlicher Autoren und Beiträge*, Abhandlungen und Materialien zur Publistik (Berlin: Colloquium, 1989)

Holmes, Deborah, '"… Die Menschheit verdient ein Massaker ohne Ende": The Warlike Pacifism of Grete Meisel-Hess', in *Pacifist and Anti-Militarist Writing in German, 1889–1928: From Bertha von Suttner to Erich Maria Remarque*, ed. by Andreas Kramer and Ritchie Robertson, London German Studies, 16 (Munich: Iudicium and London: Institute of Modern Languages Research, 2018), pp. 110–23

Hughes, Michael, *Nationalism and Society: Germany 1800–1945* (London: Edward Arnold, 1988)

Jay, Martin, 'The Weimar Left: Theory and Practice', in *Weimar Thought: A Contested Legacy*, ed. by Peter E. Gordon and John P. McCormick (Princeton, NJ: Princeton University Press, 2013), pp. 377–93

Jurt, Joseph, *Sprache, Literatur und Nationale Identität. Die Debatten über das Universelle und das Partikuläre in Frankreich und Deutschland*, Mimesis, 58 (Berlin: De Gruyter, 2014)

Kane, Michael, *Modern Men: Mapping Masculinity in English and German Literature, 1880–1930* (London: Cassell, 1999)

Kateb, George, *Patriotism and Other Mistakes* (New Haven, CT: Yale University Press, 2006)

Kets de Vries, Henriëtte, 'Mothers' Arms: Käthe Kollwitz's Women and War', in *Käthe Kollwitz and the Women of War: Femininity, Identity and Art in Germany during World Wars I and II*, ed. by Claire C. Whitner (New Haven, CT: Yale University Press, 2016), pp. 10–19

King, Ian, '"Das Bürgertum erliegt der Wucht...". Tucholsky zwischen Bürgertum und Arbeiterbewegung', in *Kurt Tucholsky und der Weltbühne-Kreis zwischen Bürgertum und Arbeiterbewegung*, ed. by Ian King, Schriftenreihe der Kurt Tucholsky-Gesellschaft, 11 (Leipzig: Ille & Riemer, 2016), pp. 25–47

Klose, Joachim, '"Heimat" als gelingende Ordnungskonstruktion', in *Die Machbarkeit politischer Ordnung. Transzendenz und Konstruktion*, ed. by Werner J. Patzelt, Edition Politik, 8 (Bielefeld: Transcript, 2013), pp. 391–416

Koszyk, Kurt, *Zwischen Kaiserreich und Diktatur. Die sozialdemokratische Presse von 1914 bis 1933* (Heidelberg: Quelle & Meyer, 1958)

— *Deutsche Presse 1914–1945. Geschichte der deutschen Presse. Teil III*, Abhandlungen und Materialien zur Publistik, 7 (Berlin: Colloquium, 1972)

Kramberger, Petra, 'Das Jahr 1929 in der deutschsprachigen Presse der Untersteiermark aus Maribor, Celje und Ptuj', in *Grenzdiskurse. Zeitungen deutschsprachiger Minderheiten und ihr Feuilleton in Mitteleuropa bis 1939*, ed. by Sibylle Schönborn (Essen: Klartext, 2009), pp. 113–26

Krauss, Marita, 'Heimat – Begriff und Erfahrung', in *Heimat, liebe Heimat. Exil und Innere Emigration (1933–1945)*, ed. by Hermann Haarmann (Berlin: Bostelmann & Siebenhaar, 2004), pp. 11–29

Lang, Markus, 'Frankreich als Vorbild. Karl Loewenstein und die Grundlagen der Weimarer Demokratie', in *Deutsche Frankreich-Bücher aus der Zwischenkriegszeit*, ed. by Alfons Söllner (Baden-Baden: Nomos, 2011), pp. 101–24

Langewiesche, Dieter, *Nation, Nationalismus, Nationalstaat in Deutschland und Europa*, Beck'sche Reihe, 1399 (Munich: Beck, 2000)

Le Bon, Gustave, *Psychologie des Foules* (Paris: Alcan, 1895)

Lethen, Helmut, *Verhaltenslehren der Kälte. Lebensversuche zwischen den Kriegen* (Frankfurt a.M.: Suhrkamp, 1994)

Mann, Golo, *Deutsche Geschichte des 19. und 20. Jahrhunderts* (Frankfurt a.M.: Fischer, 1958)

Mann, Michael, *Fascists* (Cambridge: Cambridge University Press, 2004)

Mergel, Thomas, 'High Expectations – Deep Disappointment: Structures of the Public Perception of Politics in the Weimar Republic', in *Weimar Publics/Weimar Subjects: Rethinking the Political Culture of Germany in the 1920s*, ed. by Kathleen Canning, Kerstin Barndt and Kristin McGuire, Spektrum: Publications of the German Studies Association, 2 (New York: Berghahn, 2010), pp. 192–210

Midgley, David, *Writing Weimar: Critical Realism in German Literature, 1918–1933* (Oxford: Oxford University Press, 2000)

Moltke, Johannes von, *No Place Like Home: Locations of Heimat in German Cinema*, Weimar and Now: German Cultural Criticism (Berkeley, CA: University of California Press, 2005)

Mosse, George L., *The Image of Man: The Creation of Modern Masculinity*, Studies in the History of Sexuality (Oxford: Oxford University Press, 1996)

Müller, Horst H. W., *Kurt Hiller*, Hamburger Bibliographien, 6 (Hamburg: Christians, 1969)

Müller, Jan-Werner, *Constitutional Patriotism* (Princeton, NJ: Princeton University Press, 2007)

Müller, Thomas, *Imaginierter Westen. Das Konzept des 'deutschen Westraums' im völkischen Diskurs zwischen Politischer Romantik und Nationalsozialismus* (Bielefeld: Transcript, 2009)

Onions, C. T. (ed.), *The Shorter Oxford English Dictionary* (London: Guild, 1987)

Peterson, Brent O., *History, Fiction, and Germany: Writing the Nineteenth-Century Nation*, Kritik: German Literary Theory and Cultural Studies (Detroit, MI: Wayne University Press, 2005)

Poor, Harold, 'Kurt Tucholsky and the Question of the Destructiveness of the Intellectual Left in the Weimar Republic', in *Perspectives & Personalities: Studies in Modern German Literature (Honoring Claude Hill)*, ed. by Ralph Ley and others (Heidelberg: Winter, 1978), pp. 313–19

Prettenthaler-Ziegerhofer, Anita, 'Richard Nikolaus Coudenhove-Kalergi, Founder of the Pan-European Union, and the Birth of a New Europe', in *Europe in Crisis: Intellectuals and the European Idea, 1917–1957*, ed. by Mark Hewitson and Matthew D'Auria (New York: Berghahn, 2012), pp. 89–110

Pross, Harry, *Literatur und Politik. Geschichte und Programme der politisch-literarischen Zeitschriften im deutschen Sprachgebiet seit 1870* (Olten: Walter, 1963)

Queckbörner, Peter, *'Zwischen Irrsinn und Verzweiflung'. Zum erweiterten Kulturbegriff der Zeitschrift 'Die Schaubühne'/'Die Weltbühne' im Ersten Weltkrieg*, Analysen und Dokumente, 41 (Frankfurt a.M.: Lang, 2000)

Raddatz, Fritz J., *'Das Tage-Buch'. Portrait einer Zeitschrift* (Königstein/ Taunus: Athenäum, 1981)

Rash, Felicity, *German Images of the Self and the Other: Nationalist, Colonialist and Anti-Semitic Discourse, 1871-1918* (London: Palgrave Macmillan, 2012)

Robertson, Ritchie, *Heine*, Jewish Thinkers (London: Weidenfeld & Nicolson, 1988)

Rollins, William, 'Heimat, Modernity, and Nation in the Early Heimatschutz Movement', in *Heimat, Nation, Fatherland: The German Sense of Belonging*, ed. by Jost Hermand and James Steakley, German Life and Civilization, 22 (New York: Lang, 1996), pp. 87–112

Roth, Karl Heinz, 'Schein-Alternativen im Gesundheitswesen. Alfred Grotjahn (1869–1931) – Integrationsfigur etablierter Sozialmedizin und nationalsozialistischer Rassenhygiene', in *Erfassung zur Vernichtung. Von der Sozialhygiene zum 'Gesetz über Sterbehilfe'*, ed. by Karl Heinz Roth (Berlin: Gesundheit Berlin, 1984), pp. 31–56

Ruehl, Martin A., 'Aesthetic Fundamentalism in Weimar Poetry: Stefan George and his Circle, 1918-1933', in *Weimar Thought: A Contested Legacy*, ed. by Peter E. Gordon and John P. McCormick (Princeton, NJ: Princeton University Press, 2013), pp. 240–72

Schumann, Dirk, 'Political Violence, Contested Public Space, and Reasserted Masculinity in Weimar Germany', in *Weimar Publics/Weimar Subjects: Rethinking the Political Culture of Germany in the 1920s*, ed. by Kathleen Canning, Kerstin Barndt and Kristin McGuire, Spektrum: Publications of the German Studies Association, 2 (New York: Berghahn, 2010), pp. 236–53

Schwabe, Klaus, 'Germany's Peace Aims and the Domestic and International Constraints', in *The Treaty of Versailles: A Reassessment after 75 Years*, ed. by Manfred F. Boemeke, Gerald D. Feldman and Elisabeth Glaser, Publications of the German Historical Institute (Cambridge: Cambridge University Press, 1998), pp. 37–68

Schwartz, Michael, '"Proletarier" und "Lumpen". Sozialistische Ursprünge eugenischen Denkens', *Vierteljahrshefte für Zeitgeschichte*, 42 (1994), 537–70

Sharp, Ingrid, 'Blaming the Women: Women's "Responsibility" for the First World War', in *The Women's Movement in Wartime: International Perspectives, 1914-19*, ed. by Alison Fell and Ingrid Sharp (London: Palgrave Macmillan, 2007), pp. 67–87

— 'Käthe Kollwitz's Witness to War: Gender, Authority and Reception', in *Women in German Yearbook*, 27 (2011), 87–107

Sharp, Ingrid, Judit Acsády and Nikolai Vukov, 'Internationalism, Pacifism, Transnationalism: Women's Movements and the Building of a Sustainable Peace in the Post-War World', in *Women Activists between War and Peace: Europe, 1918–1923*, ed. by Ingrid Sharp and Matthew Stibbe (London: Bloomsbury Academic, 2017), pp. 77–122 [DOI: 10.5040/9781474205894.0010]

Sluga, Glenda, *Internationalism in the Age of Nationalism*, Pennsylvania Studies in Human Rights (Philadelphia, PA: University of Pennsylvania Press, 2013)

Smale, Catherine, '"Auf uns sinken die Toten": Anti-War Sentiment in Expressionist Women's Writing from the First World War', in *Pacifist and Anti-Militarist Writing in German, 1889–1928: From Bertha von Suttner to Erich Maria Remarque*, ed. by Andreas Kramer and Ritchie Robertson, London German Studies, 16 (Munich: Iudicium and London: Institute of Modern Languages Research, 2018), pp. 77–92

Söll, Änne, *Der neue Mann. Männerporträts von Otto Dix, Christian Schad und Anton Räderscheidt 1914–1930* (Munich: Fink, 2016)

Sontheimer, Kurt, *Antidemokratisches Denken in der Weimarer Republik. Die politischen Ideen des deutschen Nationalismus zwischen 1918 und 1933* (Munich: Nymphenburger, 1962)

Steinhausen, Georg, *Geschichte der deutschen Kultur*, 2 vols (Leipzig: Bibliographisches Institut, 1904–13), II (1913)

Sternberger, Dolf, 'Verfassungspatriotismus', in *Schriften*, ed. by Dolf Sternberger, 12 vols in 13 (Frankfurt a.M.: Insel, 1977–96), X, *Verfassungspatriotismus* (1990), pp. 13–16

Takemoto, Makiko, *Die Außenpolitik und der Pazifismus der Weimarer Intellektuellen im Umkreis der Zeitschriften der Weltbühne und des Tage-Buchs in der Zeit 1926–1933* (Hiroshima: Carl von Ossietzky Universität Oldenburg, 2007)

Taylor, Ronald, *Literature and Society in Germany, 1918–1945*, Studies in Contemporary Literature and Culture, 3 (Brighton: Harvester, 1980)

Taylor Allen, Ann, *Feminism and Motherhood in Germany, 1800–1914* (New Brunswick, NJ: Rutgers University Press, 1991)

Treffry, Diana, *Collins English Dictionary*, 4th edn (2000)

Vaquas, Rida, '"Saint Francis of Assisi" by Karl Kautsky', *Cosmonaut*, 29 July 2019 <https://cosmonautmag.com/2019/07/saint-francis-of-assisi-by-karl-kautsky/> [accessed 12 April 2022]

Viel, Bernhard, *Utopie der Nation. Ursprünge des Nationalismus im Roman der Gründerzeit*, Blaue Reihe Wissenschaft, 6 (Berlin: Matthes & Seitz, 2009)

Walburga-Baumeister, Ursula, *DIE AKTION 1911–1932. Publizistische Opposition und literarischer Aktivismus der Zeitschrift im restriktiven Kontext*, Erlanger Studien, 107 (Erlangen: Palm & Enke, 1996)

Weiss-Sussex, Godela, 'The Monist Novel as Site of Female Agency: Grete Meisel-Hess' *Die Intellektuellen* (1911)', in *Biological Discourses: The Language of Science and Literature around 1900*, ed. by Robert Craig and Ina Linge, Cultural History and Literary Imagination, 27 (Oxford: Lang, 2017), pp. 111–33

Weitz, Eric D., *Creating German Communism, 1890–1990: From Popular Protests to Socialist State* (Princeton, NJ: Princeton University Press, 1997)

Wigger, Iris, *The 'Black Horror on the Rhine': Intersections of Race, Nation, Gender and Class in 1920s Germany* (London: Palgrave Macmillan, 2017)

Winkler, Heinrich August, 'Im Schatten von Versailles. Das deutsch-polnische Verhältnis während der Weimarer Republik', in *Deutsche und Polen. 100 Schlüsselbegriffe*, ed. by Ewa Kobylińska, Andreas Lawaty and Rüdiger Stephan (Munich: Piper, 1992), pp. 95–103

Wotschke, Jean, *From the Home Fires to the Battlefield: Mothers in German Expressionist Drama*, Studies in Modern German Literature, 85 (New York: Lang, 1998)

Ziemann, Benjamin, *Contested Commemorations: Republican War Veterans and Weimar Political Culture*, Studies in the Social and Cultural History of Modern Warfare, 36 (Cambridge: Cambridge University Press, 2013)

INDEX

Aktion, Die 5
Alldeutscher Verband *see* Pan-German League
Alsace 100, 121–22, 173
anti-Semitism 19, 113–14, 144, 173, 206
Austria/Austrian 35–36, 57–67, 173, 181
Austro-Hungarian Empire 36–37, 57–67

Baltic, the 47–48
    Baltic-German culture 47–57
Battle of the Teutoburg Forest *see Hermannsschlacht*, the
Bavaria 76–78, 120
Berlin 2, 4, 79, 103, 145, 165
    electricians' strike 222–23, 226
Berliner Illustrirte Zeitung (BIZ), Die 4–5
Bertram, Ernst 99–100, 127–28
    Rheingenius und Génie du Rhin 99–100, 127–28
Bismarck, Otto von 17, 86, 127, 153–54, 171, 206
Black Horror, the 112–13
borders 135, 143
    changes in 1, 22, 25, 35–68, 235
    of Germany 1, 22, 35, 39, 207–08, 217–18, 235
    kinship across 90, 94–96, 134–35, 209
    political 135, 196
Bürgertum, German 111, 191, 233–34, 238

capitalism 30, 34, 42–43, 51, 87, 163, 166, 173, 187, 190, 194, 196–97, 204, 210, 212–13, 222–23, 230–31, 237–38
colonialism 112, 117
Communism 23, 161, 166–69, 179, 182–95, 197–99, 205, 218–30, 237
Courland 47–57
Cuno, Wilhelm 209–10
Czechoslovakia 36–38, 58, 114

democracy 2, 25, 92, 108–09, 111, 115, 161, 184, 200–01, 202–03, 208, 221, 237
    direct *see also* Räte 163, 205–06
    rejection of 8–11, 16, 163
    representative 1, 8–11, 12, 73, 90, 119, 124, 166, 176, 188, 230, 231
deutschnational 18–20, 172, 224, 233
    world view 18–19
Deutschnationale Volkspartei (DNVP) 113, 209
disarmament 90, 110, 219, 237
    military 113, 142–58, 219, 235
    moral 116–42
Dolchstoßlegende, the 186, 211 n. 145
Dombrowski, Erich 11, 144–45, 146, 150, 152
Dreyfus, Alfred 155
Duisburg 70–71

East Prussia 39–40, 47, 65, 88, 217
emasculation 222, 224, 227–30
Empire, German 17–19, 44
England 4, 50, 103, 114
Erzberger, Matthias 119, 122–23
eugenics 23, 97–98, 221, 227
    biological determinism 97–99
    racist 97
    socially progressive 97–99
Europe 19, 36, 38–39, 40, 62, 75, 89–92, 95, 97, 100–03, 109, 115, 120, 125, 127, 133, 142–43, 159, 184, 187, 197, 235, 239–40

Fascism 1, 8, 14, 206, 221, 237–38
Fichte, Johann Gottlieb 58, 61–64, 67–68, 110
    Reden an die deutsche Nation 58–59, 61, 64, 67, 110
First World War 1, 25, 44–45, 51, 58, 59, 97, 101, 112, 120, 125–26, 127, 130, 141, 144, 147, 151, 154, 155, 181, 185, 196, 202, 220, 234–35

Flake, Otto 11, 36, 57–67, 71–72, 87, 90, 109–15, 118–20, 124, 126–28, 142, 156, 158, 235
Foerster, Friedrich Wilhelm 74, 130, 139
Mein Kampf gegen das militaristische und nationalistische Deutschland 131–32
Politische Ethik und Politische Pädagogik 130–31, 149
forest, German 215–18, 231
significance of 215–16
France 4, 22, 76, 90, 94–95, 100, 103, 110, 112–13, 114, 115, 117, 125, 158, 196–97, 201, 237
Germany's relationship to 92–94, 103–09
Francis of Assisi, Saint 198–99
Freiheit, Die 3
Freikorps, the 139, 163, 175–76, 181, 210, 214
French Revolution, the 25, 90, 150
Fried, Alfred Hermann 145–47, 151, 152
Friedrich II, King of Prussia 104–05

Geldern, Rudolf 173–75
Georg, Manfred 118, 133–35, 141
Gerlach, Hellmut von 9, 154
German Question, the 25, 35, 39, 47, 57, 235
Germany
culpability of 101, 120–21, 154–55, 236
economy of 41, 46, 122, 200, 201, 222
historical development of 73–76, 127, 184, 237
loyalty to 13, 18, 50–51, 74, 77, 102, 152–53, 162, 164, 168
reputation abroad 61, 93, 116, 122–23
social hierarchy in 18, 65, 234
Goethe, Johann Wolfgang von 105–06, 190–91
Gerold, Mary 48–49, 52–56, 64
Grelling, Richard 154–55
J'accuse 155 & n. 236
Großdeutschland 36 & n. 45, 37, 39, 57, 59, 62, 64, 67
Großmann, Stefan 4, 5

Hauser, Kaspar *see also* Tucholsky, Kurt 11, 48 & n. 88, 54, 169–70
'Heckerlied', Das 174 & nn. 32 & 36
Heimat 25–34, 35, 42–43, 45–47, 49, 52–53, 54–55, 57, 68–69, 71, 77–78, 79–80, 81–82, 85, 87–88, 95, 102–03, 134–35, 136, 153, 168, 185–86, 194–95, 235–36
activism 30–31, 32–33, 43
exclusionary 27–28, 33–34
inclusive 30–31, 33
as pre-condition of patriotism 31, 33
Heimatbewegung 30, 32–33
Heine, Heinrich 170, 178, 213–14, 234
Deutschland. Ein Wintermärchen 177
Doktrin 170–71
Zur Geschichte der Religion und Philosophie in Deutschland 170, 177–78, 189–90, 196
Herbers, Hein 152–53
Hermannsschlacht, the 195–97, 213, 218, 231
Hiller, Kurt 11, 23, 148–50, 155–57, 159
Hindenburg, Paul von 5, 186–88
Hitler, Adolf 1 n. 1, 14, 60, 152
Hoffmann von Fallersleben, August Heinrich 165, 175–76
Holy Roman Empire, the 64, 75–76, 127–28, 131
Hungary 38–39, 64

internationalism 21, 22, 89–92, 93, 98, 101, 109, 110, 115, 125, 133, 157–58, 161, 198, 199, 234, 237, 239

Jacobsohn, Siegfried 2, 4, 6, 209–10
journalist style 7, 125
Jünger, Ernst 44
In Stahlgewittern 44
Jurisch, Ludwig 170–71, 178, 199–200, 219, 231

Kahlenberg, Hans von *see* Keßler von Monbart, Helene
Kaiserreich, the 16–20, 23, 28, 44, 50, 52–53, 75, 87, 110, 119, 126, 128, 142, 145, 165, 169, 175, 234, 236

INDEX

Kant, Immanuel 149–50
Kapp, Wolfgang 163, 202, 230
Kapp Putsch, the 23, 163 & n. 2, 164, 185, 201–07, 227, 230
Kautsky, Karl 189–90, 198, 205–06, 219
Keßler von Monbart, Helene 90, 94–103, 109, 113, 115, 126–29, 132–33, 135–39, 141–42, 158, 236
  Der Fremde 99
  French correspondent of 94, 96
Kollwitz, Käthe 137–38
Komintern 214, 218–19
Kommunistische Partei Deutschlands (KPD) 99, 162–63, 168, 182, 194, 200–01, 209, 214, 219–21
Kreiser, Walter 3–4, 117, 153
Krische, Paul 28–31, 79, 81, 235
  Heimat! 28–31

language
  politicization of 37–39, 61–62
  status of 61–62
Latvia 36, 47–57, 185 & n. 71, 235
League of Nations 40, 133, 148, 193
Left, the 2–3, 5, 10–12, 20, 23, 29, 39, 128, 161–63, 165, 176, 188–89, 191–94, 202, 205–06, 214, 219–21, 234, 239–40
Lehmann-Rußbüldt, Otto 172–73, 175, 178, 237
Lessing, Gotthold Ephraim 105, 189
life, rural 28–31, 33–34, 64–67, 88
loyalty, national 13, 153, 168
Ludendorff, Erich 72, 125, 165, 186–87, 229
Luther, Martin 173 n. 27, 188–90, 198–99, 234
Luxemburg, Rosa 163, 190

Mann, Heinrich 106–07
  Macht und Mensch 106–07
Mann, Thomas 7, 128–30
  Betrachtungen eines Unpolitischen 107, 128–30
March Action, the 23, 218–30
Maternalism 91, 130–42
Mertens, Carl 23, 139–42, 156, 166, 204
Messianism 91, 123–30, 188

Metzler, Georg *see* Witting, Richard 120–22, 154
Meyer, Willy 147, 193–94
Michel, Wilhelm 22, 71–78, 86–87, 112, 114–15, 127, 132, 207, 214–18, 229
  Verrat am Deutschtum 71–72, 127
militarism 2, 12, 52, 54, 56, 91, 112, 118, 119, 124, 130, 147, 155, 156, 186, 193, 221, 227, 229, 230–31, 235
Mörs 70–71, 77
mothers, German 131, 133–34, 137–39
  influence of 130–31, 133–34, 135, 139–42
Mussolini, Benito 1 n. 1
'Mutter der Schmerzen' 136–39
myth, rural 29–30, 65–66

Napoleon Bonaparte 61–62, 75–76, 86, 108, 127, 171–72, 197, 213–14, 237
National Socialism *see* Nationalsozialistische Deutsche Arbeiterpartei
nationalism
  moderate 168
  state-based 16–18
  subject-based 18–20
  versus patriotism 13–21
Nationalsozialistische Deutsche Arbeiterpartei (NSDAP) 1 n. 1, 3, 8, 23, 27, 33, 97, 148, 152, 194, 206
Neue Sachlichkeit 225 & n. 206
Nicolai, Georg Friedrich 145–46, 151

October Manifesto 145–46
Ossietzky, Carl von 2, 3–4, 6–9, 116–17, 148, 153–54, 219–20, 221
  Nobel Peace Prize 8
  personality 68
  Weltbühne-Prozeß 3–4, 7

pacifism 142–58
  absolutist 143
  conditional 143, 147–48, 193
  European 143
  patriotic 11–12, 91, 142–43, 157
Palatinate, the 32–33, 71–78, 87–88, 214–18

pan-Europeanism 89
Pan-German League 20
Panter, Peter *see also* Tucholsky, Kurt
   48–53, 55–56, 152–53
patriotism
   internationalist 89–159
   progressive 34, 35, 55, 69, 165, 238, 240
   regionalist 25–88
   Socialist 161–231
   versus nationalism 13–21
Peasants' Revolt, the 173 & n. 27
Persius, Lothar 148, 192–93
Pfemfert, Franz 4, 5, 6
pioneer, the 20 & n. 88, 36, 38
Poland 39–47, 114, 182
proletariat *see* working class, the
Protestantism 18, 29, 50, 75, 173, 189–90, 198–99
Prussia 12, 16–17, 26, 29, 34, 56, 61, 95, 104–05, 187–88

Radbruch, Gustav 176
Radek, Karl 214
Radkersburg 60–66
Rathenau, Walter 119–20
   assassination of 119–20, 156, 175
Reger, Erik 69–71, 77, 165
regionalism 21, 234, 239
   border communities 35–68
   separatism 76–77, 214–15
Reichsbanner Schwarz-Rot-Gold, the 11, 124–25
Reimann, Hans 85–87
Remarque, Erich Maria 44
   Im Westen nichts Neues 44–45
reparations 113–14, 201, 208, 213, 219
republicanism 1, 7, 9, 23, 29, 55, 73, 156, 164, 184, 202, 203, 207, 234, 237
   militant 11–12, 124–25
   revolutionary aspiration 170, 174
   rhetoric of 158, 176
   symbolism 119, 176
revanchism 2, 124, 138, 150, 186, 236
revisionism 2, 39, 110, 179
   Alsace-Lorraine 121–22
   anti-Slav 36–38, 60–63
   historical 23, 173, 234, 235

revolutions of 1848 18, 168, 169–74
   as source of inspiration 169, 172, 173–74, 237
   as cautionary tale 173
Rhine, the 76, 79, 175–76, 194–95, 197, 211
   left bank of 100, 112, 175, 211, 217–18
Rhineland, the 77, 112
Right, the 11–13, 26, 28–30, 156, 188, 201, 208, 214, 224, 229, 233, 239–40
Roter Frontkämpferbund 219–21
Rothammer, Karl 125–28, 200, 208–10, 221–31
   'Der Kommunistenputsch' 225–30
Ruhr, the 69–70, 76, 110, 165, 172
Ruhr Crisis, the 110, 114–15, 201 n. 112, 206–18
Ruhraufstand 206, 211, 223, 225, 227
Russia 47–48, 119, 181, 187

Schlageter, Albert Leo 210
   cult of personality 209, 214
Schlageter Line 214
Schneckenburger, Max 175
   'Die Wacht am Rhein' 175–76
Schücking, Walther 144–45
Schwarze Reichswehr see also Mertens, Carl 139–42, 153
Schwarzschild, Leopold 4, 5, 6
Shylock (*Merchant of Venice*) 113
Shylock Peace, the 113–14
Siemsen, Hans 79–82, 87
Socialism 21, 23, 46–47, 161–63, 237–38, 239
   reformist 199–230
   revolutionary 163–99
soldiers, German 4, 11–12, 36, 48, 52, 53–55, 57, 119, 148, 150–51, 178–82, 185, 202
Sozialdemokratische Partei Deutschlands (SPD) 2, 3, 162, 165, 168, 176, 189, 192–93, 200, 202, 205–06, 221, 224, 227–29
Spartacus League 163 & n. 3, 175–76, 182, 201
Stabsoffizier, ein 178–99, 203–04
   'Das alte Heer' 178–99

INDEX

Steiniger, Alphons 10, 11, 166–69
Stennes, Walter 206
Stinnes, Hugo 69, 210, 222–23
Stössinger, Felix 11, 90, 103–09, 115, 127, 158
Ströbel, Heinrich 11, 70, 114–15, 122–23, 126, 148, 155, 192, 200, 201–02, 203–07, 219, 222, 228–29
Styria 57–67

Tage-Buch, Das 5–6
territory 36, 40, 43, 44, 48, 100
   German 25, 46, 60, 77, 114, 184
   return of 2, 22, 182
Teutonic Order, the 47 and nn. 86 & 87
Tiger, Theobald *see also* Tucholsky, Kurt 48 n. 88
Toller, Ernst 128–29
   pacifism 128–29
treason 3–4, 12–13, 71–72, 116–17, 144, 153, 157, 164, 166, 209
Treaty of Rapallo 119
Treaty of Saint-Germain-en-Laye 35, 36, 57, 60, 62, 235
Treaty of Versailles 1 n. 2, 4, 9, 22, 25, 62, 113, 146, 163 n.2, 194, 201–02, 209, 219, 235, 236
Tucholsky, Kurt 2, 3–4, 6, 7, 8, 11, 35–36, 47–57, 64, 68–69, 71, 78, 87, 91–92, 117, 118, 148, 152–53, 156, 164–65, 179, 182–84, 226, 235, 238
   Deutschland, Deutschland über alles 34, 81–82, 157, 159

Unabhängige Sozialdemokratische Partei Deutschlands (USPD) 2, 11, 192, 205, 219
Upper Silesia 37, 39–47, 51, 181–82

Varssovius, Franz 174–78
violence 116, 149, 152, 213–14, 219–20, 225, 231
   left-wing 220
   right-wing 140–41
Volk, das schaffende 140, 166, 204–07
   as National Socialist slogan 206
   as Socialist slogan 204–05

Volkskörper 23 & n. 92, 221–30
   anti-left wing rhetoric 23
   anti-right wing rhetoric 224, 226, 229
Voltaire 104–07
   significance for Heinrich Mann 106
   significance for Felix Stössinger 104–05
Vorwärts 3, 203

Warschauer, Frank 82–85, 87
Weimar Republic 8, 23, 52, 60, 73–75, 93, 115, 119, 142, 146, 158, 164–65, 174, 180, 184, 200, 206–07, 212, 217, 221, 224, 231, 237
Weltbühne, Die
   'anti-republican' 8–11, 207
   circulation 3
   moral mission 91, 116–18, 142, 237
   origins 2
   political orientation 2–3, 162
   rhetoric 12, 22, 23, 26, 72–73, 91, 110, 116, 131, 158, 162, 164, 169, 199, 208, 218, 230–31, 237
Weltbühne-Prozeß *see* Ossietzky, Carl von 3–4, 7, 12
Wilhelm II, Kaiser 17–18, 50, 108, 180, 223
Witting, Richard 120–22, 154
women
   attitudes to 54, 130–42, 222, 224, 228
   rights of 130–31
working class, the 41, 99, 165–66, 169, 170, 172–73, 193, 194, 203, 204, 205, 212, 223, 226, 228, 238
   politicization of 23, 211–12, 221
Wrobel, Ignaz *see also* Tucholsky, Kurt 4, 8, 11, 48 & n. 88, 53–55, 68, 78, 81, 129–30, 150–52, 164, 179, 181–86, 202–03, 226

Zetkin, Clara 163, 165–66, 172–73, 209
Zwehl, Hans von 206–07, 210–15, 230
Zweig, Arnold 35–36, 39–47, 51, 56, 71, 87, 235

www.ingramcontent.com/pod-product-compliance
Lightning Source LLC
Chambersburg PA
CBHW071407160426
42813CB00084B/711